POETRY AS
EXPERIENCE

POETRY AS EXPERIENCE

NORMAN C. STAGEBERG & WALLACE L. ANDERSON

Iowa State Teachers College

AMERICAN BOOK COMPANY

New York   Cincinnati   Chicago   Boston   Atlanta   Dallas   San Francisco

....

COPYRIGHT ACKNOWLEDGMENTS

BRANDT AND BRANDT for "To Jesus on His Birthday," from *The Buck in the Snow*, published by Harper and Brothers, copyright, 1928, by Edna St. Vincent Millay; for "the Cambridge ladies," from *Collected Poems of E. E. Cummings*, published by Harcourt, Brace & Co., Inc., copyright, 1923, by E. E. Cummings.

DOUBLEDAY & CO., INC. for "Trees," from *Trees and Other Poems* by Joyce Kilmer, copyright, 1914, by Doubleday & Co., Inc.; for "Danny Deever" from *Departmental Ditties and Barrack-Room Ballads* and "The Ladies" from *The Seven Seas*, copyright, 1896, by Rudyard Kipling, by permission of Mrs. George Bambridge and Doubleday & Co., Inc.; for six poems from *Leaves of Grass* by Walt Whitman, copyright, 1924, by Doubleday & Co., Inc.

ALFRED A. KNOPF, INC. for "The Wayfarer" from *Collected Poems of Stephen Crane*, copyright, 1899, 1926, by Alfred A. Knopf, Inc.; for "Cross," from *The Weary Blues* by Langston Hughes, copyright, 1926, by Langston Hughes; for "Sea Lullaby" and "Down to the Puritan Marrow" from *Collected Poems* by Elinor Wylie, copyright, 1921, 1932, by Alfred A. Knopf, Inc.; for "Dead Boy," from *Selected Poems* by John Crowe Ransom, copyright, 1927, 1945 by Alfred A. Knopf, Inc.; for "To My Small Son in Church" from *This, My Letter* by Sara Henderson Hay, copyright, 1939, by Alfred A. Knopf, Inc.

LITTLE, BROWN AND COMPANY for six poems from *Poems by Emily Dickinson*, edited by Martha Dickinson Bianchi and Alfred Leete Hampson, 1921.

THE MACMILLAN COMPANY for the selection from George Barker, *Selected Poems*, copyright, 1941, by The Macmillan Company and used with their permission; for the selection from Henry Bradley, *The Making of English*, copyright, 1925, by The Macmillan Company and used with their permission; for the selections from Thomas Hardy, *Collected Poems*, copyright, 1926, 1931 by The Macmillan Company and used with their permission; for the selections from John Masefield, *Poems, Complete Edition (1935)*, copyright, 1935, by The Macmillan Company and used with their permission; for the selection from Marianne Moore, *Selected Poems*, copyright, 1935, by The Macmillan Company and used with their permission; for the selection from James Stevens, *Collected Poems*, copyright, 1928, by The Macmillan Company and used with their permission; for the selections from William Butler Yeats, *Collected Poems*, copyright, 1940, by The Macmillan Company and used with their permission; for the selections from Edwin Arlington Robinson, *Collected Poems*, copyright, 1937, by The Macmillan Company and used with their permission.

RANDOM HOUSE, INC., for "Winter Landscape" from *Ruins and Visions*, copyright, 1942, by Stephen Spender; for "The Express" and "Landscape Near an Aerodrome" from *Poems* by Stephen Spender, copyright, 1934, by Modern Library; for "In Memory of W. B. Yeats," "Musée des Beaux Arts," and "September 1, 1939" from *Another Time*, copyright, 1940, by W. H. Auden; for "Who's Who" from *The Collected Poetry of W. H. Auden*, copyright, 1945, by W. H. Auden; for "These Days Are Misty" from *Poems, 1925–1940*, copyright, 1937, 1939, 1940, by Louis MacNeice; for "The Sunlight on the Garden" and "Precursors" from *Springboard* by Louis MacNeice, copyright, 1945, by Random House; for "Shine, Perishing Republic" from *Roan Stallion* by Robinson Jeffers, copyright, 1925, by Boni and Liveright; and for "Hurt Hawks" from *Cawdor*, copyright, 1928, by Robinson Jeffers.

RINEHART & COMPANY, INC. for "The Swan" from *Selected Poems*, copyright, 1938, by John Gould Fletcher, and reprinted with the permission of Rinehart & Company, Inc., Publishers, and for an extract from Earl Daniels, *The Art of Reading Poetry*, published 1941 by Rinehart & Company, Inc.

CHARLES SCRIBNER'S SONS for "Lucifer in Starlight," "Dirge in the Woods," and lines from "Love in the Valley" reprinted from *Selected Poems* by George Meredith; copyright 1897 by George Meredith, 1925 by William M. Meredith; used by permission of the publishers, Charles Scribner's Sons; for variant readings of several poems in Maurice Forman, *The Poetical Works and Other Writings of John Keats*, Limited Hampstead edition, 1938, Charles Scribner's Sons, Publishers; for "What Is to Come" and "Margaritae Sorori" from *Poems of W. E. Henley*, 1907, and brief quotations from Lawrence Housman, *My Brother, A. E. Housman* (1938), all published by Charles Scribner's Sons.

iv

PERSONAL
ACKNOWLEDGMENTS

The authors owe many personal debts of gratitude for assistance. Their department head, H. Willard Reninger, generously granted lighter teaching schedules during work-in-progress and was constantly on deck to aid and abet. Other staff colleagues offered helpful criticism, among them Leslie Bigelow (now of the University of Arizona), John Cowley, Louise Forest, Alden Hanson, and James Hearst. The college reference librarian, Mary Dieterich, gave valuable aid in research. Charles D. Abbott of the Lockwood Memorial Library, University of Buffalo, kindly threw open the resources of his fine collection of manuscripts and modern poetry.

Intellectual indebtedness is hard to assess. The reader will note a heavy draft upon the writings of I. A. Richards and John Dewey for concepts and terms. But without the scholarly labors of many others—Otto Jespersen, Leonard Bloomfield, Wolfgang Köhler, Henry Lanz, to name a few—little of worth could have been accomplished.

N. C. S.

W. L. A.
Iowa State Teachers College

ix

PREFACE TO THE STUDENT

Poems are not made by dreamers for dreamers. They are made—out of life experiences—by individuals who have lived actively and thought freely, who have been soldiers, athletes, revolutionaries, statesmen, farmers, musicians, business men—the list is as endless as the activities of life. But poetry is not life itself. Life as we live it is made up of innumerable experiences of every sort, often without pattern or meaning. Out of this mass the poet selects and re-arranges details and events; he orders, clarifies, and intensifies the raw material of life in such a way as to create new experiences that are coherent and meaningful.

The medium he employs is language, but not the random, casual, diluted language of every-day affairs. Instead he manipulates his medium in startling ways. He turns sentence patterns topsy-turvy; he chisels apart worn-out chains of words and hammers together new links. Always he seeks to place the exact word in the most strategic position. The language of poetry, as a result, cannot be read idly; it demands alertness and concentration. A single reading of a poem is never enough. Often many readings are required to yield a coherent and meaningful experience.

Although the understanding of poetry is not easy, the rewards are rich. Stated in the most general terms, they include a heightened

awareness of the perceptual world around us and a fuller compre-
hension of the ways human beings act and think and feel. This
generalization may have little significance for you now. But as you
read the poems in this book, you will gradually attain an awakened
realization of the many-fold values that have made poetry endure
in the hearts and minds of the race since the very dawn of history.

CONTENTS

2. THE POEM AS RESPONSE   21

New Response—21. The Stock Response—22. The Inadequate Response—27. The Sentimental Response—30.

3. CONNOTATION   40

Source of Word Meaning—40. Denotation—41. Connotation—41. Contextual Control of Connotation—43. Variability of Connotation—46. Single-Context Connotation—49.

4. IMAGERY   54

Visual Imagery and Variations—**55**. Auditory Imagery—**59**. Articulatory Imagery—**60**.

5. FIGURATIVE LANGUAGE   66

Figures of Similarity—**66**. Simile—**66**. Metaphor—**67**. Per-

sonification—69. Tenor and Vehicle—70. Uses of Figures
of Similarity—78. Symbol—81.

6. SOUND SYMBOLISM   94

Onomatopoeia—95. Ease of Articulation—98. Phonetic
Intensives—100.

9. RIME AND STANZA

12. POEMS WITH VARIANTS   238

PART II: POEMS FOR STUDY

LIST OF POEMS

CONTENTS xxi

CONTENTS

THE ESSENTIALS
OF POETRY

1

THE NATURE OF A POEM

WHAT DOES A POEM MEAN? The first question that inexperienced readers are likely to ask about a poem is "What does this poem mean?" Such a question implies that a poem contains a central thought which equals the whole meaning of the poem, and that the reader goes through the poem simply to get to the end for the sake of the little nugget of wisdom that the poem may contain. The implication that a poem can be equated with its central thought is not true. On the contrary, one reads a poem in much the same way that he watches a baseball game. Every bleacher fan is a participant in the game in the sense that he identifies himself with the players. He is thrilled with a neatly executed double-play, becomes excited whenever a home run is hit, and quarrels with the umpire over a close decision. Although he may be interested in the outcome, it is the process of the game itself, the experience of watching it develop play by play that counts. To read poetry for thought alone is like going to a baseball game to watch the scoreboard instead of the game. The final score is no more the whole game than the central thought is the whole meaning of the poem. To illustrate this point, let us compare the thought "Flying is exhilarating" with its embodiment in the following poem. The speaker is an airplane pilot.

3

High Flight

Oh! I have slipped the surly bonds of Earth   *1*
   And danced the skies on laughter-silvered wings;
Sunward I've climbed, and joined the tumbling mirth
   Of sun-split clouds,—and done a hundred things
You have not dreamed of—wheeled and soared and swung   *5*
   High in the sunlit silence. Hov'ring there,
I've chased the shouting wind along, and flung
   My eager craft through footless halls of air. . . .
Up, up the long delirious, burning blue
   I've topped the wind-swept heights with easy grace,   *10*
Where never lark, or even eagle flew—
   And, while with silent, lifting mind I've trod
   The high untrespassed sanctity of space,
Put out my hand and touched the face of God.

JOHN GILLESPIE MAGEE, JR.

The central thought is plainly present, but no one would say that it equals the poem itself. Instead of making a flat statement **about** the excitement of flying, the pilot, who is speaking, takes us up into the skies with him to participate imaginatively in the actual experience. We get a sense of the swift and unhindered movements of a plane in flight from such action words as *slipped, danced, climbed, wheeled, soared, swung, hov'ring, chased,* and *flung.* We feel the pilot's exhilaration because he has not only shown his own joy but has attributed this feeling to the things around him. It is as if the *laughter*-silvered wings, tumbling *mirth* of clouds, *shouting* winds, and *eager* craft are all sharing in the sport and fun. The rhythm also contributes to the whole meaning; for example, its regular de-dúm pattern of stresses is varied in lines three, six, and nine by the words *súnward, hígh in,* and *úp, úp;* the effect of this rhythmic variation is to emphasize our feeling of the ever-increasing height of the plane in its upward escape from earth to heaven. Enough has perhaps been said here to show that a poem "means" much more than merely its central thought. The thought, in fact, is but one of many parts, all of which interact to produce a unified and total experience. This total experience, as we shall soon see, is the whole "meaning" of a poem.

THE POEM WITHIN. When we read a poem something happens within us. The words on the page awaken a response: they bring to life a group of images, feelings, and thoughts. The nature of these is determined (1) by our own past experiences with the words, and (2) by our present mental and emotional set. This response within us—the experience caused by the words—*is* the poem.[1] A poem then is an interaction within a reader between the words of a poet and the total past experience and present set of the reader.

THE TIME-EXPERIENCE. A poem does not come, full-blown, into being. It is, on the contrary, a cumulative experience in time. It is created in the mind part by part as we read a succession of words; and not until we reach the end of the poem does the experience become a completed whole, one in which all contributory impressions are fused into one total experience. As we begin to read a poem our understanding of the first words is incomplete; we place them in the most promising context suggested by the title and the opening words, but we hold this first interpretation in suspense to see whether the words that follow will corroborate the provisional context we have adopted. As an example let us experience, step by step, a simple little lyric entitled "Upon a Child." The title itself appears to mean "about a child," thus indicating nothing except the general subject of the poem; so we go on to the first line:

Upon a Child

Here a pretty baby lies

At this point in the poem we are unsure of where the baby lies, though from past experience we should assume that it is lying in a bed or cradle. This assumption seems to be borne out by the next words of the continuing experience:

---

[1] The word *poem* is also used to refer to the words on the printed page. These words, however, are only the stimuli for the **real** poem, which is experienced within the reader. In our discussion the context will make clear in which sense the word *poem* is used.

Upon a Child

Here a pretty baby lies
Sung asleep with lullabies:

With the completion of line 2 most of us probably have in mind a picture of a rosy-cheeked babe lying peacefully asleep in its crib. The third line reinforces the first interpretation that we are holding in suspense for corroboration:

Upon a Child

Here a pretty baby lies
Sung asleep with lullabies:
Pray be silent, and not stir

But look what happens as the experience becomes a completed whole with the reading of the fourth line:

Upon a Child

Here a pretty baby lies
Sung asleep with lullabies:
Pray be silent, and not stir
Th' easy earth that covers her.
ROBERT HERRICK

Our first interpretation held in suspense, our provisional context, needs readjustment. We realize now for the first time that the experienced poem deals with death, not sleep. The first line now is seen to suggest an epitaph, *i.e.,* "Here lies—." In line 2 the word *asleep* now comes to mean *dead*. In line 3 each imperative has acquired an added meaning not present before the reading of the last line. And the title itself is no longer general; it has become specific and has taken on added meaning. In short, not until we have progressed, step by step, to the very end of this cumulative experience in time, does the poem become a completed whole.

THE WHOLE AND PARTS. Nothing in the world exists alone. Every thing is a part of a larger whole, which we call its context. The nature of any whole determines the behavior of its parts. Examples of this are apparent everywhere. The behavior of a river, for instance,—its speed, movement, and direction—is determined by the whole river system of which it is a part. The behavior of a college student is determined by the social situation in which he finds himself: he behaves differently in church, at a football game, on a date, and in the class room. Likewise, a word or word-group normally occurs in a context which determines its meaning. The meaning of the word *fast,* for example, is different in the expressions *stand fast* and *go fast,* because in each case the word is in a different context; the meaning of the sentence "A strike was called" cannot be understood until we know whether the context is a baseball game or a labor dispute.

Not only does a whole determine the behavior of its parts, but the parts in turn may exercise influence upon one another and in so doing influence the whole. This inter-relation of part and whole may be illustrated by two simple examples. Consider, in the context of a barroom, the following list of words: *alcohol, men, table, bottle, glasses, cabinet, cat.* For most persons the meanings of these words will be more or less the same. Now let us change the context from a barroom to a laboratory scene. The new context changes the meanings of all the words. "Thus the tables change from drinking tables to laboratory tables, the liquor bottles to bottles of chemicals, the house cat to a laboratory specimen, etc."[2] In short, the new whole has modified the meaning of all the parts. For a second example, consider the following group of words: *librarian, loan desk, books, crowd, seats.* These words probably call up in your mind a picture of a library. Now let us change the first two words and look at the list again: *minister, altar, books, crowd, seats.* Library books have become hymn books; the crowd of students is seen to be a congregation of worshippers; and seats in the library appear as pews in a church. The alteration of the first two words has changed the meaning of the rest of the words and of the whole.

Further illustration of this inter-relation of part and whole is furnished by the psychology of perception. In the following diagram lines BD and DF appear to be, and actually are, of the same length.

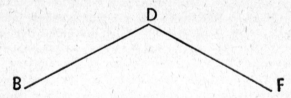

If we place these lines in a parallelogram in such a way that each line is enclosed in a separate whole, we get quite a different picture.

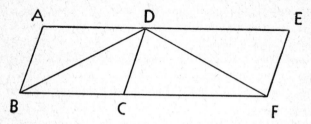

Line BD now appears to be shorter than line DF. The reason, of course, is that the different contexts into which the lines have been placed have altered their apparent lengths.

EXERCISE

The following sentences, considered in isolation, have various possible meanings. Choose one sentence and write for it a brief paragraph of context that will limit the sentence to a single meaning. Then, write another paragraph that will give a different meaning to the same sentence.

1. He is in a good position to pass.
2. The date looked promising.
3. They were now ready to ship.
4. You are losing your grip.
5. The wolf was at the door.
6. Drop me a line.

A poem too is a whole which is made up of parts. These parts may be properties of words, like rhythm, vowel sounds, and consonant sounds; or they may be evoked by words, like images, feelings, and thoughts. Each part is an integral member of a co-ordinated team. As such, it influences the action of its teammates, and the play of the team as a whole determines the movements of the players. In other words, the parts of a poem exert a mutual influence upon one another, and the whole poem determines the meaning of its parts.

But all these influences, we must remind ourselves, occur within the reader; and the reason they can occur is that the human nervous system has the power and tendency to organize stimuli into experienced wholes that are as well articulated and unified as possible.[3]

Note these influences in this poem by George Meredith.

Dirge in Woods

A wind sways the pines,   *1*
    And below
Not a breath of wild air;
Still as the mosses that glow
On the flooring and over the lines   *5*
Of the roots here and there.
The pine-tree drops its dead;
They are quiet, as under the sea.
Overhead, overhead
Rushes life in a race,   *10*
As the clouds the clouds chase;
    And we go,
And we drop like the fruits of the tree,
    Even we,
    Even so.   *15*

Reading through the first eight lines, one perhaps feels them to be nothing more than a description of the stillness of the forest. The next three are also description, presenting by way of contrast, the strong movement in the overhead clouds. But something more happens in this new section. The rime word *overhead* recalls to the reader's mind the hitherto unemphasized *dead* of the previous section; and in the following line the word *life* makes *dead* still more prominent in one's awareness because the two words are opposite in meaning. Because this life-death opposition is vivid in consciousness as one reads lines 12 and 13, one without hesitation

[3] This tendency is called the Principle of Prägnanz. See Kurt Koffka, *Principles of Gestalt Psychology* (New York: Harcourt Brace, 1935), p. 110; and M. D. Vernon, *Visual Perception* (Cambridge [England]: Cambridge University Press, 1937), p. 102.

assigns to *go* and *drop* the meanings of *live* and *die*. But the word *go*, if it were not for this contextual control, could just as well have the figurative meaning of *die*. It is the preceding whole, here, that prompts the correct reading.

VARIATIONS IN THE POETIC EXPERIENCE. The poetic experience engendered by a printed poem is somewhat different for every reader. The reason is that each reader has a unique experience-background and psychological individuality, not exactly like those of any other person in the world. Consequently, the response one reader makes to the words of the poem—his images, feelings, and thoughts—will not precisely duplicate the response of any other reader, nor will it be identical with the experience of the poet as a reader of his own poem.[4]

This concept of the uniqueness of every poetic experience has a further consequence. An individual reader himself changes in the course of time. Thus any given poem, if read at intervals of time, will create different poetic experiences in the reader to the extent that he himself has changed.[5] Many readers have testified that the re-reading of a poem may reveal new perceptions and understandings not previously observed.

To illustrate the variations in experience that a poem may evoke, let us read a poem by John Gould Fletcher:

The Swan

Under a wall of bronze,   *1*
Where beeches dip and trail
Thin branches in the water,
With red-tipped head and wings,
A beaked ship under sail,   *5*
There glides a great black swan.

---

[4] "Poetry is based on the principle of free individual interpretation; you must create the meaning of each poem out of your private experience." C. Day Lewis, "A Hope for Poetry," *Collected Poems* (New York: Random House, 1935), p. 195.

[5] Walter De la Mare, in a discussion of the nature of the poetic experience, has written that "the effect they [the words of a poem] produce on their reader . . . will vary, of course, with every individual reader and even at different readings." *Poetry in Prose* (New York: Oxford University Press, 1937), p. 40.

Under the autumn trees
He goes. The branches quiver,
Dance in the wraith-like water,
Which ripples beneath the sedge   *10*
With the slackening furrow that glides
In his wake when he is gone:
The beeches bow dark heads.

Into the windless dusk,
Where in mist great towers stand   *15*
Guarding a lonely strand
That is bodiless and dim,
He speeds with easy stride;
And I would go beside,
Till the low brown hills divide   *20*
At last, for me and him.

Let us ask ourselves two questions about this poem. (1) Considering
the first line in the light of the whole poem, what image shall we
say is called up by *a wall of bronze?* To a New Englander it might
be a low rock wall colored with autumn vines; to a Chinese it might
be a mud wall of reddish-brown hue; the possibilities are numerous.
(2) What contributions do the towers in line 15 make to the total
impression? After answering these questions let us compare our
experiences of these two items with those of the poet himself.
Fletcher has written about this poem:

I recall plainly the circumstances under which this poem was composed.
I was walking along the Thames, on a beautiful sunny October day, at a
spot where the opposite bank of the river was bordered by a row of beech
trees fringing the water, with long branches and copper-colored foliage.
Suddenly from a small creek, appeared a black swan which swam straight
down the river, breaking its perfectly still and mirror-like surface into
wide ripples. The towers of Oxford University loomed up in the distance,
softened and mellowed by the hazy sunlight of autumn. It was this scene
and the mood it evoked that I tried to convey in my verse.[6]

Now we realize that to the poet the wall of bronze is a row of beech
trees with copper-colored foliage standing on a river bank, but

[6] William Rose Benét, ed., *Fifty Poets* (New York: Duffield and Green,
1933), pp. 72–73.

probably some other image is conveyed by the words to most readers. And the sight of the towers of Oxford, ancient and hallowed with literary tradition, must have stirred up in the poet's being a set of feelings that were a part of his mood, his response to the scene. But to most readers the towers are vague and impersonal, and probably impart little warmth of feeling. In short, Fletcher's poetic experience as a reader of his own poem, we must infer from his prose statement above, is different from that of other readers of the poem.

Although it is true that a given poem will produce variations in the poetic experiences of different readers, it does not follow that a poem may be interpreted in any way that happens to please a reader's fancy. On the contrary, one's interpretation of a poem is kept within bounds by two controls: the cultural and the contextual.

CULTURAL CONTROL. Cultural control is the common body of experience that is shared by members of a given community, nation, or culture. Such commonness of experience has this consequence: the words of the language used by the group will call up images, thoughts, and feelings which are similar for most members. For example, the word *Buick* will create similar though not identical images in the minds of most Americans; the words *Four score and seven years ago* induce thoughts of Lincoln and his ideal of a people's government; the words *Pearl Harbor* stir up feelings of patriotic ardor. Thus, although one's individual experience is indeed unique, it also has much in common with that of other members of the community.

In the following poem, for example, individual variations of experience are possible in the imaging of many of the words, such as *horse* and *prairies;* however, cultural control is exerted in that most Americans have had experience, real or vicarious, with circus days, Wild West shows, Indian fighters, and pioneer life, so that their response is kept within the same general bounds.

Buffalo Bill

Boy heart of Johnny Jones—aching to-day?   *1*
Aching, and Buffalo Bill in town?
Buffalo Bill and ponies, cowboys, Indians?

Some of us know
All about it, Johnny Jones.   *5*

Buffalo Bill is a slanting look of the eyes,
   A slanting look under a hat on a horse.
He sits on a horse and a passing look is fixed
   On Johnny Jones, you and me, barelegged,
A slanting, passing, careless look under a hat on a horse.   *10*

Go clickety-clack, O pony hoofs along the street.
Come on and slant your eyes again, O Buffalo Bill.
Give us again the ache of our boy hearts.
Fill us again with the red love of prairies, dark nights, lonely
   wagons, and the crack-crack of rifles sputtering flashes   15
   into an ambush.

CARL SANDBURG

CONTEXTUAL CONTROL. Contextual control, as we have
seen above in the discussion of the whole and parts, is the limitation
of the meaning of words by their verbal environment, that is, by
the other words with which they are associated. A word in isolation
has many possible areas of meaning, but a word in a poem is necessarily a word in context. The context determines, even more precisely than cultural control, the bounds within which one's interpretation must be restricted. In the following poem, when one has read
through line 10, he finds three possible meanings of *girls that fell*.
But contextual control is exerted in lines 13 and 15, so that only one
valid interpretation is left.

The Bell

It is the bell of death I hear,   *1*
Which tells me my own time is near,
When I must join those quiet souls
Where nothing lives but worms and moles;
And not come through the grass again,   *5*
Like worms and moles, for breath or rain;
Yet let none weep when my life's through,
For I myself have wept for few.

The only things that knew me well
Were children, dogs, and girls that fell ;   *10*
I bought poor children cakes and sweets,
Dogs heard my voice and danced the streets ;
And, gentle to a fallen lass,
I made her weep for what she was.
Good men and women know not me,   *15*
Nor love nor hate the mystery.

W. H. DAVIES

ILLUSTRATIVE POEMS

Upon a Maid

Here she lies (in bed of spice)   *1*
Fair as Eve in Paradise :
For her beauty it was such
Poets could not praise too much.
Virgins come, and in a ring   *5*
Her supremest requiem sing ;
Then depart, but see ye tread
Lightly, lightly o'er the dead.

ROBERT HERRICK

Auto Wreck

Its quick soft silver bell beating, beating,   *1*
And down the dark one ruby flare
Pulsing out red light like an artery,
The ambulance at top speed floating down
Past beacons and illuminated clocks   *5*
Wings in a heavy curve, dips down,
And brakes speed, entering the crowd.
The doors leap open, emptying light ;
Stretchers are laid out, the mangled lifted
And stowed into the little hospital.   *10*
Then the bell, breaking the hush, tolls once,
And the ambulance with its terrible cargo
Rocking, slightly rocking, moves away,
As the doors, an afterthought, are closed.

We are deranged, walking among the cops   *15*
Who sweep glass and are large and composed.
One is still making notes under the light.
One with a bucket douches ponds of blood
Into the street and gutter.
One hangs lanterns on the wrecks that cling,   *20*
Empty husks of locusts, to iron poles.

Our throats were tight as tourniquets,
Our feet were bound with splints, but now,
Like convalescents intimate and gauche,
We speak through sickly smiles and warn   *25*
With the stubborn saw of common sense,
The grim joke and the banal resolution.
The traffic moves around with care,
But we remain, touching a wound
That opens to our richest horror.   *30*
Already old, the question Who shall die?
Becomes unspoken Who is innocent?
For death in war is done by hands;
Suicide has cause and stillbirth, logic;
And cancer, simple as a flower, blooms.   *35*
But this invites the occult mind,
Cancels our physics with a sneer,
And spatters all we knew of denouement
Across the expedient and wicked stones.

KARL SHAPIRO

Read the first two lines of the next poem and then jot down the possible meanings of the word *frame* in line 2. Now read the rest of the poem. At what point in your reading does it become completely clear which meaning of *frame* is the appropriate one?

Walking with God. Gen. V. 24

Oh! for a closer walk with God,   *1*
　A calm and heav'nly frame;
A light to shine upon the road
　That leads me to the Lamb!

Where is the blessedness I knew   *5*
   When first I saw the Lord?
Where is the soul-refreshing view
   Of Jesus, and his word?

What peaceful hours I once enjoyed!
   How sweet their mem'ry still!   *10*
But they have left an aching void
   The world can never fill.

Return, O holy Dove, return,
   Sweet messenger of rest!
I hate the sins that made thee mourn,   *15*
   And drove thee from my breast.

The dearest idol I have known,
   Whate'er that idol be;
Help me to tear it from thy throne,
   And worship only thee.   *20*

So shall my walk be close with God,
   Calm and serene my frame;
So purer light shall mark the road
   That leads me to the Lamb.

WILLIAM COWPER

FOURTH SONG, *Astrophel and Stella*

Only joy, now here you are,   *1*
Fit to hear and ease my care;
Let my whispering voice obtain
Sweet reward for sharpest pain;
Take me to thee, and thee to me—   *5*
'No, no, no, no, my dear, let be.'

Night hath closed all in her cloak,
Twinkling stars love-thoughts provoke,
Danger hence, good care doth keep,
Jealousy itself doth sleep;   *10*

Take me to thee, and thee to me—
'No, no, no, no, my dear, let be.'

Better place no wit can find,
Cupid's yoke to loose or bind;
These sweet flowers on fine bed too,   *15*
Us in their best language woo;
Take me to thee, and thee to me—
'No, no, no, no, my dear, let be.'

This small light the moon bestows
Serves thy beams but to disclose;   *20*
So to raise my hap more high,
Fear not else, none can us spy;
Take me to thee, and thee to me—
'No, no, no, no, my dear, let be.'

That you heard was but a mouse,   *25*
Dumb sleep holdeth all the house;
Yet asleep, me thinks they say,
Young folks, take time while you may;
Take me to thee, and thee to me—
'No, no, no, no, my dear, let be.'   *30*

Niggard time threats, if we miss
This large offer of our bliss,
Long stay ere he grant the same;
Sweet, then, while each thing doth frame,
Take me to thee, and thee to me—   *35*
'No, no, no, no, my dear, let be.'

Your fair mother is a-bed,
Candles out and curtains spread;
She thinks you do letters write;
Write, but let me first endite;   *40*
Take me to thee, and thee to me—
'No, no, no, no, my dear, let be.'

Sweet, alas, why strive you thus?
Concord better fitteth us ;
Leave to Mars the force of hands,   45
Your power in your beauty stands ;
Take thee to me, and me to thee—
'No, no, no, no, my dear, let be.'

Woe to me, and do you swear
Me to hate? but I forbear ;   50
Cursed be my destines all,
That brought me so high to fall ;
Soon with my death I will please thee—
'No, no, no, no, my dear, let be.'

SIR PHILIP SIDNEY

In the next poem note the influence of line 17 upon lines 1 and 2.

A Proper Sonnet, How Time Consumeth All Earthly Things

Ay me, ay me, I sigh to see the scythe afield,   1
Down goeth the grass, soon wrought to withered hay.
Ay me, alas! ay me, alas, that beauty needs must yield,
And princes pass, as grass doth fade away.

Ay me, ay me, that life cannot have lasting leave,   5
Nor gold take hold of everlasting joy.
Ay me, alas! ay me, alas, that time hath talents to receive,
And yet no time can make a sure stay.

Ay me, ay me, that wit cannot have wished choice,
Nor wish can win that will desires to see.   10
Ay me, alas! ay me, alas, that mirth can promise no rejoice,
Nor study tell what afterward shall be.

Ay me, ay me, that no sure staff is given to age,
Nor age can give sure wit that youth will take.
Ay me, alas! ay me, alas, that no counsel wise and sage 15
Will shun the show that all doth mar and make.

Ay me, ay me, come time, shear on and shake thy hay,
It is no boot to balk thy bitter blows.
Ay me, alas! ay me, alas, come time, take every thing away,
For all is thine, be it good or bad that grows.   *20*

ANONYMOUS

My Sweetest Lesbia

My sweetest Lesbia, let us live and love,   *1*
And though the sager sort our deeds reprove,
Let us not weigh them. Heav'n's great lamps do dive
Into their west, and straight again revive,
But soon as once set is our little light,   *5*
Then must we sleep one ever-during night.

If all would lead their lives in love like me,
Then bloody swords and armor should not be;
No drum nor trumpet peaceful sleeps should move,
Unless alarm came from the camp of love.   *10*
But fools do live, and waste their little light,
And seek with pain their ever-during night.

When timely death my life and fortune ends,
Let not my hearse be vexed with mourning friends,
But let all lovers, rich in triumph, come   *15*
And with sweet pastimes grace my happy tomb;
And Lesbia, close up thou my little light,
And crown with love my ever-during night.

THOMAS CAMPION

Ars Poetica

A poem should be palpable and mute   *1*
As a globed fruit

Dumb
As old medallions to the thumb

Silent as the sleeve-worn stone   *5*
Of casement ledges where the moss has grown—

A poem should be wordless
As the flight of birds

*   *   *

A poem should be motionless in time
As the moon climbs   *10*

Leaving, as the moon releases
Twig by twig the night-entangled trees,

Leaving, as the moon behind the winter leaves,
Memory by memory the mind—

A poem should be motionless in time   *15*
As the moon climbs

*   *   *

A poem should be equal to:
Not true

For all the history of grief
An empty doorway and a maple leaf   *20*

For love
The leaning grasses and two lights above the sea—

A poem should not mean
But be.

ARCHIBALD MACLEISH

2

THE POEM AS RESPONSE

NEW RESPONSE. The new and meaningful experiences that we go through afford us new viewpoints and new outlooks; as a result our practical and emotional adjustments to future situations can be more selective and more appropriate. This is true both of real-life experience and poetic experience. A good poem creates in us a fresh and individualized experience. It may offer new perceptions of the external world and of human behavior; it may bring about new combinations of feelings and thoughts; it may modify or readjust our attitudes. An example of the kind of experience we are talking about is produced by the following poem by Lew Sarett:

Four Little Foxes

Speak gently, Spring, and make no sudden sound ;   *1*
For in my windy valley, yesterday I found
New-born foxes squirming on the ground—
                 Speak gently.

Walk softly, March, forbear the bitter blow ;   *5*
Her feet within a trap, her blood upon the snow,
The four little foxes saw their mother go—
                 Walk softly.

Go lightly, Spring, oh, give them no alarm;
When I covered them with boughs to shelter them from harm,   *10*
The thin blue foxes suckled at my arm—
> Go lightly.

Step softly, March, with your rampant hurricane;
Nuzzling one another, and whimpering with pain,
The new little foxes are shivering in the rain—   *15*
> Step softly.

LEW SARRETT

This poem is the expression of a real-life experience which the writer has tried to transmit through his selection and arrangement of words. The reader, on his part, is able to receive the transmission satisfactorily because he probably has felt at some time the chill of March winds, has shivered in the spring rain, has observed newly born animals, and has watched foxes in the wild or in the zoo; in short, his background of common experience has been sufficient to enable him to respond to the words of the poem with a poetic experience not unlike that of the poet. Furthermore, his response will probably include a feeling of pity and sympathy, and possibly thoughts will arise about the violation of trapping laws. The total response—images and feelings and thoughts—is a new and fresh experience; and it may influence the reader's adjustment to future situations in which he meets other creatures, animal or human, who are undeservedly suffering, by creating in him a deeper sympathy and a kinder understanding. This new response is the one the poet intended his readers to have. Sarett said of this poem:

I determined . . . to establish by suggestion the general idea that I was trying to express through the little foxes. I decided to let the foxes simply *be,* and by their moving, effective, *being* suggest my thought. . . . With this poem I wish to say something not only for a litter of harried foxes, but also for all other broken, hunted, defeated outcasts and derelicts, wild and human. Creatures like that tear me apart. I know how they feel.[1]

THE STOCK RESPONSE. The value of a good poem may be lost to a reader if his response is merely his customary mode of seeing or feeling or thinking, set off accidentally by some part of

---

[1] William Rose Benét, *Fifty Poets* (New York: 1933), pp. 95–96.

the poem, instead of a new and appropriate response elicited by a keen awareness of the whole poem with all its implications. Such a customary response—automatic, ready-made, and habitual—we call a stock response. In everyday living we employ many stock responses for standard occasions. They are useful because they enable us to meet the many situations facing us daily without making ceaseless new adjustments that would exhaust our mental energy. For example, when a man meets a woman of his acquaintance on the street, his automatic response prompts him to tip his hat without pausing to debate whether or not she is deserving of this token of esteem. Or when one hears a prayer in church he may respond with his habitual feeling of reverence and humility without stopping to decide whether or not such emotions are appropriate to this minister's particular conception of the Divine Being.

But stock responses, though necessary in many practical affairs, may get in the way of, and prevent, responses that are more appropriate to particular occasions. For instance, at the sight of a little, old, gray-haired woman we are likely to respond with our "grandmother" stock response—feelings of deference and respect—even though we know she has cheated on her income tax and is ruining the married life of her daughter and son-in-law. Here our ready-made response, which is inappropriate to this particular situation, prevents a response that really fits the occasion.

Let us consider a poem in which a reader's stock response, set off by some part of the poem, might prevent an appropriate response. The following poem expresses the tragedy of the mulatto who is accepted by neither the black nor the white race:

Cross

My old man's a white old man   *1*
And my old mother's black.
If ever I cursed my white old man
I take my curses back.

If ever I cursed my black old mother   *5*
And wished she were in hell,
I'm sorry for that evil wish
And now I wish her well.

My old man died in a fine big house.
My ma died in a shack.   *10*
I wonder where I'm gonna die,
Being neither white nor black?

LANGSTON HUGHES

If this poem is read by one who has a strong prejudice against Negroes, it is not improbable that his stock response of dislike, aroused by the Negro speaker in the poem, will blank out the more appropriate response of sympathy toward the mulatto.[2]

The poet himself may also be guilty of a stock response by presenting in his poem, not a fresh perception or an individual nuance of feeling, but only a typical, standardized, stereotyped human reaction. In other words, the poem itself can be a stock response, that of the writer. This kind of poem is easily recognized: the images and feelings are unindividualized; the language is rubber-stamped; the rhythmic movement is banal and inappropriate; the whole has no mark of personality and might have been written by a committee. The next poem illustrates such a stock response on the part of a poet.

Dead Cousin

The little cousin now is dead,   *1*
   His spirit's light is quenched;
For him let bitter tears be shed,
   For him our hearts are wrenched.

His custom was around the home   *5*
   To romp and sing and play,
And with his faithful dog to roam
   In meadows sweet and gay.

His father's hope, his mother's joy,
   The last of noble kin,   *10*
The trump of death has called our boy
   To leave a world of sin.

---

[2] For an actual instance of this kind of stock response, see the footnote to "Mr. Flood's Party," pp. 79–80.

Mournfully jangles the funeral bell,
  Dolefully knelling his death.
And soon within his gloomy cell   *15*
  He'll know nor light nor breath.

We lift a sad and solemn song
  As he in earth is laid,
And pray he will not stay for long
  In Death's eternal shade.   *20*

ANONYMOUS

Although the title, "Dead Cousin," leads us to expect an elegy dealing with a personal loss, none of the main characters—the cousin or his parents—is made real. What is said about the boy, in lines 5 through 9, may well apply to any one of a thousand boys. All we learn of him is that he romped, played, and sang at home or roamed the meadows with his dog. Not a single detail, either of appearance or behavior, is given to set him apart as an individual. The chief mourners, his father and mother, are also phantom figures to whom has been attributed not an iota of personality. The poet has done nothing to make these figures appear alive to the reader.

As we look at the language, we find only a series of clichés, *i.e.,* wornout combinations of words, such as *bitter tears, trump of death, gloomy cell,* and *sad and solemn song.* These hackneyed expressions have become the rubber-stamp substitutes for fresh and vigorous language. They are the standard parts of assembly-line poems.

The rhythm is one of weary monotony. Line after line drones on in a de-dúm de-dúm rhythm that has the tick-tock regularity of a clock. The only break in this regularity occurs in lines 13 and 14. Here the rhythm becomes notably inappropriate in that the extra syllables of the new dúm-de-de pattern create an effect of lightness that is out of keeping with the sense of the lines. An appropriate rhythm at this point would move slowly, with few unstressed syllables, to suggest the slow tolling of the funeral bell.

Poems that are stock responses in themselves are often popular with uncritical readers. They touch off familiar feelings that are pleasant to experience; they require no troublesome mental adjustments; they are easy, lazy reading. The objection to them is that we are no better off after having read them; they do not help us to escape from an experiential and emotive rut; they do not provide us with new norms of perceiving and feeling that make possible finer experiences in the future.

As a contrast to "Dead Cousin" let us look at another poem which is a fresh and individualized response on the part of the poet.

Dead Boy

The little cousin is dead, by foul subtraction,   *1*
A green bough from Virginia's aged tree,
And none of the county kin like the transaction,
Nor some of the world of outer dark, like me.

A boy not beautiful, nor good, nor clever,   *5*
A black cloud full of storms too hot for keeping,
A sword beneath his mother's heart—yet never
Woman bewept her babe as this is weeping.

A pig with a pasty face, so I had said,
Squealing for cookies, kinned by poor pretense   *10*
With a noble house. But the little man quite dead,
I see the forebears' antique lineaments.

The elder men have strode by the box of death
To the wide flag porch, and muttering low send round
The bruit of the day. O friendly waste of breath!   *15*
Their hearts are hurt with a deep dynastic wound.

He was pale and little, the foolish neighbors say;
The first-fruits, saith the Preacher, the Lord hath taken;
But this was the old tree's late branch wrenched away,
Grieving the sapless limbs, the shorn and shaken.   *20*

                              JOHN CROWE RANSOM

In this poem the "little cousin" is individualized in such a way that we can see him as a real boy. He is not the vague and ideal lad whom we met in the previous poem. Instead he has been given a set of characteristics that enable the reader to get a vivid picture of a small, pasty-faced boy constantly getting into mischief and tormenting his mother. To the reality of the boy himself the poet has added the reality of the mourning situation. The mother, although she knows his shortcomings, is nevertheless overcome with grief. The narrator, although he had called him "A pig with a pasty face . . . squealing for cookies," yet feels a sense of loss. The kinfolk also have their reason to regret his death, namely, that it means the end of the family line. And this reason, a worldly and probable one, is the dominant note of the poem.

This dominant note is given emphasis by fresh and vigorous language. For example, the kin are not merely the hackneyed *noble kin* of "Dead Cousin"; instead they are the *sapless limbs* of the family tree. And the boy is *a green bough,* a *late branch,* which has been suddenly *wrenched away* by death. We notice here that, although the poet has used the stock image of a family tree, he has actualized it in fresh and striking language. Thus the tree becomes an effective vehicle for the central pathos of the poem. In addition, because the tree image opens and closes the poem, it helps to bind the parts into a unified whole.

The rhythm, though it is based on a de-dúm de-dúm pattern, has none of the clock-like monotony of the stock poem. Numerous rhythmic variations have been introduced. For instance, strong stresses are often placed side by side, as in the *wíde flág pórch* of line 14; phrasal pauses occur at varied positions within the lines, as in lines 7 and 18; run-on lines give fluidity to the movement, as in line 10. The result of such variations is to give a colloquial cast to the language which contributes to the total effect of reality.

THE INADEQUATE RESPONSE. We have seen that the words of a poem are the formula for a poetic experience, or response, which is a compound of images, feelings, and thoughts. The poet, to create a desired effect, must select and arrange his material in the poem so that the particular objective situation he composes will call forth a relatively uniform response, as far as uniformity is possible. His failure to do this will result in an uncontrolled or inadequate response in the reader. The next poem is an example.

The Red Wheelbarrow

so much depends   *1*
upon

a red wheel
barrow

glazed with rain   *5*
water

beside the white
chickens

WILLIAM CARLOS WILLIAMS

Each reader can decide for himself the adequacy of this poem by comparing his own response, or poetic experience, with the one the author tried to effect. Mr. Williams has said of this poem:

> The wheelbarrow in question stood outside the window of an old negro's house on a back street in the suburb where I live. It was pouring rain and there were white chickens walking about in it. The sight impressed me somehow as about the most important, the most integral that it had ever been my pleasure to gaze upon. And the meter though no more than a fragment succeeds in portraying this pleasure flawlessly, even it succeeds in denoting a certain unquenchable exaltation—in fact I find the poem quite perfect.[3]

Did you experience the importance, the pleasure, and the unquenchable exaltation which the poet felt? If not, your response was inadequate, and in this case the fault may be charged to the poem because the objective situation is too meager.

EXERCISE

Read the next poem and the two critical discussions of it that follow. Then prepare to discuss in class your individual response to the poem.

The Pool

Are you alive?   *1*
I touch you.

---

[3] Benét, *Fifty Poets*, p. 60.

You quiver like a sea-fish.
I cover you with my net.
What are you—banded one? *5*

H. D.

Professor Earl Daniels:

"The Pool" contains emotion. . . . Here, a reader is likely to make the too common mistake of equating poet with person speaking through the poem, to think that speaker feminine because the poet is a woman. [The initials H. D. stand for Hilda Doolittle.] But the wonder is too childish for that; this is no sophisticated adult poet bending over water. More likely, it is a simple fisher boy, rather a primitive lad, equipped with a fishing net, who has stopped for a moment, because he cannot quite believe, moved as he is by the beauty of the morning, that the water is not something more than water, has not suddenly, strangely, become alive. The poet is dramatizing a child's mood rather than her own. For the sake of that mood she omits almost everything else from the picture. The pool is not localized . . . it might be any pool, anywhere, any water flashing in the sunlight, though it seems most appropriate to think of some small pool among the rocks along a shore. Coming suddenly on it, the boy's first thought is, "It's alive," and he reaches a naturally curious finger to touch the surface. Coolness and moisture suggest at once the living creature with which he is most familiar, and he brings his net into action. But the water does not behave like a fish, does not thrash around. All he has are patches of shade made by the meshes of the net, a cause for new wonder in the same half playful mood of his first question, and the poem ends on the note with which it began.[4]

Professor I. A. Richards:

The experience evoked in the reader is not sufficiently specific. A poet may, it is true, make an unlimited demand upon his reader, and the greatest poets make the greatest claim, but the demand made must be proportional to the poet's own contribution. The reader here supplies too much of the poem. Had the poet said only, "I went and poked about for rocklings and caught the pool itself", the reader, who converts what is printed above into a poem, would still have been able to construct an experience of equal value; for what results is almost independent of the author.[5]

---

[4] *The Art of Reading Poetry* (New York: Farrar and Rinehart, 1941), p. 197.
[5] *Principles of Literary Criticism* (New York: Harcourt Brace, 1934), p. 200.

THE SENTIMENTAL RESPONSE. A poem which invites emotion in the reader should present an objective occasion—a situation or series of events—which provides an adequate source for the emotion.[6] If, however, a poem presents the reader with an expression of emotion for which he discerns no sufficient cause, he is likely to be left unmoved and unconvinced. This sort of poem, one in which the emotion expressed seems too great for the objective occasion which calls it forth, we call a sentimental response on the part of the poet. If the reader shares this excessive emotion he too is making a sentimental response. The next poem is an example.

Pensive at eve on the *hard* world I mus'd,   *1*
And *my poor* heart was sad: so at the Moon
I gaz'd—and sigh'd, and sigh'd!—for, ah! how soon
Eve darkens into night. Mine eye perus'd
With tearful vacancy the *dampy* grass   *5*
Which wept and glitter'd in the *paly* ray;
And *I did pause me* on my lonely way,
And *mused me* on those *wretched ones* who pass
O'er the black heath of Sorrow. But, alas!
Most of *Myself* I thought: when it befell   *10*
That the *sooth* Spirit of the breezy wood
Breath'd in mine ear—'All this is very well;
But much of *one* thing is for *no* thing good.'
Ah! my *poor heart's* INEXPLICABLE SWELL!

NEHEMIAH HIGGINBOTTOM[7]

We notice that much emotion is expressed in this poem. A few instances will suffice. We are told, in line 2, that the poor heart of the speaker was sad; in line 3, that he sighed and sighed; in line 5, that his eye was tearful; and throughout the poem we are presented with protestations of deep sorrow. In addition, the poet has used exclamation marks, italics, and small capital letters in an attempt to

---

[6] Cf. George Santayana, ". . . the glorious emotions with which he [the poet] bubbles over must at all hazards find or feign their correlative objects." *Interpretations in Poetry and Religion* (New York: Scribners, 1918), p. 277.

[7] This name is a pseudonym used by Samuel T. Coleridge, who wrote the sonnet as a parody.

emphasize the intensity of the words. However, when we look for an objective occasion to justify this superabundance of emotion, we learn merely that the speaker has been musing on the hard world and on some wretched and sorrowful beings, about whom we are told nothing. Sufficient cause has not been given to enable us to share in the speaker's alleged emotion. For this reason the poem is unmoving and unconvincing.

Poems themselves, we have seen, may be classified into four types of response: new, stock, inadequate, and sentimental. It must be pointed out, however, that these classes may overlap; for example, a poem may be both a stock and a sentimental response at the same time.

The reader's response to such types of poems depends not only on the poems but also on the reader himself. If he reads attentively and thoughtfully and if, of course, he has had enough relevant life experience, he will derive a new response from a good poem, and will be able to recognize the other types of poems for what they are.

ILLUSTRATIVE POEMS

A Merry Christmas and a Glad New Year

Oh, bells that chime your sweetest!   1
   Oh, world of glistening white!
Oh, breezes blithely bringing
   A message of delight!
From leafless hill and valley   5
   But one refrain I hear:
"A merry, merry Christmas
   And a glad New Year!"

From humble home and palace
   The kindly voice is breathed,   10
From forest arch and pillar,
   And meadows snowy wreathed,
An echo from the angels,
   A paean of good cheer:
Hark! "Merry, merry Christmas   15
   And a glad New Year!"

Oh, light of heavenly gladness
  That falls upon the earth!
Oh, rapture of thanksgiving
  That tells the Saviour's birth!   *20*
The golden links of kindness
  Bring heart to heart more near,
With a "Merry, merry Christmas
  And a glad New Year!"

GEORGE COOPER

To Jesus on His Birthday

For this your mother sweated in the cold,   *1*
For this you bled upon the bitter tree:
A yard of tinsel ribbon bought and sold;
A paper wreath; a day at home for me.
The merry bells ring out, the people kneel;   *5*
Up goes the man of God before the crowd;
With voice of honey and with eyes of steel
He drones your humble gospel to the proud.
Nobody listens. Less than the wind that blows
Are all your words to us you died to save.   *10*
O Prince of Peace! O Sharon's dewy Rose!
How mute you lie within your vaulted grave.
  The stone the angel rolled away with tears
  Is back upon your mouth these thousand years.

EDNA ST. VINCENT MILLAY

The Rainy Day

The day is cold, and dark, and dreary;   *1*
It rains, and the wind is never weary;
The vine still clings to the mouldering wall,
But at every gust the dead leaves fall,
  And the day is dark and dreary.   *5*

My life is cold, and dark, and dreary;
It rains, and the wind is never weary;

My thoughts still cling to the mouldering Past,
But the hopes of youth fall thick in the blast,
　And the days are dark and dreary.　　　　*10*

Be still, sad heart! and cease repining;
Behind the clouds is the sun still shining;
Thy fate is the common fate of all,
Into each life some rain must fall,
　Some days must be dark and dreary.　　*15*
HENRY WADSWORTH LONGFELLOW

The Poplar-Field

The poplars are felled; farewell to the shade;　　*1*
And the whispering sound of the cool colonnade,
The winds play no longer, and sing in the leaves,
Nor Ouse on his bosom their image receives.

Twelve years have elapsed since I first took a view　*5*
Of my favourite field, and the bank where they grew,
And now in the grass behold they are laid,
And the tree is my seat that once lent me a shade.

The blackbird has fled to another retreat
Where the hazels afford him a screen from the heat,　*10*
And the scene where his melody charmed me before,
Resounds with his sweet-flowing ditty no more.

My fugitive years are all hasting away,
And I must ere long lie as lonely as they,
With a turf on my breast, and a stone at my head,　*15*
Ere another such grove shall arise in its stead.

'Tis a sight to engage me, if anything can,
To muse on the perishing pleasures of man;
Though his life be a dream, his enjoyments, I see,
Have a being less durable even than he.　　*20*
WILLIAM COWPER

Binsey Poplars felled 1879

My aspens dear, whose airy cages quelled,   *1*
Quelled or quenched in leaves the leaping sun,
All felled, felled, are all felled ;
 Of a fresh and following folded rank
     Not spared, not one   *5*
    That dandled a sandalled
 Shadow that swam or sank
On meadow and river and wind-wandering weed-winding bank.

O if we but knew what we do
 When we delve or hew—   *10*
 Hack and rack the growing green !
  Since country is so tender
 To touch, her being só slender,
 That, like this sleek and seeing ball
 But a prick will make no eye at all,   *15*
 Where we, even where we mean
    . To mend her we end her,
 When we hew or delve :
After-comers cannot guess the beauty been.
 Ten or twelve, only ten or twelve   *20*
  Strokes of havoc únselve
    The sweet especial scene,
  Rural scene, a rural scene,
  Sweet especial rural scene.

GERARD MANLEY HOPKINS

Auld Robin Gray

When the sheep are in the fauld, and the kye at hame,   *1*
And a' the warld to rest are gane,
The waes o' my heart fa' in showers frae my e'e,
While my gudeman lies sound by me.

Young Jamie lo'ed me weel, and sought me for his bride ;   *5*
But saving a croun he had naething else beside :

To make the croun a pund, young Jamie gaed to sea ;
And the croun and the pund were baith for me.

He hadna been awa' a week but only twa,
When my father brak his arm, and the cow was stown awa' ;   *10*
My mother she fell sick,—and my Jamie at the sea—
And auld Robin Gray come a-courtin' me.

My father couldna work, and my mother couldna spin ;
I toil'd day and night, but their bread I couldna win ;
Auld Rob maintain'd them baith, and wi' tears in his e'e   *15*
Said 'Jennie, for their sakes, O, marry me !'

My heart it said nay ; I look'd for Jamie back ;
But the wind it blew high, and the ship it was a wrack ;
His ship it was a wrack—Why didna Jamie dee ?
Or why do I live to cry, Wae's me !   *20*

My father urged me sair : my mother didna speak ;
But she look'd in my face till my heart was like to break :
They gi'ed him my hand, tho' my heart was in the sea ;
Sae auld Robin Gray he was gudeman to me.

I hadna been a wife a week but only four,   *25*
When mournfu' as I sat on the stane at the door,
I saw my Jamie's wraith,—for I couldna think it he,
Till he said, 'I'm come home to marry thee.'

O sair, sair did we greet, and muckle did we say ;
We took but ae kiss, and we tore ourselves away :   *30*
I wish that I were dead, but I'm no like to dee ;
And why was I born to say, Wae's me !

I gang like a ghaist, and I carena to spin ;
I daurna think on Jamie, for that wad be a sin ;
But I'll do my best a gude wife to be   *35*
For auld Robin Gray he is kind unto me.

LADY ANNE LINDSAY

On a Faded Violet

I

The odour from the flower is gone   *1*
  Which like thy kisses breathed on me;
The colour from the flower is flown
  Which glowed of thee and only thee!

II

A shrivelled, lifeless, vacant form,   *5*
  It lies on my abandoned breast,
And mocks the heart which yet is warm,
  With cold and silent rest.

III

I weep,—my tears revive it not!
  I sigh,—it breathes no more on me;   *10*
Its mute and uncomplaining lot
  Is such as mine should be.
        PERCY BYSSHE SHELLEY

Home-Sickness

Where I am, the halls are gilded,   *1*
  Stored with pictures bright and rare;
Strains of deep melodious music
  Float upon the perfumed air:—
Nothing stirs the dreary silence   *5*
  Save the melancholy sea,
Near the poor and humble cottage
  Where I fain would be!

Where I am, the sun is shining,
  And the purple windows glow,   *10*
Till their rich armorial shadows
  Stain the marble floor below:—

Faded autumn leaves are trembling
   On the withered jasmine-tree,
Creeping round the little casement,   15
   Where I fain would be!

Where I am, the days are passing
   O'er a pathway strewn with flowers;
Song and joy and starry pleasures
   Crown the happy, smiling hours:—   20
Slowly, heavily, and sadly,
   Time with weary wings must flee,
Marked by pain, and toil, and sorrow,
   Where I fain would be!

Where I am, the great and noble   25
   Tell me of renown and fame,
And the red wine sparkles highest,
   To do honor to my name:—
Far away a place is vacant,
   By a humble hearth, for me,   30
Dying embers dimly show it,
   Where I fain would be!

Where I am are glorious dreamings,
   Science, genius, art divine;
And the great minds whom all honor   35
   Interchange their thoughts with mine:—
A few simple hearts are waiting,
   Longing, wearying, for me,
Far away where tears are falling,
   Where I fain would be!   40

Where I am, all think me happy,
   For so well I play my part,
None can guess, who smile around me,
   How far distant is my heart,—

Far away, in a poor cottage,   45
  Listening to the dreary sea,
Where the treasures of my life are,
  Where I fain would be!

ADELAIDE A. PROCTER

The Woman in the Rye

"Why do you stand in the dripping rye,   1
Cold-lipped, unconscious, wet to the knee,
When there are firesides near?" said I.
"I told him I wished him dead," said she.

"Yea, cried it in my haste to one   5
Whom I had loved, whom I well loved still;
And die he did. And I hate the sun,
And stand here lonely, aching, chill;

"Stand waiting, waiting under skies
That blow reproach, the while I see   10
The rooks sheer off to where he lies
Wrapt in a peace withheld from me!"

THOMAS HARDY

To—

The bowers whereat, in dreams, I see   1
  The wantonest singing birds,
Are lips—and all thy melody
  Of lip-begotten words—

Thine eyes, in Heaven of heart enshrined   5
  Then desolately fall,
O God! on my funereal mind
  Like starlight on a pall—

Thy heart—*thy* heart!—I wake and sigh,
  And sleep to dream till day   10
Of the truth that gold can never buy—
  Of the baubles that it may.

EDGAR ALLAN POE

Cliff Klingenhagen

Cliff Klingenhagen had me in to dine   *1*
With him one day ; and after soup and meat,
And all the other things there were to eat,
Cliff took two glasses and filled one with wine
And one with wormwood. Then, without a sign   *5*
For me to choose at all, he took the draught
Of bitterness himself, and lightly quaffed
It off, and said the other one was mine.
And when I asked him what the deuce he meant
By doing that, he only looked at me   *10*
And smiled, and said it was a way of his.
And though I know the fellow, I have spent
Long time a-wondering when I shall be
As happy as Cliff Klingenhagen is.

EDWIN ARLINGTON ROBINSON

3

CONNOTATION

SOURCE OF WORD MEANING.

Words are used not in isolation but in human situations. It is through our experiences with them in human situations that they take on meaning. As an example, let us observe an army recruit who hears his sergeant say, "You men go over to headquarters and police the grounds, and I don't want to see anyone goldbrick." The recruit is not sure what the verbs *police* and *goldbrick* mean, and not wanting to ask questions, he watches and listens. Soon he finds himself among a squad of soldiers busily picking up cigarette butts, waste paper, and refuse; and through this situation he realizes that *police* means to clean up and not, as he had suspected, to act as a police guard. In the course of the job a fellow worker may pause, look cautiously around, and say to him, "I'd sure like to take it easy and just goldbrick, but if I do I may not get my promotion." By this new situation, added to his remembrance of the sergeant's order, he learns that *goldbrick* means to shirk one's duty and that the feeling attached to the word is one of disapproval. This process by which words take on meaning may be observed by anyone who watches a college student enlarging his stock of current slang or a science major picking up the jargon of the laboratory.

The meaning of a word is often complex, having such components as a picture, an idea, a quality, a relationship, and personal feelings and associations. For convenience of discussion we divide meaning into two parts, denotation and connotation.

DENOTATION. The denotation of a word is its agreed-upon sense—what it refers to, stands for, or designates, apart from the feelings that it may call up. For example, the word *brink* refers to, or denotes, an edge; *Venus* denotes a certain Roman goddess; *glory* denotes praise and distinction; *dead* denotes the quality of being without life; *yellow, red,* and *white* denote colors.

CONNOTATION. But as we experience words in human situations they not only take on certain denotations; they often acquire individual flavors: they come to have the emotive tone, the associations, and the suggestiveness of the situations of which they have been a part. Let us examine a few examples. The word *brink* we have met in situations involving danger, in such expressions as the *brink of a cliff* or the *brink of disaster;* thus its emotive tone is one of fear, and it carries a suggestiveness of danger. To a Latinist the word *venereal* might suggest loveliness because he knows that it is derived from the word *Venus,* the goddess of beauty, whom he has met in much Latin poetry; but to most persons, who have met it only in medical or societal situations as a part of the expression *venereal disease,* its emotive tone is one of unpleasantness and it suggests repulsiveness. As a contrast to *venereal* let us consider *glorious.* This word and its companion *glory* occur in situations employing the language of the Bible and of the church, *e.g.,* "for thine is the kingdom and the power and the *glory*"; in nature descriptions emphasizing beauty, *e.g.,* "Full many a *glorious* morning have I seen"; in descriptions of deeds of martial daring and achievement, *e.g.,* "the *glory* may be thine of ending this great war." Because these words, *glory* and *glorious,* have been a part of countless such situations, their emotive tone is one of pleasantness and they have the suggestiveness of greatness and splendor. This aspect of words we are discussing—their flavor, emotive tone, clusters of associations, the vague memories they conjure up—is called connotation.

Here is an experiment in connotation which you might try. Assume that you are going to write a poem in which you wish to use the connotative power of words to suggest romance, allurement, and adventure. Which word in each of the following pairs would you choose as having the more appropriate connotation: Nineveh, Grand Rapids; galleon, ship; dollar bills, pieces of eight; horse, steed; deed, act; adventuress, prostitute; skinny, slender; king, ruler; sparrow, nightingale; emeralds, road-rails?

In the next poem observe the differences in connotation between the words of the first two stanzas and those of the last stanza. What purpose is served in the poem by these connotative differences?

Cargoes

Quinquireme of Nineveh from distant Ophir,   *1*
Rowing home to haven in sunny Palestine,
With a cargo of ivory,
And apes and peacocks,
Sandalwood, cedarwood, and sweet white wine.   *5*

Stately Spanish galleon coming from the Isthmus,
Dipping through the Tropics by the palm-green shores,
With a cargo of diamonds,
Emeralds, amethysts,
Topazes, and cinnamon, and gold moidores.   *10*

Dirty British coaster with a salt-caked smoke stack
Butting through the Channel in the mad March days,
With a cargo of Tyne coal,
Road-rails, pig-lead,
Firewood, iron-ware, and cheap tin trays.   *15*

                                        JOHN MASEFIELD

Words in poems are chosen with careful regard for their connotations. Let us consider the usual connotations of *deceased, dead,* and *defunct.* The first of these, *deceased,* is much used in legal situations and is consequently a flavorless and matter-of-fact word. The second, *dead,* is the word we use in situations concerning the loss of a loved one by death. It has an emotive tone so strong and is so poignant that many persons avoid it in such situations and use instead expressions like *gone* and *departed.* The third, *defunct,* is disrespectful and jocular; we say, for example, that an unpopular dormitory regulation is now *defunct*. These differences in connotation may be illustrated in the poem which follows. In line 7 the poet uses the word "*dead*." Try substituting the two synonyms for the poet's word and see if you feel the difference.

The Isle of Portland

The star-filled seas are smooth to-night   *1*
　　From France to England strown;
Black towers above the Portland light
　　The felon-quarried stone.

On yonder island, not to rise,   *5*
　　Never to stir forth free,
Far from his folk a dead lad lies
　　That once was friends with me.

Lie you easy, dream you light,
　　And sleep you fast for aye;   *10*
And luckier may you find the night
　　Than ever you found the day.
　　　　　　A. E. HOUSMAN

CONTEXTUAL CONTROL OF CONNOTATION. The situation in which a word is being used, *i.e.*, its context, determines the degree to which its usual connotations are aroused in our minds. In the poem above, "The Isle of Portland," the context of *dead* is such as to stir up all its connotative power. But the same word, *dead*, can be put into other contexts in which its usual connotations are absent. When, for instance, we read that a battery is *dead* or that a *dead* tennis ball is useless, the word does not have the emotive tone that it had in the poem.

EXERCISE

1. Think over the connotations that each of these three expressions has for you: 1. Be silent; 2. Keep still; 3. Keep your mouth shut. Now read the two versions of the next poem and see if you can guess why the poet made the change that you find in line two.

On Being Asked for a War Poem

(EARLIER VERSION)

I think it better that in times like these   *1*
A poet keep his mouth shut, for in truth
We have no gift to set a statesman right;
He has had enough of meddling who can please
A young girl in the indolence of her youth,   *5*
Or an old man upon a winter's night.

(LATER VERSION)

I think it better that in times like these   *1*
A poet's mouth be silent, for in truth
We have no gift to set a statesman right;
He has had enough of meddling who can please
A young girl in the indolence of her youth,   *5*
Or an old man upon a winter's night.

                    WILLIAM BUTLER YEATS

2. In the second part of the next poem the speaker expresses a desire for physical contact with his sweetheart. But to avoid any grossness of sex suggestion, the poet uses, in the first eight lines, words that connote purity and cleanness, so that the poem as a whole conveys an impression of innocence. Which are these words?

Bright Star, Would I Were Stedfast as Thou Art

Bright star, would I were stedfast as thou art—   *1*
   Not in lone splendor hung aloft the night
And watching, with eternal lids apart,
   Like nature's patient, sleepless Eremite,
The moving waters at their priestlike task   *5*
   Of pure ablution round earth's human shores,
Or gazing on the new soft-fallen mask
   Of snow upon the mountains and the moors—
No—yet still stedfast, still unchangeable,
   Pillow'd upon my fair love's ripening breast,   *10*
To feel for ever its soft fall and swell,
   Awake for ever in a sweet unrest,
Still, still to hear her tender-taken breath,
   And so live ever—or else swoon to death.

                    JOHN KEATS

3. Think over the connotations that these three words have for you: *small, wee, little.* Now read the next three poems and try all three words wherever one of them occurs. Be ready to remark in class on the appropriateness of the poet's choice in each case.

To My Small Son, in Church

In the brief space of half an hour, not more,   *1*
You have constructed paper hats, and ships;
Managed to drop my purse upon the floor,
Reduced the Bulletin to ragged strips—
And from what next will fire your nimble mind   *5*
I shrink with a maternal apprehension.
Assuredly, in church, my son, I find
Monotony the mother of invention.

Now, shorn of hymnal and collection folder,
The final hope of occupation gone;   *10*
With conversation being frowned upon,
Your interest, if possible, grows colder.
You glance despairingly at me, and yawn,
Slide glumly down and sleep against my shoulder.

SARA HENDERSON HAY

Cradle Song

Sleep, sleep, beauty bright   *1*
Dreaming o'er the joys of night;
Sleep, sleep: in thy sleep
Little sorrows sit and weep.

Sweet babe, in thy face   *5*
Soft desires I can trace
Secret joys and secret smiles
Little pretty infant wiles.

As thy softest limbs I feel
Smiles as of the morning steal   *10*
O'er thy cheek, and o'er thy breast
Where thy little heart does rest.

O, the cunning wiles that creep
In thy little heart asleep!
When thy little heart does wake,   *15*
Then the dreadful lightnings break.

From thy cheek and from thy eye
O'er the youthful harvests nigh
Infant wiles and infant smiles
Heaven and Earth of peace beguiles.   *20*

WILLIAM BLAKE

My Wife's a Winsome Wee Thing

She is a winsome wee thing,   *1*
She is a handsome wee thing,
She is a bonnie wee thing,
  This sweet wee wife o' mine.

I never saw a fairer,   *5*
I never lo'ed a dearer,
And neist my heart I'll wear her,
  For fear my jewel tine.

She is a winsome wee thing,
She is a handsome wee thing,   *10*
She is a bonnie wee thing,
  This sweet wee wife o' mine.

The warld's wrack, we share o't,
The warstle and the care o't;
Wi' her I'll blythely bear it,   *15*
  And think my lot divine.

ROBERT BURNS

VARIABILITY OF CONNOTATION. The connotations of words are not necessarily constant. A word may have various possible connotations or none at all. The reason for the variability is that the word, possessing various meanings, will have been used in various types of situations, each type having its own flavor and cluster of associations. With such a word the connotation aroused, if any, on a given occasion will depend on the context in which it is embedded. For example, in the three sentences below the word *yellow* is respectively neutral, favorable, and unfavorable in connotation because of the differing contexts:

1. Road signs are painted yellow and black.
2. The little girl smiled happily; her bright eyes sparkled and her shining yellow curls glistened in the sunshine.
3. An evil glare shone from his small yellow eyes, deepset above dark green pouches that hung upon his pitted cheeks.

EXERCISE

In the four poems below observe the differing connotations given to the word *white* by the differing contexts and be prepared to discuss these effects in class.

A White Rose

The red rose whispers of passion,   *1*
   And the white rose breathes of love;
O, the red rose is a falcon,
   And the white rose is a dove.

But I send you a cream-white rosebud   *5*
   With a flush on its petal tips;
For the love that is purest and sweetest
   Has a kiss of desire on the lips.
           JOHN BOYLE O'REILLY

Golgotha

Through darkness curves a spume of falling flares   *1*
That flood the field with shallow, blanching light.
   The huddled sentry stares
   On gloom at war with white,
   And white receding slow, submerged in gloom.   *5*
   Guns into mimic thunder burst and boom,
   And mirthless laughter rakes the whistling night.
The sentry keeps his watch where no one stirs
But the brown rats, the nimble scavengers.
           SIEGFRIED SASSOON

Neutral Tones

We stood by a pond that winter day,   *1*
And the sun was white, as though chidden of God,
And a few leaves lay on the starving sod;
  —They had fallen from an ash, and were gray.

Your eyes on me were as eyes that rove   *5*
Over tedious riddles of years ago;
And some words played between us to and fro
  On which lost the more by our love.

The smile on your mouth was the deadest thing
Alive enough to have strength to die;   *10*
And a grin of bitterness swept thereby
  Like an ominous bird a-wing. . . .

Since then, keen lessons that love deceives,
And wrings with wrong, have shaped to me
Your face, and the God-curst sun, and a tree,   *15*
  And a pond edged with grayish leaves.

THOMAS HARDY

Open the Door to Me, Oh!

Oh, open the door, some pity to shew,   *1*
  Oh, open the door to me, oh!
Tho' thou hast been false, I'll ever prove true,
  Oh, open the door to me, oh!

Cauld is the blast upon my pale cheek,   *5*
  But caulder thy love for me, oh!
The frost that freezes the life at my heart,
  Is nought to my pains frae thee, oh!

The wan moon is setting ayont the white wave,
  And time is setting with me, oh!   *10*
False friends, false love, farewell! for mair
  I'll ne'er trouble them, nor thee, oh!

She has open'd the door, she has open'd it wide;
　She sees his pale corse on the plain, oh!
My true love, she cried, and sank down by his side,   *15*
　Never to rise again, oh!

ROBERT BURNS

　William B. Yeats, who had in mind a slightly different version of these lines, made this comment: "There are no lines with more melancholy beauty than these by Burns—

　　'The white moon is setting behind the white wave,
　　And Time is setting with me, O!'

and these lines are perfectly symbolical. Take from them the whiteness of the moon and of the wave, whose relation to the setting of Time is too subtle for the intellect, and you take from them their beauty. But, when all are together, moon and wave and whiteness and setting Time and the last melancholy cry, they evoke an emotion which cannot be evoked by any other arrangement of colours and sounds and forms."[1]

　　SINGLE-CONTEXT CONNOTATION. A word may acquire specific connotations through some particular context of which it has been a part. Many a person has lively feelings and associations attached to a particular, trivial, popular song, or to a particular place, because it has been in his past life a part of some particular situation, such as a love scene. Similarly, a word may acquire feelings and associations because of a particular situation, or context, in which we have experienced it. Thus, when a poet borrows a word or expression from a definite context in the work of a previous writer in order to plant it in his own poem, the uprooted word brings with it the feelings and associations of its former context. This sort of literary borrowing is common in modern poetry.

　　EXERCISE

1. An instance of a poet's use of specific connotations occurs with the word *golden* in the two poems below. As you study the first one, you will note that in line 5 the term *golden* is rich in connotative power, suggesting such things as the following: 1. wealth, as opposed to the poverty of chimney sweepers; 2. brightness, as opposed to the blackness of chimney sweepers; 3. cleanness, as opposed to the dirtiness of chimney sweepers; 4. happiness, as opposed to the misery of chimney sweepers; 5. blond hair; 6. perfection, because gold was in Shakespeare's time considered

[1] *Ideas of Good and Evil* (New York: Macmillan, 1912), pp. 241–242.

the perfect substance; 7. sadness, because of the contrast between golden youth and the thought of death. The appearance of *golden* in the second poem will remind the literate reader of its use in Shakespeare's poem, because the two contexts are similar, and the Shakespearean connotations will be alive in the second poem.

Fear No More the Heat o' the Sun

Fear no more the heat o' the sun,   *1*
   Nor the furious winter's rages;
Thou thy worldly task hast done,
   Home art gone, and ta'en thy wages;
Golden lads and girls all must,   *5*
As chimney-sweepers, come to dust.

Fear no more the frown o' the great,
   Thou art past the tyrant's stroke:
Care no more to clothe and eat;
   To thee the reed is as the oak: *10*
The sceptre, learning, physic, must
All follow this, and come to dust.

Fear no more the lightning-flash,
   Nor the all-dreaded thunder-stone;
Fear not slander, censure rash;   *15*
   Thou has finish'd joy and moan:
All lovers young, all lovers must
Consign to thee, and come to dust.

No exorciser harm thee!
   Nor no witchcraft charm thee!   *20*
Ghost unlaid forbear thee!
   Nothing ill come near thee!
Quiet consummation have;
And renowned be thy grave!

            WILLIAM SHAKESPEARE

With Rue My Heart Is Laden

With rue my heart is laden   *1*
   For golden friends I had,
For many a rose-lipt maiden
   And many a lightfoot lad.

By brooks too broad for leaping   5
  The lightfoot boys are laid;
The rose-lipt girls are sleeping
  In fields where roses fade.

       A. E. HOUSMAN

2. The following poem is based on Milton's *Paradise Lost*. Prince Lucifer was the leader of many angels who, having revolted in Heaven against God, were cast down through space into Hell, where they were condemned to suffer. Lucifer is the ruler of this dark dominion. Study this next poem below as a preparation for the one which follows it. Be prepared to discuss the effect of the borrowed line.

Lucifer in Starlight

On a starred night Prince Lucifer uprose.   1
Tired of his dark dominion swung the fiend
Above the rolling ball in cloud part screened,
Where sinners hugged their spectre of repose.
Poor prey to his hot fit of pride were those.   5
And now upon his western wing he leaned,
Now his huge bulk o'er Afric's sands careened,
Now the black planet shadowed Arctic snows.
Soaring through wider zones that pricked his scars
With memory of the old revolt from Awe,   10
He reached a middle height, and at the stars,
Which are the brain of heaven, he looked, and sank.
Around the ancient track marched, rank on rank,
The army of unalterable law.

       GEORGE MEREDITH

Cousin Nancy

Miss Nancy Ellicott   1
Strode across the hills and broke them,
Rode across the hills and broke them—
The barren New England hills—
Riding to hounds   5
Over the cow-pasture.

Miss Nancy Ellicott smoked
And danced all the modern dances;

And her aunts were not quite sure how they felt
  about it,
But they knew that it was modern.   *10*

Upon the glazen shelves kept watch
Matthew and Waldo, guardians of the faith,
The army of unalterable law.

T. S. ELIOT

ILLUSTRATIVE POEMS

The Cambridge Ladies

the Cambridge ladies who live in furnished souls   *1*
are unbeautiful and have comfortable minds
(also, with the church's protestant blessings
daughters, unscented shapeless spirited)
they believe in Christ and Longfellow, both dead,   *5*
are invariably interested in so many things—
at the present writing one still finds
delighted fingers knitting for the is it Poles?
perhaps. While permanent faces coyly bandy
scandal of Mrs. N and Professor D   *10*
. . . the Cambridge ladies do not care, above
Cambridge if sometimes in its box of
sky lavender and cornerless, the
moon rattles like a fragment of angry candy

E. E. CUMMINGS

After Great Pain a Formal Feeling Comes

After great pain a formal feeling comes—   *1*
The nerves sit ceremonious like tombs ;
The stiff Heart questions—was it He that bore?
And yesterday—or centuries before?

The feet mechanical   *5*
Go round a wooden way
Of ground or air or Ought, regardless grown,
A quartz contentment like a stone.

This is the hour of lead
Remembered if outlived,   *10*
As freezing persons recollect the snow—
First chill, then stupor, then the letting go.

EMILY DICKINSON

4

IMAGERY

Objects of perception of all our senses may be reproduced as images in the mind. For example, you can at this minute image in your mind your class room building; you can image your favorite tune; you can image the taste of chocolate, the smell of cheese, the cold of a winter wind, the heft of a weight in your hand. And you can conjure up in your mind a medley of images of different sense perceptions, as might occur if you image a hamburger sizzling on a hot griddle; this cluster of images might include the sputtering sound, the fragrant odor, and the luscious sight of a flat, round object, crispy and brown. Such mental reproduction of sense perceptions, when called up by memory or by words, we call imagery.

The language of poetry makes much use of words which call up imagery because poets like to deal concretely with experience. When imagery is absent, as in many poor poems, we say that the poem is prosy. Two stanzas will serve as illustrations. The first, from Tennyson's *In Memoriam*, contains a series of simple images; the second is a statement of a mathematical theorem versified in the same stanza form as the first, but is almost barren of images. The first stanza is poetry; the second is metrical prose.

1. The time draws near the birth of Christ:
        The moon is hid; the night is still;
        The Christmas bells from hill to hill
    Answer each other in the mist.

2. And hence no force, however great,
        Can draw a cord, however fine,
        Into a horizontal line
    Which shall be absolutely straight.[1]

VISUAL IMAGERY AND VARIATIONS. In poetry, visual imagery is the most common kind. Individuals vary greatly in the visual imagery they create from the words of poetry—in the vividness and richness of their mind-pictures and in the details that they will image from the same words. With some the pictures are full and distinct; with others, vague and meager. In most readers, however, the mental pictures become more elaborate if the material read is such that it baffles rapid understanding—as is often the case in poetry—and if time is allowed for response to develop.[2] Because time is required for the fullest development of imagery in the mind of the reader, it is wise to read rather slowly and deliberately, and even to pause occasionally to permit the images to take form.

Highly individual imagery is sometimes called into being by words because of vivid and recent experiences of a person. An example of such individual imagery is afforded by the war veteran who had recently served in the Aleutians. There he had become accustomed to flaming red sunsets seen across the bay and reflected on the hills. Because of this experience his imaging of the following lines was largely a re-creation of the Aleutian sunsets he had known:

The splendour falls on castle walls
    And snowy summits old in story:
The long light shakes across the lakes,
    And the wild cataract leaps in glory.

ALFRED, LORD TENNYSON

---

[1] See Bliss Perry, *A Study of Poetry* (Boston: Houghton Mifflin, 1920), p. 155.

[2] These psychological data are taken from M. D. Vernon's *Visual Perception* (Cambridge [England]: Cambridge University Press, 1937).

Another student took a walk along Iowa hills beside the Cedar River. During his walk he rested and stared down upon the dark still water reflecting brown autumn trees in the light and shadow of a late afternoon in October. Upon his return home he picked up a new volume of poetry to read. The first stanza in the book was the following, and the imagery it called up was a vivid picture of the exact details of the scene he had just left:

The river this November afternoon
Rests in an equipoise of sun and cloud:
A glooming light, a gleaming darkness shroud
Its passage. All seems tranquil, all in tune.

                    C. DAY LEWIS

Variations in imaginal reproduction, however, are no cause for concern, because images created by given words may differ in the minds of different readers and yet have the same effects in directing thought and arousing emotion. That variations in the readers' visual images need not interfere with a more or less constant effect may be illustrated by the two following poems.

The Gold-Threaded Coat

Covet not the gold-threaded coat,
Grasp the years when you are young,
When the flowers open come pluck them;
Do not wait to gather a spent spray from an empty bough.

    TU CH'IU-NIANG, TRANSLATED BY SOAME JENYNS

The flowers of the third line may be imaged in many ways, *e.g.*, as cherry, elder, lilac, or hydrangea flowers, and the bough may be visualized as of any size, shape, or kind. Regardless of the precise visualization of these details, there remains the contrast of fresh and withered flowers, suggesting the differences between youth and old age, and no reader will misunderstand what the poet is saying through these images.

The next poem is filled with relatively unspecific words like *ships, towers, fields, valley, rock, river, houses,* which different readers will image in many different ways according to their individual past experiences. Yet, despite these variations in imagery, the beauty and majesty of a city in the early morning light and the feelings that this vision evokes are available to all readers.

Composed Upon Westminster Bridge Sept. 3, 1802

Earth has not anything to show more fair: *1*
Dull would he be of soul who could pass by
A sight so touching in its majesty:
This City now doth, like a garment, wear
The beauty of the morning; silent, bare,   *5*
Ships, towers, domes, theatres, and temples lie
Open unto the fields, and to the sky;
All bright and glittering in the smokeless air.
Never did sun more beautifully steep
In his first splendour, valley, rock, or hill;   *10*
Ne'er saw I, never felt, a calm so deep!
The river glideth at his own sweet will:
Dear God! the very houses seem asleep;
And all that mighty heart is lying still![3]

WILLIAM WORDSWORTH

EXERCISE

Read the following poems slowly and deliberately, imaging as fully as you can, and prepare to point out in class what senses are involved in your imagery. In the class discussion about the images in the poems, observe the variations in the imaging of different students.

Twilight

Darkness comes out of the earth   *1*
    And swallows dip into the pallor of the west;
From the hay comes the clamour of children's mirth;
    Wanes the old palimpsest.

---

[3] The following scene, described in Dorothy Wordsworth's *Journal*, may have been the inspiration for this sonnet: "We left London on Saturday morning at half past five or six. . . . It was a beautiful morning. The city, St. Paul's, with the river, and a multitude of little boats, made a most beautiful sight as we crossed Westminster Bridge. The houses were not over-hung by their cloud of smoke, and they were spread out endlessly, yet the sun shone so brightly, with such a fierce light, that there was something like the purity of one of nature's own grand spectacles."

The night-stock oozes scent,   *5*
   And a moon-blue moth goes flittering by:
All that the worldly day has meant
   Wastes like a lie.

The children have forsaken their play;
   A single star in a veil of light   *10*
Glimmers: litter of day
   Is gone from sight.

D. H. LAWRENCE

Dulce Et Decorum Est

Bent double, like old beggars under sacks,   *1*
Knock-kneed, coughing like hags, we cursed through sludge,
Till on the haunting flares we turned our backs,
And towards our distant rest began to trudge.
Men marched asleep. Many had lost their boots,   *5*
But limped on, blood-shod. All went lame, all blind;
Drunk with fatigue; deaf even to the hoots
Of gas-shells dropping softly behind.

Gas! GAS! Quick, boys!—An ecstasy of fumbling,
Fitting the clumsy helmets just in time,   *10*
But someone still was yelling out and stumbling
And floundering like a man in fire or lime.—
Dim through the misty panes and thick green light,
As under a green sea, I saw him drowning.

In all my dreams before my helpless sight   *15*
He plunges at me, guttering, choking, drowning.

If in some smothering dreams, you too could pace
Behind the wagon that we flung him in,
And watch the white eyes writhing in his face,
His hanging face, like a devil's sick of sin;   *20*
If you could hear, at every jolt, the blood
Come gargling from the froth-corrupted lungs,
Bitter as the cud
Of vile, incurable sores on innocent tongues,—

My friend, you would not tell with such high zest   *25*
To children ardent for some desperate glory,
The old Lie: Dulce et decorum est
Pro patria mori.
WILFRED OWEN

Two kinds of imagery, auditory and articulatory, are important for a special purpose—the experiencing of sound effects.

AUDITORY IMAGERY. Auditory imagery means the mental reproduction of sounds. In the silent reading of poetry we experience two kinds of auditory imagery: the imaging of the sounds that words symbolize and the imaging of the sounds of the words themselves. For example, when we read "the dog barked" we can have an image not only of the sound of barking but also of the sound of the word *barked*. This latter kind, the reproduction in our nervous systems of the sounds of words, is tremendously important, for it enables us to sense the music of poetry without the necessity of reading aloud. Let us try an example. Read the following line aloud, giving the words resonance and force:

Boomlay, boomlay, boomlay, BOOM!
VACHEL LINDSAY

Now, read it silently, trying to hear the sounds of the words. By such auditory imaging as you have just done, practiced readers of poetry enjoy the sounds of poems while reading silently.

EXERCISE
Read this poem aloud, emphasizing with your voice the words which are vividly descriptive of or imitative of sounds. Then read it silently and try to hear the same effect.

Jazz Fantasia

Drum on your drums, batter on your banjoes,   *1*
sob on the long cool winding saxophones.
Go to it, O jazzmen.

Sling your knuckles on the bottoms of the happy
tin pans, let your trombones ooze, and go husha-   *5*
husha-hush with the slippery sand-paper.

Moan like an autumn wind high in the lonesome tree-
tops, moan soft like you wanted somebody terrible,
cry like a racing car slipping away from a motorcycle
cop, bang-bang! you jazzmen, bang altogether drums,   *10*
traps, banjoes, horns, tin cans—make two people fight
on the top of a stairway and scratch each other's eyes
in a clinch tumbling down the stairs.

Can the rough stuff . . . now a Mississippi steamboat
pushes up the night river with a hoo-hoo-hoo-oo . . .   *15*
and the green lanterns calling to the high soft stars
. . . a red moon rides on the humps of the low river
hills . . . go to it, O jazzmen.

CARL SANDBURG

ARTICULATORY IMAGERY. Articulatory imagery is the
mental reproduction of movements made by the vocal apparatus in
producing speech sounds. Its main components are images of muscular strain and images of touch sensations. Such imagery is caused
by incipient movements of articulation. These movements sometimes
become perceptible. For example, if you will place your fingers
firmly on both sides of your Adam's apple and forcefully image the
SOUND of *squeak*, holding the *ea*, you may feel slight muscular
movements of your throat muscles. Another experiment may be
tried with the word *bubble:* (1) Speak the word *bubble* distinctly
three times; (2) next, image the SOUND of the word distinctly,
that is, speak it silently, three times; (3) now, stretch your mouth
wide open and image the SOUND of the word again. If your articulatory image seems distorted, the reason is that in step three you
have disturbed the normal incipient movements of articulation.
From this discussion it becomes evident that a line like Browning's

Fee, faw, fum! bubble and squeak!

is most vivid to a reader who has developed his powers of articulatory imagery.

Articulatory imagery enables us, in the silent reading of poetry,
to sense both rough and smooth qualities of the sounds of successive
words. For instance, in the following line by Browning, the rough-

ness, that is, the difficulty of articulation, may be sensed, even though the line is read silently, not aloud:

Rough iron-spiked, ripe fruit—o'ercrusted.

Likewise, the smoothness, the ease of articulation, of this line by Coleridge may be sensed in silent reading:

Alone, alone, all, all, alone.

Both articulatory and auditory imagery must be deliberately cultivated if the reader is to savor fully the music of poetry and to become aware of the effects of speech sounds, as sounds, upon meaning.

EXERCISE

The three following passages from Tennyson's "The Passing of Arthur" illustrate the skillful use of articulatory imagery. The first describes a battle between two hosts of knights in armor. The second and third describe a knight walking over rough terrain to reach the edge of a lake. Read each passage aloud and then silently. Point out the articulatory imagery. Does it at any place reinforce the meaning of the words? In passages two and three observe the change in the nature of the articulatory imagery at the end of each.

1. And ever and anon with host to host
    Shocks, and the splintering spear, the hard mail hewn,
    Shield-breakings, and the clash of brands, the crash
    Of battleaxes on shatter'd helms, . . .

2.   He, stepping down
    By zigzag paths, and juts of pointed rock,
    Came on the shining levels of the lake.

3. But the other swiftly strode from ridge to ridge,   *1*
    Clothed with his breath, and looking, as he walk'd
    Larger than human on the frozen hills.
    He heard the deep behind him, and a cry
    Before. His own thought drove him like a goad.   *5*
    Dry clash'd his harness in the icy caves

And barren chasms, and all to left and right
The bare black cliff clang'd round him, as he based
His feet on juts of slippery crag that rang
Sharp-smitten with the dint of armed heels—   *10*
And on a sudden, lo! the level lake,
And the long glories of the winter moon.

ILLUSTRATIVE POEMS

Lew Sarett, the author of the next poem, has written an explanatory note about it:

When the primitive Indian of the Canadian North went hunting in the old days, he "called" or lured moose by two methods. Sometimes with a folded piece of birch-bark at his lips he would imitate the blare and bellow of a moose. This mode of "calling" still survives among woods Indians in moose-country and is often used by white men. There was another method, however, not well-known to white men. At dusk, when the wind went down and the water was quiet, when it is the habit of moose to come out of the "bush" to the lakes, to drink, to feed upon the lily-roots, and to plunge into the water in order to shake off the moose-flies, the deer-flies and the "no-see-ums"—then the Indian would wade into the water of any quiet lake used much by moose—they have their favorite watering places. Here for hours the Indian would imitate the splashings and drippings of a feeding moose, on the theory that moose in the neighborhood in the tranquil evening would hear the sounds and would be drawn to the immediate vicinity of the hunting Indian. "Red-Rock, the Moose-Hunter," is based on this old, uncommon technique of "calling" moose.[4]

Red-Rock the Moose-Hunter

Bronze in the rose-dusted twilight,   *1*
A statue of bronze, arms uplifted,
He stands ankle-deep in the lilies
As rigidly fixed and as silent
As a red granite butte on the prairie,   *5*

---

[4] *The Collected Poems of Lew Sarett* (New York: Henry Holt, 1941), pp. 346–347.

As still as the dusk in the foot-hills—
"Ho! Red-Rock, big hunter-of-moose!
Red-Rock, him fool-um old bull!
Red-Rock, big moose-killer!—Wuh!"—
Bronze in the tranquil sunset,   *10*
Statuesque bronze in the willows.

A sudden rush through the lilies;
A splashing of flashing limbs,
Shattering his mirror of silver—
Juggling his gold-glinted rainbows,   *15*
And flinging them into the winds;
A sudden swoop through the waters,
A sudden scoop of the hands—
And bronze in the copper twilight,
With arms uplifted he stands,   *20*
Statuesque bronze in the lilies—
"Red-Rock, big caller-of-moose!—Wuh!"

Dripping, dripping, dripping
Blue-shimmering drops through his fingers;
Dripping, dripping, dripping   *25*
Thin tinkling streams from his palms;
Plashing, plashing, plashing
Cupped handfuls of silvery waters
Splashing among the lilies—
Black bronze in the purple twilight,   *30*
Statuesque bronze in the night—
"Red-Rock! Big hunter-of-moose!—Wuh!"

A long low call from the valley;
A bellow, and echoing bugle
Mellow and deep with the passion   *35*
Of lone longing male for his mate:
"Hark! Hark! sweet One-in-the-Lilies!
Ho! my Splashing-One! Ho!
I come!—with my limbs aquiver!
I come!—with a straining of flanks!"   *40*

Beat-beating, beat-beating, beat-beating,
Long-loping feet in the forest ;
A clashing of horn in the timber,
A crashing of hoofs in the brush . . .
A splash in the placid bayou,   *45*
An eager nose to the air,
And lo! a palpitant bellow,
A wild-ringing rapturous blare! . . .

Black bronze in the cool blue moonlight.
Black statuesque bronze in the night.   *50*
Cupped hands to the stars uplifted—
Dripping, dripping, dripping
Thin tinkling streamlets of silver,
Soft-plashing fountains of silver,
Shimmering-blue sprinklings of silver—   *55*
"Red-Rock! Big killer-of-moose!—Wuh!"

LEW SARETT

A Prairie Sunset

Shot gold, maroon and violet, dazzling silver, emerald, fawn,   *1*
The earth's whole amplitude and Nature's multiform power
    consign'd for once to colors ;
The light, the general air possess'd by them—colors till now
    unknown,
No limit, confine—not the Western sky alone—the high me-
    ridian—North, South, all,
Pure luminous color fighting the silent shadows to the last.   *5*

WALT WHITMAN

The Great Lover (Excerpt)

These I have loved: *1*
        White plates and cups, clean-gleaming,
Ringed with blue lines ; and feathery, faery dust ;
Wet roofs, beneath the lamplight ; the strong crust
Of friendly bread ; and many-tasting food ;   *5*
Rainbows ; and the blue bitter smoke of wood ;

And radiant raindrops couching in cool flowers;
And flowers themselves, that sway through sunny hours,
Dreaming of moths that drink them under the moon;
Then, the cool kindliness of sheets, that soon   *10*
Smooth away trouble; and the rough male kiss
Of blankets; grainy wood; live hair that is
Shining and free; blue-massing clouds; the keen
Unpassioned beauty of a great machine;
The benison of hot water; furs to touch;   *15*
The good smell of old clothes; and other such—
The comfortable smell of friendly fingers,
Hair's fragrance, and the musty reek that lingers
About dead leaves and last year's ferns. . . .

RUPERT BROOKE

Meeting at Night

The grey sea and the long black land;   *1*
And the yellow half-moon large and low;
And the startled little waves that leap
In fiery ringlets from their sleep,
As I gain the cove with pushing prow,   *5*
And quench its speed i' the slushy sand.

Then a mile of warm sea-scented beach;
Three fields to cross till a farm appears;
A tap at the pane, the quick sharp scratch
And blue spurt of a lighted match,   *10*
And a voice less loud, through its joys and fears,
Than the two hearts beating each to each!

ROBERT BROWNING

5

FIGURATIVE LANGUAGE

Poetry is written in a language which makes ample use of figures of speech. Such figures, however, are seldom merely ornamental, like gargoyles on a Gothic cathedral, but instead form an integral part of what the poet has to say. They are more like the arched windows encased in stone, giving essential support to the structure and illuminating the interior with light and color. In other words, figures of speech serve a structural purpose in poetry and make possible a richness and complexity unattainable through literal statement. To understand poetry, then, it is imperative that one learn how to interpret figurative language.

Figurative language makes use of many kinds of figures of speech, of which we shall now study the four most important: simile, metaphor, personification (called figures of similarity), and symbol.[1]

FIGURES OF SIMILARITY

SIMILE. A simile is a statement of similarity introduced by *like* or *as*, for example, Christopher Morley's "the alert faces of women shoppers, turning this way and that *like* foraging poultry."

---

[1] The figures of paradox, irony, understatement, overstatement, and inversion are dealt with in Chapter *10*.

We observe here how simple the structure of the simile is: the item under discussion is mentioned; a comparing word, *like* or *as*, is used; and a second item similar to the first in some respects is mentioned. The two items compared are usually unlike in most respects.

METAPHOR.   A metaphor is an expression used in a new sense, on the basis of similarity between its literal sense and the new thing or situation to which it is applied. It might be called an implied simile. A few examples will make this clear. In a language of the South Pacific called Melanesian Pidgin, the expression used to name the mouth of a gun is *eye-belong-musket*. Here the word *eye* is used in a new sense on the basis of similarity between an actual eye, the literal sense, and the appearance of the end of a gun. *Eye* is therefore a metaphor, just as it is in our everyday expressions, the *eye* of a needle and the *eye* of a potato. In Chinese, when an expression was needed as a name for torpedo, two existing words were combined to produce a new expression which is translated literally as *fish-thunder*. This metaphor is based on the similarity of a torpedo to the appearance and movement of a fish and to the sound of thunder. In French, the knob at the upper end of a walking stick is called the *apple* of a cane, whereas in English it is called the *head* of a cane. Here we have a French metaphor based on similarity of shape, and an English metaphor based on similarity of both shape and position. Sometimes the similarity between the two things brought together in a metaphor consists of the similar feelings that each thing arouses. When, for example, we say, "That guy is a rat," the similarity of *guy* to *rat* is not that of physical details but of the feelings that the person and the rat each arouses. This kind of metaphor, based on similarity of feelings aroused, is called an emotive metaphor. Likewise, we also have emotive similes.

Our daily language is filled with metaphors. For example, in one set of terms alone, the names of the parts of the body, we get a long list of metaphors: the *head* of a pin, the *foot* of a ladder, the *neck* of a bottle, the *shoulders* of a highway, the *lip* of a cup, the *brow* of a hill, the *elbow* of a pipe, the *knee*-action of an automobile, the *throat* of a flower, *kidney* beans, the *heart* of the argument, the *nose* of an airplane, an iron *lung*, the *veins* of a leaf, an *arterial* highway, to *stomach* a person, the *tongue* of a wagon, a line of poetry *pulses*, and many others. You are using metaphors when you *wolf* your food, feel *cocky, get a toehold* on an economics problem, *hit the jackpot* in an examination, or find a lesson *easy sailing*.

A metaphor that is commonly used may lose in our minds the element of similarity that originally prompted it. If, for example, we hear of the *face* of a cliff and think only of the cliff itself, forgetting its similarity to a human face, then the metaphor is no longer alive. Such a term is called a dead metaphor. A metaphor may, of course, be alive for one person and dead for another. For example, an Easterner visiting a friend in Wyoming might be invited to *tie up* for the night. The Easterner, for whom the expression is new, would be conscious of a similarity between his arrival by automobile and that of a man on horseback; thus, for him, the words *tie up* would be a live metaphor. But the Westerner, for whom the expression is a common one, might have in mind only the sense of *stay;* for him, then, the expression is a dead metaphor.

Dead metaphors are numerous in our everyday speech. We speak of the following, for instance, usually without any thought of similarity between two things: a *dry* book, a *brilliant* student, *shallow* thinking, *dropping* a course, and *pursuing* a subject. In the paragraph above about metaphors from names of parts of the body, most of the examples are dead metaphors.

Many common words embody metaphors that died centuries ago in the course of language change. Here are a few of them, together with their early literal meanings which show the basis of similarity: nasturtium = twisted nose; muscle = little mouse; window = wind-eye; daisy = day's eye (= the sun); thrilling = piercing; pavilion = butterfly; insipid = tasteless; grenade = pomegranate; seminary = seed garden; porpoise = pig-fish; to meander = to move like a winding river; to ponder = to weigh. Students of those languages that have contributed to the English vocabulary become acquainted with countless metaphors of this kind and gain thereby an enrichment of word-understanding that is unknown to the average reader.

A metaphor may take the following forms:

1. Noun: The boil has not yet come to a *head*.
2. Verb: He *headed* the long, black sedan into a dark alley.
3. Adjective: The navigation for the flight was done in the *head* bomber.

4. Adverb: Spinning crazily, the little plane plunged
                  headlong into the sea.
5. Word-group: [Describing a field of daffodils]
                  Ten thousand saw I at a glance
                  Tossing their heads in sprightly dance.

PERSONIFICATION. Personification is a metaphor in which a lifeless object, an animal, or abstract idea is made to act like a person. It imputes human life and attributes and motives to lifeless objects, animals, and abstract ideas and thereby endows with animation, vividness, and nearness those things which are normally thought of as impersonal and aloof from human affairs. It is used a great deal in our everyday language, as in expressions like these: the sun smiled upon the meadows; an over-powering fear clutched him by the throat; autumn put on her brightest robes; winter undressed the trees; his fingers stuttered at the typewriter; a frowning sky threatened to rain; the robin perched on the bird bath and proudly made her toilet. In poetry, too, personification is frequently used; the following examples are personifications of morning:

1. But look, the morn, in russet mantle clad,
    Walks o'er the dew of yon high eastward hill.
                    WILLIAM SHAKESPEARE

2. Full many a glorious morning have I seen
    Flatter the mountain-tops with sovereign eye,
    Kissing with golden face the meadows green,
    Gilding pale streams with heavenly alchemy.
                    WILLIAM SHAKESPEARE

3. Now morn her rosy steps in th' Eastern Clime
    Advancing, sow'd the Earth with Orient Pearl.
                    JOHN MILTON

4. The joyous morning ran and kissed the grass
    And drew his fingers through her sleeping hair.
                    JOHN FREEMAN

1. List ten figures of similarity that employ words from each of these two areas:

A.   Animal life

> *Examples:*   1. He is *chicken*-hearted.
>   2. Don't *monkey* around with my radio.
>   3. He slid through the tacklers like an *eel*.

B.   Sports

> *Examples:*   1. He has an *ace up his sleeve* in the debate.
>   2. You're *skating on thin ice* if you don't study for that test.
>   3. I've got *two strikes on me already* with that new girl; I don't think I'll even *get to first base*.

2. Many of our folk sayings are metaphors which express commonplace ideas with vividness and succinctness. Here are a few:

A. Don't put all your eggs in one basket.
B. Too many cooks spoil the broth.
C. You can't teach an old dog new tricks.

Write down ten such folk metaphors and then write in unfigurative language the meaning of each. Which are better, the metaphors or your statements of their meaning? Why?

TENOR AND VEHICLE.   In a figure of similarity, there are always two parts which are similar. For instance, in Burns'

Your locks are like the snow

the first part *locks* is similar in color to the second part *snow*. These two parts of any figure of similarity are called respectively the tenor and the vehicle. The tenor is what the poet is really talking about, the actual thing or situation. In the example above, the tenor is *locks*. The vehicle is that part brought in because of its similarity in some respect to the tenor. In the same example above, the vehicle is *snow;* it is similar to the tenor *locks* in color. Let us look at another example:

The fog comes
on little cat feet.

In this metaphor the poet is really talking about the fog, so we call *fog* the tenor. The part brought in because of its similarity to *fog* is *cat;* hence *cat* is the vehicle; it is similar to the tenor *fog* in quietness of movement.

A figure of similarity may be developed in detail so that the vehicle has numerous parts, each having a link of similarity with the tenor. These lines by W. D. Howells will illustrate:

Tossing his mane of snows, in wildest eddies and tangles,
Lion-like March cometh in, hoarse, with tempestuous breath.

We can easily chart this version of the ancient simile that "March comes in like a lion" to show how we transfer the attributes of the vehicle to the tenor:

Vehicle	Tenor
Lion	= *Month of March*
A. Tossing his mane in eddies and tangles	= With whirling snows
B. Hoarse	= With noise of wind and water
C. With tempestuous breath	= With high winds

We note here that the vehicle *lion* has numerous parts, each capable of being interpreted in terms of the tenor *March* and its parts.

In a figure of similarity either the tenor or the vehicle, or parts of each, may be understood without being expressly stated. Let us examine an illustration of this in a line by C. Day Lewis:

Sunlight and shadows in the copse play tig [=tag]

The picture is clear: in the copse, or wood, the sunlight and shadows make rapid, jerky movements like those of children playing tag. In the first half of the metaphor the tenor is *sunlight and shadows,* because this is what the poet is really talking about; the vehicle here must be *children,* though they are not mentioned, because it is children who would play tag. Here then it is the vehicle *children* which is understood, not stated. In the second half of the metaphor it is the vehicle *play tig* which is actually mentioned. But the children's game is not the real subject here; what the poet is really saying is that sunlight and shadows *make rapid jerky movements.* Here then it is the tenor which is understood, not stated. A chart will show these relationships:

Vehicle	Tenor
Children (*understood*)	= Sunlight and shadows
Play tig	= Make rapid, jerky movements (*understood*)

But a figure of similarity is not a mathematical equation of tenor-and-vehicle equivalents in which every term must be balanced by a counterpart. Sometimes it contains terms which literally apply to the vehicle but which are not to be given a figurative interpretation. In the poem below the term *haunches* is a part of the vehicle *cat* but has by itself no special figurative sense:

Fog

The fog comes   *1*
on little cat feet.

It sits looking
over harbor and city
on silent haunches   *5*
and then moves on.

    CARL SANDBURG

Again, a figure of similarity may contain words which are appropriate to the poem but which really do not belong to the figure at all. A line of Edith Sitwell's will provide a simple example:

Whinnying, neighed the maned blue wind.

In this metaphor the tenor is *wind* and the vehicle is *horse*, understood. The sound of the wind is described by *whinnying* and *neighed*, which are parts of the vehicle. But *maned*, a part of the vehicle *horse*, has no precise equivalent in the tenor *wind*, which is invisible. This will cause no difficulty to the imaginative reader. He will perhaps image a flowing mane, since a wind must be in motion, and may interpret this flowing mane as an associated image, such as trees bending before the blast or clouds swiftly scudding across a sky. In the case of the word *blue* we have a term which can actually describe neither the tenor *wind* nor the vehicle *horse*. It is really not a part of the figure at all, and must be interpreted as an associated image, perhaps descriptive of a background sky.

Occasionally the tenor and vehicle of a figure of similarity are united by only a single link of similarity. The purpose of such a figure is to illustrate, that is, to give greater clearness and definiteness to the subject. The following couplet by Pope is an example of an illustrative simile:

Words are like leaves ; and where they most abound
Much fruit of sense beneath is rarely found.

But often in poetry the tenor and vehicle are united by numerous links of similarity. Let us look at a time-proved example by Oliver W. Holmes:

If I should live to be
The last leaf on the tree
  In the spring.

As we explore this metaphor we shall find that it is rich with many possible similarities between the tenor, *an old man,* and the vehicle, *the last leaf on the tree in the spring.* We may think of a curled-up, bent shape; wrinkles and blemishes; tawniness of color; loneliness; old age; weakness against opposing forces; precarious hold on life; and other things. No two readers will perhaps be conscious of the same set of similarities, and the figure will be the most meaningful to the reader who sees the most similarities. The richness of this metaphor may be readily felt by comparing it with a similarly patterned metaphor which is merely illustrative, that is, which has but a single link of similarity between tenor and vehicle:

If I should then become
The last tooth in the gum
  Of a crone.

When tenor and vehicle are brought together in a figure of similarity, there may be innumerable links of similarity that an ingenious reader can find, but if he probes too deeply he might spoil the impression that the poet wishes to create. As an example, let us examine a metaphor by Thomas Campion:

There is a garden in her face
  Where roses and white lilies grow.

The vehicle, a garden with roses and white lilies, is used to describe the tenor, the face of a young woman. By this metaphor the poet probably intends to suggest a soft, fair complexion, pink cheeks, red lips, youthfulness, fragrance, grace, and beauty. But an over-zealous reader might go further, visualizing in the vehicle such images as spots on the lily and weeds in the garden; and he might try to interpret these incongruous details in terms of a young woman's face, considering for example the spots on the lily as freckles on her nose. Such misinterpretation will spoil the response intended by the poet, although the reading of the rest of the poem, the whole context, should correct the misinterpretation.

To restrain us from bringing incongruous details into the figure, the poet may present it in a restrictive context, which helps to guide the reader's response into the desired channel and to exclude inappropriate interpretations. An example of this is T. S. Eliot's simile:

The readers of the *Boston Evening Transcript*
Sway in the wind like a field of ripe corn.

The Boston Evening Transcript was a conservative newspaper read by conservative persons. This context helps to guide our response to the simile: we see that the readers' opinions bend in one direction just as tall corn bows before the wind, and we may even image heads nodding assent, like ripe ears of corn bobbing in the wind. Now let us change the context of the simile and see what happens:

The soldiers in the endless column dragging
Flutter with rags like a field of ripe corn.

Our points of similarity are now different. The corn is not just a large expanse; it stands in rows. We see random movements of long brownish leaves and a general weatherbeaten, ragged, and torn aspect of the corn because such details are demanded by the changed context.

When the vehicles of two or more metaphors are combined to form the vehicle of a single metaphor, we have what is called a mixed metaphor. As a flagrant example, the following from a comic strip will serve: "If we don't stop shearing the sheep that lays the golden egg, we'll pump it dry." Here the vehicles of three different metaphors are combined to express a single meaning, and because each of the three is alive, we are conscious of the incongruity of the resultant mixed metaphor. The mixed metaphor is usually the result of a writer's use of a metaphor that is dead for him but alive for some readers. For example, Stephen Spender uses a dead and a live metaphor in one line from "The Funeral" describing a factory worker as

One cog in a golden and singing hive.

Here, if the *cog* metaphor is dead for the reader, as it apparently was for the poet, *i.e.*, if he thinks of *cog* simply as an important and useful part, without reference to a wheel or machine, then he will read the line as a simple metaphor. If however the *cog* metaphor is alive for him, *i.e.*, if he thinks of the worker as a cog on a wheel, then he will realize that it would not be found in a bee hive, and for him the line will be a mixed metaphor.

EXERCISE

1. Although the following figures of similarity have been taken out of their total context in poems, each is self-sufficient enough to be studied by itself. Interpret each one, pointing out the similarities between vehicle and tenor that form the basis of the figure.

A.   The wine of life keeps oozing drop by drop.
           EDWARD FITZGERALD

B.   April, April,
         Laugh thy girlish laughter;
     Then, the moment after,
         Weep thy girlish tears.
         WILLIAM WATSON

C.   the rough male kiss
     Of blankets.
         RUPERT BROOKE

D.   Its edges foam'd with amethyst and rose,
     Withers once more the old blue flower of day.
           G. W. RUSSELL

E. Dim as the borrow'd beams of moon and stars   *1*
   To lonely, weary, wand'ring travelers
   Is Reason to the soul: and, as on high
   Those rolling fires discover but the sky,
   Not light us here; so Reason's glimmering ray   *5*
   Was lent, not to assure our doubtful way,
   But guide us upward to a better day.
   And as those nightly tapers disappear
   When day's bright lord ascends our hemisphere;
   So pale grows Reason at Religion's sight;   *10*
   So dies, and so dissolves in supernatural light.

                    JOHN DRYDEN

F.   *A little learning* is a dang'rous thing;   *1*
   Drink deep, or taste not the Pierian spring:
   There shallow draughts intoxicate the brain,
   And drinking largely sobers us again.
   Fired at first sight with what the Muse imparts,   *5*
   In fearless youth we tempt the heights of Arts,
   While from the bounded level of our mind
   Short views we take, nor see the lengths behind;
   But more advanced, behold with strange surprise
   New distant scenes of endless science rise!   *10*
   So pleased at first the tow'ring Alps we try,
   Mount o'er the vales, and seem to tread the sky,
   Th' eternal snows appear already past,
   And the first clouds and mountains seem the last;
   But, those attained, we tremble to survey   *15*
   The growing labours of the lengthened way,
   Th' increasing prospect tires our wand'ring eyes,
   Hills peep o'er hills, and Alps on Alps arise![2]

                  ALEXANDER POPE

G. The yellow fog that rubs its back upon the window-panes,   *1*
   The yellow smoke that rubs its muzzle on the window-panes
   Licked its tongue into the corners of the evening,
   Lingered upon the pools that stand in drains,

---

[2] Of this figure Samuel Johnson has made the following comment: ". . . the comparison of a student's progress in the sciences with the journey of a traveller in the Alps, is perhaps the best that English poetry can shew. . . . The simile of the Alps has no useless parts, yet affords a striking picture by itself; it makes the foregoing position better understood, and enables it to take faster hold on attention; it assists the apprehension, and elevates the fancy."

Let fall upon its back the soot that falls from chimneys,   *5*
Slipped by the terrace, made a sudden leap,
And seeing that it was a soft October night,
Curled once about the house, and fell asleep.

T. S. ELIOT

2. Interpret the following poem, which consists of an expanded simile:

Nature

As a fond mother, when the day is o'er,   *1*
Leads by the hand her little child to bed,
Half willing, half reluctant to be led,
And leave his broken playthings on the floor,
Still gazing at them through the open door,   *5*
Nor wholly reassured and comforted
By promises of others in their stead,
Which, though more splendid, may not please him more;
So Nature deals with us, and takes away
Our playthings one by one, and by the hand   *10*
Leads us to rest so gently, that we go
Scarce knowing if we wish to go or stay,
Being too full of sleep to understand
How far the unknown transcends the what we know.

HENRY WADSWORTH LONGFELLOW

3. The following poem by Robert Burns is made up of stanzas which the poet borrowed from songs of his time and modified to suit his purpose. Here is the first stanza before it was made over by Burns:

Her cheeks were like the roses
    That blossom fresh in June,
O, she's like a new strung instrument
    That's newly put in tune.

Compare this stanza with the first one below and try to decide why the poet made his changes.

My Love Is Like a Red Red Rose

My love is like a red red rose   *1*
    That's newly sprung in June:
My love is like the melodie
    That's sweetly played in tune.

So fair art thou, my bonnie lass,   *5*
  So deep in love am I:
And I will love thee still, my dear,
  Till a' the seas gang dry.

Till a' the seas gang dry, my dear,
  And the rocks melt wi' the sun: *10*
And I will love thee still, my dear,
  While the sands o' life shall run.

And fare thee weel, my only love,
  And fare thee weel awhile!
And I will come again, my love,   *15*
  Tho' it were ten thousand mile.

ROBERT BURNS

USES OF FIGURES OF SIMILARITY. In poetry figures of similarity have four uses, which often interact. First, they may be used to illustrate, to give greater clearness and definiteness to the subject. Robert Herrick's "The Watch" is an example of this use:

Man is a Watch, wound up at first, but never
Wound up again: Once down, He's down for ever.
The Watch once downe, all motions then do cease;
And Mans Pulse stopt, *All Passions sleep in Peace.*

Second, they provide means of concentration, enabling the poet to say much in few words. An example is Holmes' simile of the last leaf on the tree, discussed above on page 73. Third, they are a method of weaving into the fabric of the poem multifarious items of the material of life, giving to the poetic experience a fullness and sensory richness that might be lacking in a straightforward and unfigurative treatment of a subject. A simile from Keats' "Endymion" will exemplify this use:

For as delicious wine doth, sparkling, dive
  In nectar'd clouds and curls through water fair,
So from the arbour roof down swell'd an air
  Odorous and enlivening.

Fourth, they intensify and diversify the feelings in the poetic experience by assembling the diverse objects that naturally arouse them. The poet, by joining in a figure disparate objects that awake similar emotions, can create powerful emotional effects. And by using combinations of objects to which we attach varying or contrasting or similar but not identical feelings, he can bring to birth new and subtle blends of feelings that even he may never have experienced before. Such new emotional blends sometimes reflect life experience more truly than simple and pure emotions. The role of figures of comparison in creating new and complex combinations of feelings may be illustrated by the similes in lines 20 and 25–26 of the following poem by E. A. Robinson.

Mr. Flood's Party

Old Eben Flood, climbing alone one night   *1*
Over the hill between the town below
And the forsaken upland hermitage
That held as much as he should ever know
On earth again of home, paused warily.   *5*
The road was his with not a native near;
And Eben, having leisure, said aloud,
For no man else in Tilbury Town to hear:

"Well, Mr. Flood, we have the harvest moon
Again, and we may not have many more;   *10*
The bird is on the wing, the poet says,
And you and I have said it here before.
Drink to the bird." He raised up to the light
The jug that he had gone so far to fill,
And answered huskily: "Well, Mr. Flood,   *15*
Since you propose it, I believe I will."

Alone, as if enduring to the end
A valiant armor of scarred hopes outworn,
He stood there in the middle of the road
Like Roland's ghost winding a silent horn.   *20*
Below him, in the town among the trees,
Where friends of other days had honored him,
A phantom salutation of the dead
Rang thinly till old Eben's eyes were dim.

Then, as a mother lays her sleeping child   25
Down tenderly, fearing it may awake,
He set the jug down slowly at his feet
With trembling care, knowing that most things break;
And only when assured that on firm earth
It stood, as the uncertain lives of men   30
Assuredly did not, he paced away,
And with his hand extended paused again:

"Well, Mr. Flood, we have not met like this
In a long time; and many a change has come
To both of us, I fear, since last it was   35
We had a drop together. Welcome home!"
Convivially returning with himself,
Again he raised the jug up to the light;
And with an acquiescent quaver said:
"Well, Mr. Flood, if you insist, I might.   40

"Only a very little, Mr. Flood—
For auld lang syne. No more, sir; that will **do.**"
So, for the time, apparently it did,
And Eben evidently thought so too;
For soon amid the silver loneliness   45
Of night he lifted up his voice and sang,
Secure, with only two moons listening,
Until the whole harmonious landscape rang—

"For auld lang syne." The weary throat gave out,
The last word wavered, and the song was done.   50
He raised again the jug regretfully
And shook his head, and was again alone.
There was not much that was ahead of him,
And there was nothing in the town below—
Where strangers would have shut the many doors   55
That many friends had opened long ago.[3]

EDWIN ARLINGTON ROBINSON

---

[3] The author, Mr. Robinson, once wrote in a letter that this poem "was turned down for alcoholic reasons by *Collier's*." Ridgely Torrence, ed., *Selected Letters of Edwin Arlington Robinson* (New York: Macmillan, 1940), p. 123. This remark underscores the truth of the assertion that a poem which is itself

SYMBOL

A *symbol* is a person, place, thing, quality, or relationship that is used to stand for something other than itself. In poetry we commonly meet two kinds, conventional and nonce symbols. *Conventional symbols* are those which have been widely used and whose meanings are immediately understood. They are common in life and in art. A shoulder patch stands for a soldier's organization; a fraternity pin symbolizes membership in a particular fraternity. In Chinese art, a tortoise symbolizes long life; a lonely pine on a mountain, the scholar who has retired to solitude; a fish leaping a rapids, the student who has passed his official master's examination. In Christian art, a symbol is often used to identify holy figures; for instance, the infant John the Baptist is distinguished from the Christ child by his rude staff in the form of a cross, and Mary Magdalene is signalized among a group of women by a jar of ointment which she carries. In poetry, too, we find conventional symbols; a road or stream, for example, often symbolizes the course of life, and evening and night symbolize death.

Symbol is closely related to metaphor; usually it is simply the vehicle of a metaphor, the tenor being understood by convention or made clear by the poetic context. Occasionally, however, a symbol will have no link of similarity with what it stands for; in such a case it is not a metaphor.

The poet who employs symbols that are conventional attains immediate perspicuity in that their meanings are recognized without doubt. Of course, he must make certain that the symbolic objects are taken, not at their face value, but for what they represent. This he may do by statement or by implication. In the following poem Stephen Spender at first uses *home, evening,* and *West* in their ordinary senses; then, in the last stanza, he transforms the terms into symbols, declaring the change by the last line:

Winter Landscape

Come home with white gulls waving across gray   *1*
Fields.   Evening.   A daffodil West.
Somewhere in clefts of rock the birds hide, breast to breast.

a fresh and individualized response is capable of touching off a stock response in readers. See pages 22 ff.

I warm with fire. Curtain shrouds dying day.
Alone.   By the glowing ember   5
I shut out the bleak-tombed evenings of November.

And breast to breast, those swans. Sheep huddle and press
Close.   Each to each.   Oh,
Is there no herd of men like beasts where man may go?

Come home at last; come, end of loneliness.   10
Sea.   Evening.   Daffodil West.
And our thin dying souls against Eternity pressed.

STEPHEN SPENDER

The next poem nowhere states directly that the uphill road is a symbol of the course of life, but the growing context makes this interpretation clear as we read through the poem:

Up-Hill

Does the road wind up-hill all the way?   1
    Yes, to the very end.
Will the day's journey take the whole long day?
    From morn to night, my friend.

But is there for the night a resting-place?   5
    A roof for when the slow dark hours begin.
May not the darkness hide it from my face?
    You cannot miss that inn.

Shall I meet other wayfarers at night?
    Those who have gone before.   10
Then must I knock, or call when just in sight?
    They will not keep you standing at that door.

Shall I find comfort, travel-sore, and weak?
    Of labour you shall find the sum.
Will there be beds for me and all who seek?   15
    Yea, beds for all who come.

CHRISTINA ROSSETTI

In contrast to conventional symbols, illustrated in the two fore-going poems, we also find *nonce symbols* in poetry. A nonce symbol is one that is invented and used for a particular occasion; its interpretation is determined by the poetic context of which it is a part. These two types, conventional and nonce symbols, are simply the opposite ends of a scale of frequency of use: the more frequently any symbol is used the more conventional it becomes. The following poem by Rupert Brooke contains the nonce symbols of *waters* for life and *frost* for death. The poet makes no outright statement about the symbolic values of these words but trusts his context, with its living-dead opposition, to render this meaning clear to the reader.

The Dead

These hearts were woven of human joys and cares,   *1*
    Washed marvellously with sorrow, swift to mirth.
The years had given them kindness. Dawn was theirs,
    And sunset, and the colours of the earth.
These had seen movement, and heard music; known   *5*
    Slumber and waking; loved; gone proudly friended;
Felt the quick stir of wonder; sat alone;
    Touched flowers and furs and cheeks. All this is ended.

There are waters blown by changing winds to laughter
And lit by the rich skies, all day. And after,   *10*
    Frost, with a gesture, stays the waves that dance
And wandering loveliness. He leaves a white
    Unbroken glory, a gathered radiance,
A width, a shining peace, under the night.

RUPERT BROOKE

A symbol does not necessarily stand for just one thing; it may sometimes stand for various things. A poem by Carl Sandburg will illustrate:

Prayers of Steel

Lay me on an anvil, O God.   *1*
Beat me and hammer me into a crowbar.
Let me pry loose old walls.
Let me lift and loosen old foundations.

Lay me on an anvil, O God.   5
Beat me and hammer me into a steel spike.
Drive me into the girders that hold a skyscraper together.
Take red-hot rivets and fasten me into the central girders.
Let me be the great nail holding a skyscraper through blue
    nights into white stars.

CARL SANDBURG

The first stanza deals with demolition: steel, symbolizing a person,
wishes to be instrumental in demolishing an old structure—"old
walls" and "old foundations." The second stanza deals with con-
struction: the person symbolized wishes to be instrumental in building a new structure to replace the old. The symbolism, we observe,
is of a very general nature: something old (useless, outmoded)
should be destroyed and something new (useful, up-to-date) should
be built in its stead. But most readers will not rest content with
such a general interpretation; they will interpret the symbols in
more specific terms, such as monarchism *vs.* democracy; private
enterprise *vs.* government control; nationalism *vs.* internationalism;
paganism *vs.* Christianity; a student's old habits of careless study
vs. his new habits of systematic study; rote learning in education
vs. the problem method. There are as many possibilities as there
are old and new things that can be contrasted, and any specific
interpretation that fits the general pattern of the symbolism is certainly acceptable.

A use of symbols somewhat like the preceding occurs when a
poet presents a specific situation to symbolize a general condition,
which the reader will interpret in terms of other specific situations
according to his interests and background. The next poem illustrates
this pattern of the use of symbolism.

Ozymandias

I met a traveller from an antique land   1
Who said : Two vast and trunkless legs of stone
Stand in the desert. Near them, on the sand,
Half sunk, a shattered visage lies, whose frown,
And wrinkled lip, and sneer of cold command,   5

Tell that its sculptor well those passions read
Which yet survive, stamped on these lifeless things,
The hand that mocked them, and the heart that fed:
And on the pedestal these words appear:
"My name is Ozymandias, king of kings: *10*
Look on my works, ye Mighty, and despair!"
Nothing beside remains. Round the decay
Of that colossal wreck, boundless and bare
The lone and level sands stretch far away.

PERCY BYSSHE SHELLEY

A poem may have both a literal meaning and, for those who read
alertly, a further symbolic meaning. This duality is illustrated in the
next poem. In the last two lines the use of the word *sleep,* which
is often a conventional symbol for *die,* suggests to the alert reader
that the poem as a whole may be symbolic as well as literal in
meaning.

Stopping by Woods on a Snowy Evening

Whose woods these are I think I know.   *1*
His house is in the village though;
He will not see me stopping here
To watch his woods fill up with snow.

My little horse must think it queer   *5*
To stop without a farmhouse near
Between the woods and frozen lake
The darkest evening of the year.

He gives his harness bells a shake
To ask if there is some mistake.   *10*
The only other sound's the sweep
Of easy wind and downy flake.

The woods are lovely, dark and deep.
But I have promises to keep,
And miles to go before I sleep,   *15*
And miles to go before I sleep.

ROBERT FROST

EXERCISE

Study the following poem until the imagery and the symbolism seem clear to you. Then, and only then, read the remarks that follow the poem, which are a summary of the poet's own explanation.[4] Was your interpretation like that the poet intended you to have? If not, who was at fault, you or the poet?

Children look down upon the morning-gray   *1*
Tissue of mist that veils a valley's lap:
Their fingers itch to tear it and unwrap
The flags, the roundabouts, the gala day.
They watch the spring rise inexhaustibly—   *5*
A breathing thread out of the eddied sand,
Sufficient to their day: but half their mind
Is on the sailed and glittering estuary.
Fondly we wish their mist might never break,
Knowing it hides so much that best were hidden: *10*
We'd chain them by the spring, lest it should broaden
For them into a quicksand and a wreck.
But they slip through our fingers like the source,
Like mist, like time that has flagged out their course.

C. DAY LEWIS

1. This poem originated in a strong feeling that the poet had about his two children, a feeling of sadness that they must grow, leave their protection, and go out into a dangerous and difficult world. We note that this is a universal feeling, that is, many parents have experienced and will experience the same emotion.

2. The poem has two themes: the children's feeling of impatience and expectation, which appears in the first eight lines; and the poet's own feeling, which comes out in the last six lines. These two themes, he tells us, are intended to balance and contrast with each other.

3. The poem began with line 4, which came first into the poet's head. Thinking about this line, he noticed that it was an image of a fête or fair, the sort of thing a child looks forward to; "obviously, it symbolized . . . the grown-up world which a child is so impatient to enter." Here we observe that the poem, from its very inception, is more than a literal statement; it is symbolic. In completing the first four lines, the poet added to the symbolism the early-morning mist symbolizing the veil which the

――――――――
[4] C. Day Lewis, *Poetry for You* (New York: Oxford University Press, 1947), pp. 42–46.

children wish to tear away, the veil which shuts them off from the grown-up world.

4. In the second four lines the poet wanted a second image-sequence, as a variation on the theme of the first four lines. This he created in "the picture of a spring bubbling up out of the earth, and the children bending down to watch its 'breathing thread.'" We see here that in line 5 the poet has suddenly shifted location from the hill top of line 1 to the side of the spring. Did the words of the poem make this shift for you, or did you remain on the hill top as you read? If you remained, you will realize how difficult it is for a poet to re-create his own experience in the mind of his reader. In these four lines the use of symbols is continued: "the spring represents life near its source, *young* life; and the children are only half satisfied with it; 'half their mind' is looking forward to the time when their life will have broadened out, as a stream broadens into an estuary, and become more important and exciting."

5. The last six lines repeat the imagery of the first eight: mist, spring, estuary, and flags. This is done so that the reader "can see the two main themes from a number of different angles . . ."

ILLUSTRATIVE POEMS

John Anderson My Jo

John Anderson my jo, John,	*1*
When we were first acquent,	
Your locks were like the raven,	
Your bonnie brow was brent;	
But now your brow is beld, John,	*5*
Your locks are like the snow;	
But blessings on your frosty pow,	
John Anderson, my jo.	
John Anderson my jo, John,	
We clamb the hill thegither;	*10*
And mony a canty day, John,	
We've had wi' ane anither:	
Now we maun totter down, John,	
And hand in hand we'll go,	
And sleep thegither at the foot,	*15*
John Anderson, my jo.	

ROBERT BURNS

To an Athlete Dying Young

The time you won your town the race   *1*
We chaired you through the market-place;
Man and boy stood cheering by,
And home we brought you shoulder-high.

To-day, the road all runners come,   *5*
Shoulder-high we bring you home.
And set you at your threshold down,
Townsman of a stiller town.

Smart lad, to slip betimes away
From fields where glory does not stay   *10*
And early though the laurel grows
It withers quicker than the rose.

Eyes the shady night has shut
Cannot see the record cut,
And silence sounds no worse than cheers   *15*
After earth has stopped the ears :

Now you will not swell the rout
Of lads that wore their honours out,
Runners whom renown outran
And the name died before the man.   *20*

So set, before its echoes fade,
The fleet foot on the sill of shade,
And hold to the low lintel up
The still-defended challenge-cup.

And round that early-laurelled head   *25*
Will flock to gaze the strengthless dead,
And find unwithered on its curls
The garland briefer than a girl's.

A. E. HOUSMAN

Sea Lullaby

The old moon is tarnished   *1*
With smoke of the flood,
The dead leaves are varnished
With colour like blood,

A treacherous smiler   *5*
With teeth white as milk,
A savage beguiler
In sheathings of silk,

The sea creeps to pillage,
She leaps on her prey ;   *10*
A child of the village
Was murdered today.

She came up to greet him
In a smooth golden cloak,
She choked him and beat him   *15*
To death, for a joke.

Her bright locks were tangled,
She shouted for joy,
With one hand she strangled
A strong little boy.   *20*

Now in silence she lingers
Beside him all night
To wash her long fingers
In silvery light.

          ELINOR WYLIE

There Is a Garden in Her Face

There is a garden in her face,   *1*
    Where roses and white lilies grow ;
A heav'nly paradise is that place,
    Wherein all pleasant fruits do flow.

There cherries grow which none may buy   *5*
Till cherry-ripe themselves do cry.

Those cherries fairly do enclose
   Of orient pearl a double row;
Which when her lovely laughter shows,
   They look like rosebuds filled with snow.   *10*
Yet them nor peer nor prince can buy
Till cherry-ripe themselves do cry.

Her eyes like angels watch them still;
   Her brows like bended bows do stand,
Threat'ning with piercing frowns to kill   *15*
   All that attempt with eye or hand
Those sacred cherries to come nigh,
Till cherry-ripe themselves do cry.

THOMAS CAMPION

SELECTED STANZAS FROM *The Rubaiyat of Omar Khayyam*

Come, fill the Cup, and in the fire of spring   *1*
Your Winter-garment of Repentance fling;
   The Bird of Time has but a little way
To flutter—and the Bird is on the Wing.

Whether at Naishápúr or Babylon,   *5*
Whether the Cup with sweet or bitter run,
   The Wine of Life keeps oozing drop by drop,
The Leaves of Life keep falling one by one.

*   *   *

The Worldly Hope men set their Hearts upon
Turns Ashes—or it prospers; and anon,   *10*
   Like Snow upon the Desert's dusty Face,
Lighting a little hour or two—is gone.

*   *   *

Myself when young did eagerly frequent
Doctor and Saint, and heard great argument
   About it and about; but evermore   *15*
Came out by the same door where in I went.

With them the seed of Wisdom did I sow,
And with mine own hand wrought to make it grow;
   And this was all the Harvest that I reaped—
'I came like Water, and like Wind I go.'   *20*

       *   *   *

Oh threats of Hell and Hopes of Paradise!
One thing at least is certain— *This* Life flies;
   One thing is certain and the rest is lies—
The Flower that once has blown forever dies.

       *   *   *

We are no other than a moving row   *25*
Of Magic Shadow-shapes that come and go
   Round with the Sun-illumined Lantern held
In Midnight by the Master of the Show;

But helpless Pieces of the Game He plays
Upon this Checker-board of Nights and Days;   *30*
   Hither and thither moves, and checks, and slays,
And one by one back in the Closet lays.

The Ball no question makes of Ayes and Noes,
But Here or There as strikes the Player goes;
   And He that tossed you down into the Field,   *35*
He knows about it all—HE knows—HE knows!

The Moving Finger writes, and, having writ,
Moves on; nor all your Piety nor Wit
   Shall lure it back to cancel half a Line,
Nor all your Tears wash out a Word of it.   *40*

EDWARD FITZGERALD

Bombing Casualties in Spain

Dolls' faces are rosier but these were children   *1*
their eyes not glass but gleaming gristle
dark lenses in whose quicksilvery glances
the sunlight quivered. These blenched lips
were warm once and bright with blood   *5*
but blood
held in a moist bleb of flesh
not spilt and spatter'd in tousled hair.

In these shadowy tresses
red petals did not always   *10*
thus clot and blacken to a scar.

These are dead faces.
Wasps' nests are not so wanly waxen
wood embers not so greyly ashen.

They are laid out in ranks   *15*
like paper lanterns that have fallen
after a night of riot
extinct in the dry morning air.

HERBERT READ

Sonnet LXXIII

That time of year thou mayst in me behold   *1*
When yellow leaves, or none, or few, do hang
Upon those boughs which shake against the cold,
Bare ruin'd choirs, where late the sweet birds sang.
In me thou see'st the twilight of such day   *5*
As after sunset fadeth in the west,
Which by and by black night doth take away,
Death's second self, that seals up all in rest.

In me thou see'st the glowing of such fire,
That on the ashes of his youth doth lie,   10
As the death-bed whereon it must expire
Consum'd with that which it was nourish'd by.
This thou perceiv'st, which makes thy love more strong,
To love that well which thou must leave ere long.

WILLIAM SHAKESPEARE

6

SOUND SYMBOLISM

Sound symbolism is a natural correspondence between sound and sense. There are words, writes Otto Jespersen, eminent Danish linguist, "which we feel instinctively to be adequate to express the ideas they stand for, and others the sound of which are felt to be more or less incongruous with their signification . . . everybody must feel that the word roll . . . is more adequate than the Russian word katat'."[1] This is to say, the very sounds of the word *roll* make it more expressive of its sense than the sounds of its Russian synonym *katat'*. Psychological experiments and the study of primitive languages both affirm correspondences of sound and sense.[2] As a simple example of psychological evidence, try the following experiment on your friends. Show the two drawings reproduced below and ask your friends to match these with the meaningless words *taketa* and *naluma*. If most of them agree about which word goes with which drawing, then it appears likely that some

---

[1] *Language, its Nature, Development and Origin* (London: George Allen and Unwin, 1922), p. 398.

[2] See, for example:

Edward Sapir, "A Study in Phonetic Symbolism," *Selected Writings of Edward Sapir* (Berkeley: University of California Press, 1949), pp. 61–72.

Wolfgang Köhler, *Gestalt Psychology* (New York: Liveright Publishing Corporation, 1929), p. 242.

correspondence does exist between the sounds and the visual impressions.[3]

A 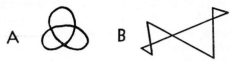 B

Sound symbolism in poetry is of three kinds: (1) speech sounds which imitate actual sounds; (2) speech sounds which have been so arranged as to make them difficult or easy to articulate; (3) speech sounds which in themselves suggest meaning; these are called phonetic intensives.

ONOMATOPOEIA.   The simplest kind of sound symbolism consists of speech sounds which imitate actual sounds, such as we hear in the words *sizz* and *roar*. Such imitation is called onomatopoeia. Onomatopoetic words are found in many languages. For example, the meaning of the English onomatopoetic word *murmur* is expressed by *omumu* in Tahitian, by *murmuru* in Tamil, and by *marmara-* in Sanskrit. In Zulu the word *bomboloza* means to rumble in the bowels.

The human speech organs, however, are incapable of articulating with exactness many of the sounds of nature; hence the speech sounds used to represent natural sounds are often only approximate. For instance the English *whisper*, the French *chuchoter*, the German *flüstern*—the English *bow-wow* and the French *gnaf-gnaf*—are all attempts, inexact but suggestive, to represent natural sounds. The reason for the success of such inexactly imitative sounds has been explained by the English philologist Henry Bradley, who has pointed out that the resemblance of an onomatopoetic word to the sound it names

. . . consists not so much in similarity of impression on the ear as in similarity of mental suggestion. For instance, it is not at all literally true

---

[3] Adapted from Wolfgang Köhler, *Gestalt Psychology* (New York: Liveright Publishing Company, 1929), pp. 242–243. See also G. W. Hartmann, *Gestalt Psychology* (New York: Ronald Press, 1935), pp. 147–148.

Also: "There is no doubt that synaesthetic combinations and associations permeate all languages and that these correspondences have been, quite rightly, exploited and elaborated by the poets." René Wellek and Austin Warren, *Theory of Literature* (New York: Harcourt, Brace, 1949), p. 164.

that a gun, or a heavy body impinging on a door, 'says bang.' But the sequence of the three sounds of which the word consists is of such a nature that it can easily be uttered with force, so as to suggest the startling effect of a sudden violent noise, while the final consonant admits of being prolonged to express the notion of the continued resonance. In this instance and in many others, the so-called 'imitative' word represents an inarticulate noise not so much by way of echo as symbolically. That is to say, the elements composing the sound of the word combine to produce a mental effect which we recognize as analogous to that produced by the noise.[4]

As examples of onomatopoeia in poetry we may cite Pope's *the torrent roars;* Nashe's bird calls, *cuckoo, jug-jug, pu-we, to-witta woo;* and Poe's description of the susurrus of silk, *the silken sad uncertain rustling.*

An onomatopoetic word may express, not only a sound, but the being which produces the sound, as in the English *peeweet,* in the Australian *twonk,* which means frog, and in the Annamese *cupcup,* which means a tiger, the sounds resembling those made by the tiger when stalking his prey. An onomatopoetic word may also express the sound plus the movement that causes it, as in *tap* and *bubble,* *e.g.,* Tennyson's

Bubbled the nightingale and heeded not.[5]

Words sometime lose their onomatopoetic quality as in the course of time they undergo changes of sound. For example, the Latin *pipio,* a peeping bird, is now English *pigeon,* its original imitative force having been lost through a series of sound changes. But language also takes on new onomatopoetic words as human beings invent new combinations of sounds that seem expressive of meaning. If, for instance, we should be told that a car *whooshed* by or that a *yakity-yak* issued from a room in the women's dormitory, we should

---

[4] *The Making of English* (New York: The Macmillan Company, and London: Macmillan & Company, Ltd., 1925), p. 156.

[5] Of this line from *The Princess,* Tennyson remarked:

"When I was in a friend's garden, I heard a nightingale singing with such a frenzy of passion that it was unconscious of everything else, and not frightened though I came and stood quite close beside it. I saw its eye flashing and felt the air bubble in my ear through the vibration." *The Works of Tennyson,* with notes by the author, ed. by Hallam, Lord Tennyson (New York: Macmillan, 1923 edition), p. 916.

have no difficulty in understanding these imitative words, even though we had never heard them before.

EXERCISE

Point out the onomatopoetic words in the following passages.

1. [DESCRIPTION OF THE SOUNDS OF SERPENTS]
   A dismal universal hiss
         JOHN MILTON

2. . . . the sea, playing on the yellow sand,
   Sends forth a rattling murmur to the land.
         CHRISTOPHER MARLOWE

3. [DESCRIPTION OF THE SOUND OF ICE-LADEN BRANCHES]
   . . . they click upon themselves.
         ROBERT FROST

4. The myriad shriek of wheeling ocean-fowl,
   The league-long roller thundering on the reef,
   The moving whisper of huge trees that branched
   And blossomed in the zenith, or the sweep
   Of some precipitous rivulet to the wave.
         ALFRED, LORD TENNYSON

5. When the hounds of spring are on winter's traces,
      The mother of months in meadow or plain
   Fills the shadows and windy places
      With lisp of leaves and ripple of rain.
         ALGERNON C. SWINBURNE

6. I hear lake water lapping with low sounds by the shore.
         WILLIAM BUTLER YEATS

7. And the plashing of waterdrops
   In the marble fountain
   Comes down the garden paths.
         AMY LOWELL

8. The moan of doves in immemorial elms
      And murmuring of innumerable bees.[6]
         ALFRED, LORD TENNYSON

---

[6] If the sounds in these lines are reproduced in a line of different meaning, *e.g.*,
      More ordure never will renew our midden's pure manure,
the suggestiveness of the original is lost. The lesson is clear: onomatopoeia cannot by itself convey meaning; it can only fortify the sound impressions described by meaningful words. This example is taken from Laura Riding and Robert Graves, *A Survey of Modernist Poetry* (Garden City, New York: Doubleday Doran, 1928), p. 37.

9.   How often, these hours, have I heard the monotonous
        crool of a dove.

WALTER DE LA MARE

EASE OF ARTICULATION.   The second kind of sound
symbolism consists of speech sounds which have been so arranged
as to make them difficult or easy to articulate. Clusters of consonant
sounds which require difficult or labored muscular effort seem appropriate for the description of difficult or violent movement, or for
harsh effects, *e.g.*, Pope's

When Ajax strives some rock's vast weight to throw.

On the other hand, words that move easily in utterance, unimpeded
by difficulty of articulation, seem fitting for the description of
smooth and easy movement, *e.g.*, Milton's description of the road
from the universe to Hell,

Smooth, easy, inoffensive down to Hell.

Here the effortless transitions between *smooth* and *easy* and *inoffensive* suggest the easiness of the descent.

Closely related to this mode of sound symbolism are metrical
effects, such as the employment of added stressed syllables to brake
a line, or added unstressed syllables to accelerate it. These are discussed on pages 146 and 147.

EXERCISE

1. Of the two passages below by Milton the first describes the opening
of the gates of Hell; the second, the opening of the gates of Heaven.
Point out how the sounds help to indicate the manner of the opening of
each.

A.

<pre>
                    Then in the key-hole turns   1
Th' intricate wards, and every bolt and bar
Of massy iron or solid rock with ease
Unfast'ns. On a sudden op'n fly,
With impetuous recoil and jarring sound,   5
Th' infernal doors, and on their hinges grate
Harsh thunder.
</pre>

B.
> Heaven op'n'd wide
> Her ever-during gates, harmonious sound
> On golden hinges moving.

2. The two following passages by Milton deal with movement. The first describes Satan's struggle as he makes his difficult way through a turbulent chaos. The second describes a dance of nature. In what parts of these lines do the sounds themselves seem to reinforce the sense?

A.
> So he with difficulty and labour hard,
> Moved on, with difficulty and labour he.

B.
> The sounds and seas with all their finny drove,
> Now to the moon in wavering morrice move,
> And on the tawny sands and shelves
> Trip the pert fairies and the dapper elves;

3. In the following poem by Thomas Hardy there are many consonant combinations that are hard to say. These consist of the end group in a word plus the beginning consonants of the following word. Read the poem aloud to find out these consonant clusters and see what purpose they serve in the poem as a whole.

In Tenebris, I

> Wintertime nighs;   *1*
> But my bereavement-pain
> It cannot bring again:
>   Twice no one dies.
>
> Flower-petals flee;   *5*
> But, since it once hath been,
> No more that severing scene
>   Can harrow me.
>
> Birds faint in dread:
> I shall not lose old strength   *10*
> In the lone frost's black length:
>   Strength long since fled!

Leaves freeze to dun;
But friends cannot turn cold
This season as of old   *15*
  For him with none.

Tempests may scath;
But love cannot make smart
Again this year his heart
  Who no heart hath.   *20*

Black is night's cope;
But death will not appal
One who, past doubtings all,
  Waits in unhope.

THOMAS HARDY

PHONETIC INTENSIVES. The third kind of sound symbolism consists of speech sounds which in themselves suggest meaning; these are called phonetic intensives.[7] An example occurs in the word *flare,* whose initial sounds, [fl], carry a suggested meaning of moving light.[8] The origin of the association between phonetic intensives and their meanings is unclear. For instance, we do not know whether the initial [fl] in some words suggests moving light because of some inherent fitness between the sounds [fl] and their meaning, or because the accidents of linguistic history have produced words like *flash, flare, flame, flicker,* whose initial [fl]'s and similar meanings have caused [fl] to become associated with moving light. Nevertheless, words containing such phonetic intensives may have a special intensity because the denotation of the word as a whole is strengthened by the suggested meanings of some of the sounds it contains. Let us examine the word *glimmer* as an example. Its [gl] has behind it a meaning of light, borne out by such words

_____

[7] For information on this kind of sound symbolism, see the following sources: Leonard Bloomfield, *Language* (New York: Henry Holt, 1933), pp. 244–245; Otto Jespersen, *Language: its Nature, Development and Origin* (London: George Allen and Unwin, 1922), pp. 396–411; Edgar H. Sturtevant, *An Introduction to Linguistic Science* (New Haven: Yale University Press, 1947), pp. 110–112; Stanley S. Newman, "Further Experiments in Phonetic Symbolism," *American Journal of Psychology,* XLV, 57–75.

[8] For the pronunciation of the symbols given in brackets, see Table of Phonetic Symbols on page 454.

as *glow, glare, glint, gleam, glisten;* its [ɪ] suggests smallness, as in *dim, bit, sip, pin, chip, slim;* its [ɝ] indicates repetition, as in *twitter, flicker, flutter, sputter, chatter.* Thus these three sounds in *glimmer* suggest the meaning of a small, repeatedly moving light, and in so doing intensify the denotative sense of the word as a whole.

Of the many phonetic intensives found in poetry, we shall discuss only a few here.

Three pairs of sounds are employed with great frequency. The vowels [u], as in *doom,* and [o], as in *woe,* are used to suggest a state of feeling that may be loosely described by terms like *melancholy, unhappiness,* and *mournfulness;* thus words like *gloom, forlorn, moan, sorrow* are in frequent use, and the [u] or [o] sounds may dominate a passage concerned with unhappiness. The vowels [i], as in *peep,* and [ɪ], as in *drip,* suggest smallness, exemplified in *wee, teeny, thin, wink, flicker, trickle.* At the ends of words the sounds [l], spelt -*le,* and [ɝ], spelt -*er,* suggest the frequent repetition of an action. Of these our language has countless examples, such as *clatter, jingle, glitter, sparkle, twinkle, ripple, mutter, shatter, trickle.* In some words, a closing [l] suggests the repetition not of an action but of some visual detail, as in *dapple, stipple, freckle, bramble, bristle.*

Of the consonants used as phonetic intensives we have already mentioned [fl] for moving light and [gl] for light. Among others at the beginnings of words, [b] gives the impression of impact, as in *bang, bump, bounce, bat;* [bl] carries the idea of impetus and use of breath or air, as in *blow, blast, bluster, blizzard;* [gr] suggests roughness and coarseness, as in *grind, grit, gravel, gride, grate;* [skr] indicates a grating impact or sound, as in *scratch, scrape, scrabble, scrannel;* [sp] indicates a point, as in *spire, spark, spot, spout, spike, spade;* [str] has the sense of thinness and narrowness, as in *strait, strip, stream, strap, street.*

Of the consonants at the end of words [p], [t], and [k] give the sense of an abrupt stoppage of movement, whereas [ʃ], spelt -*sh,* indicates an unabrupt stoppage of movement. These contrasting effects become evident when we compare *clap* with *clash, bat* with *bash,* and *smack* with *smash.* In the end position an [n] or [ŋ], spelt -*ng,* after a vowel suggests resonance, as in *clang.*

Knowledge of the meanings of phonetic intensives is sometimes helpful in understanding why particular words in poems seem to be especially appropriate and even inevitable. A double caution, however, is needed. First, we must bear in mind that this kind of sound symbolism is operative only when the sense of the word as a whole is related to the sense of the phonetic intensive which it contains. The [fl] in *flea,* for example, and the [ɪ] in *big* have no suggestive power because the potential meanings of these sounds, respectively moving light and smallness, are outside the areas of meaning of the words themselves. Second, we must understand that an automatic stimulus-response relationship does not exist between the phonetic intensives and their imputed meanings. Rather, the meanings are latent, and rise to the surface of consciousness only when the enclosing context—its sense, feeling, and general import—offers conditions favorable to their emergence. Such conditions may be brought about by a poet's delicate and sensitive handling of language, and it is then that these intensives flash into life and help create that vividness and intensity of experience that is sometimes attributed to "word magic." For example, the atmosphere of the next poem, with its slow rhythm and low-keyed imagery, builds up a feeling of sadness. In this context the [o] sounds release their latent suggestiveness to reinforce the total impression.

All Day I Hear

All day I hear the noise of waters   *1*
    Making moan,
Sad as the sea-bird is, when going
    Forth alone,
He hears the winds cry to the waters'   *5*
    Monotone.

The grey winds, the cold winds are blowing
    Where I go.
I hear the noise of many waters
    Far below.   *10*
All day, all night, I hear them flowing
    To and fro.

                JAMES JOYCE

On the contrary, the [o] sounds have no suggestion of melancholy in

More hope arose within his joyous heart
As, note by note, the bugles nearer blew.

because the context is not sympathetic to such a meaning.

The phonetic intensive in a word may be given special emphasis by the repetition of the sound in other words in the passage. A. E. Housman, for example, uses this means of strengthening the effect of *snap:* "And sharp the link of life will *snap.*"

EXERCISE

In the italicized words of the following quotations point out each phonetic intensive and its suggested meaning.

1. She is a winsome *wee* thing.
                    ROBERT BURNS

2. Now fades the *glimmering* landscape on the sight.
                    THOMAS GRAY

3. A late lark *twitters* from the quiet skies.
                    WILLIAM E. HENLEY

4. . . . crickets *jingle* there.
                    WILFRED OWEN

5. *Blow, blow,* thou winter wind.
                    WILLIAM SHAKESPEARE

6. The *moan* of multitudes in *woe.*
                    JOHN MASEFIELD

7. The birds sit *chittering* in the thorn.
                    ROBERT BURNS

8. The naked stars . . . *glinting* on the puddles.
                    SIEGFRIED SASSOON

9. Down the road someone is practicing scales,
   The notes like little fishes vanish with a *wink*
        of tails.
                    LOUIS MACNEICE

10. [A FOLK PRAYER]
    From ghoulies and ghosties and long-legged beasties
    And things that go *bump* in the night,
    Good Lord, deliver us.
                    ANONYMOUS

11.   . . . the *flickering* gunnery rumbles.

WILFRED OWEN

12.   [DESCRIPTION OF THE SONG OF A WOODLARK]
      Teevo, cheevo cheevio chee:
      O where, what can that be?
      Weedio-weedio: there again!
      So tiny a *trickle* of song-strain.

GERARD MANLEY HOPKINS

13.   This is the way the world ends
      Not with a *bang* but a *whimper.*

T. S. ELIOT

14.   I turned about and looked where branches break
      The *glittering* reaches of the flooded lake.

WILLIAM BUTLER YEATS

15.   Three jolly gentlemen
         At break of day
      Came *clitter-clatter* down the stairs
         And galloped away.

WALTER DE LA MARE

16.   The mugger *cracked* his whip and sang.

W. W. GIBSON

17.   The moon, *dwindled* and *thinned* to a fringe of
         a fingernail held to the candle.

GERARD MANLEY HOPKINS

18.   When will return the glory of your prime?
         No more— Oh, never *more!*

PERCY BYSSHE SHELLEY

19.   [DESCRIPTION OF A SALOON BAR]
                              . . . the *glush* of
      squirting taps plus *slush* of foam knocked off.

E. E. CUMMINGS

20.   Water *ruffled* and *speckled* by galloping wind.

F. S. FLINT

21.   What sound was dearest in his native dells?
      The mellow *lin-lan-lone* of evening bells.

ALFRED, LORD TENNYSON

22.   A full sea *glazed* with muffled moonlight.

ALFRED, LORD TENNYSON

23.   The street-lamp *sputtered,*
      The street-lamp *muttered.*

T. S. ELIOT

24. [DESCRIPTION OF THE STRIDENT PIPES OF SHEPHERDS]
    And when they list, their lean and flashy songs
    Grate on their *scrannel* pipes of wretched straw.
                                            JOHN MILTON

25. [DESCRIPTION OF A SNAKE AT A WATER TROUGH]
    And where the water had *dripped* from the tap,
        in a small clearness,
    He sipped with his *straight* mouth . . .
    And *flickered* his two-forked tongue from his
        lips, and mused a moment.
                                        D. H. LAWRENCE

26. [DESCRIPTION OF A KNIGHT, ENTERING A DARK CAVE]
            His *glist'ring* armour made
    A little *glooming* light, much like a shade.
                                        EDMUND SPENSER

27. [DESCRIPTION OF THE CHARIOT OF THE SUN OF GOD]
    And from about him fierce Effusion roll'd
    Of smoke and *bickering* fire, and *sparkles* dire.
                                            JOHN MILTON

ILLUSTRATIVE POEMS

In the following poem the word *pied* means "blotched with two
or more colors; spotted; mottled." What phonetic intensives in the
words of the poem reinforce the impression of spottiness?

Pied Beauty

Glory be to God for dappled things—   *1*
    For skies of couple-colour as a brinded cow;
        For rose-moles all in stipple upon trout that swim;
Fresh-firecoal chestnut-falls; finches' wings;
    Landscape plotted and pieced—fold, fallow, and plough;   *5*
        And all trades, their gear and tackle and trim.

All things counter, original, spare, strange;
    Whatever is fickle, freckled (who knows how?)
        With swift, slow; sweet, sour; adazzle, dim;
He fathers-forth whose beauty is past change: *10*
            Praise him.
                            GERARD MANLEY HOPKINS

My Star

All that I know   *1*
  Of a certain star
Is, it can throw
  (Like the angled spar)
Now a dart of red,   *5*
  Now a dart of blue;
Till my friends have said
  They would fain see, too,
My star that dartles the red and blue!
Then it stops like a bird; like a flower, hangs furled: *10*
  They must solace themselves with the Saturn above it.
What matter to me if their star is a world?
  Mine has opened its soul to me; therefore I love it.

ROBERT BROWNING

Bredon Hill

In summertime on Bredon   *1*
  The bells they sound so clear;
Round both the shires they ring them
  In steeples far and near,
  A happy noise to hear.   *5*

Here of a Sunday morning
  My love and I would lie,
And see the coloured counties,
  And hear the larks so high
  About us in the sky.   *10*

The bells would ring to call her
  In valleys miles away:
'Come all to church, good people;
  Good people, come and pray.'
  But here my love would stay.   *15*

And I would turn and answer
   Among the springing thyme,
'Oh, peal upon our wedding,
   And we will hear the chime,
   And come to church in time.'   *20*

But when the snows at Christmas
   On Bredon top were strown,
My love rose up so early
   And stole out unbeknown
   And went to church alone.   *25*

They tolled the one bell only,
   Groom there was none to see,
The mourners followed after,
   And so to church went she,
   And would not wait for me.   *30*

The bells they sound on Bredon,
   And still the steeples hum.
'Come all to church, good people,'—
   Oh, noisy bells, be dumb;
   I hear you, I will come.   *35*

            A. E. HOUSMAN

STANZAS FROM *In Memoriam*

[*The first group describes calmness; the second, a "wild unrest" in
nature. Show how sounds are used to contribute to the impression
of the whole. The grief mentioned is that of the poet for a friend
who has died.*]

XI

Calm is the morn without a sound,   *1*
   Calm as to suit a calmer grief,
   And only thro' the faded leaf
The chestnut pattering to the ground:

Calm and deep peace on this high wold,　　　*5*
　　And on these dews that drench the furze,
　　And all the silvery gossamers
That twinkle into green and gold:

Calm and still light on yon great plain
　　That sweeps with all its autumn bowers,　　*10*
　　And crowded farms and lessening towers,
To mingle with the bounding main:

Calm and deep peace in this wide air,
　　These leaves that redden to the fall;
　　And in my heart, if calm at all,　　　*15*
If any calm, a calm despair:

Calm on the seas, and silver sleep,
　　And waves that sway themselves in rest,
　　And dead calm in that noble breast
Which heaves but with the heaving deep.　　*20*

xv

To-night the winds begin to rise　　　*1*
　　And roar from yonder dropping day:
　　The last red leaf is whirled away,
The rooks are blown about the skies;

The forest crack'd, the waters curl'd,　　*5*
　　The cattle huddled on the lea;
　　And wildly dash'd on tower and tree
The sunbeam strikes along the world:

And but for fancies, which aver
　　That all thy motions gently pass　　*10*
　　Athwart a plane of molten glass,
I scarce could brook the strain and stir

That makes the barren branches loud;
　　And but for fear it is not so,
　　The wild unrest that lives in woe　　*15*
Would dote and pore on yonder cloud

That rises upward always higher,
  And onward drags a labouring breast,
  And topples round the dreary west,
A looming bastion fringed with fire.   *20*
       ALFRED, LORD TENNYSON

i was sitting in mcsorley's

i was sitting in mcsorley's.   outside it was New   *1*
York and beatifully snowing.

Inside snug and evil.   the slobbering walls filthily
push witless creases of screaming warmth chuck pil-
lows are noise funnily swallows swallowing revolv-   *5*
ingly pompous a the swallowed mottle with smooth
or a but of rapidly goes gobs the and of flecks of and a
chatter sobbings intersect with which distinct disks of
graceful oath, upsoarings the break on   ceiling-
flatness   *10*

the Bar. tinking luscious jigs dint of ripe silver with
warmlyish wetflat splurging smells waltz the glush of
squirting taps plus slush of foam knocked off and a
faint piddle-of-drops she says I ploc spittle what the
lands thaz me kid in no sir hopping sawdust you kiddo   *15*
he's a palping wreaths of badly Yep cigars who jim
him why gluey grins topple together eyes pout gestures stickily point made glints squinting who's a wink
bum-nothing and money fuzzily mouths take big
wobbly foot-steps every goggle cent of it get out ears   *20*
dribbles soft right old feller belch the chap hic sum-
more eh chuckles skulch . . .

and i was sitting in the din thinking drinking the ale,
which never lets you grow old blinking at the low
ceiling my being pleasantly was punctuated by the al-   *25*
ways retchings of a worthless lamp.

when With a minute terrif   iceffort one dirty squeal
of soiling light yanKing from bushy obscurity a bald
greenish foetal head established It suddenly upon the
huge neck around whose unwashed sonorous muscle   *30*
the filth of a collar hung gently.

(spattered) by this instant of semiluminous nausea A
vast wordless nondescript genie of trunk trickled firmly in to one exactly-multilated ghost of a chair,

a; domeshaped interval of complete plasticity, shoul-   *35*
ders, sprouted the extraordinary arms through an an-
gle of ridiculous velocity commenting upon an un-
clean table. and, whose distended immense Both paws
slowly loved a dinted mug

gone Darkness   it was so near to me, i ask of shad- *40*
ow won't you have a drink?

(the eternal perpetual question)

Inside snugandevil.   i was sitting in mcsorley's
It, did not answer.

outside. (it was New York and beautifully, snowing. . . . *45*
E. E. CUMMINGS

An Essay on Criticism, LINES 337–373

But most by Numbers judge a Poet's song;   *1*
And smooth or rough, with them is right or wrong:
In the bright Muse though thousand charms conspire,
Her voice is all these tuneful fools admire;
Who haunt Parnassus but to please their ear,   *5*
Not mend their minds; as some to Church repair,
Not for the doctrine, but the music there.
These equal syllables alone require,
Though oft the ear the open vowels tire;

While expletives their feeble aid do join;   *10*
And ten low words oft creep in one dull line:
While they ring round the same unvaried chimes,
With sure returns of still expected rhymes;
Where'er you find "the cooling western breeze,"
In the next line, it "whispers through the trees:"   *15*
If crystal streams "with pleasing murmurs creep,"
The reader's threatened (not in vain) with "sleep:"
Then, at the last and only couplet fraught
With some unmeaning thing they call a thought,
A needless Alexandrine ends the song   *20*
That, like a wounded snake, drags its slow length along.
Leave such to tune their own dull rhymes, and know
What's roundly smooth or languishingly slow;
And praise the easy vigour of a line,
Where Denham's strength, and Waller's sweetness join.   *25*
True ease in writing comes from art, not chance,
As those move easiest who have learned to dance.
'Tis not enough no harshness gives offence,
The sound must seem an Echo to the sense:
Soft is the strain when Zephyr gently blows,   *30*
And the smooth stream in smoother numbers flows;
But when loud surges lash the sounding shore,
The hoarse, rough verse should like the torrent roar:
When Ajax strives some rock's vast weight to throw,
The line too labours, and the words move slow;   *35*
Not so, when swift Camilla scours the plain,
Flies o'er th' unbending corn, and skims along the main.

ALEXANDER POPE

7

ALLITERATION AND ASSONANCE

People have always delighted in playing with the sounds of language. Particularly is this noticeable in the frequency with which repeated consonant and vowel sounds are used in everyday life. Advertisers, for example, knowing the attractive power of repeated sounds, bombard us with such appeals as *Better Buy Bird's Eye, The Flavor Lingers Longer, In League With Leisure,* and *Irresistible Crystal.* In the exuberant and capricious world of slang, with such expressions as *flat-foot, lame-brain,* and *eager-beaver,* it is the repetition that packs the punch. In addition to the ephemeral expressions of slang, there are many stock phrases containing sound repetitions that are kept in current use as part and parcel of our standard language. A few examples are the following: *busy as a bee* (Never, *busy as an ant*), *from top to toe, fuss and fume, might and main, kith and kin, leave in the lurch; high and mighty, free and easy, hit or miss; fair and square, highways and byways, make or break.* Sound repetitions, however, are not limited to the language of daily life. In poetry, too, we derive much enjoyment from the artistic use of the repetition of consonant and vowel sounds.

ALLITERATION

Alliteration is the repetition of identical consonant sounds. It performs two functions in poetry: 1. it provides the aural pleasure of repeated sounds; 2. it helps to structure the poem.

ALLITERATION FOR AURAL PLEASURE. In poetry the skillful use of alliteration to provide aural pleasure may be illustrated by these lines of G. K. Chesterton:

Strong gongs groaning as the guns boom far,   1
Don John of Austria is going to the war;
Stiff flags straining in the night-blasts cold
In the gloom black-purple, in the glint old-gold,
Torchlight crimson on the copper kettle-drums,   5
Then the tuckets, then the trumpets, then the cannon, and he
    comes.

If, however, a consonant sound is insistently overplayed, it may introduce an unpleasing instead of a pleasurable effect, as in Swinburne's

Welling waters winsome word
Wind in warm wan weather.

More subtle effects are produced when the alliterating sounds are so subordinated that they are but dimly perceived and yet make a musical contribution to the poetic experience. This passage from Tennyson's "Song of the Lotos-Eaters" is an example of such subdued alliteration, involving *d, w, f, l,* and *b:*

Lo! in the middle of the wood,
The folded leaf is woo'd from out the bud
With winds upon the branch.

ALLITERATION OF PATTERN. Poets often play an alliteration of several sounds in the same passage; these sounds may fall into patterns, which form slender threads in the total fabric of sound. Among the many patterns possible, here are some of the more simple that may occur:

1. *Ternary alliteration:* an initial consonant sound to be alliterated, a shift to other alliterated consonant sounds, and a return to the first sound; *e.g.,*

*D*own sunk a hollow *b*ottom *b*roa*d* and *d*eep.

JOHN MILTON

2. *Cancrizans alliteration:* a series of consonant sounds repeated in reverse; *e.g.,*

The thundering ra*tt*le of s*latt*ing shook the sheaves.

JOHN MASEFIELD

3. *Augmentative alliteration:* two consonant sounds in juxtaposition, repeated in the same order but separated by a vowel; *e.g.,*

So *fl*ashed and *f*e*ll* the brand Excalibur.

ALFRED, LORD TENNYSON

4. *Diminutive alliteration:* the opposite of augmentative; *e.g.,*

To *fi*elds where *fl*ies no sharp and sided hail.

GERARD MANLEY HOPKINS[1]

5. *Rondo alliteration:* alternation of two or more consonants; *e.g.,*

The *l*eague-*l*ong *roll*er *th*undering on the *r*eef.

ALFRED, LORD TENNYSON

Patterns that are complex and too individual to be easily classified will frequently occur, like Louis MacNeice's

The luck and pluck and plunge of blood,
The wealth and spilth and sport of breath.

Alliterative patterns, whether consciously observed or but vaguely felt, can be both a source of musical pleasure and a help in giving a sense of orderliness to the poem.

Our study of alliterative patterns, however, does not imply that the poet deliberately chooses particular patterns in creating his verse. On the contrary, the poet writes by ear, adjusting his words until the total sequence of sounds represents the aural effects that he desires. But the student, through analyzing these effects, can train

---

[1] The classifications of augmentative and diminutive alliteration are taken from Kenneth Burke, "On Musicality in Verse," *The Philosophy of Literary Form* (Louisiana State University Press, 1941), p. 372 ff. This article contains an interesting theory of "concealed alliteration."

himself to become more sensitive to the role of sound in poetry. This is applicable to alliteration, sound symbolism, and also to assonance, which will be taken up later in this chapter.

EXERCISE

Underline the alliterated consonants in the following quotations, and name or describe any patterns that you observe. The patterns discussed above are not mutually exclusive, and you may find that the same alliterative passage may represent more than one pattern.

1. The portly presence of potentates goodly in girth.
   JOHN MASEFIELD

2. He saw himself
   Balanced as Blondin, more headstrong
   Than baby Hercules.
   C. DAY LEWIS

3. Soldiers are sworn to action; they must win
   Some flaming, fatal climax with their lives.
   SIEGFRIED SASSOON

4. . . . to lulle him in his slumber soft.
   EDMUND SPENSER

5. A mighty fountain momently was forced.
   SAMUEL T. COLERIDGE

6. Were it not wise if I fled from the place and the pit and the fear?
   ROBERT BROWNING

7. [DESCRIPTION OF THE RISING SUN]
   Stands tiptoe on the misty mountain tops.
   WILLIAM SHAKESPEARE

8. She sent the gentle sleep from Heaven,
   That slid into my soul.
   SAMUEL T. COLERIDGE

9. . . . like starry light
   Which, sparkling on the silent waves, does seem more bright.
   EDMUND SPENSER

10. His earliest memory, the mood
    Fingered and frail as maidenhair,
    Was this.
    C. DAY LEWIS

11.　Over the dark Abyss, whose boiling Gulf
　　　Tamely endur'd a Bridge of wondrous length.
　　　　　　　　　　　　　JOHN MILTON

12.　[DESCRIPTION OF A BATTLE IN HEAVEN BETWEEN THE
　　　HOST OF GOOD ANGELS AND THE HOST OF BAD ANGELS]
　　　. . . dire was the noise
　　　Of conflict; overhead the dismal hiss
　　　Of fiery Darts in flaming volleys flew,
　　　And flying vaulted either Host with fire.
　　　　　　　　　　　　　JOHN MILTON

13.　[DESCRIPTION OF THE SEPARATION OF LAND AND WATER
　　　DURING THE CREATION OF THE WORLD]
　　　Immediately the Mountains huge appear　　　　*1*
　　　Emergent, and their broad bare backs upheave
　　　Into the Clouds, their tops ascend the sky:
　　　So high as heav'd the tumid Hills, so low
　　　Down sunk a hollow bottom broad and deep,　　*5*
　　　Capacious bed of Waters.
　　　　　　　　　　　　　JOHN MILTON

14.　So fierce a foe to frenzy.
　　　　　　SAMUEL T. COLERIDGE

15.　[DESCRIPTION OF THE ALLEGORICAL FIGURE OF LECH-
　　　ERY. *Note in particular the treatment of the f's and l's.*]
　　　In a greene gowne he clothed was full faire,　　　*1*
　　　Which underneath did hide his filthinesse,
　　　And in his hand a burning hart he bare,
　　　Full of vaine follies, and new fanglenesse:
　　　For he was false, and fraught with ficklenesse,　　*5*
　　　And learned had to love with secret lookes,
　　　And well could daunce, and sing with ruefulnesse,
　　　And fortunes tell, and read in loving bookes,
　　　And thousand other wayes, to bait his fleshly hookes.
　　　　　　　　　　　　EDMUND SPENSER

16.　The bare black cliff clanged round him.
　　　　　　ALFRED, LORD TENNYSON

17.　Run the rapid and leap the fall.
　　　　　　SIDNEY LANIER

18.   Dreamland lies forlorn of light.

D. G. ROSSETTI

19.   Stark 'neath the star stood the dead-still Mill.

WALTER DE LA MARE

ALLITERATION FOR STRUCTURE.   The second function of alliteration is to help structure the poem, that is, to help weld the poetic experience of the reader into a coherent and unified whole. This it accomplishes through the added emphasis that alliterated words usually have. Such emphasis may serve various purposes:

1. It may strengthen the effect of the key words; *e.g.*, Pope's

The *b*ookfu*l* *bl*ockhead, ignorant*l*y read,
With *l*oads of *l*earned *l*umber in his head.

2. It may call attention to a contrast; *e.g.*, Dryden's

Depth of *p*ains, and height of *p*assion.

3. It may link together words that are related in image, thought, or feeling; *e.g.*, Milton's description of the eating of the forbidden fruit by Eve:

*Gr*eedily she in*g*or*g*'*d* without restraint.

Such linkage may sometimes bring about a more subtle reciprocity of meanings, such as we see in the chiasmic arrangement of Tennyson's

I heard the ri*pp*le *w*ashing in the reeds,
And the *w*i*l*d *w*aters *l*a*pp*ing on the crag.

These lines, as mere statement, tell us of the *ripple washing* and the *waters lapping*, but the alliteration of the *p*'s and *l*'s and *w*'s brings about a psychological interplay of meanings whereby we sense also the *ripple lapping* and the *waters washing*.

EXERCISE

Underline the alliterated consonants in the following quotations, and ascertain the structural purpose of all alliteration that seems to have a further aim than to furnish aural pleasure.

1.   Then shall the new yeares joy forth freshly send
      Into the glooming world his gladsome ray.

EDMUND SPENSER

2. Plum-purple waŝ the west; but spikes of light
Spear'd open lustrous gashes, crimson-white.
GERARD MANLEY HOPKINS

3. So doe I now myselfe a prisoner yeeld,
To sorrow and to solitary pain:
From presence of my dearest deare exylde,
Longwhile alone in languor to remaine.
EDMUND SPENSER

4. [DESCRIPTION OF THE VAST HALL OF PANDEMONIUM IN
HELL AFTER THE DEMONS HAD BEEN TURNED INTO SER-
PENTS]
. . . dreadful was the din
Of hissing through the Hall.
JOHN MILTON

5. And though that he were worthy he was wys
And of his port as meeke as is a mayde.
GEOFFREY CHAUCER

6. And deeper than did ever plummet sound
I'll drown my book.
WILLIAM SHAKESPEARE

7. . . . and over them the sea-wind sang
Shrill, chill, with flakes of foam.
ALFRED, LORD TENNYSON

8. And my pulses closed their gates with a shock on my heart as I
heard
The shrill-edged shriek of a mother divide the shuddering night.
ALFRED, LORD TENNYSON

9. [*In Paradise, after Eve had eaten the forbidden fruit, Adam, not
at all deceived about the outcome, also partook because he was
foolishly smitten with her charms. In this quotation the word*
fondly *means foolishly.*]
. . . [Adam was] not deceiv'd
But fondly overcome with Female charm.
JOHN MILTON

10. There many Minstrales maken melody,
To drive away the dull melancholy.
EDMUND SPENSER

11. [DESCRIPTION OF ACTION OF THE SUN]
     And hurld his glistring beames through gloomy aire.
                              EDMUND SPENSER

ASSONANCE

VOWEL TONES. A spoken vowel is a complex voice tone consisting of two basic parts. The first part is the tone of the speaking voice, which is produced by the vibration of the vocal cords.

The second part is a cluster of tones which are produced, not by the vibration of the vocal cords, but by the shape of the throat and mouth cavities in a manner not fully understood. You can hear them by whispering any vowel, for in the act of whispering the vocal cords do not vibrate and therefore the speaking voice is absent. Every vowel has a somewhat different set of these tones; and each tone has its own frequency of vibration, causing its fixed pitch, and its own intensity. By the use of scientific instruments the frequency of vibration and the degree of intensity of the component tones of every vowel can be ascertained and plotted on paper. Now, among these component tones there is one, different for every vowel, which stands out prominently over all others, which receives most of the sound energy, and whose fixed pitch gives the individual tone quality, or timbre, that distinguishes each vowel from all others. This tone is called the formant of a vowel. It is our hearing of this formant that "forms" for us the identity of any particular vowel, that enables us to distinguish, for example, the vowel in *beet* from the vowel in *bet*. And since each formant, giving a distinctive character to its vowel, has a definite frequency of vibration, which we experience as pitch, we may consider each vowel as a musical tone.[2]

Vowels, then, are musical tones. Furthermore, they form a scale when arranged from high to low in terms of the frequencies of their formants. This scale, based on a long list of experiments, is reproduced below. The "characteristic frequency" assigned to each vowel represents a mean frequency obtained by analyzing a large number of cases where the same vowel was uttered. This procedure was necessary because any given vowel is different in every utterance, though the differences are often not noticeable to the human ear.

---

[2] The pitch of a vowel formant, which is invariable within limits, is a thing apart from the pitch of the speaking voice, which is variable.

Vowel	As pronounced in	Characteristic frequency of formant
1. [i]	bee	3100
2. [ɪ]	hit	――
3. [e]	they	2461
4. [ɛ]	pet	1958
5. [æ]	at	1840
6. [ɑ]	father	900
7. [ɔ]	law	732
8. [o]	no	461
9. [ʊ]	pull	――
10. [u]	gloom	326[3]

This vowel scale constitutes a tonal frame of reference that we shall use a little later on for the study of vowel melodies. Because of lack of adequate data, it does not include all the vowels and diphthongs (two adjoining vowels that make up one speech sound) in American speech. The complete list will be found in the Table of Phonetic Symbols on page 454.

ASSONANCE FOR MUSICAL PLEASURE.   Assonance usually means the repetition of identical vowel or diphthong tones, especially in stressed syllables, as in low moan and light lies. This type of assonance is called *assonance of identity.*

One of the functions of assonance in poetry is to furnish musical pleasure. From the psychology of music it is known that musical tone is a direct emotional stimulus, setting up in the body the precise physical changes that underlie or accompany emotion. Such an affective condition caused by tonal stimulation is a general mood. In poetry this mood can be transformed into more specific feelings by the meanings of the words and their connotative and emotive charge.

---

[3] This table is that of D. C. Miller, in Henry Lanz, *The Physical Basis of Rime* (Stanford University, California: Stanford University Press, 1931), p. 22. The frequencies are those found by D. C. Miller, tabulated by Mark H. Liddell. The vowels [ɪ] and [ʊ] have been interpolated. The vowels [e] and [o], though diphthongized in American speech, may for our purposes be considered as pure vowels, because the second element of each as a diphthong adjoins it on the scale.

This emotional power possessed by the vowels of poetry, as musical tones, can be intensified by repetition.[4]

EXERCISE

To sharpen your perception of vowel sounds, read the following passages aloud. Listen carefully to the sounds you utter and locate the identical vowels and diphthongs. Do not let your eyes deceive you; *parch, heart, sergeant,* for example, contain identical vowels though spelt differently.

1. Slow the low gradual moan came in the snowing.
    JOHN MASEFIELD

2. I arise from dreams of thee,
    In the first sweet sleep of night.
    PERCY BYSSHE SHELLEY

3. The viol, the violet, and the vine.
    EDGAR ALLAN POE

4. Oh, broken is the golden bowl! the spirit flown forever.
    EDGAR ALLAN POE

5. Larch-heart that chars to a chalk-white glow.
    ROBERT BROWNING

6. No freedom till the sleep that sets me free.
    SIEGFRIED SASSOON

---

[4] Why the repetition of sounds affords pleasure has been given a reasonable explanation by De Witt Parker:

"All word-sounds as we utter or hear them leave memory traces in the mind, which are not pure images . . . , but also motor sets, tendencies, or impulses to the remaking of sounds. The doing of any deed—a word is also a deed—creates a will to its doing again; hence the satisfaction when that will is fulfilled in the repeated sound. . . . And the same law that rules in music and design holds here also: there must not be too much of consonance, of repetition, else the will becomes satiated and fatigued; there must be difference as well as identity,—the novelty and surprise which accompany the arousal of a still fresh and unappeased impulse." *The Principles of Aesthetics* (New York: Silver, Burdett, 1920), pp. 196–197.

This explanation of the satisfaction we derive from hearing repeated sounds applies not only to assonance but also to alliteration and rime.

7. And bowery hollows crowned with summer sea.

ALFRED, LORD TENNYSON

8. How sweet the moonlight sleeps upon this bank!
   Here will we sit, and let the sounds of night
   Creep in our ears; soft stillness and the night
   Become the touches of sweet harmony.

WILLIAM SHAKESPEARE

Love in the Valley

(FIRST STANZA)

Under yonder beech-tree single on the green-sward,   *1*
  Couched with her arms behind her golden head,
Knees and tresses folded to slip and ripple idly,
  Lies my young love sleeping in the shade.
Had I the heart to slide an arm beneath her,   *5*
  Press her parting lips as her waist I gather slow,
Waking in amazement she could not but embrace me:
  Then would she hold me and never let me go?

GEORGE MEREDITH

In addition to assonance of identity, other types of assonance are also used to furnish musical pleasure.

1. *Assonance of contrast* is a series of contrasting assonanted vowels chosen from the top and bottom of the vowel scale, usually [u] or [o] as opposed to [i] or [e], as in *noon-day dreams* and *sedate and slow and gay.*

2. *Assonance of similarity* is a vowel sequence that moves along in only a limited section of the scale, as in

On that lone shore loud moans the sea.[5]

3. *Assonance of pattern* is the arrangement of assonanted vowels in a fairly definite patterning, as in Shakespeare's

a b   c   d   e d   c b   a   d
Making their tomb the womb wherein they grew.

---

[5] This line is cited by Gerard M. Hopkins in his *Notebooks* as an example of "*vowelling off* or changing of vowel down some scale. . . ." *Notebooks and Papers,* ed. by Humphry House (London: Oxford University Press, 1937), p. 243.

This line contains a pattern of perfect symmetry, with a final *d* to close off the line. Assonance of pattern may be clearly observed by the reader or but vaguely felt. In either case it can, like alliteration, be both a source of musical pleasure and a help in giving a sense of orderliness to the poem.

EXERCISE

Study the accented vowels of the following lines in relation to the vowel scale on page 120 and classify each as assonance of contrast, assonance of similarity, or assonance of pattern. Some passages will come under more than one classification.

1.   *Pace*-horn, *chase*-horn, *race*-horn.
        VACHEL LINDSAY

2.   To deep and deeper blue.
        JAMES JOYCE

3.   Far from the valleys of Hall.
        SIDNEY LANIER

4.   The weary way-worn wanderer bore
     To his own native shore.
        EDGAR ALLAN POE

5.   In Xanadu did Kubla Khan.
        SAMUEL T. COLERIDGE

6.   . . . the sleek, sharp, dark-leaved holly tree.
        WALTER DE LA MARE

7.   Laborious orient ivory sphere on sphere.
        ALFRED, LORD TENNYSON

8.   Drink deep or taste not the Pierian spring.
        ALEXANDER POPE

9.   If aught of oaten stop, or pastoral song.[6]
        WILLIAM COLLINS

---

[6] Of this line John Livingston Lowes has remarked, "The music of the line . . . is due to the nice conjunction of recurring consonants with subtly varying vowels." *Convention and Revolt in Poetry* (Boston: Houghton Mifflin, 1930), p. 244.

10.   The mellow ouzel fluted in the elm.[7]

       ALFRED, LORD TENNYSON

11.   The ploughman homeward plods his weary way.

       THOMAS GRAY

12.   Wind whines and whines the shingle,
    The crazy pierstakes groan;
    A senile sea numbers each single
    Slimesilvered stone.

       JAMES JOYCE

13.   Philomel with melody.

       WILLIAM SHAKESPEARE

ASSONANCE FOR STRUCTURE.   In addition to giving musical pleasure, assonance has a second function: to help structure the poem, that is, to help fuse the poetic experience into an integrated whole. Assonanted vowels give words special emphasis, and this emphasis may serve to fulfill certain structural purposes:

1. It may strengthen the effect of important words; *e.g.*, Tennyson's

Petals from *blown roses* on the grass.

2. It may call attention to a contrast; *e.g.*, Joyce's

In the deep *cool* shadow
    At *noon* of day.

3. It may give an aural nexus to words that are related in image, thought, or feeling; *e.g.*, Sandburg's

Passing through *huddled* and *ugly* walls.

EXERCISE

In the following lines point out instances of assonance of structure, and explain the purpose of each. In some cases more than one purpose may be served.

---

[7] Of this line Tennyson has remarked, " 'The merry blackbird sang among the trees' would seem quite as good a line to nine-tenths of all English men and women. Who knows but that the Cockney may come to read it: 'The meller housel fluted i' the helm.' Who knows what English may come to?" *The Works of Tennyson,* with notes by the author, ed. by Hallam, Lord Tennyson (New York: Macmillan, 1923 edition), p. 916.

1. Music that brings sweet sleep down from the blissful skies.

ALFRED, LORD TENNYSON

2. Fills the shadows and windy places
       With lisp of leaves and ripple of rain.

ALGERNON C. SWINBURNE

3. 'Mid hushed cool-rooted flowers, fragrant-eyed.

JOHN KEATS

4. In Stygian cave forlorn
       'Mongst horrid shapes, and shrieks, and sights unholy.

JOHN MILTON

5.   . . . Not poppy, nor mandragora,
    Nor all the drowsy syrups of the world,
    Shall ever medicine thee to that sweet sleep
    Which thou owedst yesterday.

WILLIAM SHAKESPEARE

6. The curfew tolls the knell of parting day,
    The lowing herd wind slowly o'er the lea.

THOMAS GRAY

7. I wander by the edge
    Of this desolate lake
    Where wind cries in the sedge.

WILLIAM BUTLER YEATS

ILLUSTRATIVE POEMS

ALLITERATION

A Consecration

Not of the princes and prelates with periwigged charioteers   *1*
Riding triumphantly laurelled to lap the fat of the years,—
Rather the scorned—the rejected—the men hemmed in with
     the spears:

The men of the tattered battalion which fights till it dies,
Dazed with the dust of the battle, the din and the cries,   *5*
The men with the broken heads and the blood running into
     their eyes.

Not the be-medalled Commander, beloved of the throne,
Riding cock-horse to parade when the bugles are blown,
But the lads who carried the koppie and cannot be known.

Not the ruler for me, but the ranker, the tramp of the road,   *10*
The slave with the sack on his shoulders pricked on with the
      goad,
The man with too weighty a burden, too weary a load.

The sailor, the stoker of steamers, the man with the clout,
The chantyman bent at the halliards putting a tune to the
      shout,
The drowsy man at the wheel and the tired lookout.   *15*

Others may sing of the wine and the wealth and the mirth,
The portly presence of potentates goodly in girth;—
Mine be the dirt and the dross, the dust and the scum of the
      earth!

THEIRS be the music, the color, the glory, the gold;
Mine be a handful of ashes, a mouthful of mold.   *20*
Of the maimed, of the halt and the blind in the rain and the
      cold—
Of these shall my songs be fashioned, my tales be told.

JOHN MASEFIELD

SONNET XLVII, *Amoretti*

Trust not the treason of those smyling lookes,   *1*
    untill ye have theyr guylefull traynes well tryde:
    for they are lyke but unto golden hookes,
    that from the foolish fish theyr bayts doe hyde:
So she with flattring smyles weake harts doth guyde   *5*
    unto her love, and tempte to theyr decay,
    whome being caught she kills with cruell pryde,
    and feeds at pleasure on the wretched pray:
Yet even whylst her bloody hands them slay,
    her eyes looke lovely and upon them smyle: *10*
    that they take pleasure in her cruell play,
    and dying doe them selves of payne beguyle.

O mighty charm which makes men love theyr bane,
and thinck they dy with pleasure, live with payne.

EDMUND SPENSER

Lepanto

White founts falling in the Courts of the sun,   *1*
And the Soldan of Byzantium is smiling as they run;
There is laughter like the fountains in that face of all men
    feared,
It stirs the forest darkness, the darkness of his beard;
It curls the blood-red crescent, the crescent of his lips;   *5*
For the inmost sea of all the earth is shaken with his ships.
They have dared the white republics up the capes of Italy,
They have dashed the Adriatic round the Lion of the Sea,
And the Pope has cast his arms abroad for agony and loss,
And called the kings of Christendom for swords about the
    Cross.   *10*
The cold queen of England is looking in the glass;
The shadow of the Valois is yawning at the Mass;
From evening isles fantastical rings faint the Spanish gun,
And the Lord upon the Golden Horn is laughing in the sun.
Dim drums throbbing, in the hills half heard,   *15*
Where only on a nameless throne a crownless prince has
    stirred,
Where, risen from a doubtful seat and half-attainted stall,
The last knight of Europe takes weapons from the wall,
The last and lingering troubadour to whom the bird has
    sung,
That once went singing southward when all the world was
    young.   *20*
In that enormous silence, tiny and unafraid,
Comes up along a winding road the noise of the Crusade.
Strong gongs groaning as the guns boom far,
Don John of Austria is going to the war;
Stiff flags straining in the night-blasts cold   *25*
In the gloom black-purple, in the glint old-gold,
Torchlight crimson on the copper kettle-drums,
Then the tuckets, then the trumpets, then the cannon, and
    he comes.

Don John laughing in the brave beard curled,
Spurning of his stirrups like the thrones of all the world,   *30*
Holding his head up for a flag of all the free.
Love-light of Spain—hurrah!
Death-light of Africa!
Don John of Austria
Is riding to the sea.   *35*

Mahound is in his paradise above the evening star,
(*Don John of Austria is going to the war.*)
He moves a mighty turban on the timeless houri's knees,
His turban that is woven of the sunsets and the seas.
He shakes the peacock gardens as he rises from his ease,   *40*
And he strides among the tree-tops and is taller than the
    trees;
And his voice through all the garden is a thunder sent to
    bring
Black Azrael and Ariel and Ammon on the wing.
Giants and the Genii,
Multiplex of wing and eye,   *45*
Whose strong obedience broke the sky
When Solomon was king.

They rush in red and purple from the red clouds of the morn,
From the temples where the yellow gods shut up their eyes in
    scorn;
They rise in green robes roaring from the green hells of the
    sea   *50*
Where fallen skies and evil hues and eyeless creatures be,
On them the sea-valves cluster and the gray sea-forests curl,
Splashed with a splendid sickness, the sickness of the pearl;
They swell in sapphire smoke out of the blue cracks of the
    ground,—
They gather and they wonder and give worship to Mahound.   *55*
And he saith, "Break up the mountains where the hermit-
    folk can hide,
And sift the red and silver sands lest bone of saint abide,
And chase the Giaours flying night and day, not giving rest,
For that which was our trouble comes again out of the west.

We have set the seal of Solomon on all things under sun,   *60*
Of knowledge and of sorrow and endurance of things done.
But a noise is in the mountains, in the mountains; and I know
The voice that shook our palaces—four hundred years ago:
It is he that saith not 'Kismet'; it is he that knows not Fate;
It is Richard, it is Raymond, it is Godfrey at the gate!   *65*
It is he whose loss is laughter when he counts the wager
    worth,
Put down your feet upon him, that our peace be on the
    earth."
For he heard drums groaning and he heard guns jar,
(*Don John of Austria is going to the war.*)
Sudden and still—hurrah!   *70*
Bolt from Iberia!
Don John of Austria
Is gone by Alcalar.

St. Michael's on his Mountain in the sea-roads of the north
(*Don John of Austria is girt and going forth.*)   *75*
Where the gray seas glitter and the sharp tides shift
And the sea-folk labor and the red sails lift.
He shakes his lance of iron and he claps his wings of stone;
The noise is gone through Normandy; the noise is gone
    alone;
The North is full of tangled things and texts and aching
    eyes,   *80*
And dead is all the innocence of anger and surprise,
And Christian killeth Christian in a narrow dusty room,
And Christian dreadeth Christ that hath a newer face of
    doom,
And Christian hateth Mary that God kissed in Galilee,—
But Don John of Austria is riding to the sea.   *85*
Don John calling through the blast and the eclipse,
Crying with the trumpet, with the trumpet to his lips,
Trumpet that sayeth *ha!*
    Domino Gloria!
Don John of Austria   *90*
Is shouting to the ships.

King Philip's in his closet with the Fleece about his neck
(*Don John of Austria is armed upon the deck.*)
The walls are hung with velvet that is black and soft as sin,
And little dwarfs creep out of it and little dwarfs creep in.   *95*
He holds a crystal phial that has colors like the moon,
He touches, and it tingles, and he trembles very soon,
And his face is as a fungus of a leprous white and gray
Like plants in the high houses that are shuttered from the
    day,
And death is in the phial and the end of noble work,   *100*
But Don John of Austria has fired upon the Turk.

Don John's hunting, and his hounds have bayed—
Booms away past Italy the rumor of his raid.
Gun upon gun, ha! ha!
Gun upon gun, hurrah!   *105*
Don John of Austria
Has loosed the cannonade.

The Pope was in his chapel before day or battle broke,
(*Don John of Austria is hidden in the smoke.*)
The hidden room in man's house where God sits all the year,   *110*
The secret window whence the world looks small and very
    dear.
He sees as in a mirror on the monstrous twilight sea
The crescent of his cruel ships whose name is mystery;
They fling great shadows foe-wards, making Cross and
    Castle dark,
They veil the plumèd lions on the galleys of St. Mark;   *115*
And above the ships are palaces of brown, black-bearded
    chiefs,
And below the ships are prisons, where with multitudinous
    griefs,
Christian captives, sick and sunless, all a laboring race re-
    pines
Like a race in sunken cities, like a nation in the mines.
They are lost like slaves that swat, and in the skies of morn-
    ing hung   *120*
The stair-ways of the tallest gods when tyranny was young.

They are countless, voiceless, hopeless as those fallen or flee-
    ing on
Before the high Kings' horses in the granite of Babylon.
And many a one grows witless in his quiet room in hell
Where a yellow face looks inward through the lattice of his
    cell,   125
And he finds his God forgotten, and he seeks no more a
    sign—
(*But Don John of Austria has burst the battle-line!*)
Don John pounding from the slaughter-painted poop,
Purpling all the ocean like a bloody pirate's sloop,
Scarlet running over on the silvers and the golds,   130
Breaking of the hatches up and bursting of the holds,
Thronging of the thousands up that labor under sea
White for bliss and blind for sun and stunned for liberty.
Vivat Hispania!
Domino Gloria!   135
Don John of Austria
Has set his people free!

Cervantes on his galley sets the sword back in the sheath
(*Don John of Austria rides homeward with a wreath.*)
And he sees across a weary land a straggling road in Spain,   140
Up which a lean and foolish knight for ever rides in vain,
And he smiles, but not as Sultans smile, and settles back the
    blade . . .
(*But Don John of Austria rides home from the Crusade.*)
GILBERT   KEITH   CHESTERTON

ASSONANCE

The poems that follow contain varied types of assonance. Study
each poem until you understand it. Then reread it, focusing your attention on the sounds of the vowels to ascertain what assonance has
been used and, especially, why it has been used. Since American
speech contains only about twenty vowels and diphthongs, some ac-
cidental repetitions of vowels will necessarily occur. Try to separate
these chance appearances from what seems to be a purposed and
artistic employment of assonance. Do not expect to find purposed assonance in every line, for it is a device that is rather sparingly used
in much poetry.

Chill of the Eve

A long green swell   *1*
Slopes soft to the sea ;
And a far-off bell
Swings sweet to me ;
As the grey   *5*
Chill day
Slips away
From the lea.

Spread cold and far,
Without one glow   *10*
From a mild pale star,
Is the sky's steel bow ;
And the grey
Chill day
Slips away   *15*
Below.

Yon green tree grieves
To the air around ;
And the whispering leaves
Have a lonely sound ;   *20*
As the grey
Chill day
Slips away
From the ground.

And dark, more dark,   *25*
The shades settle down ;
Far off is a spark
From the lamp-lit town ;
And the grey
Chill day   *30*
Slips away
With a frown.

                JAMES STEPHENS

Winter

Clouded with snow   *1*
 The cold winds blow,
And shrill on leafless bough
The robin with its burning breast
 Alone sings now.   *5*

The rayless sun,
 Day's journey done,
Sheds its last ebbing light
On fields in leagues of beauty spread
 Unearthly white.   *10*

Thick draws the dark,
 And spark by spark,
The frost-fires kindle, and soon
Over that sea of frozen foam
 Floats the white moon.   *15*

                    WALTER DE LA MARE

The Twilight Turns from Amethyst

The twilight turns from amethyst   *1*
 To deep and deeper blue,
The lamp fills with a pale green glow
 The trees of the avenue.

The old piano plays an air,   *5*
 Sedate and slow and gay;
She bends upon the yellow keys,
 Her head inclines this way.

Shy thoughts and grave wide eyes and hands
 That wander as they list—   *10*
The twilight turns to darker blue
 With lights of amethyst.

                        JAMES JOYCE

In each stanza of the next poem occurs a kind of assonance of pattern called "cross-assonance." Reading aloud will be helpful in locating this pattern.

Bombers

Through the vague morning, the heart preoccupied,   *1*
A deep in air buried grain of sound
Starts and grows, as yet unwarning—
The tremor of baited deep sea line.

Swells the seed, and now tight sound-buds   *5*
Vibrate, upholding their paean flowers
To the sun. There are bees in sky-bells droning,
Flares of crimson at the heart unfold.

Children look up, and the elms spring-garlanded
Tossing their heads and marked for the axe.   *10*
Gallant or woebegone, alike unlucky—
Earth shakes beneath us : we imagine loss.

Black as vermin, crawling in echelon
Beneath the cloud-floor, the bombers come :
The heavy angels, carrying harm in   *15*
Their wombs that ache to be rid of death.

This is the seed that grows for ruin,
The iron embryo conceived in fear.
Soon or late its need must be answered
In fear delivered and screeching fire.   *20*

Choose between your child and this fatal embryo.
Shall your guilt bear arms, and the children you want
Be condemned to die by the powers you paid for
And haunt the houses you never built?

C. DAY LEWIS

The next poem is an account of Eve's description of Paradise, from Milton's *Paradise Lost,* IV, lines 641–656.

Paradise

Sweet is the breath of morn, her rising sweet,   1
With charm of earliest Birds ; pleasant the Sun
When first on this delightful Land he spreads
His orient Beams, on herb, tree, fruit, and flow'r,
Glist'ring with dew ; fragrant the fertile earth   5
After soft showers ; and sweet the coming on
Of grateful Ev'ning mild, then silent Night
With this her solemn Bird and this fair Moon,
And these the Gems of Heav'n, her starry train :
But neither breath of Morn when she ascends   10
With charm of earliest Birds, nor rising Sun
On this delightful land, nor herb, fruit, flow'r,
Glist'ring with dew, nor fragrance after showers,
Nor grateful Ev'ning mild, nor silent Night
With this her solemn Bird, nor walk by Moon,   15
Or glittering Star-light without thee is sweet.

JOHN MILTON

Inversnaid

This darksome burn, horseback brown,   1
His rollrock highroad roaring down,
In coop and in comb the fleece of his foam
Flutes and low to the lake falls home.

A windpuff-bonnet of fawn-froth   5
Turns and twindles over the broth
Of a pool so pitchblack, fell-frowning,
It rounds and rounds Despair to drowning.

Degged with dew, dappled with dew
Are the groins of the braes that the brook treads through,   10
Wiry heathpacks, flitches of fern,
And the beadbonny ash that sits over the burn.

What would the world be, once bereft
Of wet and of wildness? Let them be left,

O let them be left, wildness and wet;   15
Long live the weeds and the wilderness yet.

GERARD MANLEY HOPKINS

The Harbor

Passing through huddled and ugly walls   1
By doorways where women haggard
Looked from their hunger-deep eyes,
Haunted with shadows of hunger-hands,
Out from the huddled and ugly walls,   5
I came sudden, at the city's edge,
On a blue burst of lake,
Long lake waves breaking under the sun
On a spray-flung curve of shore;
And a fluttering storm of gulls,   10
Masses of great gray wings
And flying white bellies
Veering and wheeling free in the open.

CARL SANDBURG

8

R H Y T H M

Rhythm dominates our lives. The heart beat with rhythmic regularity sends life-bearing blood pulsing through our arteries and veins. The revolution of the earth around the sun brings about the cycle of changing seasons. The alternation of day and night, the ebb and flow of tides, the recurrence of the phases of the moon—all attest the presence of rhythm in nature. Man-made objects, too, provide instances of rhythm at every hand—in the tick of a clock, the hammering of pistons, and the chug of a locomotive. And in many of man's activities, such as the patterned movements of a marching band, the shift in a T-formation, the gyrations of a jitter-bug, we find evidence of both the presence of rhythm and the pleasure which it gives. From these examples we may rightly infer that rhythm means regularity of recurrence.

The word *rhythm,* as applied to language, means the regular re-currence of time-patterns and stress-patterns. As an illustration let us examine a verse from the *Song of Solomon* (4:6):

Until the day break, and the shadows flee
away, I will get me to the mountain of myrrh,
and to the hill of frankincense.

137

In this verse the recurring time-patterns will stand out more clearly if we print the lines like this:

Until the day break,
and the shadows flee away,
I will get me to the mountain of myrrh,
and to the hill of frankincense.

Here we observe that lines one and two are roughly equivalent to each other in the length of time required for utterance, and that lines three and four, each a little longer than the first two lines, are also equivalents in time. These equivalences form a simple rhythm of time-patterns. Now let us observe the stresses of the lines:

Until the day break,

and the shadows flee away,

I will get me to the mountain of myrrh,

and to the hill of frankincense.

Each line has a three-stress pattern, with the time intervals between these stresses somewhat variable. Thus the passage may be said to have a rough stress-pattern in addition to the time-pattern witnessed above, and we therefore say that it has rhythm.

EXERCISE

The following passage is the beginning of the Sermon on the Mount, *Matthew*, Chapter V. Read the selection aloud so as to bring out the time-patterns and stress-patterns. Since this is prose, though it verges toward poetry, the rhythm is not sustained throughout.

1   And seeing the multitudes, he went up into a mountain; and when he was set, his disciples came unto him:

2   And he opened his mouth, and taught them, saying,

3   Blessed are the poor in spirit: for their's is the kingdom of heaven.

4   Blessed are they that mourn: for they shall be comforted.

5   Blessed are the meek: for they shall inherit the earth.

6   Blessed are they which do hunger and thirst after righteousness: for they shall be filled.

7   Blessed are the merciful: for they shall obtain mercy.

8   Blessed are the pure in heart: for they shall see God.

9   Blessed are the peacemakers: for they shall be called the children
of God.

10   Blessed are they which are persecuted for righteousness' sake:
for their's is the kingdom of heaven.

11   Blessed are ye, when men shall revile you, and persecute you, and
shall say all manner of evil against you falsely, for my sake.

12   Rejoice, and be exceeding glad: for great is your reward in heaven:
for so persecuted they the prophets which were before you.

METER.   The word *rhythm* is also used in a more limited
sense to mean the arrangement of words in such a way that the
stressed syllables recur at regular intervals, the time between stresses
being occupied with unstressed syllables or pauses. For this narrower sense of the word to denote stress patterns, we use the term
meter. The following quotations illustrate meter:

1.   Should auld acquaintance be forgot

    And never brought to mind?

ROBERT BURNS

2.   For the moon never beams without bringing me dreams

    Of the beautiful Annabel Lee.

EDGAR ALLAN POE

3.   There they are, my fifty men and women,

    Naming me the fifty poems finished!

ROBERT BROWNING

4.   Take her up tenderly,

    Lift her with care;

Fashioned so slenderly,

    Young and so fair.

THOMAS HOOD

The basic unit of meter is the *foot,* a short section of the verse containing one stressed syllable and one or more unstressed syllables,

or, in lieu of the latter, a pause. In any given kind of meter each foot is theoretically of the same length regardless of the number of unstressed syllables or the pause that it contains. There are four common kinds of metrical feet: the iambus, the anapest, the trochee, and the dactyl.

The foot called an iambus consists of one unstressed syllable followed by one stressed syllable, as in *awáke*. A meter in which the iambus is the most frequently used foot is called iambic. The following lines are in iambic meter:

'Tis hárd to sáy if greáter wánt of skíll
Appéar in wríting ór in júdging íll.
ALEXANDER POPE

The foot called an anapest consists of two unstressed syllables followed by one stressed syllable, as in *overtáke*. A meter in which the anapest is the most frequently used foot is called anapestic. The following lines are in anapestic meter:

But our lóve it was strónger by fár than the lóve
Of thóse who were ólder than wé.
EDGAR ALLAN POE

The foot called a trochee consists of one stressed syllable followed by one unstressed syllable, as in *húrry*. A meter in which the trochee is the most frequently used foot is called trochaic. The following line is in trochaic meter:

Pánsies, lílies, kíngcups, dáisies.
WILLIAM WORDSWORTH

The foot called a dactyl consists of one stressed syllable followed by two unstressed syllables, as in *mótherly*. A meter in which the dactyl is the most frequently used foot is called dactylic. The following lines are in dactylic meter:

Whíte were the moórlands

And frózen befóre her,

Greén were the moórlands

And bloóming behínd her.

CHARLES KINGSLEY

In addition to these four kinds of metrical feet, there are two kinds of irregular feet that may be used to vary a meter, the spondee and the pyrrhic. The spondee consists of two stressed syllables, as in *Jóhn Smíth.* The pyrrhic consists of two unstressed syllables, as the first two words in *to the greát déep.* In the following lines the first two feet of the second line are a pyrrhic and a spondee respectively:

'Tis nót a líp, or eýe, we beaúty cáll,

But the joínt fórce and fúll resúlt of áll.

ALEXANDER POPE

EXERCISE

Practice reading the following passages aloud to catch the swing of the meter. Write an accent mark over each syllable that you stress in your reading. Note that the stress pattern of the basic meter is not always adhered to with exactness.

1. Dactylic meter:

Come from the hills where your hirsels are grazing,
  Come from the glen of the buck and the roe;
Come to the crag where the beacon is blazing,
  Come with the buckler, the lance, and the bow.

SIR WALTER SCOTT

2. Trochaic meter:

Now the day is over,
  Night is drawing nigh,
Shadows of the evening
  Steal across the sky.

SABINE BARING-GOULD

3. Iambic meter:

The bookful blockhead, ignorantly read,
With loads of learned lumber in his head,
With his own tongue still edifies his ears,
And always list'ning to himself appears.

ALEXANDER POPE

4. Anapestic meter:

The blackbird has fled to another retreat,
Where hazels afford him a screen from the heat.

WILLIAM COWPER

5. Iambic meter:

There lived a wife at Usher's well,
    And a wealthy wife was she;
She had three stout and stalwart sons,
    And sent them o'er the sea.

ANONYMOUS

6. Trochaic or iambic meter:

Tasks in hours of insight willed
Can be through hours of gloom fulfilled.

MATTHEW ARNOLD

7. Iambic meter:

When I see birches bend from left to right
Across the line of straighter, darker trees,
I like to think some boy's been swinging them.

ROBERT FROST

8. Dactylic meter:

Could I but live again
    Twice my life over,
Would I not strive again?

ROBERT BROWNING

The classification of all syllable stresses into only two groups,
stressed and unstressed, *i.e.*, heavily stressed and lightly stressed, is

not in exact accord with the facts of spoken poetry but is a matter of analytical convenience. In actual speech many degrees of stress are used. For example in the line

On thy cold grey stones, O sea.

the word *grey* has more stress than *on* but may have less than *cold* or *stones*, and may be indicated as either stressed or unstressed, according to one's individual reading. Thus, because all the varying degrees of stress must be classed, in analysis, as either stressed or unstressed, there will occur legitimate differences of opinion about the stresses of a metrical pattern.

A meter of perfect regularity seldom continues for long in a good poem, but it does persist in the nervous organism of the reader as a clocklike pattern of auditory expectancies, which we call the subjective meter. Against this subjective meter the poet, according to his expressive purpose, varies his metrical design, introducing pauses, adding or suppressing syllables, and substituting for the expected metrical feet those of another meter.

If the subjective meter in the reader's mind is realized by a sequence of words exactly corresponding to it in the placement of stresses, the result is a chain of experienced satisfactions that soon become metrically tiresome. The following poem, with an iambic meter of almost perfect regularity, is an example:

Intelligence Test

The most uninteresting chap   *1*
   I think I ever knew
Had thousands of remarks on tap
   And all of them were true.
He bored me to a final tear   *5*
   Before he went away,
Because he didn't care to hear
   The things I had to say.

The woman I've enjoyed the most
   Had neither charm nor wit;   *10*
She didn't even have the ghost
   Of knowledge to transmit.

But with what grace she gently bent—
  A flower upon its stalk,
And listened meek and reverent   *15*
  When I desired to talk.

The dullest people, as a rule,
  Possess the largest brains;
The cleverest man may be a fool
  Because the fact remains   *20*
That brilliance not at all descends
  From erudition's tree—
One joins my group of clever friends
  By listening to ME!

CEDRIC ADAMS

If, on the other hand, the stresses show variations from the subjective meter, the result is a series of satisfactions, disappointments, postponements, and surprisals that are a part of the emotive effect of meter. The following lines by John Keats, based on a subjective iambic meter, will illustrate such variations.

Keen, fitful gusts are whispering here and there   *1*

Among the bushes half leafless, and dry;   *2*

The stars look very cold about the sky,   *3*

And I have many miles on foot to fare,   *4*

Yet feel I little of the cool bleak air,   *5*

Or of the dead leaves rustling drearily.   *6*

JOHN KEATS

In line 1 the stress on *keen* gives us a spondee for a forceful opening. In line 2 *leafless* is a trochee substituted for the expected iambus. Lines 3 and 4 foot it along in regular iambics. Line 5 is greatly varied in that it begins and ends with a spondee and has a pyrrhic for the third foot. Line 6 forms an interesting contrast to line 5: it begins and ends with a pyrrhic and has a spondee for the third foot. These metrical variations to the iambic pattern—eight of them in six lines—give life to the meter and prevent it from becoming tiresome.

Our purpose in the study of poetic meters is twofold: to learn how to read poetry aloud with effectiveness and to discover the functions of meter.

READING ALOUD.   Poetry read aloud should sound neither metronomic nor prosy. Rather, effective reading requires a compromise between the regular stresses of the subjective meter and the stresses needed to make clear the sense of the words; the latter stresses are called rhetorical stresses. If the reading follows exactly the subjective meter, it will become sing-song and may obscure the shades of meaning and feeling intended by the poet. If, on the other hand, the reading follows only the prose sense of the words, it may diminish the intended rhythmic effect. As a useful rule of thumb, this suggestion has been found helpful: read mainly to bring out the sense, using the punctuation as a guide and stressing the words that need rhetorical emphasis; at the same time adjust your stresses to the subjective meter whenever such adjustment does not interfere with the sense.

To illustrate this kind of reading let us look at two lines taken from Polonius' advice to Laertes, *Hamlet*, I, iii, lines 68 and 78. The basic meter is iambic.

Gíve évery mán thy éar, but féw thy vóice.

Thís above áll: to thíne ówn sélf be trúe.

In the first line the sense requires a stress on the first syllable, which otherwise, according to the basic iambic pattern, would be unstressed. In the rest of the line, rhetorical stresses are needed on *évery* and *féw*, and *éar* and *vóice*, in order to bring out the contrasts of sense expressed by these words; and these rhetorical stresses are the same as the basic iambic stresses. The word *man*, though rhetorically weak and therefore requiring no stress, is nevertheless given stress to fit the subjective iambic meter. In the second line the case is different. Here the words that need rhetorical stresses are *this, all, own, self;* the result of this stressing is that only two iambic feet are left, the second and the fifth, and no adjustment for meter is possible without doing violence to the sense.

FUNCTIONS OF METER.   Meter performs three functions in poetry: 1. it provides rhythmic pleasure; 2. it controls tempo and movement; 3. it gives emphasis to particular words. Through these three functions it can create a great variety of effects.

The rhythmic pleasure provided by meter is but one instance of the universal human enjoyment of rhythm, as witnessed in such activities as dancing, running, giving college yells, and playing music. Among poems, those which march in strong meters are often the most popular. Most high school students, for instance, have thrilled to Lindsay's "The Congo" and Noyes' "The Highwayman," each of which thumps along with a drum-beat meter.

Tempo control can be explained by a comparison of two excerpts from Milton's *Paradise Lost*, both based on a simple metrical pattern, a five-stress iambic line:

[DESCRIPTION OF MULCIBER'S LONG FALL FROM HEAVEN TO EARTH]

Dropt from the Zenith like a falling star.   I, 745

[DESCRIPTION OF SATAN'S DIFFICULT JOURNEY THROUGH CHAOS]
                    So eagerly the fiend

O'er bog or steep, through strait, rough, dense, or rare,

With head, hands, wings, or feet pursues his way.   II, 947–948

The first has been given a rapid tempo, which agrees with and reinforces the sense of the words. This rapidity is produced by the over-normal number of unstressed syllables: there are six, with only four stressed syllables, instead of the usual pattern of five of each in the five-stress iambic line. In the second excerpt, the two lines have been given a slow tempo, which supports the sense of the words. The slowness is produced by the over-normal number of stressed syllables: there are six, with only four unstressed syllables in each line, just the reverse of the preceding example. The principle is clear: excess of unstressed syllables accelerates the pace, but excess of stressed syllables brakes the line.

Emphasis is given, ordinarily, by the use of metrical feet different from those of the basic pattern. In Shakespeare's line

To stánd agaínst the deép, dréad-bólted thúnder.

the sense stress requires the weighting of *dread,* so that the fourth foot becomes a spondee instead of the iambus of the basic pattern; this change of metrical pattern gives added emphasis to *dread-bolted.* Another kind of foot change is made in the following poem:

The Villain

While joy gave clouds the light of stars,   *1*
  That beamed where'er they looked;
And calves and lambs had tottering knees,
  Excited, while they sucked;
While every bird enjoyed his song,   *5*
Without one thought of harm or wrong—
I turned my head and saw the wind,
  Not far from where I stood,
Drágging the corn by her golden hair,
  Into a dark and lonely wood.   *10*
W. H. DAVIES

In this poem the first eight lines are nearly regular iambic meter, and the first foot of every line is iambic. But at the beginning of the ninth line there is a sudden change from an iambus to a trochee in the word *drágging.* The effect is to give emphasis to the word, thereby strengthening the antithetic and climactic force of the line.

In the next quotation the feeling evoked by the words is intensified by metrical emphasis:

Móst wéary seémed the séa, wéary the áir,

Wéary the wándering fíelds of bárren fóam.
ALFRED, LORD TENNYSON

To some readers a feeling of weariness seems to inhere in the very sounds themselves. But the fact is that the second and third appearance of *weary* have great prominence because of the meter: they follow pauses, and the poetic foot of each has been changed from the iambus of the basic pattern to a trochee. Thus it is only the added emphasis given these words which causes the effect.

Now let us look at a less simple example of effects created by meter:

He is not here; but far away
　　The noise of life begins again,
　　And ghastly through the drizzling rain
On the bald street breaks the blank day.
　　　　ALFRED, LORD TENNYSON

The *he* of this stanza refers to a friend who has died. We note that the last line, instead of continuing the iambic pattern, has five stressed syllables to three unstressed, and that the new arrangement has produced two spondees, *bald street* and *blank day*. The result is complex. In the first place, the line has been braked to a slow speed, permitting time for a fuller response to take effect in the reader. Secondly, *bald* and *blank* have been given emphasis by their dislocation in the established iambic metrical scheme. Thirdly, *bald* and *blank* have been linked together by their metrical prominence, as well as by the repetition of *b* and *l*. This metrical linkage, fusing the words together in the reader's consciousness, causes their meanings to interchange; that is, each word, *bald* and *blank*, becomes applicable to both *street* and *day*. In addition, each word, emphasized by the meter, is descriptive of the feelings of emptiness, desolation, and sorrow that have been engendered by the imagery.

Poetry that does not steadily maintain a meter is usually called free verse. Although free verse cannot be accurately defined, we may say roughly that free verse is language which is printed in the form of poetry and which employs a rhythm of time-patterns, that is, of timed word-groupings, with occasional passages in meter. In free verse established line lengths and stanza patterns are not followed and rime is but sparingly used; the other characteristics of poetry, however, are maintained.

In the next poem the printing of the lines is such as to show the time-patterns, and some lines have been put into meter.

The Wayfarer

The wayfarer,   *1*
Perceiving the pathway to truth,
Was struck with astonishment.
It was thickly grown with weeds.
"Ha," he said,   *5*
"I see that no one has passed here
In a long time."
Later he saw that each weed
Was a singular knife.
"Well," he mumbled at last,   *10*
"Doubtless there are other roads."

STEPHEN CRANE

ILLUSTRATIVE POEMS

The two selections which follow are written in five-stress lines of iambic meter without rime. This measure is called blank verse. Practice reading these passages aloud; observe how naturally an iambic movement seems to convey the flow of English speech.

FROM *The Prelude*, BOOK I

[*The poet is describing a boyhood experience: led by Nature, he stole a boat one summer evening to go rowing across a moonlit lake.*]

One summer evening (led by her) I found   *1*
A little boat tied to a willow tree
Within a rocky cave, its usual home.
Straight I unloosed her chain, and stepping in
Pushed from the shore. It was an act of stealth   *5*
And troubled pleasure, nor without the voice
Of mountain-echoes did my boat move on;
Leaving behind her still, on either side,

Small circles glittering idly in the moon,
Until they melted all into one track   *10*
Of sparkling light. But now, like one who rows,
Proud of his skill, to reach a chosen point
With an unswerving line, I fixed my view
Upon the summit of a craggy ridge,
The horizon's utmost boundary; far above   *15*
Was nothing but the stars and the gray sky.
She was an elfin pinnace; lustily
I dipped my oars into the silent lake,
And, as I rose upon the stroke, my boat
Went heaving through the water like a swan;   *20*
When, from behind that craggy steep, till then
The horizon's bound, a huge peak, black and huge,
As if with voluntary power instinct,
Upreared its head. I struck and struck again,
And growing still in stature the grim shape   *25*
Towered up between me and the stars, and still,
For so it seemed, with purpose of its own
And measured motion like a living thing
Strode after me. With trembling oars I turned,
And through the silent water stole my way   *30*
Back to the covert of the willow tree;
There in her mooring-place I left my bark,—
And through the meadows homeward went, in grave
And serious mood.

WILLIAM   WORDSWORTH

FROM *The Task*, BOOK VI

Knowledge and wisdom, far from being one,   *1*
Have oft-times no connexion. Knowledge dwells
In heads replete with thoughts of other men;
Wisdom in minds attentive to their own.
Knowledge, a rude unprofitable mass,   *5*
The mere materials with which wisdom builds,
Till smooth'd and squar'd and fitted to its place,

Does but encumber whom it seems t'enrich.
Knowledge is proud that he has learn'd so much;
Wisdom is humble that he knows no more.   *10*
Books are not seldom talismans and spells,
By which the magic art of shrewder wits
Holds an unthinking multitude enthrall'd.
Some to the fascination of a name
Surrender judgment, hood-wink'd. Some the style   *15*
Infatuates, and through labyrinths and wilds
Of error leads them by a tune entranc'd.
While sloth seduces more, too weak to bear
The insupportable fatigue of thought,
And swallowing, therefore, without pause or choice,   *20*
The total grist unsifted, husks and all.

WILLIAM COWPER

Most of the illustrative poems which follow are markedly rhythmical. Read them aloud and exaggerate the metrical stresses a little so as to catch more easily the beat of the meter. Then reread them aloud, with careful regard for the meaning, and try to achieve the compromise between sense stressing and meter stressing that makes an effective reading.

AIR XXI, *The Beggar's Opera*

If the heart of a man is deprest with cares,   *1*
The mist is dispell'd when a woman appears;
Like the notes of a fiddle, she sweetly, sweetly
Raises the spirits, and charms our ears.
  Roses and lillies her cheeks disclose,   *5*
  But her ripe lips are more sweet than those.
    Press her,
    Caress her,
    With blisses,
    Her kisses   *10*
Dissolve us in pleasure, and soft repose.

JOHN GAY

Upon Some Women

Thou who wilt not love, doe this;   *1*
Learne of me what Woman is.
Something made of thred and thrumme;
A meere Botch of all and some.
Pieces, patches, ropes of haire;   *5*
In-laid Garbage ev'ry where.

Out-side silk, and out-side Lawne;
Sceanes to cheat us neatly drawne.
False in legs, and false in thighes;
False in breast, teeth, haire, and eyes: *10*
False in head, and false enough;
Onely true in shreds and stuffe.

ROBERT HERRICK

O, Ay My Wife She Dang Me

CHORUS

O, ay my wife she dang me,   *1*
An' aft my wife she bang'd me!
If ye gie a woman a' her will,
Guid faith! she'll soon o'ergang ye.

I

On peace an' rest my mind was bent,   *5*
   And, fool I was! I married;
But never honest man's intent
   Sae cursedly miscarried.

II

Some sairie comfort at the last,
   When a' thir days are done, man: *10*
My 'pains o' hell' on earth is past,
   I'm sure o' bliss aboon, man.

O, ay my wife she dang me,
An' aft my wife she bang'd me!
If ye gie a woman a' her will,   15
Guid faith! she'll soon o'ergang ye.

ROBERT BURNS

Hornpipe

Now the peak of summer's past, the sky is overcast   *1*
And the love we swore would last for an age seems deceit:
Paler is the guelder since the day we first beheld her
In blush beside the elder drifting sweet, drifting sweet.

Oh quickly they fade—the sunny esplanade,   *5*
Speed-boats, wooden spades, and the dunes where we've lain:
Others will be lying amid the sea-pinks sighing
For love to be undying, and they'll sigh in vain.

It's hurrah for each night we have spent our love so lightly
And never dreamed there might be no more to spend at all.   *10*
It's goodbye to every lover who thinks he'll live in clover
All his life, for noon is over soon and night-dews fall.

If I could keep you there with the berries in your hair
And your lacy fingers fair as the may, sweet may,
I'd have no heart to do it, for to stay love is to rue it   *15*
And the harder we pursue it, the faster it's away.

C. DAY LEWIS

Ballad

Spring it is cheery,   *1*
  Winter is dreary,
Green leaves hang, but the brown must fly;
  When he's forsaken,
  Wither'd and shaken—   *5*
What can an old man do but die?

  Love will not clip him,
  Maids will not lip him,

Maud and Marian pass him by;
   Youth it is sunny,   *10*
   Age has no honey,—
What can an old man do but die?

   June it was jolly,
   O for its folly!
A dancing leg and a laughing eye;   *15*
   Youth may be silly,
   Wisdom is chilly,—
What can an old man do but die?

   Friends, they are scanty,
   Beggars are plenty,   *20*
If he has followers, I know why;
   Gold's in his clutches,
   (Buying him crutches!)—
What can an old man do but die?

THOMAS HOOD

Summum Bonum

All the breath and the bloom of the year in the bag of one bee: *1*
   All the wonder and wealth of the mine in the heart of one
      gem:
In the core of one pearl all the shade and the shine of the sea:
   Breath and bloom, shade and shine,—wonder, wealth, and
      —how far above them—
         Truth, that's brighter than gem,   *5*
         Trust, that's purer than pearl,—
Brightest truth, purest trust in the universe—all were for me
      In the kiss of one girl.

ROBERT BROWNING

Wet Windy Night on a Pavement

Light drunkenly reels into shadow;   *1*
Blurs, slurs uneasily;
Slides off the eyeballs:
The segments shatter.

Tree-branches cut arc-light in ragged   5
Fluttering wet strips.
The cup of the sky-sign is filled too full:
It spills wine over.

The street-lamps dance a tarantella
And zigzag down the street;   10
They lift and fly away
In a wind of lights.

A. S. J. TESSIMOND

[CLERIMONT'S] *Song*

Still to be neat, still to be drest,   1
As, you were going to a feast;
Still to be pou'dred, still perfum'd:
Lady, it is to be presum'd,
Though arts hid causes are not found,   5
All is not sweet, all is not sound.

Give me a looke, give me a face,
That makes simplicitie a grace;
Robes loosely flowing, haire as free:
Such sweet neglect more taketh me,   10
Than all th' adulteries of art.
They strike mine eyes, but not my heart.

BEN JONSON

Margaritae Sorori

A late lark twitters from the quiet skies;   1
And from the west,
Where the sun, his day's work ended,
Lingers in content,
There falls on the old, grey city   5
An influence luminous and serene,
A shining peace.

The smoke ascends
In a rosy-and-golden haze. The spires
Shine and are changed. In the valley   *10*
Shadows rise. The lark sings on. The sun,
Closing his benediction,
Sinks, and the darkening air
Thrills with a sense of the triumphing night—
Night with her train of stars   *15*
And her great gift of sleep.

So be my passing!
My task accomplished and the long day done,
My wages taken, and in my heart
Some late lark singing,   *20*
Let me be gathered to the quiet west,
The sundown splendid and serene,
Death.

WILLIAM ERNEST HENLEY

The Twenty-Third Psalme

The God of love my Shepherd is,   *1*
   And He that doth me feed,
While He is mine, and I am His,
   What can I want or need?

He leads me to the tender grasse,   *5*
   Where I both feed and rest;
Then to the streams that gently passe:
   In both I have the best.

Or if I stray, He doth convert,
   And bring my minde in frame: *10*
And all this not for my desert,
   But for His holy name.

Yea, in Death's shadie black abode
   Well may I walk, not fear;
For Thou art with me, and Thy rod   *15*
   To guide, Thy staffe to bear.

Nay, Thou dost make me sit and dine
   Ev'n in my enemies' sight;
My head with oyl, my cup with wine
   Runnes over day and night.   *20*

Surely Thy sweet and wondrous love
   Shall measure all my dayes;
And as it never shall remove,
   So neither shall my praise.
             GEORGE HERBERT

Psalm 23 [KING JAMES VERSION]

The Lord is my shepherd;   *1*
I shall not want.

He maketh me to lie down in green pastures:
He leadeth me beside the still waters.
He restoreth my soul: *5*
He leadeth me in the paths of righteousness
For his name's sake.

Yea, though I walk
Through the valley of the shadow of death,
I will fear no evil: *10*
For thou art with me;
Thy rod and thy staff
They comfort me.

Thou preparest a table before me
In the presence of mine enemies: *15*
Thou anointest my head with oil;
My cup runneth over.

Surely goodness and mercy shall follow me
All the days of my life:
And I will dwell in the house of the Lord   *20*
For ever.

9

RIME AND STANZA

From early childhood we have all been acquainted with rime and stanza. The zestful titillation of rime has delighted us in nursery tales and playground calls. Stanzaic repetition has been made familiar to us by the singing of carols, hymns, and camp songs. In this chapter we shall see how rime may operate both as a source of pleasure and as an architectonic means of creating in the reader's mind the segment of poetic experience that we call a stanza.

RIME

Rime is usually defined as the identity or similarity, in two or more words, of the accented vowels and the sounds which follow, with different consonant sounds immediately preceding the accented vowels, *e.g., flowers:showers* and *pare:leer*. Of the many varieties of rime we shall consider three: perfect rimes, near-rimes, and para-rimes.

Perfect rimes contain riming sounds that are identical, as in *cry: buy; daisy:lazy; regretfully:forgetfully*. However, rimes that were perfect for the poet may be imperfect for the reader. This lack of perfect correspondence may be caused by sound changes that have occurred in English since the poem was written, by dialect differences between poet and reader, or by individual habits of pronunciation peculiar to the poet or the reader. For example, *was:pass*—[wæs]:[pæs]—were perfect rimes for Pope in the 18th century but are imperfect to the reader of the 20th century. Similarly, the *oar in:law in* of a contemporary poem are perfect rimes to some Englishmen and Eastern Americans but are imperfect for millions of readers.

Near-rimes contain accented vowels that are similar but not identical; the consonants immediately preceding these accented vowels are different but the sounds following are the same.[1] Examples of near-rimes are *response:stance; star:fur; yawns:stones.*

Para-rimes contain differing vowels in a constant consonantal framework.[2] Examples of para-rimes are *sipped:supped; knive us: nervous; glib:globe.*

Other varieties of rime that occur may be illustrated by the following: *peep-show:rickshaw; lie:memory; pare:pair; fall:dial.* Sometimes assonance takes the place of rime in the riming words, as in *feet:leap.*[3]

Rimes other than perfect rimes are in frequent use in modern poetry. By adding to the number of riming combinations and by allowing greater dissimilarity and variety in the rimed words, they offer new and exciting sound effects, particularly to readers sated with perfect rimes.

POSITION OF RIMES. Riming words are most often used at the ends of lines, although they may occupy any position in a poem. It is sometimes convenient, in analyzing a poem, to diagram the end rimes of a stanza. For this purpose one uses letters—*a, b, c,* etc.—to represent the words which rime, in the manner indicated below. The following excerpts illustrate rime in various positions.

END RIME

I am unable, yonder begger cries,   a
To stand, or move; if he say true, hee *lies.*   a

> JOHN DONNE

---

[1] Near-rimes are also called oblique rimes, slant rimes, and chiming.

[2] Para-rimes are also called consonance, consonantal rime, and consonantal dissonance.

[3] For assonance see Chapter 7.

The Worldly Hope men set their Hearts upon   a
Turns Ashes—or it prospers; and anon,   a
   Like Snow upon the Desert's dusty Face,   b
Lighting a little hour or two—is gone.   a

              EDWARD FITZGERALD

Condemn'd to Hope's delusive mine,   a
   As on we toil from day to day,   b
By sudden blasts or slow decline   a
   Our social comforts drop away.   b

           SAMUEL JOHNSON

INTERNAL RIME

Their tricks and craft hae put me daft,
   They've ta'en me in, and a' that;
But clear your decks, and *Here's the sex!*
   I like the jades for a' that.

             ROBERT BURNS

[A CLOUD IS REPRESENTED AS SPEAKING]
I bring fresh showers for the thirsting flowers,
   From the seas and the streams;
I bear light shade for the leaves when laid
   In their noonday dreams.

           PERCY BYSSHE SHELLEY

Lilly O'Grady
Silly and shady.

      EDITH SITWELL

The sunlight on the garden
Hardens and grows cold,
You cannot cage the minute
Within its nets of gold.

      LOUIS MACNEICE

Rime is not essential to poetry, and its value has long been a subject of debate. Milton, for example, disparaged rime, terming it "the jingling sound of like endings," and wrote his great epic, *Paradise Lost,* in unrimed verse. But although much fine poetry has been written without rime, rime has been and still is an important element in many poems and therefore requires thoughtful consideration.

USES OF RIME. Rime performs three functions: 1. it provides musical pleasure; 2. it sets off the lines; 3. it helps to bind the poem together.

The first function of rime is to provide the pleasure of hearing repeated sounds, usually at regular intervals. This pleasure has two sources. One of these, mentioned in our discussion of assonance on page 121, is the satisfaction attendant upon a fulfilled expectation. The second has been described by John L. Lowes, who says that rime ". . . by a . . . merging of sameness with difference, gives a specific sort of aesthetic pleasure, and that, I take it, is its *raison d'être*."[4] Lowes means that in all kinds of rime (except identical rime, *e.g.*, *lane:lain*) some of the consonant and vowel sounds are the same while others are different. In serious poetry such a merging is a minor source of musical pleasure. However, in humorous verse, a verbal play upon sameness and differences in sound may be the chief source of the pleasurable effect. The following poem is a good illustration.

If You Stick A Stock of Liquor

If you stick a stock of liquor in your locker, 1
It is slick to stick a lock upon your stock,
Or some joker who is slicker's going to trick you of your liquor;
Though you snicker you'll feel sicker from the shock.
Be a piker though your clubmates mock and bicker, 5
For like brokers round a ticker they will flock
To your locker full of liquor, and your stock will vanish quicker
If you fail to lock your liquor with a lock.

NEWMAN LEVY

The second function of rime is to set off the lines. A poem without rime would be heard as a single continuum, save for the pauses and stops required by the metrical and rhetorical design; its phrases

---

[4] *Convention and Revolt in Poetry* (Boston: Houghton Mifflin, 1930), p. 245.

"would run away from one another in a rapid and irrevocable flux."[5]
The presence of end-rime segments the flow of sound into the integral parts that we call lines. Even if the sense of a line at its end calls for an uninterrupted continuation with the following line, an end-rime may bring about a slight pause after the riming word, or an added emphasis to its sound, which may combine with the rime itself to help frame the line. To experience for yourself this dividing function of rime, listen observantly to your own reading of the following stanzas. The first is from William Henley's "Margaritae Sorori"; the second is Robert Herrick's "Upon Julia's Clothes."

1.

The smoke ascends   *1*
In a rosy-and-golden haze. The spires
Shine and are changed. In the valley
Shadows rise. The lark sings on. The sun,
Closing his benediction,   *5*
Sinks, and the darkening air
Thrills with a sense of the triumphing night—
Night with her train of stars
And her great gift of sleep.

WILLIAM ERNEST HENLEY

2.

Whenas in silks my Julia goes,   *1*
Then, then, methinks how sweetly flows
The liquefaction of her clothes!

Next, when I cast mine eyes and see
That brave vibration each way free,   *5*
—O how that glittering taketh me!

ROBERT HERRICK

The third function of rime is to link the lines together and bind them into the line-groups that we call stanzas, "for the first sound still echoes in the ear when its counterpart occurs, and the two link together, in varying degrees according to the interval, their respective lines."[6] Occasionally rime is also used to link stanzas together.

---

[5] George Santayana, *The Sense of Beauty* (New York: Scribners, 1896), p. 173.

[6] Lowes, *Convention and Revolt*, p. 245.

Rime, then, is structural; it provides a system of relationships between the different lines of the stanza or poem, thereby helping to give a structural unity to the poetic experience. To experience for yourself this binding function of rime, listen observantly to your own reading of the two poems that follow. The first is without rime. The second uses rime not only to bind the lines of each stanza together, but to link together the first and second, and the third and fourth stanzas.

1.

A touch of cold in the Autumn night—   *1*
I walked abroad,
And saw the ruddy moon lean over a hedge
Like a red-faced farmer.
I did not stop to speak, but nodded,   *5*
And round about were the wistful stars
With white faces like town children.

T. E. HULME

2.

Autumn

I love to see, when leaves depart,   *1*
The clear anatomy arrive,
Winter, the paragon of art,
That kills all forms of life and feeling
Save what is pure and will survive.   *5*

Already now the clanging chains
Of geese are harnessed to the moon:
Stripped are the great sun-clouding planes:
And the dark pines, their own revealing,
Let in the needles of the noon.   *10*

Strained by the gale the olives whiten
Like hoary wrestlers bent with toil
And, with the vines, their branches lighten
To brim our vats where summer lingers
In the red froth and sun-gold oil.   *15*

Soon on our hearth's reviving pyre
Their rotted stems will crumble up:
And like a ruby, panting fire,
The grape will redden on your fingers
Through the lit crystal of the cup.   *20*

ROY CAMPBELL

STANZA

Many stanza forms in English poetry follow conventional rime schemes. For example, the Spenserian stanza always has a scheme of end rimes that may be diagrammed as *a b a b b c b c c*. If a reader, through previous acquaintance with a particular stanza form, has learned to expect a certain order of end rimes, such expectancy will make him more conscious of the repeated riming words, thereby heightening his aural pleasure and helping to shape his poetic experience. Hence it is desirable that a student of poetry become acquainted with the rime schemes of the frequently used stanzas. Then, when he reads a new poem in a familiar stanza form, he will more readily derive a pleasurable and coherent experience. To illustrate, we now turn to a consideration of four stanza forms that are very common in English and American poetry: the ballad stanza, the heroic couplet, the English sonnet, and the Italian sonnet.

BALLAD STANZA.   The ballad stanza is a simple four-line unit with rimes at the end of the second and fourth lines. The meter is iambic. The lines have alternately four and three stresses. As you read the following old English ballad, notice that the appearance of the second rime in each stanza acts as a sign of closure.

Katharine Jaffray

There livd a lass in yonder dale,   *1*
   And doun in yonder glen, O
And Katharine Jaffray was her name,
   Well known by many men. O

Out came the Laird of Lauderdale,   *5*
   Out frae the South Countrie,
All for to court this pretty maid,
   Her bridegroom for to be.

He has teld her father and mither baith,
    And a' the rest o her kin,   *10*
And has teld the lass hersell
    And her consent has win.

Then came the Laird of Lochinton,
    Out frae the English border,
All for to court this pretty maid,   *15*
    Well mounted in good order.

He's teld her father and mither baith,
    As I hear sindry say,
But he has nae teld the lass her sell,
    Till on her wedding day.   *20*

When day was set, and friends were met,
    And married to be,
Lord Lauderdale came to the place
    The bridal for to see.

'O are you came for sport, young man?   *25*
    Or are you come for play?
Or are you come for a sight o our bride,
    Just on her wedding day?'

'I'm nouther come for sport,' he says,
    'Nor am I come for play;   *30*
But if I had one sight o your bride,
    I'll mount and ride away.'

There was a glass of the red wine
    Filld up them atween,
And ay she drank to Lauderdale,   *35*
    Wha her true-love had been.

Then he took her by the milk-white hand,
    And by the grass-green sleeve,
And he mounted her high behind him there,
    At the bridegroom he askt nae leive.   *40*

Then the blude run down by the Cowden Banks,
   And down by Cowden Braes,
And ay she gard the trumpet sound,
   'O this is foul, foul play!'

Now a' ye that in England are,   *45*
   Or are in England born,
Come nere to Scotland to court a lass,
   Or else ye'l get the scorn.

They haik ye up and settle ye by,
   Till on your weddin day,   *50*
And gie ye frogs instead o fish,
   And play ye foul, foul play.
     ANONYMOUS (CHILD BALLAD NO. 221)

     HEROIC COUPLET.   The heroic couplet consists of a pair of riming lines in five-stress iambic meter. In a poem made up of heroic couplets each couplet is usually a fairly complete entity, and the second rime word signals its completion. Notice in the following selection that the rimes serve to set apart each individual couplet.

An Essay on Criticism, LINES 233–246

   A perfect Judge will read each work of Wit   *1*
With the same spirit that its author writ:
Survey the WHOLE, not see slight faults to find
Where nature moves, and rapture warms the mind:
Nor lose, for that malignant dull delight,   *5*
The gen'rous pleasure to be charmed with Wit.
But in such lays as neither ebb, nor flow,
Correctly cold, and regularly low,
That shunning faults, one quiet tenour keep;
We cannot blame indeed—but we may sleep.   *10*
In wit, as nature, what affects our hearts
Is not th' exactness of peculiar parts;
'Tis not a lip, or eye, we beauty call,
But the joint force and full result of all.
                  ALEXANDER POPE

ENGLISH SONNET. The English sonnet consists of three four-line units, called quatrains, and a concluding couplet.[7] The meter is five-stress iambic. The rime scheme is *a b a b c d c d e f e f g g*. Each quatrain is unconnected by rime with what precedes or follows it, and tends to be an individual unit within the whole. Its completion is marked by the second occurrence of its second rime. The couplet, which completes the sonnet, also tends to be individual, and often gives an epigrammatic finish to the poem. The individuality of the couplet is indicated formally in the 1607 edition of Shakespeare's sonnets by indentation, which sets apart the last two lines from the rest of the poem.

As you read the following English sonnets notice how the foreknown rime scheme helps to guide your reading.

Sonnet LXXI

No longer mourn for me when I am dead   *1*
Than you shall hear the surly sullen bell
Give warning to the world that I am fled
From this vile world, with vilest worms to dwell:
Nay, if you read this line, remember not   *5*
The hand that writ it; for I love you so,
That I in your sweet thoughts would be forgot,
If thinking on me then should make you woe.
O! if, I say, you look upon this verse,
When I perhaps compounded am with clay,   *10*
Do not so much as my poor name rehearse,
But let your love even with my life decay;
  Lest the wise world should look into your moan,
  And mock you with me after I am gone.

       WILLIAM SHAKESPEARE

The Lemmings

Once in a hundred years the Lemmings come   *1*
Westward, in search of food, over the snow,
Westward, until the salt sea drowns them dumb,
Westward, till all are drowned, those Lemmings go.

---

[7] This kind of sonnet is also called Shakespearean or Elizabethan.

Once, it is thought, there was a westward land,   *5*
(Now drowned) where there was food for those starved things,
And memory of the place has burnt its brand
In the little brains of all the Lemming Kings.
Perhaps, long since, there was a land beyond
Westward from death, some city, some calm place,   *10*
Where one could taste God's quiet and be fond
With the little beauty of a human face;
But now the land is drowned, yet still we press
Westward, in search, to death, to nothingness.

JOHN MASEFIELD

ITALIAN SONNET. The Italian sonnet, also called Petrarchan, is a complex stanza form, in five-stress iambic meter,
fourteen lines long, divided into two parts of eight and six lines
each. The first part, called the octave, has a rime scheme of
a b b a a b b a. The second *a* signals a stop or a strong pause and the
fourth *a* a complete stop. The second part, called the sestet, employs
three new rimes in any one of various schemes, such as *c d e c d e*
or *c d d c e e.* Because in the sestet no one scheme is to be expected,
the reader has no expectancies to guide his reading, as he had in the
octave. But the beginning of the sestet is itself a sign—a sign that a
new aspect of the thought or image or feeling is to be taken up.[8]

As you read the following Italian sonnets notice that the second
and fourth *a* rimes coincide with and reinforce the meaningful stops
in the wording and that a turn in the poem begins with the sestet.

Remember

Remember me when I am gone away,   *1*
Gone far away into the silent land;
When you can no more hold me by the hand,
Nor I half turn to go yet turning stay.

---

[8] For a fuller discussion of the Italian sonnet, see Norman C. Stageberg, "The
Aesthetic of the Petrarchan Sonnet," *Journal of Aesthetics and Art Criticism,*
VII (December, 1948), 132–137.

Remember me when no more day by day   5
   You tell me of our future that you planned:
   Only remember me; you understand
It will be late to counsel then or pray.
Yet if you should forget me for a while
   And afterwards remember, do not grieve: 10
   For if the darkness and corruption leave
   A vestige of the thoughts that once I had,
Better by far you should forget and smile
   Than that you should remember and be sad.

                 CHRISTINA ROSSETTI

Holy Sonnet x

Death be not proud, though some have called thee   1
Mighty and dreadfull, for, thou art not soe,
For, those, whom thou think'st, thou dost overthrow,
Die not, poore death, nor yet canst thou kill mee.
From rest and sleepe, which but thy pictures bee,   5
Much pleasure, then from thee, much more must flow,
And soonest our best men with thee doe goe,
Rest of their bones, and soules deliverie.
Thou art slave to Fate, Chance, kings, and desperate men,
And dost with poyson, warre, and sicknesse dwell,   10
And poppie, or charmes can make us sleepe as well,
And better then thy stroake; why swell'st thou then?
One short sleepe past, wee wake eternally,
And death shall be no more; death, thou shalt die.

                 JOHN DONNE

The Clerks

I did not think that I should find them there   1
When I came back again; but there they stood,
As in the days they dreamed of when young blood
Was in their cheeks and women called them fair.
Be sure, they met me with an ancient air,—   5
And yes, there was a shop-worn brotherhood
About them; but the men were just as good,
And just as human as they ever were.

And you that ache so much to be sublime,
And you that feed yourself with your descent,   *10*
What comes of all your visions and your fears?
Poets and kings are but the clerks of Time,
Tiering the same dull webs of discontent,
Clipping the same sad alnage of the years.

EDWIN ARLINGTON ROBINSON

In writing sonnets, poets often do not follow with exactness the forms that we have just examined. Instead, they may compose variations of their own upon the English or the Italian sonnet. Observe in the two sonnets below what departures from conventional sonnet form, English or Italian, have been employed.

Who's Who

A shilling life will give you all the facts: *1*
How Father beat him, how he ran away,
What were the struggles of his youth, what acts
Made him the greatest figure of his day:
Of how he fought, fished, hunted, worked all night,   *5*
Though giddy, climbed new mountains; named a sea:
Some of the last researchers even write
Love made him weep his pints like you and me.

With all his honours on, he sighed for one
Who, say astonished critics, lived at home;   *10*
Did little jobs about the house with skill
And nothing else; could whistle; would sit still
Or potter round the garden; answered some
Of his long marvellous letters but kept none.

W. H. AUDEN

The Zebras

From the dark woods that breathe of fallen showers,   *1*
Harnessed with level rays in golden reins,
The zebras draw the dawn across the plains
Wading knee-deep among the scarlet flowers.

The sunlight, zithering their flanks with fire,   5
Flashes between the shadows as they pass
Barred with electric tremors through the grass
Like wind along the gold strings of a lyre.

Into the flushed air snorting rosy plumes
That smoulder round their feet in drifting fumes,   10
With dove-like voices call the distant fillies,
While round the herds the stallion wheels his flight,
Engine of beauty volted with delight,
To roll his mare among the trampled lilies.

ROY CAMPBELL

STANZAIC POEMS. In the process of reading a stanzaic
poem, with each stanza having the same rime scheme, one learns the
rime scheme for himself in the first few stanzas, and if the poem is of
considerable length his experience becomes better controlled by the
riming words as he gets further into the poem. The following poem
will furnish an illustration. As you read it for the first time note how
quickly you become familiar with the rime scheme, how the rimes
set off each line, and how the second *b* rime helps to produce a feeling of closure at the end of each stanza.

An Elegy on the Death of a Mad Dog

Good people all, of every sort,   1
   Give ear unto my song;
And if you find it wondrous short,—
   It cannot hold you long.

In Islington there was a man,   5
   Of whom the world might say,
That still a godly race he ran,—
   Whene'er he went to pray.

A kind and gentle heart he had,
   To comfort friends and foes;   10
The naked every day he clad,—
   When he put on his clothes.

And in that town a dog was found,
   As many dogs there be,
Both mongrel, puppy, whelp, and hound,   *15*
   And curs of low degree.

This dog and man at first were friends;
   But when a pique began,
The dog, to gain some private ends,
   Went mad, and bit the man.   *20*

Around from all the neighbouring streets,
   The wondering neighbours ran,
And swore the dog had lost his wits,
   To bite so good a man.

The wound it seemed both sore and sad   *25*
   To every Christian eye;
And while they swore the dog was mad,
   They swore the man would die.

But soon a wonder came to light,
   That showed the rogues they lied;   *30*
The man recovered of the bite,
   The dog it was that died.

OLIVER GOLDSMITH

The next three poems, with a less simple stanza form, will give us further illustration. Observe, as you read, how soon the stanza form, controlled by the rimes, becomes familiar, how the rime words set off the lines, and how the appearance of the expected rimes of the closing couplet becomes a signal for the completion of the stanza.

At Tea

The kettle descants in a cozy drone,   *1*
And the young wife looks in her husband's face,
And then at her guest's and shows in her own
Her sense that she fills an envied place;

And the visiting lady is all abloom,   5
And says there was never so sweet a room.

And the happy young housewife does not know
That the woman beside her was first his choice,
Till the fates ordained it could not be so . . .
Betraying nothing in look or voice   10
The guest sits smiling and sips her tea,
And he throws her a stray glance yearningly.

By her Aunt's Grave

"Sixpence a week," says the girl to her lover,   1
"Aunt used to bring me, for she could confide
In me alone, she vowed. 'Twas to cover
The cost of her headstone when she died.
And that was a year ago last June;   5
I've not yet fixed it. But I must soon."

"And where is the money now, my dear?"
"O, snug in my purse . . . Aunt was *so* slow
In saving it—eighty weeks, or near.". . .
"Let's spend it," he hints. "For she won't know.   10
There's a dance tonight at the Load of Hay."
She passively nods. And they go that way.

Outside the Window

"My stick!" he says, and turns in the lane   1
To the house just left, whence a vixen voice
Comes out with the firelight through the pane,
And he sees within that the girl of his choice
Stands rating her mother with eyes aglare   5
For something said while he was there.

"At last I behold her soul undraped!"
Thinks the man who had loved her more than himself;
"My God!—'tis but narrowly I have escaped.—
My precious porcelain proves it delf."   10

His face has reddened like one ashamed,
And he steals off, leaving his stick unclaimed.

THOMAS HARDY

Poets often employ an original arrangement of rimes instead of following a conventional scheme. In such poems the reader is liable to overlook riming words, especially if they are separated from each other by more than two or three lines, and unusual alertness is necessary if one is to feel the full force of the rimes. The next poem will illustrate.

Musée des Beaux Arts

About suffering they were never wrong,   *1*
The Old Masters: how well they understood
Its human position; how it takes place
While someone else is eating or opening a window or just
     walking dully along;
How, when the aged are reverently, passionately waiting   *5*
For the miraculous birth, there always must be
Children who did not specially want it to happen, skating
On a pond at the edge of the wood:
They never forgot
That even the dreadful martyrdom must run its course   *10*
Anyhow in a corner, some untidy spot
Where the dogs go on with their doggy life and the torturer's
     horse
Scratches its innocent behind on a tree.
In Brueghel's *Icarus*, for instance: how everything turns away
Quite leisurely from the disaster; the ploughman may   *15*
Have heard the splash, the forsaken cry,
But for him it was not an important failure; the sun shone
As it had to on the white legs disappearing into the green
Water; and the expensive delicate ship that must have seen
Something amazing, a boy falling out of the sky,   *20*
Had somewhere to get to and sailed calmly on.

W. H. AUDEN

ILLUSTRATIVE POEMS

Breake of Day

[*This poem is an aubade, that is, a morning song, a less familiar type than the serenade, or evening song. A woman is represented as speaking.*]

'Tis true, 'tis day; what though it be?   *1*
O wilt thou therefore rise from me?
Why should we rise, because 'tis light?
Did we lie downe, because 'twas night?
Love which in spight of darknesse brought us hether,   *5*
Should in despight of light keepe us together.

Light hath no tongue, but is all eye;
If it could speake as well as spie,
This were the worst, that it could say,
That being well, I faine would stay,   *10*
And that I lov'd my heart and honor so,
That I would not from him, that had them, goe.

Must businesse thee from hence remove?
Oh, that's the worst disease of love,
The poore, the foule, the false, love can   *15*
Admit, but not the busied man.
He which hath businesse, and makes love, doth doe
Such wrong, as when a maryed man doth wooe.
                                        JOHN DONNE

Green Grow the Rashes

Green grow the rashes O,   *1*
    Green grow the rashes O;
The sweetest hours that e'er I spend,
    Are spent amang the lasses O!

There's nought but care on ev'ry han',   *5*
   In ev'ry hour that passes O ;
What signifies the life o' man,
   An' 'twere na for the lasses O.

The warly race may riches chase,
   An' riches still may fly them O ;   *10*
An' tho' at last they catch them fast,
   Their hearts can ne'er enjoy them O.

But gie me a canny hour at e'en,
   My arms about my dearie O ;
An' warly cares, an' warly men,   *15*
   May a' gae tapsalteerie O !

For you sae douce, ye sneer at this,
   Ye're nought but senseless asses O:
The wisest man the warl' saw,
   He dearly lov'd the lasses O.   *20*

Auld nature swears, the lovely dears
   Her noblest work she classes O ;
Her prentice han' she tried on man,
   An' then she made the lasses O.

ROBERT BURNS

I Like to See It Lap the Miles

I like to see it lap the miles,   *1*
And lick the valleys up,
And stop to feed itself at tanks ;
And then, prodigious, step

Around a pile of mountains,   *5*
And, supercilious, peer
In shanties by the sides of roads ;
And then a quarry pare

To fit its sides, and crawl between,
Complaining all the while   10
In horrid, hooting stanza;
Then chase itself down hill

And neigh like Boanerges;
Then, punctual as a star,
Stop—docile and omnipotent—   15
At its own stable door.

EMILY DICKINSON

Sonnet XXIX

When in disgrace with fortune and men's eyes   1
I all alone beweep my outcast state,
And trouble deaf heaven with my bootless cries,
And look upon myself, and curse my fate:
Wishing me like to one more rich in hope,   5
Featur'd like him, like him with friends posses't,
Desiring this man's art, and that man's scope,
With what I most enjoy contented least:
Yet in these thoughts myself almost despising,
Haply I think on thee,—and then my state,   10
Like to the lark at break of day arising
From sullen earth, sings hymns at heaven's gate;
    For thy sweet love remember'd such wealth brings
    That then I scorn to change my state with kings.

WILLIAM SHAKESPEARE

Sonnet

Down to the Puritan marrow of my bones   1
There's something in this richness that I hate.
I love the look, austere, immaculate,
Of landscapes drawn in pearly monotones.
There's something in my very blood that owns   5
Bare hills, cold silver on a sky of slate,
A thread of water, churned to milky spate
Streaming through slanted pastures fenced with stones.

I love those skies, thin blue or snowy gray,
Those fields sparse-planted, rendering meager sheaves ;   *10*
That spring, briefer than apple-blossom's breath,
Summer, so much too beautiful to stay,
Swift autumn, like a bonfire of leaves,
And sleepy winter, like the sleep of death.

ELINOR WYLIE

Exposure

Our brains ache, in the merciless iced east winds that knive
      us . . .   *1*
Wearied we keep awake because the night is silent . . .
Low, drooping flares confuse our memory of the salient . . .
Worried by silence, sentries whisper, curious, nervous,
      But nothing happens.   *5*

Watching, we hear the mad gusts tugging on the wire,
Like twitching agonies of men among its brambles.
Northward, incessantly, the flickering gunnery rumbles,
Far off, like a dull rumour of some other war.
      What are we doing here?   *10*

The poignant misery of dawn begins to grow . . .
We only know war lasts, rain soaks, and clouds sag stormy.
Dawn massing in the east her melancholy army
Attacks once more in ranks on shivering ranks of gray,
      But nothing happens.   *15*

Sudden successive flights of bullets streak the silence.
Less deadly than the air that shudders black with snow,
With sidelong flowing flakes that flock, pause, and renew,
We watch them wandering up and down the wind's noncha-
      lance,
      But nothing happens.   *20*

Pale flakes with fingering stealth come feeling for our faces—
We cringe in holes, back on forgotten dreams, and stare,
      snow-dazed,

Deep into grassier ditches. So we drowse, sun-dozed,
Littered with blossoms trickling where the blackbird fusses.
  Is it that we are dying?   *25*

Slowly our ghosts drag home: glimpsing the sunk fires, glozed
With crusted dark-red jewels; crickets jingle there;
For hours the innocent mice rejoice: the house is theirs;
Shutters and doors, all closed: on us the doors are closed,—
  We turn back to our dying.   *30*

Since we believe not otherwise can kind fires burn;
Nor ever suns smile true on child, or field, or fruit.
For God's invincible spring our love is made afraid;
Therefore, not loath, we lie out here; therefore were born,
  For love of God seems dying.   *35*

To-night, His frost will fasten on this mud and us,
Shrivelling many hands, puckering foreheads crisp.
The burying-party, picks and shovels in their shaking grasp,
Pause over half-known faces. All their eyes are ice,
  But nothing happens.   *40*

        WILFRED OWEN

Softly Now Are Sifting

Softly now are sifting   *1*
Snows on landscapes frozen.
Thickly fall the flakelets,
Feathery-light together,
Shower of silver pouring, *5*
Soundless, all around us,
Field and river folding
Fair in mantle rarest.
   GEORGE P. MARSH

The Sunlight on the Garden

The sunlight on the garden   *1*
Hardens and grows cold,
We cannot cage the minute

Within its nets of gold;
When all is told   5
We cannot beg for pardon.

Our freedom as free lances
Advances towards its end;
The earth compels, upon it
Sonnets and birds descend;   10
And soon, my friend,
We shall have no time for dances.

The sky was good for flying
Defying the church bells
And every evil iron   15
Siren and what it tells:
The earth compels,
We are dying, Egypt, dying

And not expecting pardon,
Hardened in heart anew,   20
But glad to have sat under
Thunder and rain with you,
And grateful too
For sunlight on the garden.

LOUIS MACNEICE

I Spend My Days Vainly

I spend my days vainly,   1
    Not in delight;
Though the world is elate
    And tastes her joys finely.

Here wrapped in slow musing   5
    Lies my dark mind,
To no music attuned
    Save its own, and despising

The lark for remoteness,
  The thrush for bold lying,   *10*
The soft wind for blowing,
  And the round sun for brightness.

O tarry for me, sweet;
  I shall stir, I shall wake!
And the melody you seek   *15*
  Shall be lovely, though late.

FRANK KENDON

Get Up and Bar the Door

It fell about the Martinmas time,   *1*
  And a gay time it was then,
When our goodwife got puddings to make,
  And she's boild them in the pan.

The wind sae cauld blew south and north,   *5*
  And blew into the floor;
Quoth our goodman to our goodwife,
  'Gae out and bar the door.'

'My hand is in my hussyfskap,
  Goodman, as ye may see;   *10*
An it shoud nae be barrd this hundred year,
  It's no be barrd for me.'

They made a paction tween them twa,
  They made it firm and sure,
That the first word whaeer should speak,   *15*
  Shoud rise and bar the door.

Then by there came two gentlemen,
  At twelve o clock at night,
And they could neither see house nor hall,
  Nor coal nor candle-light.   *20*

'Now whether is this a rich man's house,
  Or whether is it a poor?'
But neer a word wad ane o them speak,
  For barring of the door.

And first they ate the white puddings,   *25*
  And then they ate the black;
Tho muckle thought the goodwife to hersel,
  Yet neer a word she spake.

Then said the one unto the other,
  'Here, man, tak ye my knife;   *30*
Do ye tak aff the auld man's beard,
  And I'll kiss the goodwife.'

'But there's nae water in the house,
  And what shall we do than?'
'What ails ye at the pudding-broo,   *35*
  That boils into the pan?'

O up then started our goodman,
  An angry man was he:
'Will ye kiss my wife before my een,
  And scad me wi pudding-bree?'   *40*

Then up and started our goodwife,
  Gied three skips on the floor:
'Goodman, you've spoken the foremost word,
  Get up and bar the door.'

ANONYMOUS (CHILD BALLAD NO. 275)

Essay on Man, EPISTLE II, LINES 1–18.

Know then thyself, presume not God to scan;   *1*
The proper study of Mankind is Man.
Placed on this isthmus of a middle state,
A Being darkly wise, and rudely great:
With too much knowledge for the Sceptic side,   *5*
With too much weakness for the Stoic's pride,

He hangs between; in doubt to act, or rest;
In doubt to deem himself a God, or Beast;
In doubt his Mind or Body to prefer;
Born but to die, and reas'ning but to err;   *10*
Alike in ignorance, his reasons such,
Whether he thinks too little, or too much:
Chaos of Thought and Passion, all confused;
Still by himself abused, or disabused;
Created half to rise, and half to fall;   *15*
Great lord of all things, yet a prey to all;
Sole judge of Truth, in endless Error hurled:
The glory, jest, and riddle of the world!

ALEXANDER POPE

10

INDIRECTION

Devices of indirection are not unfamiliar to us. In our discussion of figurative language in Chapter 5 we met several —simile, metaphor, personification, and symbol. By means of such devices, poets are enabled to achieve greater concentration and suggestiveness than would be possible by the use of literal statement. In addition to the figures mentioned above, poets use other devices of indirection, of which we shall now discuss five: *paradox, irony, understatement, overstatement,* and *inversion.*

PARADOX. Paradox is a statement which seems to be self-contradictory or opposed to common sense, but which may be essentially true. Many of our familiar expressions are paradoxical, *e.g.,* "The pen is mightier than the sword"; or the Biblical passage "For whosoever will save his life shall lose it: and whosoever will lose his life for my sake shall find it." An examination of these statements will be helpful in discovering how paradox operates.

Let us consider the first statement literally. If one were to take up his pen and sally forth to battle against a man armed with a sword, he would be even more foolish than Don Quixote was in tilting against windmills. To say that a pen as an instrument of fighting is more powerful than a sword is nonsense. In this sense the statement is obviously untrue. Yet, in another sense, the pen as an instrument of ideas *is* mightier than the sword.[1] The paradox hinges on the word *mightier*. In the sense of physical might the pen is not mightier than the sword, and the statement is self-contradictory. However, in the sense of non-physical but ideational might, the statement is not contradictory but true. A paradox, then, turns on at least one key term which has a multiple meaning.

The Biblical passage quoted above is more complex, partly because the term *life* is used four times, twice as the pronoun *it*. But the same principle is in operation. From the context it is clear that the key term, *life,* is used in two senses. Sense one is material or physical life, which is temporal; sense two is spiritual life, which is eternal. These two meanings are used alternately in the passage. If they had been stated explicitly, the passage would read: "For whosoever will save his material-physical life, which is only temporal, shall lose his spiritual life, which is eternal: and whosoever will lose his material-physical life, which is temporal, for my sake shall find his spiritual life, which is eternal." With the substitution of the explicit meaning the revised passage has lost much of the interest of the original. The paradox is made more complex because the contraries physical and spiritual are also applied alternately to the other key terms *save, lose,* and *find.*

The effect of paradox derives from the tantalizing suggestiveness of its indirect method, from the realization that what is false in one sense is true in another, from the simultaneous recognition of both the "contradiction" and the truth in what is said.

The effectiveness of paradox in poetry may be illustrated by Richard Lovelace's "To Lucasta. Going to the Wars."

Tell me not, sweet, I am unkind,   *1*
    That from the nunnery
Of thy chaste breast and quiet mind,
    To war and arms I fly.

---

[1] "The pen is mightier than the sword" also illustrates another rhetorical device, *metonymy,* a figure of speech which substitutes for the exact name of something the name of something which is closely associated with it, *e.g.,* the part for the whole, the cause for the effect, the instrument for the accomplishment. In this case "pen" is a substitute for "ideas" or "thoughts" (written down by pen); "sword" is a substitute for "war."

True, a new mistress now I chase,   5
   The first foe in the field;
And with a stronger faith embrace
   A sword, a horse, a shield.

Yet this inconstancy is such
   As you too shall adore;   10
I could not love thee, dear, so much,
   Loved I not honor more.

          RICHARD LOVELACE

The paradox hinges on the key term *inconstancy*, which has a double sense in terms of the object toward which it is directed. The situation is that of a lover leaving his mistress to go off to war. Since he is leaving by his own choice, he faces the delicate problem of reconciling her to his departure and persuading her that he is not being inconstant to her. He anticipates her remonstrance: "You are unkind. You are leaving me for a new mistress. You don't love me." He agrees with her, in the second stanza, admitting that he is inconstant in leaving her for a new mistress, war. In the last stanza the paradox enters. By being inconstant to her, he is being constant to honor, which is inclusive of their love, as was suggested in the first stanza by the terms *nunnery* and *chaste*. Therefore he is constant to her because of his inconstancy.

The effect of the paradox—juxtaposing in a playful way a pure and a physical love, and punning on the words *arms, chase,* and *embrace*—is a mental exhilaration that is an integral part of the poetic experience.

IRONY. Closely allied to paradox is the device of irony. Irony is a disparity or opposition between appearance and actuality, and/or between expectation and realization. The most familiar form of irony is irony of statement. Calling a fat friend "Slim," or referring to a hamburger joint as "The 'Ritz" are examples of irony of statement. In this kind of irony, then, words are designed to convey a meaning opposite to the literal sense. The funeral oration of Mark Antony in *Julius Caesar* is a good example in literature.

The situation is this. After the killing of Caesar, Brutus, although sincere in his belief that he and the conspirators had done right, was fearful of the reaction of the mob. He felt, however, that when he explained to them that Caesar had been assassinated to protect the interests of the people they, too, would recognize the necessity of the act. When Mark Antony asked for permission to speak to the people, Brutus, against the wishes of the other conspirators, agreed; for he thought it would help their cause. Brutus insisted, however, that Antony speak after Brutus himself had given his explanation. Furthermore he directed Antony as follows: "You shall not in your funeral speech blame us,/ But speak all good you can devise of Caesar,/ And say you do't by our permission."

It was Mark Antony's intention, of course, to inflame the people against Brutus and the conspirators. Seemingly he followed Brutus' directions to the letter. The speech begins:

Friends, Romans, countrymen, lend me your ears;   *1*
I come to bury Caesar, not to praise him.
The evil that men do lives after them;
The good is oft interred with their bones;
So let it be with Caesar. The noble Brutus   *5*
Hath told you Caesar was ambitious:
If it were so, it was a grievous fault,
And grievously hath Caesar answer'd it.
Here, under leave of Brutus and the rest—
For Brutus is an honourable man;   *10*
So are they all, all honourable men—
Come I to speak in Caesar's funeral. . . .

                                        (III, ii)

The words sound sincere, and the ironical import of *not to praise him* (line 2), *noble Brutus* (line 5), and *honourable man* (line 10) is not immediately apparent; for Antony knew that any direct attempt to vilify Brutus, particularly after the crowd had just acclaimed Brutus, would have been ineffective. He chose instead the subtle indirectness of irony of statement to achieve his ends, and as his speech progressed the crowd gradually realized that Antony really meant the opposite of what he was saying. And when he reached the following words the irony was evident to all:

  O, masters, if I were disposed to stir   *1*
Your hearts and minds to mutiny and rage,

I should do Brutus wrong, and Cassius wrong,
Who, you all know, are honourable men:
I will not do them wrong; I rather choose   *5*
To wrong the dead, to wrong myself and you,
Than I will wrong such honourable men.

The people were persuaded, more convincingly than if he had
attacked the conspirators directly, that they were not *noble* and
honourable but ignoble and dishonorable.

Antony's speech also illustrates another form of irony, irony of
situation, that is, an opposition, in the situation itself, between
expectation and fulfillment. Brutus expected nothing but praise for
permitting Antony to speak. He felt that the people would be paci-
fied by his letting a friend of Caesar's speak at the funeral, especially
when that friend, without blaming Brutus and his companions, was
to speak praise of Caesar. But his expectation was not fulfilled.
Instead the opposite occurred: the mob swore to avenge Caesar's
death, and Brutus and the conspirators were forced to flee. Instead
of helping their cause, Antony's oration ruined it.

Further insight into the nature of irony may be gained by exam-
ining the following poem by Robinson:

Richard Cory

Whenever Richard Cory went down town,   *1*
We people on the pavement looked at him:
He was a gentleman from sole to crown,
Clean favored, and imperially slim.

And he was always quietly arrayed,   *5*
And he was always human when he talked;
But still he fluttered pulses when he said,
"Good-morning," and he glittered when he walked.

And he was rich—yes, richer than a king—
And admirably schooled in every grace: *10*
In fine, we thought that he was everything
To make us wish that we were in his place.

So on we worked, and waited for the light,
And went without the meat, and cursed the bread;
And Richard Cory, one calm summer night,   *15*
Went home and put a bullet through his head.

EDWIN ARLINGTON ROBINSON

The poem is a brief character sketch of a wealthy man who is admired and envied by those who consider themselves less fortunate than he. In spite of his good fortune he unexpectedly commits suicide. Thus the poem is an example of irony of situation. The situation is ironic to the reader because he has expected a different outcome. It is also ironic to the townspeople of the poem.

Moreover, the irony of situation is intensified by a second kind of irony, irony of character, an opposition between what a character seems to be and what he really is.[2] In lines 4 and 9 Cory is described specifically in regal terms: he is IMPERIALLY *slim* and *richer than a* KING. Even line 3, in this context, takes on an added suggestion of royalty: *He was a* GENTLE*man from sole to* CROWN. In line 6 there is the implication that he is regarded as more than human, an individual set apart from most mortals. He is, in their opinion, a kingly figure in contrast to his admiring subjects, the *people on the pavement.* Nowhere are we given direct evidence of the real character of Richard Cory. Throughout we have only the comments of the people about him except for Cory's last act, which is left uninterpreted. This act, however, speaks for itself. Not only is Richard Cory not the ruler of the people, despite their admiration and envy; but by committing suicide he has revealed that he is, ironically, not even ruler of himself.

The irony of situation and of character make evident certain implications. Until the last stanza Cory appears to be superior to the people. This has been achieved by emphasizing in the first three stanzas the respectful and admiring attitude of the townspeople toward him and by stressing his seemingly regal qualities. Cory's suicide, however, actually brings about a complete reversal of roles in the poem: as Cory is dethroned, the people are correspondingly

---

[2] When irony of character appears in poetry, it is generally limited to narrative-dramatic poetry. Because of its nature it is a much more common device in drama.

elevated. This reversal will be clear if we consider the reason for Cory's final act. Though not directly stated, the reason is implicit in the last stanza. The contrast between the townspeople and Cory, stressed throughout the first three stanzas, has been carried out in the final one. The people *worked, and waited for the light;* they *went without the meat, and cursed the bread;* but they went on living. Cory, on the other hand, who was in much better circumstances, did not live; instead he *put a bullet through his head.* This we are told occurred *one* CALM *summer night.* Though the night was calm to the people, it assuredly was not so to Richard Cory. *Calm* here suggests not only the quiet and peacefulness of the summer evening but by contrast points up the unexpressed violence of Cory's mind on that fateful night.

It might seem at first that because the people *went without the meat, and cursed the bread* life was not only difficult but meaningless to them. The context, however, refutes such a conclusion. The juxtaposition of *meat* and *bread* has Biblical overtones which provide a general background for the stanza.[3] That the people *cursed the bread* is not a denial of life; the fact remains that they lived. We are reminded here of Jesus' remark "It is written that man shall not live by bread alone, but by every word of God." (Luke 4:4). Even more revealing is the same thought as it is expressed in the Old Testament: "And he humbled thee, and suffered thee to hunger, and fed thee with manna, which thou knewest not, neither did thy fathers know; that he might make thee know that man doth not live by bread only, but by every word that proceedeth out of the mouth of the Lord doth man live." (Deuteronomy 8:3). This, of course, is almost identical to the situation of the townspeople. The parallel is too close to be merely coincidental, and the implication is clear. Instead of a denial of life, the line is suggestive of an affirmation of life based not on bread alone but on something more meaningful.

What is it, then, that makes life meaningful to the townspeople? The answer is given in line 13: they *waited for the* LIGHT. *Light,* like *meat* and *bread,* is used as a symbol, as it has often been used

---

[3] See, for example, Genesis 45:23. The word *meat* in its earliest sense referred to food in general.

in both literary and religious contexts.[4] It symbolizes such things as wisdom, insight, goodness, and hope. In the Bible, for example, we recall such passages as: "Ye are the light of the world;"[5] and "In the beginning was the Word . . . and the Word was God. . . . In him was *life;* and the *life* was the *light* of men. And the light shineth in darkness; and the darkness comprehended it not."[6] It is not necessary, however, to restrict *light* to any specific allusion. It is enough that it is a positive symbol with connotations of a spiritual nature. In opposition to meat and bread, symbols of physical nourishment and of material values, it suggests a spiritual sustenance of greater value. As such it clarifies the intent of the poem: it reveals the inner strength of the people and the inadequacy of Cory. Robinson has not oversimplified his case: the people do not have the light; they are working and waiting for it. The implication is that the light does exist and that it acts as a sustaining force to the people. As a goal to work for, it makes life meaningful.

Belief in the light is the one thing the people had; it is also the one thing which Cory did not have. Life had no meaning for him because he lacked spiritual values; he lived only on a material level.

The materialism of Cory is further stressed by Robinson's use of a third kind of irony, irony of anticipation. Irony of anticipation is the use of details whose ironical implications are not realized until later in a work. We have already seen that the "kingly" references, in stanzas one through three, become ironic in the light of Cory's suicide at the end. But the "kingly" references do not exhaust the irony produced in this way. The townspeople looked upon Cory as a gentleman *from sole to crown* (dress); he was *clean favored* and *slim* (physical appearance); he was *quietly arrayed* (dress); he was *human when he talked* (manner); he *glittered* when he walked (appearance); he was *rich* (material possessions); and he was admirably *schooled* in every *grace* (manner). The word *glittered* is doubly charged. It not only emphasizes the aura of regality and

---

[4] *Light,* in one form or another, is in fact the dominant symbol in all of Robinson's poetry.

[5] Matthew 5:14. The context here is the Sermon on the Mount. Compare also Matthew 5:6: "Blessed are they which do hunger and thirst after righteousness: for they shall be filled."

[6] John 1:1–5.

stresses Cory's wealth but also conveys the suggestion of speciousness, of appearance value only. The word *schooled* also takes on a special significance; it shows that Cory's manner, which seemed at first to be a manifestation of innate human quality, is only a characteristic which has been acquired. All these details about Cory are concerned solely with external qualities; and our retarded realization, at the end of the poem, of their implications is the result of Robinson's skillful use of irony of anticipation.

In conclusion, we realize that the effectiveness of the whole poem is the result of the subtle and delicate interplay of ironies, which give it a concentration and suggestiveness that could never have been achieved by direct means.

UNDERSTATEMENT. We have seen that the devices of paradox and irony make it possible to achieve powerful and complex effects in poetry, that often compression and indirection achieve more than any direct statement could do. Another device which has these qualities is understatement. In its most general sense understatement is a statement which falls below the truth or fact, which represents something as less important than it actually is, or which states something with less force than the facts warrant. The result of understatement is often the opposite of what one would expect from its definition. Though the understatement itself falls short of the truth, its effect is to increase one's awareness of the situation as it actually is. For example, in *Romeo and Juliet*, as Mercutio, wounded by a sword thrust, lies dying, his friend Benvolio asks, "What, art thou hurt?" And Mercutio replies, "Ay, ay, a scratch, a scratch; marry, 'tis enough."

It is not so much what is said but what is left unsaid that makes such understatement so effective. The recognition of the discrepancy between what is stated and the actual situation gives understatement its effect. The last line of the following poem by Robert Frost will illustrate the point.

Fire and Ice

Some say the world will end in fire,   *1*
Some say in ice.
From what I've tasted of desire
I hold with those who favor fire.

But if it had to perish twice,   5
I think I know enough of hate
To say that for destruction ice
Is also great
And would suffice.

ROBERT FROST

OVERSTATEMENT. The opposite of understatement is overstatement, a statement which, if taken literally, exceeds the limits of fact or truth, which represents something as greater or more important than it actually is, or which states something more strongly than the facts warrant. It is another device of indirection, for it is not to be taken literally. Its purpose is to emphasize or intensify a statement or situation by means of exaggeration. For example, if instead of saying "Go ahead, I am listening intently," you were to say "Go ahead, I'm *all ears*," you would be using overstatement to convey the intensity of your attention. Or, if after hiking most of the day, you were to say "I'm *dead tired*," again you would be exaggerating by means of overstatement the extent of your fatigue.

An examination of a familiar poem will help to clarify these remarks. As a sincere expression of the beauty and restorative powers of nature, Wordsworth's "I Wandered Lonely as a Cloud" has given delight to many readers. Although not immediately apparent, much of the effect is the result of Wordsworth's use of overstatement.

I Wandered Lonely as a Cloud

I wandered lonely as a cloud   1
That floats on high o'er vales and hills,
When all at once I saw a crowd,
A host, of golden daffodils;
Beside the lake, beneath the trees,   5
Fluttering and dancing in the breeze.

Continuous as the stars that shine
And twinkle on the milky way,
They stretched in never-ending line
Along the margin of a bay: 10

Ten thousand saw I at a glance,
Tossing their heads in sprightly dance.

The waves beside them danced; but they
Out-did the sparkling waves in glee:
A poet could not but be gay,   *15*
In such a jocund company:
I gazed—and gazed—but little thought
What wealth the show to me had brought:

For oft, when on my couch I lie
In vacant or in pensive mood,   *20*
They flash upon that inward eye
Which is the bliss of solitude;
And then my heart with pleasure fills,
And dances with the daffodils.

                    WILLIAM WORDSWORTH

Paraphrased literally the poem simply says: "I was lonely. Walking about aimlessly, I chanced to come upon a field in which there were a great many daffodils. It was a breezy day and the daffodils were moving. The sight made a great impression on me, and I lost my sense of loneliness. Now whenever I feel lonely and meditative all I have to do is to call to mind the picture of the field of daffodils and my mood changes to one of pleasure." But this paraphrase is not the poem. It is flat and ineffective. It tells little of why the poet felt as he did and gives us no real idea of the depth and intensity of his feelings. To externalize these feelings Wordsworth painted a vivid and exaggerated picture. In the first place, the daffodils are personified. They are a *crowd,* a *host* of daffodils, and they are *dancing* and *tossing their heads.* The giving of human characteristics to the flowers is in itself an instance of overstatement. Moreover it is important that the daffodils be given these human qualities. The poet is lonely; the *jocund company* of daffodils seem to him like human companions. They are the means by which his sense of loneliness is dispelled. Furthermore the effect of this experience is not just a temporary one. So great was the impression on the poet that the mere remembrance of the scene achieves the same effect as actually seeing it. Therefore in order to give greater credibility to the concluding stanza, Wordsworth had to give some indication in the poem that this was more than an ordinary sight. This he also accomplished by means of overstatement.

By comparing the daffodils to the *stars that shine/ And twinkle on the milky way,* and by emphasizing *continuous* and *never-ending line,* he suggests a vast field and an infinite number of daffodils in constant motion. And he saw ten thousand *at a glance.* How many more, then, were there to be seen! The sense of infinite number and joyous movement is intensified in lines 13 and 14, comparing the motion of the daffodils to the *sparkling waves;* countless and unceasing in motion as the waves must have been, the daffodils *outdid* the waves in glee.

Although Wordsworth could have stated in more literal terms what he saw, it is by indirection, in this case by overstatement, that he has been so convincing.

INVERSION. In English prose the normal word order is subject-verb-object or modifier. In poetry, however, this grammatical pattern may be distorted; for instance, the object may precede the verb or the verb may precede the subject. Such distortion of the normal grammatical pattern is called inversion. An example occurs in the first three lines of the following stanza from Gray's "Elegy Written in a Country Church-Yard":

The boast of heraldry, the pomp of pow'r,
And all that beauty, all that wealth e'er gave,
Awaits alike th'inevitable hour.
The paths of glory lead but to the grave.

Here we find a complete reversal of the ordinary pattern. The grammatical objects named in the first two lines precede the verb, *awaits;* and both the objects and the verb precede the subject, *hour.* To the reader who thinks of poetry as a kind of metrical prose, inversion appears to be misleading and confusing. Why, he may ask, does the poet distort the normal pattern of speech? Why does he attempt to make it more difficult for the reader to understand what he is saying?

The poet uses inversion for four reasons. First, it helps him to achieve a desired effect of rime and rhythm. Second, it provides variety. Third, it creates emphasis because, being unusual, it draws attention. Fourth, it gives suspense by delaying the completion of the thought.

Inversion for the sake of inversion alone is meaningless. Like all other poetic devices, its effectiveness is determined by its relation to the whole context of which it is a part. To illustrate, let us turn once more to Gray's stanza. Consider, first of all, what happens when these lines are rearranged in the normal word order:

Th'inevitable hour awaits alike
The boast of heraldry, the pomp of pow'r,
And all that beauty, all that wealth e'er gave.
The paths of glory lead but to the grave.

The sense of the passage may, for the moment, seem to be more immediately apparent; but much of that which contributes to the effectiveness of the original stanza has been lost in the rearrangement.

Gray's "Elegy" is composed of a series of quatrains in five-stress iambic meter, having a rime scheme of *a b a b*. In each stanza there is a delicate balance of sound and sense. By means of the inversion in the first three lines the expected musical pleasure of the rime scheme has been maintained. Furthermore the riming of *pow'r* and *hour,* resulting from the inversion, serves to bind the two lines together and to point up the contrast in thought and feeling between the worldly power of the lordly, aristocratic class and their lack of power to do anything about the inevitable hour of death. The same effect is achieved by bringing together by means of the rime words the contrasting thoughts of *all that wealth e'er* GAVE and *but to the* GRAVE.

Inversion actually makes the stanza easier to understand. Although it distorts the normal grammatical order, it presents details in the same order as given in the last line, which summarizes the three preceding lines. This summary statement is presented in the usual order of subject-verb-modifier. The subject of this statement, *paths of glory,* sums up the objects which introduce the stanza; the verb *lead* parallels *awaits;* and the adverbial modifier *to the grave* corresponds both in thought and in rhetorical position to the subject of the first statement, *th'inevitable hour.* By means of inversion, then, Gray has created a balance and parallelism of thought and expres-

sion which help to unify the stanza and which is in keeping with
the other stanzas of the poem.

Nor is this all. The effectiveness of the inversion can be seen more
fully in relation to what has gone before. The poem is a meditation
on life and death. The setting is a country church-yard at evening.
The speaker, captivated by the quiet charm of the scene, has been
thinking of the simple dignity of the country folk who are buried
there and who are no longer able to enjoy the homely, commonplace
labors and pleasures they had while alive. In the stanza just preceding the speaker has stated:

Let not Ambition mock their useful toil,
Their homely joys, and destiny obscure;
Nor Grandeur hear with a disdainful smile,
The short and simple annals of the poor.

By beginning the next stanza, not with the subject, *th'inevitable
hour,* but with the objects, *The boast of heraldry, the pomp of
pow'r,* Gray has created a dramatic contrast between the obscure
poor, at the end of this stanza, and the upper classes, at the beginning of the next. This contrast is further emphasized by the
alliteration of the *p*'s, linking together *simple* and *poor* with *pomp*
and *pow'r,* an effect also made possible by the inversion. In contrast
to the humble poor, the wealthy and powerful momentarily occupy
a more elevated position, which is accentuated by the terms *boast*
and *pomp,* suggesting vainglorious pride, puffed up by a sense of
importance. This contrast gives great power to the concluding
thought that rich and poor alike come to the same end. The final
effect of the inversion is that, by delaying the completion of the
thought, it has held our attention in suspense and given emphasis to
the key term *hour.*

ILLUSTRATIVE POEMS

The Golf Links

The golf links lie so near the mill
    That almost every day
The laboring children can look out
    And see the men at play.

SARAH N. CLEGHORN

A Lame Begger

I am unable, yonder begger cries,
To stand, or move; if he say true, hee *lies*.

JOHN DONNE

The Day

The day was a year at first	*1*

The day was a year at first   *1*
When children ran in the garden;
The day shrank down to a month
When the boys played ball.

The day was a week thereafter   *5*
When young men walked in the garden;
The day was itself a day
When love grew tall.

The day shrank down to an hour
When old men limped in the garden;   *10*
The day will last forever
When it is nothing at all.

THEODORE SPENCER

West London

Crouched on the pavement, close by Belgrave Square,   *1*
A tramp I saw, ill, moody, and tongue-tied.
A babe was in her arms, and at her side
A girl; their clothes were rags, their feet were bare.
Some laboring men, whose work lay somewhere there,   *5*
Passed opposite; she touched her girl, who hied
Across, and begged, and came back satisfied.
The rich she had let pass with frozen stare.
Thought I: "Above her state this spirit towers;
She will not ask of aliens, but of friends,   *10*
Of sharers in a common human fate.
She turns from that cold succor, which attends
The unknown little from the unknowing great,
And points us to a better time than ours."

MATTHEW ARNOLD

To Roses in the Bosom of Castara

Ye blushing virgins happy are   *1*
In the chaste nunn'ry of her breasts,
For he'd profane so chaste a fair,
Who'er should call them Cupid's nests.

Transplanted thus how bright ye grow,   *5*
How rich a perfume do ye yield!
In some close garden cowslips so
Are sweeter than i' th' open field.

In those white cloisters live secure
From the rude blasts of wanton breath,   *10*
Each hour more innocent and pure,
Till you shall wither into death.

Then that which living gave you room,
Your glorious sepulcher shall be;
There wants no marble for a tomb,   *15*
Whose breast hath marble been to me.

WILLIAM HABINGTON

The Mill

The miller's wife had waited long,   *1*
    The tea was cold, the fire was dead;
And there might yet be nothing wrong
    In how he went and what he said:
"There are no millers any more,"   *5*
    Was all that she had heard him say;
And he had lingered at the door
    So long that it seemed yesterday.

Sick with a fear that had no form
    She knew that she was there at last;   *10*
And in the mill there was a warm
    And mealy fragrance of the past.

What else there was would only seem
 To say again what he had meant;
And what was hanging from a beam   *15*
 Would not have heeded where she went.

And if she thought it followed her,
 She may have reasoned in the dark
That one way of the few there were
 Would hide her and would leave no mark: *20*
Black water, smooth above the weir
 Like starry velvet in the night,
Though ruffled once, would soon appear
 The same as ever to the sight.
    EDWIN ARLINGTON ROBINSON

Song

No, no, fair heretic, it needs must be   *1*
 But an ill love in me,
 And worse for thee.
For were it in my power
To love thee now this hour   *5*
 More than I did the last,
I would then so fall,
 I might not love at all.
Love that can flow, and can admit increase,
Admits as well an ebb, and may grow less. *10*

True love is still the same; the torrid zones,
 And those more frigid ones,
 It must not know;
For love, grown cold or hot,
Is lust or friendship, not   *15*
 The thing we have;
For that's a flame would die,
 Held down or up too high.
Then think I love more than I can express,
And would love more, could I but love thee less. *20*
    SIR JOHN SUCKLING

In Church

"And now to God the Father," he ends,   *1*
And his voice thrills up to the topmost tiles:
Each listener chokes as he bows and bends,
And emotion pervades the crowded aisles.
Then the preacher glides to the vestry-door,   *5*
And shuts it, and thinks he is seen no more.

The door swings softly ajar meanwhile,
And a pupil of his in the Bible class,
Who adores him as one without gloss or guile,
Sees her idol stand with a satisfied smile   *10*
And re-enact at the vestry-glass
Each pulpit gesture in deft dumb-show
That had moved the congregation so.

THOMAS HARDY

Sonnet XLIII

When most I wink, then do mine eyes best see,   *1*
For all the day they view things unrespected;
But when I sleep, in dreams they look on thee,
And darkly bright, are bright in dark directed.
Then thou, whose shadow shadows doth make bright,   *5*
How would thy shadow's form form happy show
To the clear day with thy much clearer light,
When to unseeing eyes thy shade shines so!
How would, I say, mine eyes be blessed made
By looking on thee in the living day,   *10*
When in dead night thy fair imperfect shade
Through heavy sleep on sightless eyes doth stay!
  All days are nights to see till I see thee,
  And nights bright days when dreams do show thee me.

WILLIAM SHAKESPEARE

11

CULTURAL BACKGROUND

To most people today the following lines are meaningless:

Oft him anhaga   are gebideð,
Metudes miltse,   þeah þe he modcearig
geong lagulade   longe sceolde
hreran mid hondum   hrimcealde sæ,
wadan wræclastas: wyrd bið ful aræd.[1]

Yet to the eighth-century Englishman, listening to the scop recite "The Wanderer," a story of a man's loneliness and desolation, these lines were both meaningful and moving. And although many will recognize in the following passage an earlier form of English poetry, most people will consider it merely as a curiosity:

Whan that Aprille with hise shoures soote
The droghte of March hath perced to the roote,

---

[1] Often the lonely one awaits a favor, the mercy of the Creator, though, soul-grieved, throughout the ocean-way he long must stir with his hands the rime-cold sea, must travel the tracks of exile: fate is completely inexorable!

And bathed every veyne in swich licour
Of which vertu engendred is the flour ;[2]

These lines are the beginning of Chaucer's *The Canterbury Tales,* and to the fifteenth-century reader or listener they would immediately evoke a vivid picture of spring showers, of budding trees, and of flowers blossoming after the cold of winter had passed.

Nothing has happened to the form of these poems. They contain the same images, feelings, and thoughts that they had centuries ago; yet they have lost their power for modern readers. With the passage of time the English language has changed—changed to such an extent that most English literature before 1500 cannot be understood without considerable study. Yet even to those who have studied Old English and Middle English, the poems of those times as experienced today are not the same as they were during the time of their composition.[3] Nor can they ever really be the *same.* A poet necessarily writes first of all for his own times. He writes in the language he knows; his thoughts and feelings, though uniquely his own, are conditioned by the cultural environment into which he was born. He assumes in his contemporary audience the same general intellectual and emotional patterns as his own.

From our study of the previous chapters, we have seen that to experience a poem fully is not a lazy man's job. The reader must

---

[2] When April with its sweet showers
Has pierced to the root the drought of March
And bathed every vein in such liquid⋅
Through the power of which the flower is engendered.

[3] Even Dryden, two hundred and fifty years closer to Chaucer than we are, though he had great respect for Chaucer's work, was unable to experience Chaucer's poetry fully because he was not familiar enough with the language of Chaucer's time. In his *Preface to Fables,* Dryden made the following comment about Chaucer's poetry: "The verse of Chaucer, I confess, is not harmonious to us; . . . common sense . . . must convince the reader, that equality of numbers, in every verse which we call *heroic,* was either not known, or not always practiced, in Chaucer's age. It were an easy matter to produce some thousands of his verses, which are lame for want of half a foot, and sometimes a whole one, and which no pronunciation can make otherwise." Scholarly research has enabled modern readers to read Chaucer with greater understanding and pleasure than Dryden could.

be constantly aware of what is going on in the poem; he must pay attention to the sense-meanings of words, to the implications of figurative language, and to the effects of sound devices. In other words, he must consider all those parts which constitute the verbal context of a poem. However, just as a word in a poem exists only in relation to the total verbal context, so a poem exists as a part of a larger context, its cultural background; it is the product of a particular time, a particular place, and a particular mind. The reader, then, in order to experience a poem as fully as possible, must also take into account the cultural background as well. This background we shall discuss under three headings: the language factor, the historical factor, and the personal factor.

The purpose in considering the cultural background of a poem, however, is not to shift the emphasis from the poem to its background. A poem may be *used* to gain a greater understanding of the time and place of its composition and of the mind of the author who wrote it; but in such a case the emphasis is not on the poem as an artistic creation but as an historical document. Our purpose is the reverse; it is to recover the larger context, linguistic, historical, and personal, in order to make the poem itself more meaningful.

THE LANGUAGE FACTOR.   The poems in this volume have all been written since 1500, in what we call Modern English. Because of this a few readers may conclude that the language is, in all cases, understandable. However, anyone acquainted with the literature of the sixteenth century, or even of the nineteenth century, is aware that the language of one period differs from that of another, and certainly from the language of today. The English language is constantly changing. New words are added, old words are dropped or altered in meaning, and many words change in pronunciation. In addition, a few changes in grammar have occurred since 1500. Because of these language changes, a reader may misunderstand poems of an earlier period unless he knows what changes have occurred.

Changes in the sounds of words are of three sorts. First, a word may be shortened or lengthened, that is, the number of syllables a word contains may be decreased or increased. For example, during the time of Shakespeare the words *nation* and *ocean* were often pronounced as having three syllables: *na-ti-on* and *o-ce-an*. Similarly the word *occasion* was often pronounced as having four syllables: *o-cca-si-on*. On the other hand, such words as *ever, evil, hither, other,* and *whether* frequently were pronounced as monosyllables. Obviously the experience of a modern reader will be somewhat marred in reading poetry of an earlier period if he fails to recognize changes in the length of words.

Consider, for example, the following lines, all from Shakespeare:

1. *Whether,* if you yield not to your father's choice.
2. Incenses them to send *destruction.*
3. Fearing to strengthen that *impatience.*
4. To groan and sweat under the *business.*

According to our way of pronunciation, line 1 has eleven syllables, and lines 2–4 have each nine syllables. As Shakespeare pronounced the underlined words, however, *whether* had only one syllable, *de-struc-ti-on* and *im-pa-ti-ence* each had four syllables, and *bu-si-ness* had three. Read accordingly, each line is found to be an example of regular five-stress iambic meter. It should be apparent, then, that changes in the number of syllables will affect the meter of a poem.

A second change which affects the meter is a shift in the position of the accent. A syllable which at one time received the primary stress may at a different time become an unstressed syllable as the accent shifts to another position. Most of us ordinarily pronounce the word *cónfiscate* with the primary accent on the first syllable. This is a recent development. From the early sixteenth century until the middle of the nineteenth century the usual pronunciation was *confíscate.* The same is true of many other words ending in *-ate,* such as *concéntrate, contémplate,* and *compénsate.* Moreover this shift of accent toward the front of the word has occurred in other words, *e.g., aspéct, liquór, perséver, pleasánt, siníster.* And even at the present time there are words whose accent is in the process of change. *Cigarette, Detroit, robust,* and *romance,* for example, may be accented either on the last or the first syllable.

The reader may ask at this point: If the accentuation of words has changed in the past and if changes are still going on, how am I ever going to know how to pronounce a word in reading poetry? The task is not so difficult as it may seem, and the number of words affected is relatively small. There is a simple and easy way to determine where the stress is to be placed. This can best be shown by illustration. Each of the following passages contains one word in which there has been a shift in the position of the accent:

1.   Again, if any Syracusian born
     Come to the bay of Ephesus, he dies,
     His goods *confiscate* to the duke's dispose.
                              WILLIAM SHAKESPEARE

2.   Ay, do, *persever*, counterfeit sad looks,
     Make mouths upon me when I turn my back;
     Wink each at other; hold the sweet jest up.
                              WILLIAM SHAKESPEARE

3.   His words here ended, but his meek *aspect*
     Silent yet spake, and breathed immortal love
     To mortal men, above which only shone
     Filial obedience.

                              JOHN MILTON

4.   *Contemplate* all this work of Time,
        The giant laboring in his youth;
        Nor dream of human love and truth,
     As dying Nature's earth and lime.
                     ALFRED, LORD TENNYSON

To read the underlined words as they are normally pronounced today is to destroy the basic metrical pattern of each passage. Most questions, then, about the position of the accent are answered by the demands of the meter.

Changes may occur not only in the length and accentuation of words but also in the quality of consonant and vowel sounds. Since consonant changes after 1500 have been few and unimportant, we shall confine our discussion to vowel changes, those which are especially important for the reading of poetry. Such changes, if not noticed, can mar the musical pleasure of older poetry for the modern reader.

Although we are not always sure of the exact pronunciation of a given vowel, yet it is possible to point out the usual pronunciation of certain vowel sounds in older poetry.

1. Before the nineteenth century, the vowel in *ea* words like *clean* and *lean* often had the quality of [e][4] as in *mane* or *rain, e.g.,*

In general spring, beneath the quiv'ring *shade,*
Where cooling vapours breathe along the *mead.*
ALEXANDER POPE

2. The sound of *oo* has three pronunciations, as shown by *food, good,* and *blood.* In older poetry the pronunciation will sometimes vary from that of today, *e.g.,*

I saw a third—I heard his voice: *1*
It is the Hermit *good!*
He singeth loud his godly hymns
That he makes in the *wood.*
He'll shrieve my soul, he'll wash away   *5*
The Albatross's *blood.*
SAMUEL T. COLERIDGE

3. The combination *er* in words like *serve* had three pronunciations: A. as the vowel sound in *at* plus the *r*-sound in *father* [æɝ]; B. as the *ar* in *hark* [ɑɝ]; C. as the *er* in *person* [ɝ], *e.g.,*

But still the Great have kindness in re*serve,*
He helped to bury whom he helped to *starve.*
ALEXANDER POPE

4. The sound of *oi* in words like *join* often was pronounced somewhat like the diphthong [ɑɪ] as in *mine* or *shine, e.g.,*

But these were random bolts; no form'd de*sign,*
Nor interest made the factious crowd to *join.*
JOHN DRYDEN

The reader will also meet other variations. For example, *wound,* an injury, may rime with *hound; again* with *rain;* and *wind* with *dined.* The following passage, for instance, loses much of its effectiveness unless the word *wind* is read so as to rime with *behind:*

---

[4] Phonetic symbols are bracketed. See p. 454.

" 'But *why drives* on that ship so fast
Without or wave or *wind?*'
" 'The air is cut away before,
And closes from *behind.*' "

SAMUEL T. COLERIDGE

Not only is the rime destroyed but the reciprocal sound reinforcement of the assonanted [aɪ] in *why* and *drives* is lost if *wind* is read as if it rimed with *thinned*.

When the pronunciation of a vowel is in doubt, the reader can sometimes find help by studying the vowels in the words that rime with it.

To understand a poem, the reader must know the meanings of all the words. As one moves farther and farther away from the twentieth century, this becomes increasingly difficult. In the poetry of the past, we meet two kinds of words which offer difficulty: words which are obsolete, and words which have changed in meaning. The following lines contain examples of obsolete words:

1. Whoso *list* to hunt, I know where is an hind.

SIR THOMAS WYATT

2. My doubtful hope and *eke* my hot desire.

HENRY HOWARD, EARL OF SURREY

3. You courtly *wights* that wants your pleasant choice.

RICHARD EDWARDS

4. Her mouth foamed, and the grass, therewith *besprent*.[5]

JOHN KEATS

Although with the passage of time many words have become obsolete, many more have come down to us unchanged in form but changed in meaning. For example, in the seventeenth century the word *awful* had the denotation, that is, the literal meaning, of full of awe, as in Milton's "Heaven's *awful* Monarch." Also the connotation, that is, the suggestiveness, of a word may change. The word

---

[5] Because a word has become obsolete in general speech does not mean that such words will not occur in the poetry of a later date. Many poets, especially during the nineteenth century, used obsolete words for special effects.

brat, for example, denoted children and had no derogatory connotations, *e.g.,*

O Israel, O household of the Lord,
O Abraham's *brats,* O brood of blessed seed.
                    GEORGE GASCOIGNE

If in this passage we think of the children of Israel with the present derogatory connotation of *brat,* we miss the feeling of reverence in the lines. Failure to recognize that a word has changed its meaning, then, results in misunderstanding. The way to avoid such misunderstanding is simple: look up the word in an unabridged dictionary and then use the context to establish both the denotation and the connotation.[6]

EXERCISE

With the help of an unabridged dictionary and the poetic context, ascertain the meanings of the underlined words.

1.   . . . children young
    Their *wanton* sports and childish mirth did play.
                    EDMUND SPENSER

2.   His haughtie helmet, *horrid* all with gold,
    Both glorious brightness, and great terrour bred.
                    EDMUND SPENSER

3.   The beast . . .
    Thought with his wings to *stye* above the ground.
                    EDMUND SPENSER

4.   The *silly* prentice, bound for many years,
    Doth hope that time his service will release.
                    GILES FLETCHER

5.   Lo, here the state of every mortal *wight,*
    See here the *fine* of all their gallant joys;
    Behold their pomp, their beauty, and delight,
    Whereof they vaunt as safe from all *annoys.*
                    THOMAS PROCTER

---

[6] The *Oxford English Dictionary,* also called the *New English Dictionary,* is the best source for older words.

6.   Mine eye play'd the painter and hath *stell'd*
     Thy beauty's form in *table* of my heart.

WILLIAM SHAKESPEARE

7.   Oh, Thou, who didst with pitfall and with *gin*
     Beset the Road I was to wander in.

EDWARD FITZGERALD

Change in meaning may result in the loss of a concept about which was clustered a group of attitudes. Consider, for instance, the following lines from *Othello,* in which the professional soldier, Othello, tells of his fortunes of war, mentioning

. . . most *disastrous* chances,
Of moving accidents [= occurrences] by flood and field.

Seemingly the meaning is clear. But what does Othello mean by *disastrous* chances? Does he mean that he took chances which were calamitous in their outcome? Before answering this question, let us look at another passage from Shakespeare, the context of which may help us to understand the concept of *disaster.*

. . . stars with trains of fire and dews of blood,
Disasters in the sun.

The word *disaster* here obviously has something to do with misfortune or calamity, but the context suggests more. Etymologically the word *disaster,* from the Latin *dis,* having a negative or sinister quality, plus *astrum,* star, carries with it the idea of an unlucky star. And behind the use of *disaster* and *disastrous* in the passages above lies the concept that the world and fortunes of men are controlled by the positions of the planets.[7] The *disastrous* chances of Othello, then, were not only calamitous in their outcome but were beyond his control. If the reader understands this concept, his admiration and sympathy for Othello are increased.

Changes in grammar that English has gone through will seldom interfere with our understanding of older poetry. Such words as *hath, doth, ye, thou, drinkest, singeth* are entirely clear, although

---

[7] Cf. Shakespeare's "It is the stars,/The stars above us, govern our conditions." Underlying our expression "guiding star" is this concept of planetary control.

they sound old-fashioned to the modern reader. Consider also the following lines:

1. He on a sudden *clinged* her so about.
    CHRISTOPHER MARLOWE

2. In pain and in pleasure
    The *most truest* measure.
    ANONYMOUS

3. That fish that is not *catched* thereby
    Alas, is wiser far than I.
    JOHN DONNE

Although one may be tempted to smile at these grammatical constructions, he should nevertheless realize that they were usually normal at the time the poem was written, and should not allow them to disturb the effect of the poem.

THE HISTORICAL FACTOR. In poetry one often finds allusions to events, persons, places, or things—real or imaginary, past or present. References of this sort make up what we have called the historical factor. Knowing the meaning of all the words in a poem includes a knowledge of whatever historical references may be made.

Some of these references may be simple ones, such as those in the following lines from Walt Whitman's "Passage to India" describing the scenery of the western United States:

I see over my own continent the Pacific railroad surmount-
    ing every barrier,   *1*
I see continual trains of cars winding along the Platte carry-
    ing freight and passengers,
I hear the locomotives rushing and roaring, and the shrill
    steam-whistle,
I hear the echoes reverberate through the grandest scenery
    in the world,
I cross the Laramie plains, I note the rocks in grotesque
    shapes, the buttes,   *5*

I see the plentiful larkspur and wild onions, the barren, color-
  less, sage-deserts,
I see in glimpses afar or towering immediately above me the
  great mountains, I see the Wind river and the Wah-
  satch mountains,
I see the Monument mountain and the Eagle's Nest, I pass
  the Promontory, I ascend the Nevadas,
I scan the noble Elk mountain and wind around its base,
I see the Humboldt range, I thread the valley and cross the
  river,   *10*
I see the clear waters of lake Tahoe, I see forests of majestic
  pines,

Or crossing the great desert, the alkaline plains, I behold en-
  chanting mirages of waters and meadows,
Marking through these and after all, in duplicate slender
  lines,
Bridging the three or four thousand miles of land travel,
Tying the Eastern to the Western sea,   *15*
The road between Europe and Asia.

                                        WALT WHITMAN

Here, if one does not know the places named, it is an easy matter
to find out: consult an atlas or a gazetteer. Mere identification, however, may not be enough. One must still determine what function
the references have in the poem. In the passage above, Whitman is
sketching a picture of some of *the grandest scenery in the world,*
starting with Nebraska and moving across to Wyoming, Colorado,
Utah, Nevada, and into California, places which are associated with
the route of the *Pacific railroad,* and which are important to his
idea of *Tying the Eastern to the Western sea.*

  Keats' poem, "Lines on the Mermaid Tavern," contains less simple
allusions and requires more extensive knowledge from the reader:

Souls of Poets dead and gone,   *1*
What Elysium have ye known,
Happy field or mossy cavern,
Choicer than the Mermaid Tavern?
Have ye tippled drink more fine   *5*
Than mine host's Canary wine?

Or are fruits of Paradise
Sweeter than those dainty pies
Of venison? O generous food!
Drest as though bold Robin Hood   *10*
Would, with his maid Marian,
Sup and bowse from horn and can.

   I have heard that on a day
Mine host's sign-board flew away,
Nobody knew whither, till   *15*
An astrologer's old quill
To a sheepskin gave the story,
Said he saw you in your glory,
Underneath a new old sign
Sipping beverage divine,   *20*
And pledging with contented smack
The Mermaid in the Zodiac.

   Souls of Poets dead and gone,
What Elysium have ye known,
Happy field or mossy cavern,   *25*
Choicer than the Mermaid Tavern?

JOHN KEATS

The poem itself makes little sense until we know certain facts about
the Mermaid Tavern: that it was a famous London inn, over whose
door swung a sign portraying a mermaid, and that it was the gathering place for many Elizabethan poets, including Shakespeare,
Jonson, Raleigh, Beaumont, Fletcher, and Donne. These habitués
of the Mermaid and their friends are the poets mentioned in line 1.
A feeling of conviviality and camaraderie prevailed at the Mermaid
Tavern, as is apparent in Beaumont's lines from "Master Francis
Beaumont's Letter to Ben Jonson":

      . . . in this warm shine   *1*
I lie, and dream of your full Mermaid wine.

*   *   *

      What things have ye seen
Done at the Mermaid! heard words that have been

So nimble, and so full of subtle flame,   5
As if that every one from whence they came
Had meant to put his whole wit in a jest,
And had resolved to live a fool the rest
Of his dull life.

These bits of information about the Mermaid help to make the poem
more meaningful, and the more one learns about this subject the
more complete his poetic experience will be.

But still more knowledge is required: What is Elysium? Who are
Robin Hood and Marian? Why is the beverage in line 20 called
divine? What is the Zodiac? What is the function of all these references in the poem? Until these and similar questions are answered
the reader's response will be inadequate.

The necessity of recovering historical information is not limited
to poems written in the distant past. The following contemporary
poem makes heavy demands on the reader. The poem demands a
knowledge of the incidents upon which it is based, and in addition
a knowledge of certain allusions, classical ones especially, and their
function in the poem.

These Days Are Misty

These days are misty, insulated, mute   1
   Like a faded tapestry and the soft pedal
Is down and the yellow leaves are falling down
   And we hardly have the heart to meddle
Any more with personal ethics or public calls ;   5
   People have not recovered from the crisis,
Their faces are far away, the tone of the words
   Belies their thesis.
For they say that now it is time unequivocally to act,
   To let the pawns be taken,   10
That criticism, a virtue previously,
   Now can only weaken
And that when we go to Rome
   We must do as the Romans do, cry out together
For bread and circuses ; put on your togas now   15
   For this is Roman weather.

Circuses of death and from the topmost tiers
   A cataract of goggling, roaring faces;
On the arena sand
   Those who are about to die try out their paces.   *20*
Now it is night, a cold mist creeps, the night
   Is still and damp and lonely;
Sitting by the fire it is hard to realise
   That the legions wait at the gates and that there is only
A little time for rest though not by rights for rest,   *25*
   Rather for whetting the will, for calculating
A compromise between necessity and wish,
   Apprenticed late to learn the trade of hating.
Remember the sergeant barking at bayonet practice
   When you were small;   *30*
To kill a dummy you must act a dummy
   Or you cut no ice at all.
Now it is morning again, the 25th of October,
   In a white fog the cars have yellow lights;
The chill creeps up the wrists, the sun is sallow,   *35*
   The silent hours grow down like stalactites.
And reading Plato talking about his Forms
   To damn the artist touting round his mirror,
I am glad that I have been left the third best bed
   And live in a world of error.   *40*
His world of capital initials, of transcendent
   Ideas is too bleak;
For me there remain to all intents and purposes
   Seven days in the week
And no one Tuesday is another and you destroy it   *45*
   If you subtract the difference and relate
It merely to the Form of Tuesday. This is Tuesday
   The 25th of October, 1938.
Aristotle was better who watched the insect breed,
   The natural world develop,   *50*
Stressing the function, scrapping the Form in Itself,
   Taking the horse from the shelf and letting it gallop.
Education gives us too many labels
   And clichés, cuts too many Gordian knots;

Trains us to keep the roads nor reconnoitre   55
  Any of the beauty-spots or danger-spots.
Not that I would rather be a peasant; the Happy Peasant
  Like the Noble Savage is a myth;
I do not envy the self-possession of an elm-tree
  Nor the aplomb of a granite monolith.   60
All that I would like to be is human, having a share
  In a civilised, articulate and well-adjusted
Community where the mind is given its due
  But the body is not distrusted.
As it is, the so-called humane studies   65
  May lead to cushy jobs
But leave the men who land them spiritually bankrupt
  Intellectual snobs.
Not but what I am glad to have my comforts,
  Better authentic mammon than a bogus god;   70
If it were not for Lit. Hum. I might be climbing
  A ladder with a hod.
And seven hundred a year
  Will pay the rent and the gas and the 'phone and the
    grocer;
(The Emperor takes his seat beneath the awning,   75
  Those who are about to die . . .) Come, pull the curtains
    closer.

LOUIS MACNEICE

We sense at once a note of intense feeling about a contemporary
situation. We know that the poem is a comment on *personal ethics*
and *public calls* (line 5), and that it is concerned with facing reality.
But there are two questions that the reader must answer before he
can begin to come to a full understanding of the poem. What is the
crisis referred to in line 6? Twice in the poem reference is made to
a specific date. What happened on October 25, 1938?

The poem is number XII in a volume entitled *Autumn Journal*.
In a preface to the volume, the poet tells us that "I was writing what
I have called a Journal. In a journal or a personal letter a man writes
what he feels at the moment; . . . [*Autumn Journal*] is something
half-way between the lyric and the didactic poem. In as much as it

is half-way towards a didactic poem I trust that it contains some 'criticism of life' or implies some standards which are not merely personal. I was writing it from August 1938 until the New Year and have not altered any passages relating to public events in the light of what happened after the time of writing."[8] "These Days Are Misty," then, is part of a record of the poet's thoughts and feelings about some of the events which led up to World War II. Since the *crisis* occurred after August 1938 and before October 25, 1938, we can safely conclude that the reference is to the Munich crisis. For some time the civilized world had been watching with fearful uneasiness the growing power of Hitler in Germany, afraid that his demands for *lebensraum,* "living space" for a greater German Reich, would lead to war. In February 1938, Austria had submitted to Hitler's demands. Not satisfied with this, Hitler began making demands on Czechoslovakia. Some of the leaders of England and France, instead of following a course of firm action, adopted a policy of appeasement in the hope that it might avert war. In September 1938, the English Prime Minister, Neville Chamberlain, on his own initiative, made an overture to Hitler; he asked if he could come to see him for the purpose of discussing a peaceful solution to the situation. Hitler immediately issued an ultimatum that the Sudetenland of Czechoslovakia be incorporated as part of Germany. Chamberlain, upon being assured by Hitler at Munich that this was "the last of his territorial ambitions," agreed to Hitler's demands and returned to England to declare "peace with honour," "peace for our time." On October 1, 1938, German troops moved in to begin the occupation of Czechoslovakia. Thus, Czechoslovakia, like Austria, became another pawn (line 10) lost in the vain attempt to save others from going to war.

The success of Hitler, coupled with the acquiescent attitude of England and France at that time, was an immediate invitation for other powers to make aggressive moves. Shortly after the Munich crisis, Poland and Hungary made additional demands on Czechoslovakia. On October 25, 1938, Japanese invaders bent on conquering China invaded Hankow and, in keeping with the Berlin-Rome-Tokio axis, announced a program for the control of China. This program,

---

[8] Louis MacNeice, *Autumn Journal* (New York: Random House, 1939), p. 7.

which was designed to compel China to "cooperate" with Japan culturally, economically, and politically, stated that China must join the anti-Communist accord of Japan, Germany, and Italy, and give up "all policies and forms of education likely to destroy amity" with Japan.

With this knowledge of the contemporary incidents involved, we come closer to understanding the poem. We have still to consider, however, the classical allusions in the poem and the part they play. Lines 13 through 20 shift the scene from the present to the time of the Roman Empire in its decadence. The central image is that of the Roman circus. From the reference to *circuses of death* (line 17), it should be clear that the poet is not speaking of the familiar circuses of today. In Roman times the circus was a flat oblong area surrounded by tiers of seats on three sides and divided lengthwise by a barrier around which was a track for chariot races, games, and gladiatorial combats. Circus days were festive occasions in Rome, especially for the lower classes. On these public holidays, huge crowds, sometimes as many as 150,000, would gather at the Circus Maximus or at the Colosseum to see the "sport": chariot races in which fouling was permitted; battles in which wild animals were pitted against one another or against criminals condemned to death (it is reported that nine thousand wild beasts were killed at the opening of the Colosseum); and especially gladiatorial combats, in which armed men fought to the death for the amusement of the crowds. Often gladiatorial shows were given by politicians who wanted to curry favor with the mob. These circuses were in fact "circuses of death." The customary greeting of the gladiator to the Roman Emperor was *Morituri te salutamus*, "We who are about to die salute you." It is no wonder that Juvenal, a famous Roman satirist, appalled at the degeneracy of the people, the irresponsibility of those in authority, the general lack of human values in Roman society, wrote with great scorn that there were only two things needed to make the Romans happy, *panem et circenses,* "bread and circuses" (line 15).

The allusions to Rome are significant. The opening lines of the poem, which have a contemporary setting, carry a suggestion of unreality; the people are unwilling or unable to face the reality of the present. In addition, these lines, with their *misty* days, the *faded* tapestry, and the *far away* looks of the people, begin to carry us backward in time up to *this is Roman weather,* at which point present and past become identified. The so-called "civilized" world becomes barbaric; for whatever is attributed to Roman times is attributable to the present: the lack of concern for the lives of other people, the irresponsibility and emphasis on self-interest, the general lack of ethical standards. These qualities are pointed up in the poem by the echo of the gladiators' greeting (lines 20 and 76), which MacNeice has purposely altered; it is not "We" but *"Those* who are about to die."

The poem then shifts again to the present. In lines 29–32, there is a brief reference to World War I, and then suddenly we are carried farther back in time to the Grecian era of Plato and Aristotle. Again it is necessary to know something about these men and their ideas to make the poem more meaningful. Both Plato and Aristotle were philosophers who were concerned with *personal ethics* and *public calls.* Plato was especially interested in the essential and absolute nature of Reality and man's knowledge of it. However, Reality to Plato, was not the objective world about us but the world of Ideas. Because the objective world is constantly changing and because man's senses are not completely reliable, there is no way by which man can know by his senses what Reality is. But even though a perfect circle, for example, does not exist in nature, it is possible for man in his mind to conceive of a perfect circle. An Idea or Form of a circle, then, does exist; but it is not a material or physical circle. According to Plato, there is an Idea, which is perfect and eternal, for everything. These Ideas or Forms, Plato arranged in a pyramidal system of values at the top of which, summarizing all lesser Forms, was the Idea of the highest good and ultimate Reality. Although man can never actually attain the highest good, he should nevertheless by the use of reason try to escape from the actual world of appearance. The more perfect he becomes the closer will he be to Wisdom, Truth, Beauty—to essential Reality.

The comment about the *artist touting round his mirror,* lines 38–40, is a reference to Plato's *Republic,* a discussion of justice and the Ideal State. Book X of the *Republic* is concerned in part with the nature of the artist and his relationship to the State. The discussion is carried on in terms of a bed. There is only one bed which is perfect and eternal and that is the Idea of a bed. The carpenter can make an actual bed, but his bed is only an imitation of the Bed. An artist who paints a bed copies or mirrors an actual bed; his bed therefore is an imitation of an imitation. Since the poet and the painter are imitators of the same sort, both are thrice removed from Reality and are indeed in error.

It might seem strange that the poet should prefer to live in a *world of error.* But in contrast to Plato's Ideal world, which is perfect and unattainable, the *world of error* is the actual objective world in which men and women must live as ordinary human beings. By referring to the Roman world, which emphasized the physical in man, the poet points out what should not be; by referring to Plato's *world of capital initials,* which overemphasized the intellect, he indicates what cannot be. MacNeice likewise thinks that *the Noble Savage is a myth* (line 58). The reference is not a classical one; it is, however, an allusion to another conception of man and society. The "noble savage" refers to an idea popular in the late eighteenth century and early nineteenth century that the uncivilized peoples of the world were nobler than the civilized people because they were closer to the original state of nature. In essence it also was an attempt to escape from this *world of error* to an ideal world. In contrast to these, the poet prefers Aristotle.

Aristotle, a pupil of Plato, was a scientist as well as philosopher. He wrote on agriculture, anthropology, astronomy, biology, botany, mathematics, mechanics, meteorology, optics, physics, physiology, and psychology. His major work in science was in the field of biology and was based on actual observation and experimentation. He did watch *the insect breed,/The natural world develop.* His major philosophic works, *The Politics* and *The Nichomachean Ethics,* are concerned with what the practices of men should be in an actual state. Men may be imperfect, but they are nonetheless morally responsible for their actions. An Ideal State is impossible to attain, but it is possible to attain a just state.

To attain this just state, sketched in lines 61–64, men must weigh carefully the consequences of their actions in terms of good and evil; it cannot be attained by cutting *Gordian knots* (line 54). Here again MacNeice has used a classical reference to make his point. Those who know the story will realize that much has been said in a few words. The reference is to the Greek myth of Gordius, the peasant king of Phrygia, who tied a hard knot about the yoke of his chariot. According to the oracle, the man who could loosen the knot would rule all Asia. Alexander the Great succeeded simply by cutting it in two with his sword. Hence to cut the Gordian knot has come to mean to dispose of a difficult matter in summary fashion. Thus there is both a direct and an ironic relationship to the contemporary situation which is the basis of the poem. Though MacNeice's point is not limited to one specific incident, there is a direct relationship to the way the Czechoslovakian situation was handled at Munich, as if such a move would suddenly solve the problem. It is also ironic, for in the original story the one who cut the knot would rule all Asia. At Munich, however, the English and French leaders cut the knot, increasing the possibility that Hitler might rule all Europe, precisely what the others wanted to prevent.

One more reference may need a word of explanation. *Lit. Hum.*, in line 71, is an abbreviation for *Literae Humaniores,* Latin for the more humane letters; at Oxford University it refers to a course of studies, commonly called "Greats," which consists of a study of the history, thought, and literature of Greek and Roman times, as well as a study of logic and philosophy both in the Greek and in the modern world. MacNeice is a classical scholar as well as poet. The classical allusions in the poem, then, are used with full consciousness of their implications.

It should be clear from the preceding discussion that only when one has recovered the historical context and has made it a part of his own experience will he be able to understand MacNeice's poem. A careful re-study of the poem in the light of the facts given above will show how important the historical factor may sometimes be in the reading of poetry.

THE PERSONAL FACTOR. A poem is not only the product of a particular time and place; it is also the creative work of a unique personality. We have seen that at times one's understanding of a poem can be increased by placing the poem in its historical context. Similarly the context of a poet's life and work may be of help in understanding a poem. Often a study of this context will reveal informative facts, patterns of thought, and characteristic ways of handling material, which will shed light on an individual poem. But the poem, it will be remembered, is always the center of attention.

To illustrate, let us examine Gerard Manley Hopkins' poem "Harry Ploughman." The poem presents special problems of diction and imagery, of form, rhythm, and thought. Although it is difficult, it should in the end prove to be a fresh and rewarding experience.

Harry Ploughman

Hard as hurdle arms, with a broth of goldish flue	*1*
Breathed round; the rack of ribs; the scooped flank; lank	*2*
Rope-over thigh; knee-nave; and barrelled shank—	*3*
Head and foot, shoulder and shank—	*3R*
By a grey eye's heed steered well, one crew, fall to;	*4*
Stand at stress. Each limb's barrowy brawn, his thew	*5*
That onewhere curded, onewhere sucked or sank—	*6*
Soared or sank—	*6R*
Though as a beechbole firm, finds his, as at a rollcall, rank	*7*
And features, in flesh, what deed he each must do—	*8*
His sinew-service where do.	*8R*
He leans to it, Harry bends, look. Back, elbow, and liquid waist	*9*
In him all quail to the wallowing o' the plough. 'S cheek crimsons; curls	*10*
Wag or crossbridle, in a wind lifted, windlaced:	*11*
See his wind- lilylocks -laced;	*11R*
Churlsgrace, too, child of Amansstrength, how it hangs or hurls	*12*
Them—broad in bluffhide his frowning feet lashed! raced	*13*
With, along them, cragiron under and cold furls,	*14*
With-a-fountain's shining-shot furls.	*14R*

GERARD MANLEY HOPKINS

It may seem at first that Hopkins has used a great many strange words that make it difficult to arrive at even a literal sense-meaning of the poem. Actually there are few totally unfamiliar words in the poem. The difficulty arises from the unusual figurative way in which Hopkins uses them, singly or in combination, to build up his picture of Harry Ploughman.

The title itself is a part of the poem and gives us our initial clue. The poem is a description of a ploughman; and the words and images used to describe him are naturally heavily loaded with rural associations. Literally this is what the poem says:

Harry Ploughman is as hard and strong as the arms of a hurdle [an open frame of uprights, crossbars, and a diagonal bar used in the country to form temporary fences, sheep pens, and similar enclosures]. A cloud of soft golden steam-like flue [fluff, down] surrounds him. His ribs are solid like a fodder rack. His flank is hollowed; over his lank thigh is the guide-rope leading to his horse; his knee is knobby like the nave [hub] of a wheel; and the shank of his leg is rounded and firm as a barrel. All the parts of his body as one crew prepare to work; they stand at stress, that is, they are delicately balanced and ready for action. Each limb's set of undulating muscles, its sinew that in one place is knotted up and in another place hollowed, though firm as the trunk of a beech tree, finds its task to do—as if in answer to a roll call—and each features [makes noticeable], in the flesh, what its particular job is.

Harry leans, bends forward to begin ploughing. Look at him. His back, elbow, and waist—flowing with muscles—yield with the rolling movement of the plough. His cheek becomes red; the curls of his hair wave and bridle like a spirited horse, lifted in the wind, laced [lashed and/or interlaced] by the wind. See his lily-locks laced by the wind. His rustic, powerful gracefulness, the product of Aman's rugged terrain, how it propels forward his feet clad in wrinkled leather shoes, as they race along with the cragiron [ploughshare] nosed under the soil and with the coils of cold earth shot up from the iron like streams of water from a fountain.

Hopkins has built up his portrait of the countryman by presenting detail after detail, like the coarse brushwork of a Hals, to be fused by the reader into a poetic picture.[9] The opening image—*Hard as hurdle arms*—exemplifies the rural character of the images used throughout the poem. *With a broth of goldish flue/Breathed round* is a painter's image. In the sunlight the steam from the breaths of horse and man would have a yellowish tinge, which a painter would, and which the poet does, exaggerate for artistic effect. At this point the reader may question, "But is not the whole picture of Harry

---

[9] Hopkins said of this poem, "I want Harry Ploughman to be a vivid figure before the mind's eye." *The Letters of Gerard Manley Hopkins to Robert Bridges*, edited with notes & an introduction by Claude Colleer Abbott (London: Oxford University Press, 1935), p. 265.

exaggerated?" It is indeed. The anatomical exactness of the details presented would be observable only in a nude, or through light clothing in a strong wind. If one accepts the evidence of the poem Harry is wearing nothing but shoes. Obviously the poet has presented not what he sees but what he knows. Moreover, not only has Hopkins stripped Harry but he has used details to describe him which are equally applicable to the horse. Certainly the words *flank* and *shank* are strongly suggestive of an animal. Much of this is puzzling and gives rise to questions: Was Hopkins aware of what he was doing? If so, how is his selection of details to be accounted for? Is the poem more than a mere description of Harry?

At this point a brief study of pertinent facts about Hopkins' life and thought will help us to understand "Harry Ploughman." Hopkins was fascinated by form, pattern, structure of all kinds, or to give it his own term, by inscape. His early notebooks are filled with observations concerning the inscape of clouds, rocks, leaves, flowers —inscape in terms of line, color, light-and-dark, and mass. He saw with a graphic artist's eye, with keen accuracy and delight, and this he carried over into his art. In a letter to his friend Robert Bridges, Hopkins discussed pattern as an aim of his own verse:

> But as air, melody, is what strikes me most of all in music and design in painting, so design, pattern or what I am in the habit of calling 'inscape' is what I above all aim at in poetry. Now it is the virtue of design, pattern, or inscape to be distinctive and it is the vice of distinctiveness to become queer. This vice I cannot have escaped.[10]

These words indicate that Hopkins was aware of what he was doing in describing Harry Ploughman as he did. The pictorial and structural quality of the description can be accounted for by Hopkins' intense interest in form, in this case the physical form and muscular coordination of the ploughman.

Hopkins' interest in form was not limited to a delight in form as subject matter only; he was equally interested in the formal qualities of stanza, rhythm, and sound. He had disciplined himself in the handling of artistic form in several media: he was a painter and musician as well as poet; and he wrote verse in Latin, Greek, and Welsh as well as in English. And in all these arts he liked to

---

[10] *Ibid.*, p. 66.

experiment to see what new effects he could achieve. The student of Hopkins' poetry, then, should give serious consideration to the formal qualities of his work.

What can we say of the stanza form of "Harry Ploughman?" It seems to be a nineteen-line poem with an unusual rime scheme, and with a rhythm that does not conform to the usual practices of most poets. The rime scheme, *a b b b a a b b b a a c d c c d c d d* , is suggestive of the sonnet form. On closer examination it will be seen that the lines marked 3R, 6R, 8R, 11R, and 14R are refrain lines, and that the poem is in fact a variation of the Italian sonnet, a form that Hopkins held in high regard. In a discussion about the sonnet form, Hopkins wrote to Dixon in October 1881:

Now in the form of any work of art the intrinsic measurements, the proportions, that is, of the parts to one another and to the whole, are no doubt the principal point, but still the extrinsic measurements, the absolute quantity or size goes for something. . . . Now if the Italian sonnet is one of the most successful forms of composition known, as it is reckoned to be, its proportions, inward and outward, must be pretty near perfection.[11]

Why, then, did Hopkins attempt to vary the form in writing "Harry Ploughman"? His answer, given in the same letter, will help us to understand why Hopkins deviated from the orthodox form:

The reason why the sonnet has never been so effective or successful in England as in Italy I believe to be this: it is not so long as the Italian sonnet: it is not long enough, . . . The English sonnet has the same inward proportions, 14 lines, 5 feet to the line, and the rhymes and so on may be made as in the strictest Italian type. Nevertheless it is notably shorter and would therefore appear likely to be unsuccessful, from want not of comparative but of absolute length.[12]

Hopkins then went on to show that the Italian sonnet has more syllables to the line and that the syllables themselves are often longer. The English sonnet, he felt, was "light, tripping, and trifling" in comparison with the Italian sonnet, and that the best sonnets

---

[11] *The Correspondence of Gerard Manley Hopkins and Richard Watson Dixon,* edited with notes & an introduction by Claude Colleer Abbott (London: Oxford University Press, 1935), pp. 85–86. For another letter of Hopkins about the sonnet form, see the note to "The Windhover," pp. 493 ff.

[12] *Ibid.*

written in English "shew various devices successfully employed to make up for the shortcoming."[13] By the use of refrain lines and extra syllables Hopkins accomplished the enlargement which he felt was necessary.

The mention of extra syllables raises the question of rhythm.[14] In addition to deviating from the usual length and rime scheme of the Italian sonnet Hopkins has also broken away from the expected five-stress iambic pattern. In this poem, as in many others, Hopkins wrote in what he called "sprung" rhythm, which he described as follows:

> I had long had haunting my ear the echo of a new rhythm which now I realised on paper. To speak shortly, it consists in scanning by accents or stresses alone, without any account of the number of syllables, so that a foot may be one strong syllable or it may be many light and one strong.[15]

And the explanation of why he wrote in sprung rhythm is given in the same letter: ". . . to me it appears, I own, to be a better and more natural principle than the ordinary system, much more flexible, and capable of much greater effects."[16] The reader can best experience these effects by reading the poem aloud. In fact Hopkins himself frequently insisted that his poems were meant for recital, not for mere eye-reading.

If "Harry Ploughman" is read aloud, musical qualities other than rhythm also become apparent. The poem is filled with alliteration and assonance, which contribute to the musical pleasure. Alliteration for musical pleasure is so evident as to need no pointing out. Some of the assonance, however, is subtle. For example, in line 1, we find *broth of goldish flue,* which contains the vowel gradations of [ɔ], [o], [u]. This is an instance of what Hopkins called "*vowelling off* or changing of vowel down some scale. . . ."[17] Line 3 con-

---

[13] *Ibid.,* p. 86.

[14] "The rhythm of this sonnet . . . is very highly studied." *Hopkins to Bridges,* October 11, 1887, *op. cit.,* p. 263.

[15] *Hopkins and Dixon,* October 5, 1878, *op. cit.,* p. 14. For Hopkins' fuller discussion of sprung rhythm, see the note to "The Windhover," pp. 493 ff.

[16] *Ibid.*

[17] *The Notebooks and Papers of Gerard Manley Hopkins,* edited with notes and a preface by Humphry House (London: Oxford University Press, 1937), p. 243.

tains another example in *thigh; knee-nave,* followed in line 4 by *grey eye's heed,* in which the same three vowels are employed in a different sequence. Sound in "Harry Ploughman" has another function: it is used structurally to reinforce the sense of the poem. Alliteration is frequently used to link together related words, as in *Hard as hurdle* and *shining-shot.* Also, at the beginning of the sestet, in lines 9 and 10, where the imagery changes from static to kinetic, the sense of movement is given added vividness by the prominent use of the continuant sounds *l, n,* and *w.*

We return now to the question raised earlier: Is the poem merely a pictorial presentation of a man ploughing, or is there a further meaning? The answer is given in lines 8 and 8R: every sinew has its own deed to do, which is its *service.* The word *service* here has the sense of divine service.[18] Each thew, each element of Harry's body, in doing its own job well, is glorifying God; and Harry Ploughman, the composite of these parts, also serves his Maker in ploughing well. Within the poem there is more evidence to support this view. We have already seen that Hopkins has stressed the sense of action in the sestet. That this action is service in a higher sense than mere physical movement is further suggested in line 10 by the word *quail.* Harry *quails to the wallowing o' the plough,* but it suggests also that he submits to the will of God.[19] Moreover, *Churlsgrace,* in line 12, might bear, to a man of Hopkins' background, a hint of spiritual grace.

This interpretation is borne out by certain biographical facts and by other works of Hopkins. In a letter to Bridges in 1886, Hopkins made a revealing comment about his own attitude toward his work: "This leads me to say that a kind of touchstone of the highest or most living art is seriousness; not gravity but the being in earnest with your subject—reality."[20] This statement has special significance, for to Hopkins, who was a Jesuit, the reality he speaks of is spiritual reality. Born a Protestant, Hopkins became converted to Catholicism in 1866 and two years later entered the Jesuit novitiate. He dedi-

---

[18] *Service* carries both the general sense of service to God, which we discuss here, and the particular sense of a church service.

[19] Compare Hopkins' use of the word *Buckle* in the sestet of "The Windhover," p. 496.

[20] *Hopkins to Bridges,* June 1, 1886, *op. cit.,* p. 225.

cated his life to God. The intensity of his religious devotion is indicated in a letter which he wrote to Dixon:

> What I had written I burnt before I became a Jesuit and resolved to write no more, as not belonging to my profession, unless it were by the wish of my superiors; so for seven years I wrote nothing but two or three little presentation pieces which occasion called for.[21]

Hopkins began to write again only after he had reconciled the relationship between his art and his life. His poetry too he dedicated to the service of God. Every thing, he felt, had its own peculiar beauty and function, its spiritual reality as part of God's creation. And it was this which he tried to capture in all of his work. The poems themselves are substantiation. In "Pied Beauty," for example, he writes *Glory be to God for dappled things;* in "God's Grandeur," he says *The world is charged with the grandeur of God;* and in an untitled poem, he expresses the same idea:

As kingfishers catch fire, dragonflies dráw fláme;   *1*
As tumbled over rim in roundy wells
Stones ring; like each tucked string tells, each hung bell's
Bow swung finds tongue to fling out broad its name;
Each mortal thing does one thing and the same: *5*
Deals out that being indoors each one dwells;
Selves—goes itself; *myself* it speaks and spells;
Crying *Whát I dó is me: for that I came.*

Í say móre: the just man justices;
Kéeps gráce: thát keeps all his goings graces;   *10*
Acts in God's eye what in God's eye he is—
Christ—for Christ plays in ten thousand places,
Lovely in limbs, and lovely in eyes not his
To the Father through the features of men's faces.

GERARD   MANLEY   HOPKINS

Although attracted by the outward beauty of the universe in all its form, Hopkins was concerned more with the inner individuality of every thing and the expression of this individuality in the service of God. Hence the description of Harry Ploughman. Hopkins has purposely stripped him in an attempt to show what individually

---

[21] *Hopkins and Dixon,* October 5, 1878, *op. cit.,* p. 14.

distinguishes Harry and makes him a good ploughman: the superb muscular development and coordination of the man under the control of a mind intent on performing the task he was set to do. Even though animal-like in appearance, he is nonetheless fulfilling his divine service.

The foregoing remarks on "Harry Ploughman" show that in order to understand a poem adequately one must sometimes have information not commonly known by most readers. A poem, we remember, is an interaction between the words on a printed page and the total experience of the reader. If, then, the reader's experience does not include the knowledge necessary to a full understanding of the printed words, he must acquire the missing information before he can have a meaningful poetic experience.

ILLUSTRATIVE POEMS

Upon Lazarus His Tears

Rich Lazarus! richer in those gems, thy tears,
    Than Dives in the robes he wears;
He scorns them now, but oh, they'll suit full well
    With th' purple he must wear in hell.

RICHARD CRASHAW

Sonnet XXX

When to the sessions of sweet silent thought   *1*
I summon up remembrance of things past,
I sigh the lack of many a thing I sought,
And with old woes new wail my dear time's waste:
Then can I drown an eye, unus'd to flow,   *5*
For precious friends hid in death's dateless night,
And weep afresh love's long since cancell'd woe,
And moan th' expense of many a vanish'd sight:
Then can I grieve at grievances foregone,
And heavily from woe to woe tell o'er   *10*
The sad account of fore-bemoaned moan,
Which I new pay as if not paid before.
    But if the while I think on thee, dear friend,
    All losses are restor'd and sorrows end.

WILLIAM SHAKESPEARE

SONNET IV, *Fair Virtue*

Shall **I** wasting in despair   *1*
Die because a woman's fair?
Or make pale my cheeks with care
'Cause another's rosy are?
Be she fairer than the day,   *5*
Or the flow'ry meads in May,
   If she be not so to me,
    What care **I** how fair she be?

Shall my heart be grieved or pined
'Cause **I** see a woman kind?   *10*
Or a well-disposed nature
Joined with a lovely feature?
Be she meeker, kinder, than
Turtle-dove or pelican,
   If she be not so to me   *15*
    What care **I** how kind she be?

Shall a woman's virtues move
Me to perish for her love?
Or her well-deserving known
Make me quite forget mine own?   *20*
Be she with that goodness blest
Which may gain her name of best,
   If she be not such to me,
    What care **I** how good she be?

'Cause her fortune seems too high,   *25*
Shall **I** play the fool and die?
Those that bear a noble mind,
Where they want of riches find,
Think what with them they would do,
That without them dare to woo;   *30*
   And unless that mind **I** see,
    What care **I** how great she be?

Great, or good, or kind, or fair,
I will ne'er the more despair;
If she love me, this believe,   *35*
I will die ere she shall grieve;
If she slight me when I woo,
I can scorn and let her go;
   For if she be not for me,
   What care I for whom she be?   *40*
GEORGE WITHER

Description of Spring, *Wherein Each Thing Renews Save Only the Lover*

The soote season that bud and bloom forth brings   *1*
With green hath clad the hill and eke the vale,
The nightingale with feathers new she sings,
The turtle to her make hath told her tale.
Summer is come, for every spray now springs,   *5*
The hart hath hung his old head on the pale,
The buck in brake his winter coat he flings,
The fishes float with new repaired scale,
The adder all her slough away she slings,
The swift swallow pursueth the flyes smale,   *10*
The busy bee her honey now she mings,—
Winter is worn, that was the flowers' bale:
And thus I see, among these pleasant things
Each care decays—and yet my sorrow springs.
HENRY HOWARD, EARL OF SURREY

SONNET XXIV, *Astrophel and Stella*

Rich fools there be whose base and filthy heart   *1*
Lies hatching still the goods wherein they flow,
And damning their own selves to Tantal's smart,
Wealth breeding want, more rich, more wretched grow:
Yet to those fools Heav'n doth such wit impart,   *5*
As what their hands do hold, their heads do know,
And knowing, love; and loving, lay apart
As sacred things, far from all danger's show.

But that rich fool, who by blind fortune's lot
The richest gem of love and life enjoys,　　　　　　*10*
And can with foul abuse such beauties blot;
Let him, depriv'd of sweet but unfelt joys,
Exil'd for aye from those high treasures which
He knows not, grow in only folly Rich!

SIR PHILIP SIDNEY

The Good-Morrow

I wonder by my troth, what thou, and I　　　　　　*1*
Did, till we lov'd? were we not wean'd till then?
But suck'd on countrey pleasures, childishly?
Or snorted we in the seaven sleepers den?
T'was so; But this, all pleasures fancies bee.　　　*5*
If ever any beauty I did see,
Which I desir'd, and got, t'was but a dreame of thee.

And now good morrow to our waking soules,
Which watch not one another out of feare;
For love, all love of other sights controules,　　*10*
And makes one little roome, an every where.
Let sea-discoverers to new worlds have gone,
Let Maps to other, worlds on worlds have showne,
Let us possesse one world, each hath one, and is one.

My face in thine eye, thine in mine appeares,　　*15*
And true plain hearts doe in the faces rest,
Where can we finde two better hemispheares
Without sharpe North, without declining West?
What ever dyes, was not mixt equally;
If our two loves be one, or, thou and I　　　　　　*20*
Love so alike, that none doe slacken, none can die.

JOHN DONNE

SONNET LV, *Amoretti*

So oft as I her beauty doe behold,　　　　　　　　*1*
　　and therewith doe her cruelty compare,
　　　I marvaile of what substance was the mould
　　　the which her made attonce so cruell faire.

Not earth; for her high thoghts more heavenly are,   *5*
    not water; for her love doth burne like fyre:
    not ayre; for she is not so light or rare,
    not fyre; for she doth friese with faint desire.
Then needs another Element inquire
    whereof she mote be made; that is the skye.   *10*
    for to the heaven her haughty lookes aspire:
    and eke her mind is pure immortal hye.
Then sith to heaven ye lykened are the best,
    be lyke in mercy as in all the rest.

EDMUND SPENSER

Thomas Rymer

True Thomas lay oer yond grassy bank,   *1*
    And he beheld a ladie gay,
A ladie that was brisk and bold,
    Come riding oer the fernie brae.

Her skirt was of the grass-green silk,   *5*
    Her mantel of the velvet fine,
At ilka tett of her horse's mane
    Hung fifty silver bells and nine.

True Thomas he took off his hat,
    And bowed him low down till his knee: *10*
'All hail, thou mighty Queen of Heaven!
    For your peer on earth I never did see.'

'O no, O no, True Thomas,' she says,
    'That name does not belong to me;
I am but the queen of fair Elfland,   *15*
    And I'm come here for to visit thee.

*   *   *

'But ye maun go wi me now, Thomas,
    True Thomas, ye maun go wi me,
For ye maun serve me seven years,
    Thro weel or wae as may chance to be.'   *20*

She turned about her milk-white steed,
   And took True Thomas up behind,
And aye wheneer her bridle rang,
   The steed flew swifter than the wind.

For forty days and forty nights   *25*
   He wade thro red blude to the knee,
And he saw neither sun nor moon,
   But heard the roaring of the sea.

O they rade on, and further on,
   Until they came to a garden green: *30*
'Light down, light down, ye ladie free,
   Some of that fruit let me pull to thee.'

'O no, O no, True Thomas,' she says,
   'That fruit maun not be touched by thee,
For a' the plagues that are in hell   *35*
   Light on the fruit of this countrie.

'But I have a loaf here in my lap,
   Likewise a bottle of claret wine,
And now ere we go farther on,
   We'll rest a while, and ye may dine.'   *40*

When he had eaten and drunk his fill,
   'Lay down your head upon my knee,'
The lady sayd, 'ere we climb yon hill,
   And I will show you fairlies three.

'O see not ye yon narrow road,   *45*
   So thick beset wi thorns and briers?
That is the path of righteousness,
   Tho after it but few enquires.

'And see not ye that braid braid road,
   That lies across yon lillie leven?   *50*
That is the path of wickedness,
   Tho some call it the road to heaven.

'And see not ye that bonny road,
  Which winds about the fernie brae?
That is the road to fair Elfland,   *55*
  Whe[re] you and I this night maun gae.

'But Thomas, ye maun hold your tongue,
  Whatever you may hear or see,
For gin ae word you should chance to speak,
  You will neer get back to your ain countrie.'   *60*

He has gotten a coat of the even cloth,
  And a pair of shoes of velvet green,
And till seven years were past and gone
  True Thomas on earth was never seen.
    ANONYMOUS (CHILD BALLAD NO. 37)

The Wild Swans at Coole

The trees are in their autumn beauty,   *1*
The woodland paths are dry,
Under the October twilight the water
Mirrors a still sky;
Upon the brimming water among the stones   *5*
Are nine-and-fifty swans.

The nineteenth autumn has come upon me
Since I first made my count;
I saw, before I had well finished,
All suddenly mount   *10*
And scatter wheeling in great broken rings
Upon their clamorous wings.

I have looked upon those brilliant creatures,
And now my heart is sore.
All's changed since I, hearing at twilight,   *15*
The first time on this shore,
The bell-beat of their wings above my head,
Trod with a lighter tread.

Unwearied still, lover by lover,
They paddle in the cold   *20*
Companionable streams or climb the air ;
Their hearts have not grown old ;
Passion or conquest, wander where they will,
Attend upon them still.

But now they drift on the still water,   *25*
Mysterious, beautiful ;
Among what rushes will they build,
By what lake's edge or pool
Delight men's eyes when I awake some day
To find they have flown away?   *30*

WILLIAM BUTLER YEATS

You, Andrew Marvell

And here face down beneath the sun   *1*
And here upon earth's noonward height
To feel the always coming on
The always rising of the night

To feel creep up the curving east   *5*
The earthy chill of dusk and slow
Upon those under lands the vast
And ever climbing shadow grow

And strange at Ecbatan the trees
Take leaf by leaf the evening strange   *10*
The flooding dark about their knees
The mountains over Persia change

And now at Kermanshah the gate
Dark empty and the withered grass
And through the twilight now the late   *15*
Few travelers in the westward pass

And Baghdad darken and the bridge
Across the silent river gone
And through Arabia the edge
Of evening widen and steal on   *20*

And deepen on Palmyra's street
The wheel rut in the ruined stone
And Lebanon fade out and Crete
High through the clouds and overblown

And over Sicily the air   *25*
Still flashing with the landward gulls
And loom and slowly disappear
The sails above the shadowy hulls

And Spain go under and the shore
Of Africa the gilded sand   *30*
And evening vanish and no more
The low pale light across that land

For now the long light on the sea

And here face downward in the sun
To feel how swift how secretly   *35*
The shadow of the night comes on . . .
                ARCHIBALD MACLEISH

12

POEMS WITH VARIANTS

A study of the changes made by poets in their work can be useful to the student in two ways. It can furnish valuable training in critical judgment, and it can give insight into the operation of the creative process. Hopkins' "Harry Ploughman" offers a good example. In Chapter 11 (pages 222–229) we studied the finished poem. Now, through an examination of the holograph on p. 239, let us study the most significant changes made by the poet in working out the final form.

Line 3. *Knee-bank* becomes *knee-nave*. This change serves three purposes. The metaphor *nave*, that is, the hub of a wheel, suggests strength and presents an image of the round, knob-like character of Harry's knee. The initial *n* brings into the poem another alliteration. The substitution also creates an assonance of similarity in the words *thigh; knee-nave*.

Line 4. *Grey* is added to describe *eye*. It may be helpful here to consider the appropriateness of blue, brown, green, or grey as descriptive of the eyes of a man of strength. But *grey* has also a phonetic purpose. In combination with *eye* and *heed* it repeats with variation the assonance of *thigh; knee-nave* in line 3, making a subtle addition to the musical pleasure.

Line 11. *Windloft or* becomes *in a wind lifted*. Since the word *loft*,

Harry Ploughman

Hard as hurdle arms, with a broth of goldish flue
Breathed round; the rack of ribs; the scooped flank;
            lank
Rope-over thigh; knee-bank, and barrelled shank—
          Head and foot, shoulder and shank—
By a grey eye's heel stirred, one crew, fall to;
stand at stress. Each limb's barrowy brawn, his thew
that onewhere curded, onewhere sucked or sank—
                soared or sank—
Though as a beechbole firm, finds his, as at a rollcall,
          rank
and features, in flesh, what deed he each must do—
          His sinew-service there do.

He leans to it, Harry bends, look. Back, elbow, and
         liquid waist
In him, all quail to the wallowing o' the plough. 'S
          cheek crimsons; curls
Wag or crossbridle, in a wind lifted, windlaced—
          see his wind- lilylocks-laced;
Churlsgrace, too, child of Amansstrength, how it
         hangs or hurls

these   Broad in bluff hide his frowning feet lashed!
them   raced
With, along them, cragiron under and cold furls—
         With-a-wet-fire-flushed furls.

Dromore Sept. 1887

meaning raised aloft, is obsolete, the change produces greater intelligibility. Furthermore the strong stresses on *wind* and *loft* are too heavy for the sense; whereas the new phrase with two light stresses at the beginning and another light stress at the end is more appropriate to the sense of the words.

Lines 14 and 14R. *Flame* becomes *cold* and *With-a-wet-fire-flushed-furls* becomes *With-a-fountain's shining-shot furls.* Here is a complete change of imagery. In the older version *flame furls* conveys vividly the movement of the rolls of earth rising from the plow. *Wet-fire-flushed* is a daring paradoxical metaphor; *Wet* describes the glistening moisture of the earth, and *fire-flushed* perhaps suggests a ruddiness reflected from the sky. However, the poet may have felt that the words *flame* and *fire,* with their suggestions of heat, were inappropriate because the rest of the poem pictures a cold scene. In the revised version the word *cold* fits the scene. And the fountain metaphor, with wholly different imagery, retains the movement, wetness, and shininess of the original picture.

One can never be sure, in studying variants, why a poet has made his revisions. But the process of evaluating the effects produced by different versions can help to increase one's sensitivity to poetry. It is with this thought in mind that the following poems with variants are offered. Only the more significant variants are included here. Words that have been rejected by the poet are enclosed in brackets following the wording finally chosen. Complete lines that have been rejected are bracketed and designated by R after the line number. Other editorial matter is self-explanatory.

She Dwelt Among the Untrodden Ways

[First stanza rejected:]
[My hope was one, from cities far,
Nursed on a lonesome heath;
Her lips were red as roses are,
Her hair a woodbine wreath.]

She dwelt among the untrodden ways	*1*
Beside the springs of Dove,	*2*
A Maid whom there were none to praise	*3*
And very few to love:	*4*
A violet by a mossy stone	*5*

Half hidden from the eye!   *6*
—Fair as a star, when only one   *7*
  Is shining in the sky.   *8*
    [Fourth stanza rejected:]

[And she was graceful as the broom
That flowers by Carron's side;
But slow distemper checked her bloom,
And on the Heath she died.]

She lived unknown, and few could know   *9*
  When Lucy ceased to be;   *10*
But she is in her grave, and oh,   *11*
[Long time before her head lay low   **9R**
Dead to the world was she: **10R**
But now she's etc.]   **11R**
  The difference to me!   *12*

    WILLIAM WORDSWORTH

The Lads in Their Hundreds

The lads in their hundreds to Ludlow come in for the fair,   *1*
  There's men from the barn and the forge and the mill
    and the fold,   *2*
The lads for the girls and the lads for the liquor are there, *3*
  And there with the rest are the lads that will never be old. *4*

There's chaps from the town and the field and the till and
    the cart,   *5*
  And many to count are the stalwart, and many the brave, *6*
And many the handsome of face and the handsome of heart,   *7*
  And few that will carry their looks or their truth to the
    grave.   *8*

I wish one could know them, I wish there were tokens to tell *9*
  The fortunate fellows that now you can never discern; *10*
And then one could talk with them friendly and wish them
    farewell   *11*
  And watch them depart on the way that they will not re-
    turn.   *12*

But now you may stare as you like and there's nothing to
    scan ;   *13*
    And brushing your elbow unguessed-at and not to be told   *14*
They carry back bright to the coiner the mintage of man,   *15*
[They carry unspoilt into safety the honour of man,]   **15R**
    The lads that will die in their glory and never be old.   *16*

A. E. HOUSMAN

Sailing to Byzantium [FINAL VERSION]

I

That is no country for old men. The young   *1*
In one another's arms, birds in the trees   *2*
—Those dying generations—at their song,   *3*
The salmon-falls, the mackerel-crowded seas,   *4*
Fish, flesh, or fowl, commend all summer long   *5*
Whatever is begotten, born, and dies.   *6*
Caught in that sensual music all neglect   *7*
Monuments of unaging intellect.   *8*

II

An aged man is but a paltry thing,   *9*
A tattered coat upon a stick, unless   *10*
Soul clap its hands and sing, and louder sing   *11*
For every tatter in its mortal dress,   *12*
Nor is there singing school but studying   *13*
Monuments of its own magnificence ;   *14*
And therefore I have sailed the seas and come   *15*
To the holy city of Byzantium.   *16*

III

O sages standing in God's holy fire   *17*
As in the gold mosaic of a wall,   *18*
Come from the holy fire, perne in a gyre,   *19*
And be the singing-masters of my soul.   *20*
Consume my heart away ; sick with desire   *21*
And fastened to a dying animal   *22*
It knows not what it is ; and gather me   *23*
Into the artifice of eternity.   *24*

IV

Once out of nature I shall never take	25
My bodily form from any natural thing,	26
But such a form as Grecian goldsmiths make	27
Of hammered gold and gold enamelling	28
To keep a drowsy Emperor awake;	29
Or set upon a golden bough to sing	30
To lords and ladies of Byzantium	31
Of what is past, or passing, or to come.	32

WILLIAM BUTLER YEATS

Sailing to Byzantium [EARLY VERSIONS]

FIRST STANZA

A.   All in this land—my Maker that is play
　　 Or else asleep upon His Mother's knees,
　　 Others that as the mountain people say
　　 Are at their hunting and their gallantries
　　 Under the hills, as in our fathers' day
　　 The changing colours of the hills and seas
　　 All that men know or think they know, being young,
　　 Cry that my tale is told, my story sung.

B.   Here all is young; the chapel walls display
　　 An infant sleeping on his Mother's knees,
　　 Weary with toil Teig sleeps till break of day
　　 This other wearied with night's gallantries
　　 Sleeps the morning and the noon away
　　 And I have toiled and loved until I slept
　　 A slumbering labyrinth and leaves a snail
　　 Scrawl upon the mirror of the soul.

SECOND STANZA

A.   I therefore travel towards Byzantium
　　 Among these sun-brown pleasant mariners
　　 Another dozen days and we shall come
　　 Under the jetty and the marble stair

B.   But now these pleasant dark-skinned mariners
     Carry me towards that great Byzantium
     Where all is ancient, singing at the oars
     That I may look in the great church's dome
     On gold-embedded saints and emperors
     After the mirroring waters and the foam
     Where the dark drowsy fins a moment rise
     Of fish that carry souls to paradise.

THIRD STANZA

Transfigured saints that move amid the fire
As in the gold mosaic of a wall
Reform this heart and make it what you were
Unwavering, (unfaltering), indifferent, fanatical,
It faints upon the road sick with desire
But fastened to this dying animal
Or send the dolphins back and gather me
Into the artifice of eternity.

FOURTH STANZA

The sensuous dream being past I shall not take
A guttering form of nature's fashioning
But rather that the Grecian smithies make
Of hammered gold and gold enamelling
At the Emperor's order for his lady's sake
And set upon a golden bough to sing
To lords and ladies of Byzantium
Of what is past or passing or to come.

                                    WILLIAM BUTLER YEATS

Leda and the Swan

A sudden blow: the great wings beating still   *1*
Above the staggering girl, her thighs caressed   *2*
By the dark webs, her nape caught in his bill,   *3*
He holds her helpless breast upon his breast.   *4*

How can those terrified vague fingers push   5
The feathered glory from her loosening thighs?   6
And how can body, laid in that white rush,   7
But feel the strange heart beating where it lies?   8

[A rush, a sudden wheel and hovering still   *1R*
The bird descends, and her frail thighs are pressed   *2R*
By the webbed toes, and that all powerful bill   *3R*
Has laid her helpless face upon his breast.   *4R*
How can those terrified vague fingers push   *5R*
The feathered glory from her loosening thighs!   *6R*
All the stretched body's laid on the white rush   *7R*
And feels the strange heart beating where it lies.]   *8R*

A shudder in the loins engenders there   9
The broken wall, the burning roof and tower   10
And Agamemnon dead.   11
        Being so caught up,
So mastered by the brute blood of the air,   *12*
Did she put on his knowledge with his power   *13*
Before the indifferent beak could let her drop?   *14*

WILLIAM BUTLER YEATS

On First Looking into Chapman's Homer

Much have I travell'd in the realms of gold,   *1*
   And many goodly states and kingdoms seen;   *2*
   Round many western islands have I been   *3*
Which bards in fealty to Apollo hold.   *4*
Oft of one wide expanse had I been told   5
   That deep- [low-] brow'd Homer rul'd as his desmesne;   6
   Yet did I never breathe its pure serene   7
   [Yet could I never judge what men could mean][1]   *7R*
Till I heard Chapman speak out loud and bold: 8

---

[1] Charles Cowden Clark said that the seventh line stood originally:
     "Yet could I never tell what men could mean"
and that Keats made a change to the present reading because he considered
the first reading "bald, and too simply wondering."

Then felt **I** like some watcher of the skies   *9*
  When a new planet swims into his ken;   *10*
Or like stout Cortez when with eagle [wond'ring] eyes[2]   *11*
  He star'd at the Pacific—and all his men   *12*
Look'd at each other with a wild surmise—   *13*
  Silent, upon a peak in Darien.   *14*

JOHN KEATS

To Autumn

1

Season of mists and mellow fruitfulness,   *1*
  Close bosom-friend of the maturing sun;   *2*
Conspiring with him how to load and bless   *3*
  With fruit the vines that round the thatch-eves run;   *4*
  [The vines with fruit that round the thatch eves run;]   *4R*
To bend with apples the moss'd cottage-trees,   *5*
  And fill all fruit [fruits] with ripeness [sweetness] to
    the core;   *6*
    To swell the gourd, and plump the hazel shells   *7*
  With a sweet [white] kernel; to set budding more,   *8*
And still more, later flowers for the bees,   *9*
Until they think warm days will never cease,   *10*
    For summer has o'erbrimm'd their clammy cells.   *11*

2

Who hath not seen thee oft amid thy store [stores]?   *1*
[Who hath not seen thee? for thy haunts are many]   *1R*
Sometimes whoever seeks abroad [for thee] may find   *2*
Thee sitting careless on a granary floor,   *3*
  Thy hair soft-lifted by the winnowing wind;   *4*
Or on a half-reap'd furrow sound asleep,   *5*
  Drows'd [Dos'd] with the fume of poppies, while thy
    hook   *6*
    Spares the next swath [sheath] and all its twined
      [honied] flowers: *7*
    [Spares for some slumbrous minutes the next swath;]   *7R*

---

[2] The editors of Keats, H. Buxton Forman and Maurice Buxton Forman, quote Leigh Hunt: "His 'eagle eyes' [those of Cortez] are from life, as may be seen by Titian's portrait of him."

Cancelled passage after line 4:

> [While bright the Sun slants through the husky barn;—
>   Or sound asleep in a half-reaped field
> Dosed with red poppies; while thy reaping hook
>   Spares form some slumbrous minutes while warm slumbers creep]

And sometimes like a gleaner thou dost keep	*8*
Steady thy laden [leaden] head across a brook;	*9*
Or by a cyder-press, with patient look,	*10*
Thou watchest the last oozings hours by hours.	*11*

3

Where are the songs of Spring? Ay, where are they?	*1*
Think not of them, thou hast thy music too,—	*2*
While barred clouds bloom the soft-dying day,	*3*
And touch the stubble-plains with rosy hue;	*4*
[While a gold cloud gilds the soft dying day	*3R*
Touching the the stubble plains with rosy hue—]	*4R*
Then in a wailful choir the small gnats mourn	*5*
Among the river sallows, borne aloft	*6*
Or sinking as the light wind lives or dies;	*7*
And full-grown lambs loud bleat from hilly bourn;	*8*
Hedge-crickets sing; and now with treble soft [now again full soft]	*9*
The red-breast whistles from a garden-croft;	*10*
And gathering swallows twitter in the skies.	*11*

JOHN KEATS

Ode to a Nightingale

1

My heart aches, and a drowsy [painful] numbness pains	*1*
My sense, as though of hemlock I had drunk,	*2*
Or emptied some dull opiate to the drains	*3*
One minute past [hence], and Lethe-wards had sunk:	*4*

'Tis not through envy of thy happy lot,   *5*
  But being too happy in thine happiness,—   *6*
    That thou, light-winged Dryad of the trees,   *7*
      In some melodious plot   *8*
  Of beechen green, and shadows numberless,   *9*
    Singest of summer in full-throated ease.   *10*

2

O, for a draught of vintage! that hath been   *1*
  Cool'd a long age in the deep-delved earth,   *2*
Tasting of Flora and the country green,   *3*
  Dance, and Provençal song, and sunburnt mirth!   *4*
O for a beaker full of the warm South,   *5*
  Full of the true, the blushful Hippocrene,   *6*
    With beaded [cluster'd] bubbles winking at the brim,   *7*
      And purple-stained mouth;   *8*
  That I might drink, and leave the world unseen,   *9*
    And with thee fade away into the forest dim:[3]   *10*

3

Fade far away, dissolve, and quite forget   *1*
  What thou among the leaves hast never known,   *2*
The weariness, the fever, and the fret   *3*
  Here, where men sit and hear each other groan;   *4*
Where palsy shakes a few, sad, last gray hairs,   *5*
  Where youth grows pale, and spectre-thin, and dies;   *6*
  [Where youth grows pale and thin and old and dies]   *6R*
    Where but to think is to be full of sorrow [grief]   *7*
      And leaden-eyed despairs,   *8*
  Where Beauty cannot keep her lustrous eyes,   *9*
    Or new Love pine at them beyond to-morrow.   *10*

4

Away! away! for I will fly to thee,   *1*
  Not charioted by Bacchus and his pards,   *2*
But on the viewless wings of Poesy,   *3*
  Though the dull brain perplexes and retards: *4*

---

[3] The word *away* is absent from some versions, but was included in the
version finally given forth by Keats.

Already with thee! tender is the night,   *5*
  And haply the Queen-Moon is on her throne,   *6*
    Cluster'd around by all her starry Fays;   *7*
      But here there is no light,   *8*
Save what from heaven is with the breezes blown   *9*
  [Sidelong] Through verdurous glooms and winding
    mossy ways.   *10*

5

I cannot see [tell] what flowers are at my feet,   *1*
  Nor what sweet incense hangs upon the boughs,   *2*
But, in embalmed darkness, guess each sweet   *3*
  Wherewith the seasonable month endows   *4*
The grass, the thicket, and the fruit-tree wild;   *5*
  White hawthorn, and the pastoral eglantine;   *6*
    Fast fading violets cover'd up in leaves;   *7*
      And mid-May's eldest child,   *8*
  The coming musk-rose, full of dewy [sweetest] wine,   *9*
    The murmurous haunt of flies on summer eves.   *10*

6

Darkling I listen; and, for many a time   *1*
  I have been half in love with easeful Death,   *2*
Call'd him soft names in many a mused rhyme,   *3*
  To take into the air my quiet [painless] breath;   *4*
Now more than ever seems it rich to die,   *5*
  To cease upon the midnight with no pain,   *6*
    While thou are pouring forth thy soul abroad   *7*
      In such an ecstasy!   *8*
  Still wouldst thou sing, and I have ears in vain—   *9*
    To thy high requiem become a sod.   *10*

7

Thou wast not born for death, immortal Bird!   *1*
  No hungry generations tread thee down;   *2*
The voice I hear this passing night was heard   *3*
  In ancient days by emperor and clown: *4*

Perhaps the self-same song [voice] that found a path 5
  Through the sad heart of Ruth, when, sick for home, 6
    She stood in tears amid the alien corn; 7
      The same that oft-times hath 8
  Charm'd magic [the wide] casements, opening on the
    foam 9
    Of perilous [keelless] seas, in faery [fairy] lands for-
      lorn. 10

8

Forlorn! the very word is like a bell 1
  To toll me back from thee to my sole self! 2
  [To toll me back from thee unto myself] 2R
Adieu! the fancy cannot cheat so well 3
  As she is fam'd to do, deceiving [deceitful] elf. 4
Adieu! adieu! thy plaintive anthem fades 5
  Past the near meadows, over the still stream, 6
    Up the hill-side; and now 'tis buried deep 7
      In the next valley-glades: 8
  Was it a vision, or a waking dream? 9
    Fled is that music:—Do I wake or sleep? 10

JOHN KEATS

The Tiger [FINAL VERSION]

Tiger! Tiger! burning bright   1
In the forests of the night,
What immortal hand or eye
Could frame thy fearful symmetry?

In what distant deeps or skies   2
Burnt the fire of thine eyes?
On what wings dare he aspire?
What the hand dare seize the fire?

And what shoulder, and what art,   3
Could twist the sinews of thy heart?
And when thy heart began to beat,
What dread hand? and what dread feet?

What the hammer? what the chain?   *4*
In what furnace was thy brain?
What the anvil? what dread grasp
Dare its deadly terrors clasp?

When the stars threw down their spears,   *5*
And water'd heaven with their tears,
Did he smile his work to see?
Did he who made the Lamb make thee?

Tiger! Tiger! burning bright   *6*
In the forests of the night,
What immortal hand or eye,
Dare frame thy fearful symmetry?

WILLIAM BLAKE

The Tiger

[ORIGINAL DRAFT FROM ROSSETTI MANUSCRIPT]

Tyger Tyger burning bright   *1*
In the forests of the night
What immortal hand & eye
                   or
~~Could~~ frame thy fearful symmetry
~~Dare~~

~~In what~~ distant deeps or skies   *2*
~~Burnt in~~
~~Burnt the~~ fire of thine eyes
~~The cruel~~
On what wings dare he aspire
What the hand dare sieze the fire

[Revised]   *2*
~~Burnt in distant deeps or skies~~
~~The cruel fire of thine eyes~~
~~Could heart descend or wings aspire~~
~~What the hand dare sieze the fire~~

And what shoulder & what art   *3*
Could twist the sinews of thy heart
And when thy heart began to beat
What dread hand & what dread feet

~~Could fetch it from the furnace deep~~
~~And in thy horrid ribs dare steep~~
~~In the well of sanguine woe~~
~~In what clay & in what mould~~
~~Were thy eyes of fury rolld~~

~~What~~ the hammer ~~what~~ the chain   *4*
~~Where~~   ~~where~~
In what furnace was thy brain
What the anvil What ~~the arm~~
              ~~arm~~
              ~~grasp~~
              ~~clasp~~
        dread grasp
~~Could~~ its deadly terrors ~~clasp~~
Dare   ~~grasp~~
           clasp

And ~~did he laugh~~ his work to see   *3*   *5*
     dare he ~~smile~~
        ~~laugh~~
~~What the shoulder~~ ~~what the knee~~
       ~~ankle~~
~~Did~~ he who made the lamb make thee   *4*
Dare
When the stars threw down their spears   *1*
And waterd heaven with their tears   *2*

Tyger Tyger burning bright   *6*
In the forests of the night
What immortal hand & eye
Dare ~~form~~ thy fearful symmetry
    frame

WILLIAM BLAKE

Lightning [FINAL VERSION]

I felt the lurch and halt of her heart	*1*
Next my breast, where my own heart was beating;	*2*
And I laughed to feel it plunge and bound,	*3*
And strange in my blood-swept ears was the sound	*4*
Of the words I kept repeating,	*5*
Repeating with tightened arms, and the hot blood's blindfold art.	*6*

Her breath flew warm against my neck,	*7*
Warm as a flame in the close night air;	*8*
And the sense of her clinging flesh was sweet	*9*
Where her arms and my neck's thick pulse could meet.	*10*
Holding her thus, could I care	*11*
That the black night hid her from me, blotted out every speck?	*12*

I leaned in the darkness to find her lips	*13*
And claim her utterly in a kiss,	*14*
When the lightning flew across her face	*15*
And I saw her for the flaring space	*16*
Of a second, like snow that slips	*17*
From a roof, inert with death, weeping "Not this! Not this!"	*18*

A moment there, like snow in the dark	*19*
Her face lay pale against my breast,	*20*
Pale love lost in a thaw of fear	*21*
And melted in an icy tear,	*22*
And open lips, distressed;	*23*
A moment; then darkness shut the lid of the sacred ark.	*24*

And I heard the thunder, and felt the rain,	*25*
And my arms fell loose, and I was dumb.	*26*
Almost I hated her, sacrificed;	*27*
Hated myself, and the place, and the iced	*28*
Rain that burnt on my rage; saying: Come	*29*
Home, come home, the lightning has made it too plain!	*30*

D. H. LAWRENCE

Lightning

[EARLY VERSION]

I felt the lurch and halt of her heart   *1*
  Next my breast, where my own heart was beating;   *2*
And I laughed to feel it plunge and bound,   *3*
And strange in my blood-swept ears was the sound   *4*
  Of the words I kept repeating,   *5*
Repeating with tightened arms, and the hot blood's blindfold
    art.   *6*

Her breath flew warm against my neck,   *7*
  Warm as a flame in the close night air;   *8*
And the sense of her clinging flesh was sweet   *9*
Where her arms and my neck's blood-surge could meet.   *10*
  Holding her thus, did I care   *11*
That the black night hid her from me, blotted out every
    speck?   *12*

I leaned me forward to find her lips,   *13*
  And claim her utterly in a kiss,   *14*
When the lightning flew across her face,   *15*
And I saw her for the flaring space   *16*
  Of a second, afraid of the clips   *17*
Of my arms, inert with dread, wilted in fear of my kiss.   *18*

A moment, like a wavering spark,   *19*
  Her face lay there before my breast,   *20*
Pale love lost in a snow of fear,   *21*
And guarded by a glittering tear,   *22*
  And lips apart with dumb cries;   *23*
A moment, and she was taken again in the merciful dark.   *24*

I heard the thunder, and felt the rain,   *25*
  And my arms fell loose, and I was dumb.   *26*
Almost I hated her, she was so good,   *27*

Hated myself, and the place, and my blood,   *28*
    Which burned with rage, as I bade her come   *29*
Home, away home, ere the lightning floated forth again.   *30*

D. H. LAWRENCE

The House on the Hill

They are all gone away,   *1*
    The House is shut and still,   *2*
There is nothing more to say.   *3*

Through broken walls and gray   *4*
    The winds blow bleak and shrill: *5*
They are all gone away.   *6*

Nor is there one to-day   *7*
    To speak them good or ill: *8*
There is nothing more to say.   *9*

[Malign them as we may,   *4R*
    We cannot do them ill,   *5R*
They are all gone away.   *6R*

Are we more fit than they   *7R*
    To meet the Master's will?   *8R*
There is nothing more to say.]   *9R*

Why is it then we stray   *10*
    Around the sunken sill?   *11*
They are all gone away,   *12*

And our poor fancy-play   *13*
    For them is wasted skill: *14*
There is nothing more to say.   *15*

There is ruin and decay   *16*
    In the House on the Hill: *17*
They are all gone away,   *18*
There is nothing more to say.   *19*

EDWIN ARLINGTON ROBINSON

Elegy Written in a Country Church-Yard

The following is the final version of Gray's elegy as it appeared in the first collected edition, published by Dodsley in 1768. The variants here given in brackets are taken from those of two manuscripts and three printed versions which stand between the Eton text and the present one. The Eton text begins on page 260.

The Curfew tolls the knell of parting day,	*1*
The lowing herd wind slowly o'er the lea,	*2*
The plowman homeward plods his weary way,	*3*
And leaves the world to darkness and to me.	*4*
Now fades the glimmering landscape on the sight,	*5*
And all the air a solemn stillness holds,	*6*
Save where the beetle wheels his droning flight,	*7*
And drowsy tinklings lull the distant folds;	*8*
Save that from yonder ivy-mantled tow'r	*9*
The mopeing owl does to the moon complain	*10*
Of such, as wand'ring near her secret [sacred] bow'r,	*11*
Molest her ancient solitary reign.	*12*
Beneath those rugged elms, that yew-tree's shade,	*13*
Where heaves the turf in many a mould'ring heap,	*14*
Each in his narrow cell for ever laid,	*15*
The rude Forefathers of the hamlet sleep.	*16*
The breezy call of incense-breathing Morn,	*17*
The swallow twitt'ring from the straw-built shed,	*18*
The cock's shrill clarion, or the echoing horn,	*19*
No more shall rouse [wake] them from their lowly bed.	*20*
For them no more the blazing hearth shall burn,	*21*
Or busy housewife ply her evening care:	*22*
No children run to lisp their sire's return,	*23*
Or climb his knees the envied kiss to share.	*24*

Oft did the harvest to their sickle yield,   *25*
Their furrow oft the stubborn glebe has broke;   *26*
How jocund did they drive their team afield!   *27*
How bow'd the woods beneath their sturdy stroke!   *28*

Let not Ambition mock their useful toil,   *29*
Their homely joys, and destiny obscure;   *30*
Nor Grandeur hear with a disdainful smile,   *31*
The short and simple annals of the poor.   *32*

The boast of heraldry, the pomp of pow'r,   *33*
And all that beauty, all that wealth e'er gave,   *34*
Awaits alike th' inevitable hour.   *35*
The paths of glory lead but to the grave.   *36*

Nor you, ye Proud, impute to These the fault,   *37*
If Mem'ry o'er their Tomb no Trophies raise,   *38*
Where thro' the long-drawn isle and fretted vault   *39*
The pealing anthem swells the note of praise.   *40*

Can storied urn or animated bust   *41*
Back to its mansion call the fleeting breath?   *42*
Can Honour's voice provoke the silent dust,   *43*
Or Flatt'ry sooth the dull cold ear of Death?   *44*

Perhaps in this neglected spot is laid   *45*
Some heart once pregnant with celestial fire;   *46*
Hands, that the rod of empire might have sway'd,   *47*
Or wak'd to extasy the living lyre.   *48*

But Knowledge to their eyes her ample page   *49*
Rich with the spoils of time did ne'er unroll;   *50*
Chill Penury repress'd their noble rage,   *51*
And froze the genial current of the soul.   *52*

Full many a gem of purest ray serene,   *53*
The dark unfathom'd caves of ocean bear: *54*
Full many a flower is born to blush unseen,   *55*
And waste its sweetness on the desert air.   *56*

Some village-Hampden, that with dauntless breast   *57*
The little Tyrant of his fields [lands] withstood;   *58*
Some mute inglorious Milton here may rest,   *59*
Some Cromwell guiltless of his country's blood.   *60*

Th'applause of list'ning senates to command,   *61*
The threats of pain and ruin to despise,   *62*
To scatter plenty o'er a smiling land,   *63*
And read their hist'ry in a nation's eyes,   *64*

Their lot forbad: nor circumscrib'd alone   *65*
Their growing virtues, but their crimes confin'd;   *66*
Forbad to wade through slaughter to a throne,   *67*
And shut the gates of mercy on mankind,   *68*

The struggling pangs of conscious truth to hide,   *69*
To quench the blushes of ingenuous shame,   *70*
Or heap the shrine of Luxury and Pride   *71*
With incense kindled at the Muse's flame.   *72*

Far from the madding crowd's ignoble strife,   *73*
Their sober wishes never learn'd to stray;   *74*
Along the cool sequester'd vale of life   *75*
They kept the noiseless tenor of their way.   *76*

Yet ev'n these bones from insult to protect   *77*
Some frail memorial still erected nigh,   *78*
With uncouth rhimes and shapeless sculpture deck'd,   *79*
Implores the passing tribute of a sigh.   *80*

Their name, their years, spelt by th'unletter'd muse,   *81*
The place of fame and elegy [Epitaph] supply: *82*
And many a holy text around she strews,   *83*
That teach the rustic moralist to die.   *84*

For who to dumb Forgetfulness a prey,   *85*
This pleasing anxious being e'er resigned,   *86*
Left the warm precincts of the chearful day,   *87*
Nor cast one longing ling'ring look behind?   *88*

On some fond breast the parting soul relies,   *89*
Some pious drops the closing eye requires;   *90*
Ev'n from the tomb the voice of Nature cries,   *91*
Ev'n in our Ashes live their wonted Fires.   *92*
[And in our ashes glow their wonted Fires.]   *92R*
[Awake, and faithful to her wonted Fires.]   *92R*

For thee, who mindful of th'unhonour'd Dead   *93*
Dost in these lines their artless tale relate;   *94*
If chance, by lonely contemplation led,   *95*
Some kindred [hidden] Spirit shall inquire thy Fate, *96*

Haply some hoary-headed Swain may say,   *97*
'Oft have we seen him at the peep of dawn   *98*
'Brushing with hasty steps the dews away   *99*
'To meet the sun upon the upland lawn.   *100*

'There at the foot of yonder nodding beech   *101*
'That wreathes its old fantastic roots so high,   *102*
'His listless length at noontide would he stretch,   *103*
'And pore upon the brook that babbles by.   *104*

'Hard by yon wood, now smiling [frowning] as in scorn,   *105*
'Mutt'ring his wayward fancies he would rove,   *106*
'Now drooping, woeful wan, like one forlorn,   *107*
'Or craz'd with care, or cross'd in hopeless love.   *108*

'One morn I miss'd him on the custom'd hill,   *109*
'Along the heath and near his fav'rite tree;   *110*
'Another came; nor yet beside the rill,   *111*
'Nor up the lawn, nor at the wood was he;   *112*

'The next with dirges due in sad array   *113*
'Slow thro' the church-way path we saw him born.   *114*
'Approach and read (for thou can'st read) the lay,   *115*
'Grav'd on the stone beneath yon aged thorn.'   *116*

THE EPITAPH

Here rests his head upon the lap of Earth	*117*
A Youth to Fortune and to Fame unknown.	*118*
Fair Science frown'd not on his humble birth,	*119*
And Melancholy mark'd him for her own.	*120*
Large was his bounty, and his soul sincere,	*121*
Heav'n did a recompence as largely send:	*122*
He gave to Mis'ry all he had, a tear,	*123*
He gain'd from Heav'n ('twas all he wish'd) a friend.	*124*
No farther seek his merits to disclose,	*125*
Or draw his frailties from their dread abode,	*126*
(There they alike in trembling hope repose,)	*127*
The bosom of his Father and his God.	*128*

THOMAS GRAY

Elegy Written in a Country Church-Yard

The following version of Gray's famous elegy is an early or first draft, preserved in Gray's handwriting in the Eton MS. The printing here corresponds with this manuscript in its indication of deletions and in its placement of added words below or above the line or in the margin. The line numbering is not a part of the original.

Stanzas Wrote in a Country Church-Yard

The Curfeu tolls the Knell of parting Day,	*1*
The lowing Herd wind slowly o'er the Lea,	*2*
The Plowman homeward plods his weary Way,	*3*
And leaves the World to Darkness & to me.	*4*
Now fades the glimm'ring Landscape on the Sight,	*5*
And now the Air a solemn Stillness holds;	*6*
Save, where the Beetle wheels his droning Flight,	*7*
Or drowsy Tinklings lull the distant Folds.	*8*

Save, that from yonder ivy-mantled Tower	*9*
The mopeing Owl does to the Moon complain	*10*

stray too

Of such as wand'ring near her secret Bower	*11*
& pry into	
Molest her ancient solitary Reign.	*12*

Beneath those rugged Elms, that Yewtree's Shade,	*13*
Where heaves the Turf in many a mould'ring Heap,	*14*
Each in his narrow Cell for ever laid	*15*

Hamlet

The rude Forefathers of the ~~Village~~ sleep.	*16*

For ever sleep: the breezy Call of Morn,	*17*
Or Swallow twitt'ring from the strawbuilt Shed,	*18*
Or Chaunticleer so shrill or ecchoing Horn,	*19*
No more shall rouse them from their lowly Bed.	*20*

For them no more the blazeing Hearth shall burn,	*21*
Or busy Huswife ply her Evening Care;	*22*
No children run to lisp their Sire's Return,	*23*

envied

Nor climb his Knees the coming Kiss to share.	*24* doubtful

Oft did the Harvest to their Sickle yield;	*25*
Their Furrow oft the stubborn Glebe has broke;	*26*
How jocund did they drive their Team a-field!	*27*
How bow'd the Woods beneath their sturdy Stroke!	*28*

Let not Ambition mock their useful Toil,	*29* homely
Their rustic Joys & Destiny obscure:	*30*
Nor Grandeur hear with a disdainful Smile	*31*
The short & simple Annals of the Poor.	*32*

The Boast of Heraldry the Pomp of Power,	*33*
And all, that Beauty, all that Wealth, e'er gave	*34*
Awaits alike th' inevitable Hour.	*35*
The Paths of Glory lead but to the Grave.	*36*

Forgive, ye Proud, th' involuntary Fault,   *37*
If Memory to these no Trophies raise,   *38*
Where thro' the long-drawn Ile, & fretted Vault   *39*
The pealing Anthem swells the Note of Praise.   *40*

Can storied Urn, or animated Bust,   *41*
Back to its Mansion call the fleeting Breath?   *42*
Can Honour's voice awake the silent dust,   *43* provoke
Or Flattery sooth the dull cold Ear of Death?   *44*

Perhaps in this neglected Spot is laid   *45*
Some Heart, once pregnant with celestial Fire,   *46*
Hands, that the Reins of Empire might have sway'd,   *47*
Or waked to Ecstasy the living Lyre: *48*

Some Village Cato   with dauntless Breast[4]   *49*
The little Tyrant of his Fields withstood;   *50*
Some mute inglorious Tully here may rest;   *51*
Some Caesar, guiltless of his Country's Blood.   *52*

But Knowledge to their eyes her ample Page,   *53*
Rich with the Spoils of Time, did ne'er unroll: *54*
                    repress'd
                    depress'd
Chill Penury had damp'd their noble Rage,   *55*
And froze the genial Current of the Soul.   *56*

Full many a Gem of purest Ray serene   *57*
The dark unfathom'd Caves of Ocean bear.   *58*
Full many a Flower is born to blush unseen   *59*
And wast its Sweetness on the desert Air.   *60*

Th'Applause of listening Senates to command,   *61*
The Threats of Pain & Ruin to despise,   *62*
To scatter Plenty o'er a smiling Land   *63*
And read their Hist'ry in a Nation's Eyes,   *64*

---

[4] Word lost in this line.

      Lot
Their Fate forbad: nor circumscribed alone   *65*
      growing
Their struggling Virtues, but their Crimes confined;   *66*
Forbad to wade thro' Slaughter to a Throne,   *67*
And shut the Gates of Mercy on Mankind   *68*

The struggleing Pangs of conscious Truth to hide,   *69*
To quench the Blushes of ingenuous Shame,   *70*
      crown
And at the Shrine of Luxury & Pride   *71*
With   by
~~Burn~~ Incense hallowd in the Muse's Flame.   *72*
      Kindled at

[The thoughtless World to Majesty may bow   *1R*
Exalt the brave, & idolize Success   *2R*
But more to Innocence their Safety owe   *3R*
Than Power & Genius e'er conspired to bless   *4R*

And thou, who mindful of the unhonour'd Dead   *5R*
      eir
Dost in these Notes th~~y~~ artless Tale relate   *6R*
By Night & lonely Contemplation led   *7R*
To linger in the gloomy Walks of Fate   *8R*

Hark how the sacred Calm, that broods around   *9R*
Bids ev'ry fierce tumultuous Passion cease   *10R*
In still small Accents whisp'ring from the Ground   *11R*
A grateful Earnest of eternal Peace   *12R*

No more with Reason & thyself at Strife;   *13R*
Give anxious Cares & endless Wishes room   *14R*
But thro' the cool sequester'd Vale of Life   *15R*
Pursue the silent Tenour of thy Doom.]   *16R*

Far from the madding Crowd's ignoble Strife,   *73*
Their sober Wishes never knew to stray: *74*
Along the cool sequester'd Vale of Life   *75*
      noiseless
They kept the silent Tenour of their Way.   *76*

Yet even these Bones from Insult to protect	*77*
Some frail Memorial still erected nigh	*78*
With uncouth Rhime, & shapeless Sculpture deckt	*79*
Implores the passing Tribute of a Sigh.	*80*

Their Name, their Years, spelt by th'unletter'd Muse	*81*
The Place of Fame, & Epitaph supply	*82*
And many a holy Text around she strews,	*83*
That teach the rustic Moralist to die.	*84*

For who to dumb Forgetfulness, a Prey,	*85*
This pleasing anxious Being e'er resign'd;	*86*
Left the warm Precincts of the chearful Day,	*87*
Nor cast one longing lingring Look behind?	*88*

On some fond Breast the parting Soul relies,	*89*
Some pious Drops the closing Eye requires:	*90*
Even from the Tomb the Voice of Nature cries,	*91*
And buried Ashes glow with Social Fires.	*92*

For Thee, who mindful of the unhonour'd Dead	*93*
Dost in these Notes their artless Tale relate	*94*
By Night & lonely Contemplation led	*95*
To linger in the gloomy Walks of Fate	*96*

If chance that e'er some pensive Spirit more,	*97*
By sympathetic Musings here delay'd,	*98*
With vain, tho' kind, Enquiry shall explore	*99*
Thy once-loved Haunt, this long-deserted Shade.	*100*

Haply some hoary headed Swain shall say,	*101*
Oft have we seen him at the Peep of Dawn	*102*
With hasty Footsteps brush the Dews away	*103*
On the high Brow of yonder hanging Lawn	*104*

Him have we seen the Green-wood Side along	*105*
While o'er the Heath we hied, our Labours done,	*106*
Oft as the Woodlark piped her farewell Song	*107*
With whistful Eyes pursue the setting Sun.	*108*

spreading
Oft at the Foot of yonder hoary Beech   *109* nodding
That wreathes its old fantastic Roots so high   *110*
His listless Length at Noontide would he stretch,   *111*
And pore upon the Brook that babbles by.   *112*

With Gestures quaint now smileing as in Scorn   *113*
                would he
          wayward fancies loved
Mutt'ring his fond Conceits wont to rove   *114*
     drooping
Now woeful wan, he droop'd, as one forlorn,   *115*
Or crazed with Care, or cross'd in hopeless Love.   *116*

One Morn we miss'd him on th' accustomed Hill,   *117*
Along
By the Heath-side and at his fav'rite Tree.   *118*
Another came, nor yet beside the Rill,   *119*
                by
Nor up the Lawn, nor at the Wood was he.   *120*

[There scatter'd oft, the earliest]   *R*

The next with Dirges meet in sad Array   *121*
     by
Slow thro the Church-way Path we saw him born   *122*
Approach & read, for thou can'st read the Lay   *123*
Graved carved   yon
Wrote on the Stone beneath that ancient Thorn: *124*
                Year
[There scatter'd oft the earliest of ye Spring   *1R*
                showers of
By Hands unseen are frequent Vi lets found   *2R*
     Redbreast
The Robin loves to build & warble there[5]   *3R*
And little Footsteps lightly print the Ground.]   *4R*
                The Epitaph

---

[5] Another copy of this stanza in Gray's handwriting gives *bill* for *build*.

Here rests his Head upon the Lap of Earth   *125*
A Youth to Fortune & to Fame unknown   *126*
Fair Science frown'd not on his humble birth   *127*
And Melancholy mark'd him for her own   *128*

Large was his Bounty & his Heart sincere;   *129*
Heaven did a Recompense as largely send.   *130*
He gave to Mis'ry all he had, a Tear.   *131*
He gained from Heav'n ; twas all he wish'd, a Friend   *132*

No further seek his Merits to disclose,   *133*
    think
Nor seek to draw them from their dread Abode   *134*
(His frailties there in trembling Hope repose)   *135*
The Bosom of his Father & his God.   *136*

THOMAS GRAY

POEMS FOR STUDY

Bonny Barbara Allan

It was in and about the Martinmas time,   *1*
   When the green leaves were a falling,
That Sir John Graeme, in the West Country,
   Fell in love with Barbara Allan.

He sent his man down through the town,   *5*
   To the place where she was dwelling:
'O haste and come to my master dear,
   Gin ye be Barbara Allan.'

O hooly, hooly rose she up,
   To the place where he was lying,   *10*
And when she drew the curtain by,
   'Young man, I think you're dying.'

'O it's I'm sick, and very, very sick,
   And 't is a' for Barbara Allan:'
'O the better for me ye's never be,   *15*
   Tho your heart's blood were a spilling.

'O dinna ye mind, young man,' said she,
   'When ye was in the tavern a drinking,
That ye made the healths gae round and round,
   And slighted Barbara Allan?'   *20*

He turnd his face unto the wall,
   And death was with him dealing:
'Adieu, adieu, my dear friends all,
   And be kind to Barbara Allan.'

And slowly, slowly raise she up,   *25*
   And slowly, slowly left him,
And sighing said, she coud not stay,
   Since death of life had reft him.

She had not gane a mile but twa,
   When she heard the dead-bell ringing,   *30*
And every jow that the dead-bell geid,
   It cry'd, Woe to Barbara Allan!

'O mother, mother, make my bed!
  O make it saft and narrow!
Since my love died for me to-day,   *35*
  I'll die for him to-morrow.'
     ANONYMOUS (CHILD BALLAD NO. 84)

Edward

'Why dois your brand sae drap wi bluid,   *1*
        Edward, Edward,
Why dois your brand sae drap wi bluid,
  And why sae sad gang yee O?'
'O I hae killed my hauke sae guid,   *5*
        Mither, mither,
O I hae killed my hauke sae guid,
  And I had nae mair bot hee O.'

'Your haukis bluid was nevir sae reid,
        Edward, Edward,   *10*
Your haukis bluid was nevir sae reid,
  My deir son I tell thee O.'
'O I hae killed my reid-roan steid,
        Mither, mither,
O I hae killed my reid-roan steid,   *15*
  That erst was sae fair and frie O.'

'Your steid was auld, and ye hae gat mair,
        Edward, Edward,
Your steid was auld, and ye hae gat mair,
  Sum other dule ye drie O.'   *20*
'O I hae killed my fadir deir,
        Mither, mither,
O I hae killed my fadir deir,
  Alas, and wae is mee O!'

'And whatten penance wul ye drie for that, *25*
        Edward, Edward?
And whatten penance will ye drie for that?
  My deir son, now tell me O.'

'Ile set my feit in yonder boat,
>> Mither, mither,   *30*
Ile set my feit in yonder boat,
  And Ile fare ovir the sea O.'

'And what wul ye doe wi your towirs and your ha,
>> Edward, Edward?
And what wul ye doe wi your towirs and your ha,   *35*
  That were sae fair to see O?'
'Ile let thame stand tul they doun fa,
>> Mither, mither,
Ile let thame stand tul they doun fa,
  For here nevir mair maun I bee O.'   *40*

'And what wul ye leive to your bairns and your wife,
>> Edward, Edward?
And what wul ye leive to your bairns and your wife,
  Whan ye gang ovir the sea O?'
'The warldis room, late them beg thrae life,   *45*
>> Mither, mither,
The warldis room, late them beg thrae life,
  For thame nevir mair wul I see O.'

'And what wul ye leive to your ain mither deir,
>> Edward, Edward?   *50*
And what wul ye leive to your ain mither deir?
  My deir son, now tell me O.'
'The curse of hell frae me sall ye beir,
>> Mither, mither,
The curse of hell frae me sall ye beir,   *55*
  Sic counseils ye gave to me O.'

ANONYMOUS (CHILD BALLAD NO. 13)

Fearewell Love and All Thy Lawes for Ever

Fearewell Love and all thy lawes for ever: *1*
  Thy bayted hookes shall tangill me no more;
  Senec and Plato call me from thy lore,
  To perfaict welth my wit for to endever.

In blynde error when I did persever,   5
   Thy sherpe repulse that pricketh ay so sore
   Hath taught me to sett in tryfels no store
   And scape fourth, syns libertie is lever.
Therefore farewell: goo trouble yonger hertes
   And in me clayme no more authoritie;   10
   With idill youth goo use thy propertie
And theron spend thy many brittil dertes;
   For hetherto though I have lost all my tyme
   Me lusteth no lenger rotten boughes to clymbe.

SIR THOMAS WYATT

SONNET LXXXI, *Amoretti*

Fayre is my love, when her fayre golden heares,   1
   with the loose wynd ye waving chance to marke:
   fayre when the rose in her red cheekes appeares,
   or in her eyes the fyre of love does sparke.
Fayre when her brest lyke a rich laden barke,   5
   with pretious merchandize she forth doth lay:
   fayre when that cloud of pryde, which oft doth dark
   her goodly light with smiles she drives away.
But fayrest she, when so she doth display,
   the gate with pearles and rubyes richly dight: 10
   throgh which her words so wise do make their way
   to beare the message of her gentle spright.
The rest be works of natures wonderment,
   but this the worke of harts astonishment.

EDMUND SPENSER

The Faerie Queene, BOOK II, CANTO XII

70

Eftsoones they heard a most melodious sound,   1
   Of all that mote delight a daintie eare,
   Such as attonce might not on living ground,
   Save in this Paradise, be heard elswhere:

Right hard it was, for wight, which did it heare,   5
To read, what manner musicke that mote bee:
For all that pleasing is to living eare,
Was there consorted in one harmonee,
Birdes, voyces, instruments, windes, waters, all agree.

71

The ioyous birdes shrouded in chearefull shade,   10
    Their notes unto the voyce attempred sweet;
Th'Angelicall soft trembling voyces made
To th'instruments divine respondence meet:
The silver sounding instruments did meet
With the base murmure of the waters fall: 15
The waters fall with difference discreet,
    Now soft, now loud, unto the wind did call:
The gentle warbling wind low answered to all.

72

There, whence that Musick seemed heard to bee,
    Was the faire Witch her selfe now solacing,   20
With a new Lover, whom through sorceree
And witchcraft, she from farre did thither bring:
There she had him now layd a slombering,
In secret shade, after long wanton ioyes:
Whilst round about them pleasauntly did sing   25
    Many faire Ladies, and lascivious boyes,
That ever mixt their song with light licentious toyes.

73

And all that while, right over him she hong,
    With her false eyes fast fixed in his sight,
As seeking medicine, whence she was stong,   30
Or greedily depasturing delight:
And oft inclining downe with kisses light,
    For feare of waking him, his lips bedewd,
And through his humid eyes did sucke his spright,
Quite molten into lust and pleasure lewd;   35
Wherewith she sighed soft, as if his case she rewd.

74

The whiles some one did chaunt this lovely lay;
   Ah see, who so faire thing doest faine to see,
   In springing flowre the image of thy day;
   Ah see the Virgin Rose, how sweetly shee   *40*
   Doth first peepe forth with bashfull modestee,
   That fairer seemes, the lesse ye see her may;
   Lo see soone after, how more bold and free
   Her bared bosome she doth broad display;
Loe see soone after, how she fades, and falles away.   *45*

75

So passeth, in the passing of a day,
   Of mortall life the leafe, the bud, the flowre,
   Ne more doth flourish after first decay,
   That earst was sought to decke both bed and bowre,
   Of many a Ladie, and many a Paramowre: *50*
   Gather therefore the Rose, whilest yet is prime,
   For soone comes age, that will her pride deflowre:
   Gather the Rose of love, whilest yet is time,
Whilest loving thou mayst loved be with equall crime.

76

He ceast, and then gan all the quire of birdes   *55*
   Their diverse notes t'attune unto his lay,
   As in approvance of his pleasing words.
   The constant paire heard all, that he did say,
   Yet swarved not, but kept their forward way,
   Through many covert groves, and thickets close,   *60*
   In which they creeping did at last display
   That wanton Ladie, with her lover lose,
Whose sleepie head she in her lap did soft dispose.

EDMUND SPENSER

Prothalamion

1

Calme was the day, and through the trembling ayre,   *1*
Sweet breathing *Zephyrus* did softly play
A gentle spirit, that lightly did delay
Hot *Titans* beames, which then did glyster fayre:

When I whom sullein care,   *5*
Through discontent of my long fruitlesse stay
In Princes Court, and expectation vayne
Of idle hopes, which still doe fly away,
Like empty shaddowes, did aflict my brayne,
Walkt forth to ease my payne   *10*
Along the shoare of silver streaming *Themmes*,
Whose rutty Bancke, the which his River hemmes,
Was paynted all with variable flowers,
And all the meades adornd with daintie gemmes,
Fit to decke maydens bowres,   *15*
And crowne their Paramours,
Against the Brydale day, which is not long:
    Sweete *Themmes* runne softly, till I end my Song.

2
There, in a Meadow, by the Rivers side,
A Flocke of *Nymphes* I chaunced to espy,   *20*
All lovely Daughters of the Flood thereby,
With goodly greenish locks all loose untyde,
As each had bene a Bryde,
And each one had a little wicker basket,
Made of fine twigs entrayled curiously,   *25*
In which they gathered flowers to fill their flasket:
And with fine Fingers, cropt full feateously
The tender stalkes on hye.
Of every sort, which in that Meadow grew,
They gathered some; the Violet pallid blew,   *30*
The little Dazie, that at evening closes,
The virgin Lillie, and the Primrose trew,
With store of vermeil Roses,
To decke their Bridegromes posies,
Against the Brydale day, which was not long: *35*
    Sweete *Themmes* runne softly, till I end my Song.

3
With that, I saw two Swannes of goodly hewe,
Come softly swimming downe along the Lee;
Two fairer Birds I yet did never see:

The snow which doth the top of *Pindus* strew,   *40*
Did never whiter shew,
Nor *Jove* himselfe when he a Swan would be
For love of *Leda*, whiter did appeare:
Yet *Leda* was they say as white as he,
Yet not so white as these, nor nothing neare;   *45*
So purely white they were,
That even the gentle streame, the which them bare,
Seem'd foule to them, and bad his billowes spare
To wet their silken feathers, least they might
Soyle their fayre plumes with water not so fayre   *50*
And marre their beauties bright,
That shone as heavens light,
Against their Brydale day, which was not long:
    Sweete *Themmes* runne softly, till I end my Song.

4

Eftsoones the *Nymphes*, which now had Flowers their fill,   *55*
Ran all in haste, to see that silver brood,
As they came floating on the Christal Flood.
Whom when they sawe, they stood amazed still,
Their wondring eyes to fill,
Them seem'd they never saw a sight so fayre,   *60*
Of Fowles so lovely, that they sure did deeme
Them heavenly borne, or to be that same payre
Which through the Skie draw *Venus* silver Teeme,
For sure they did not seeme
To be begot of any earthly Seede,   *65*
But rather Angels or of Angels breede:
Yet were they bred of *Somers-heat* they say,
In sweetest Season, when each Flower and weede
The earth did fresh aray,
So fresh they seem'd as day,   *70*
Even as their Brydale day, which was not long:
    Sweete *Themmes* runne softly, till I end my Song.

5

Then forth they all out of their baskets drew,
Great store of Flowers, the honour of the field,
That to the sense did fragrant odours yeild,   *75*

All which upon those goodly Birds they threw,
And all the Waves did strew,
That like old *Peneus* Waters they did seeme,
When downe along by pleasant *Tempes* shore
Scattred with Flowres, through *Thessaly* they streeme,   *80*
That they appeare through Lillies plenteous store,
Like a Brydes Chamber flore:
Two of those *Nymphes*, meane while, two Garlands bound,
Of freshest Flowres which in that Mead they found,
The which presenting all in trim Array,   *85*
Their snowie Foreheads therewithall they crownd,
Whil'st one did sing this Lay,
Prepar'd against that Day,
Against their Brydale day, which was not long:
    Sweete *Themmes* runne softly, till I end my Song.   *90*

6

Ye gentle Birdes, the worlds faire ornament,
And heavens glorie, whom this happie hower
Doth leade unto your lovers blisfull bower,
Ioy may you have and gentle hearts content
Of your loves couplement: *95*
And let faire *Venus*, that is Queene of love,
With her heart-quelling Sonne upon you smile,
Whose smile they say, hath vertue to remove
All Loves dislike, and friendships faultie guile
For ever to assoile.   *100*
Let endlesse Peace your steadfast hearts accord,
And blessed Plentie wait upon your bord,
And let your bed with pleasures chast abound,
That fruitfull issue may to you afford,
Which may your foes confound,   *105*
And make your ioyes redound,
Upon your Brydale day, which is not long:
    Sweete *Themmes* run softlie, till I end my Song.

7

So ended she; and all the rest around
To her redoubled that her undersong,   *110*
Which said, their bridale daye should not be long.

And gentle Eccho from the neighbour ground,
Their accents did resound.
So forth those ioyous Birdes did passe along,
Adowne the Lee, that to them murmurde low,   *115*
As he would speake, but that he lackt a tong
Yeat did by signes his glad affection show,
Making his streame run slow.
And all the foule which in his flood did dwell
Gan flock about these twaine, that did excell   *120*
The rest, so far, as *Cynthia* doth shend
The lesser starres. So they enranged well,
Did on those two attend,
And their best service lend,
Against their wedding day, which was not long: *125*
    Sweete *Themmes* run softly, till I end my song.

8

At length they all to mery *London* came,
To mery London, my most kyndly Nurse,
That to me gave this Lifes first native sourse:
Though from another place I take my name,   *130*
An house of auncient fame.
There when they came, whereas those bricky towres,
The which on *Themmes* brode aged backe doe ryde,
Where now the studious Lawyers have their bowers
There whylome wont the Templer Knights to byde,   *135*
Till they decayd through pride:
Next whereunto there standes a stately place,
Where oft I gayned giftes and goodly grace
Of that great Lord, which therein wont to dwell,
Whose want too well now feeles my freendles case: *140*
But Ah here fits not well
Olde woes but ioyes to tell
Against the bridale daye, which is not long:
    Sweete *Themmes* runne softly, till I end my Song.

9

Yet therein now doth lodge a noble Peer,   *145*

Great *Englands* glory and the Worlds wide wonder,
Whose dreadfull name, late through all *Spaine* did thunder,
And *Hercules* two pillors standing neere,
Did make to quake and feare:
Faire branch of Honor, flower of Chevalrie,   *150*
That fillest *England* with thy triumphs fame,
Ioy have thou of thy noble victorie,
And endlesse happinesse of thine owne name
That promiseth the same:
That through thy prowesse and victorious armes,   *155*
Thy country may be freed from forraine harmes:
And great *Elisaes* glorious name may ring
Through al the world, fil'd with thy wide Alarmes,
Which some brave muse may sing
To ages following,   *160*
Upon the Brydale day, which is not long:
    Sweete *Themmes* runne softly, till I end my Song.

10

From those high Towers, this noble Lord issuing,
Like Radiant *Hesper* when his golden hayre
In th'*Ocean* billowes he hath Bathed fayre,   *165*
Descended to the Rivers open vewing,
With a great traine ensuing.
Above the rest were goodly to bee seene
Two gentle Knights of lovely face and feature
Beseeming well the bower of anie Queene,   *170*
With gifts of wit and ornaments of nature,
Fit for so goodly stature:
That like the twins of *Iove* they seem'd in sight,
Which decke the Bauldricke of the Heavens bright.
They two forth pacing to the Rivers side,   *175*
Received those two faire Brides, their Loves delight,
Which at th'appointed tyde,
Each one did make his Bryde,
Against their Brydale day, which is not long:
    Sweete *Themmes* runne softly, till I end my Song.   *180*

The Passionate Shepherd to his Love

Come live with me and be my love,   *1*
And we will all the pleasures prove
That valleys, groves, hills, and fields,
Woods, or steepy mountain yields.

And we will sit upon the rocks,   *5*
Seeing the shepherds feed their flocks,
By shallow rivers to whose falls
Melodious birds sings madrigals.

And I will make thee beds of roses
And a thousand fragrant posies,   *10*
A cap of flowers, and a kirtle
Embroidered all with leaves of myrtle;

A gown made of the finest wool
Which from our pretty lambs we pull;
Fair lined slippers for the cold,   *15*
With buckles of the purest gold;

A belt of straw and ivy buds,
With coral clasps and amber studs:
And if these pleasures may thee move,
Come live with me, and be my love.   *20*

The shepherds' swains shall dance and sing
For thy delight each May morning:
If these delights thy mind may move,
Then live with me and be my love.

CHRISTOPHER MARLOWE

The Nymph's Reply to the Shepherd

If all the world and love were young,   *1*
And truth in every shepherd's tongue,
These pretty pleasures might me move
To live with thee and be thy love.

Time drives the flocks from field to fold   *5*
When rivers rage and rocks grow cold,
And Philomel becometh dumb;
The rest complains of cares to come.

The flowers do fade, and wanton fields
To wayward winter reckoning yields;   *10*
A honey tongue, a heart of gall,
Is fancy's spring, but sorrow's fall.

Thy gowns, thy shoes, thy beds of roses,
Thy cap, thy kirtle, and thy posies
Soon break, soon wither, soon forgotten,—   *15*
In folly ripe, in reason rotten.

Thy belt of straw and ivy buds,
Thy coral clasps and amber studs,
All these in me no means can move
To come to thee and be thy love.   *20*

But could youth last and love still breed,
Had joys no date nor age no need,
Then these delights my mind might move
To live with thee and be thy love.
                    SIR WALTER RALEIGH

SONNET VII, *Astrophel and Stella*

When nature made her chief work, Stella's eyes,   *1*
    In color black why wrapped she beams so bright?
    Would she in beamy black, like painter wise,
    Frame daintiest luster mixed of shades and light?
Or did she else that sober hue devise   *5*
    In object best to knit and strength our sight,
    Lest, if no veil these brave gleams did disguise,
    They, sunlike, should more dazzle than delight?
Or would she her miraculous power show,
    That, whereas black seems beauty's contrary,   *10*
    She even in black doth make all beauties flow?

Both so, and thus,—she, minding Love should be
    Placed ever there, gave him this mourning weed
    To honor all their deaths who for her bleed.

SIR PHILIP SIDNEY

SPRING, *Love's Labour's Lost*

When daisies pied and violets blue   *1*
    And lady-smocks all silver-white
And cuckoo-buds of yellow hue
    Do paint the meadows with delight,
The cuckoo then, on every tree,   *5*
Mocks married men; for thus sings he,
                        Cuckoo;
Cuckoo, cuckoo: O, word of fear,
Unpleasing to a married ear!

When shepherds pipe on oaten straws,   *10*
    And merry larks are ploughmen's clocks,
When turtles tread, and rooks, and daws,
    And maidens bleach their summer smocks,
The cuckoo then, on every tree,
Mocks married men; for thus sings he,   *15*
                        Cuckoo;
Cuckoo, cuckoo: O, word of fear,
Unpleasing to a married ear!

WILLIAM SHAKESPEARE

WINTER, *Love's Labour's Lost*

When icicles hang by the wall,   *1*
    And Dick the shepherd blows his nail,
And Tom bears logs into the hall,
    And milk comes frozen home in pail,
When blood is nipp'd, and ways be foul,   *5*
Then nightly sings the staring owl,
                        Tu-who;
Tu-whit, tu-who—a merry note,
While greasy Joan doth keel the pot.

When all aloud the wind doth blow,   *10*
  And coughing drowns the parson's saw,
And birds sit brooding in the snow,
  And Marian's nose looks red and raw,
When roasted crabs hiss in the bowl,
Then nightly sings the staring owl,   *15*
               Tu-who;
Tu-whit, tu-who—a merry note,
While greasy Joan doth keel the pot.
          WILLIAM SHAKESPEARE

Sonnet XXXIII

Full many a glorious morning have I seen   *1*
Flatter the mountain-tops with sovereign eye,
Kissing with golden face the meadows green,
Gilding pale streams with heavenly alchemy;
Anon permit the basest clouds to ride   *5*
With ugly rack on his celestial face,
And from the forlorn world his visage hide,
Stealing unseen to west with this disgrace.
Even so my sun one early morn did shine
With all-triumphant splendour on my brow;   *10*
But, out! alack! he was but one hour mine,
The region cloud hath mask'd him from me now.
  Yet him for this my love no whit disdaineth;
  Suns of the world may stain when heaven's sun staineth.
          WILLIAM SHAKESPEARE

Sonnet CXXX

My mistress' eyes are nothing like the sun;   *1*
Coral is far more red than her lips' red:
If snow be white, why then her breasts are dun;
If hairs be wires, black wires grow on her head.
I have seen roses damask'd, red and white,   *5*
But no such roses see I in her cheeks;
And in some perfumes is there more delight
Than in the breath that from my mistress reeks.

I love to hear her speak, yet well I know
That music hath a far more pleasing sound: *10*
I grant I never saw a goddess go,—
My mistress, when she walks, treads on the ground.
    And yet, by heaven, I think my love as rare
    As any she belied with false compare.

WILLIAM SHAKESPEARE

Song. To Celia

Drinke to me, onely, with thine eyes,   *1*
    And I will pledge with mine;
Or leave a kisse but in the cup,
    And Ile not looke for wine.
The thirst, that from the soule doth rise,   *5*
    Doth aske a drinke divine:
But might I of JOVE's *Nectar* sup,
    I would not change for thine.

I sent thee, late, a rosie wreath,
    Not so much honoring thee,   *10*
As giving it a hope, that there
    It could not withered bee.
But thou thereon did'st onely breath,
    And sent'st it backe to mee:
Since when it growes, and smells, I sweare,   *15*
    Not of it selfe, but thee.

BEN JONSON

Song

Goe, and catche a falling starre,   *1*
    Get with child a mandrake roote,
Tell me, where all past yeares are,
    Or who cleft the Divels foot,
Teach me to heare Mermaides singing,   *5*
    Or to keep off envies stinging,
            And finde
            What winde
Serves to advance an honest minde.

If thou beest borne to strange sights,   *10*
   Things invisible to see,
Ride ten thousand daies and nights,
   Till age snow white haires on thee,
Thou, when thou retorn'st, wilt tell mee
All strange wonders that befell thee,   *15*
       And sweare
       No where
Lives a woman true, and faire.

If thou findst one, let mee know,
   Such a Pilgrimage were sweet;   *20*
Yet doe not, I would not goe,
   Though at next doore wee might meet,
Though shee were true, when you met her,
And last, till you write your letter,
       Yet shee   *25*
       Will bee
False, ere I come, to two, or three.
             JOHN DONNE

The Baite

Come live with mee, and bee my love,   *1*
And we will some new pleasures prove
Of golden sands, and christall brookes,
With silken lines, and silver hookes.

There will the river whispering runne   *5*
Warm'd by thy eyes, more then the Sunne.
And there the'inamor'd fish will stay,
Begging themselves they may betray.

When thou wilt swimme in that live bath,
Each fish, which every channell hath,   *10*
Will amorously to thee swimme,
Gladder to catch thee, then thou him.

If thou, to be so seene, beest loath,
By Sunne, or Moone, thou darknest both,

And if my selfe have leave to see,   *15*
I need not their light, having thee.

Let others freeze with angling reeds,
And cut their legges, with shells and weeds,
Or treacherously poore fish beset,
With strangling snare, or windowie net: *20*

Let coarse bold hands, from slimy nest
The bedded fish in banks out-wrest,
Or curious traitors, sleavesilke flies
Bewitch poore fishes wandring eyes.

For thee, thou needst no such deceit,   *25*
For thou thy selfe art thine owne bait;
That fish, that is not catch'd thereby,
Alas, is wiser farre then I.

                              JOHN DONNE

The Canonization

For Godsake hold your tongue, and let me love,   *1*
  Or chide my palsie, or my gout,
My five gray haires, or ruin'd fortune flout,
  With wealth your state, your minde with Arts improve,
    Take you a course, get you a place,   *5*
    Observe his honour, or his grace,
Or the Kings reall, or his stamped face
  Contemplate, what you will, approve,
    So you will let me love.

Alas, alas, who's injur'd by my love?   *10*
  What merchants ships have my sighs drown'd?
Who saies my teares have overflow'd his ground?
  When did my colds a forward spring remove?
    When did the heats which my veines fill
    Adde one more to the plaguie Bill?   *15*
Soldiers finde warres, and Lawyers finde out still
  Litigious men, which quarrels move,
    Though she and I do love.

Call us what you will, wee are made such by love;
  Call her one, mee another flye,   *20*
We'are Tapers too, and at our owne cost die,
  And wee in us finde the'Eagle and the Dove.
    The Phoenix ridle hath more wit
    By us, we two being one, are it.
So to one neutrall thing both sexes fit,   *25*
  Wee dye and rise the same, and prove
  Mysterious by this love.

Wee can dye by it, if not live by love,
  And if unfit for tombes and hearse
Our legend bee, it will be fit for verse;   *30*
  And if no peece of Chronicle wee prove,
    We'll build in sonnets pretty roomes;
    As well a well wrought urne becomes
The greatest ashes, as halfe-acre tombes,
  And by these hymnes, all shall approve   *35*
  Us *Canoniz'd* for Love:

And thus invoke us; You whom reverend love
  Made one anothers hermitage;
You, to whom love was peace, that now is rage;
  Who did the whole worlds soule contract, and drove   *40*
    Into the glasses of your eyes
    So made such mirrors, and such spies,
That they did all to you epitomize,
  Countries, Townes, Courts: Beg from above
  A patterne of your love!   *45*

JOHN DONNE

A Valediction: Forbidding Mourning

As virtuous men passe mildly away,   *1*
  And whisper to their soules, to goe,
Whilst some of their sad friends doe say,
  The breath goes now, and some say, no:

So let us melt, and make no noise,   *5*
   No teare-floods, nor sigh-tempests move,
T'were prophanation of our joyes
   To tell the layetie our love.

Moving of th'earth brings harmes and feares,
   Men reckon what it did and meant,   *10*
But trepidation of the spheares,
   Though greater farre, is innocent.

Dull sublunary lovers love
   (Whose soule is sense) cannot admit
Absence, because it doth remove   *15*
   Those things which elemented it.

But we by a love, so much refin'd,
   That our selves know not what it is,
Inter-assured of the mind,
   Care lesse, eyes, lips, and hands to misse.   *20*

Our two soules therefore, which are one,
   Though I must goe, endure not yet
A breach, but an expansion,
   Like gold to ayery thinnesse beate.

If they be two, they are two so   *25*
   As stiffe twin compasses are two,
Thy soule the fixt foot, makes no show
   To move, but doth, if the'other doe.

And though it in the center sit,
   Yet when the other far doth rome,   *30*
It leanes, and hearkens after it,
   And growes erect, as that comes home.

Such wilt thou be to mee, who must
   Like th'other foot, obliquely runne;
Thy firmnes makes my circle just,   *35*
   And makes me end, where I begunne.

                    JOHN DONNE

To the Virgins, to Make Much of Time

Gather ye Rose-buds while ye may,   *1*
   Old Time is still a flying:
And this same flower that smiles to day,
   To morrow will be dying.

The glorious Lamp of Heaven, the Sun,   *5*
   The higher he's a getting;
The sooner will his Race be run,
   And neerer he's to Setting.

That Age is best, which is the first,
   When Youth and Blood are warmer;   *10*
But being spent, the worse, and worst
   Times, still succeed the former.

Then be not coy, but use your time;
   And while ye may, goe marry:
For having lost but once your prime,   *15*
   You may for ever tarry.
              ROBERT HERRICK

Cherrie-Ripe

Cherrie-Ripe, Ripe, Ripe, I cry,   *1*
Full and faire ones; come and buy:
If so be, you ask me where
They doe grow? I answer, There,
Where my *Julia's* lips doe smile;   *5*
There's the Land, or Cherry-Ile:
Whose Plantations fully show
All the yeere, where Cherries grow.
              ROBERT HERRICK

To Phillis to Love, and Live with Him

Live, live with me, and thou shalt see   *1*
The pleasures Ile prepare for thee:

What sweets the Country can afford
Shall blesse thy Bed, and blesse thy Board.
The soft sweet Mosse shall be thy bed,   *5*
With crawling Woodbine over-spread:
By which the silver-shedding streames
Shall gently melt thee into dreames.
Thy clothing next, shall be a Gowne
Made of the Fleeces purest Downe.   *10*
The tongues of Kids shall be thy meate;
Their Milke thy drinke; and thou shalt eate
The Paste of Filberts for thy bread
With Cream of Cowslips buttered:
Thy Feasting-Tables shall be Hills   *15*
With *Daisies* spread, and *Daffadils;*
Where thou shalt sit, and *Red-brest* by,
For meat, shall give thee melody.
Ile give thee Chaines and Carkanets
Of *Primroses* and *Violets.*   *20*
A Bag and Bottle thou shalt have;
That richly wrought, and This as brave;
So that as either shall expresse
The Wearer's no meane Shepheardesse.
At Sheering-times, and yearely Wakes,   *25*
When *Themilis* his pastime makes,
There thou shalt be; and be the wit,
Nay more, the Feast, and grace of it.
On Holy-dayes, when Virgins meet
To dance the Heyes with nimble feet;   *30*
Thou shalt come forth, and then appeare
The *Queen of Roses* for that yeere.
And having danc't ('bove all the best)
Carry the Garland from the rest.
In Wicker-baskets Maids shal bring   *35*
To thee, (my dearest Shephardling)
The blushing Apple, bashfull Peare,
And shame-fac't Plum, (all simp'ring there).
Walk in the Groves, and thou shalt find
The name of *Phillis* in the Rind   *40*

Of every straight, and smooth-skin tree;
Where kissing that, Ile twice kisse thee.
To thee a Sheep-hook I will send,
Be-pranckt with Ribbands, to this end,
This, this alluring Hook might be   *45*
Lesse for to catch a sheep, then me.
Thou shalt have Possets, Wassails fine,
Not made of Ale, but spiced Wine;
To make thy Maids and selfe free mirth,
All sitting neer the glitt'ring Hearth.   *50*
Thou sha't have Ribbands, Roses, Rings,
Gloves, Garters, Stockings, Shooes, and Strings
Of winning Colours, that shall move
Others to Lust, but me to Love.
These (nay) and more, thine own shal be,   *55*
If thou wilt love, and live with me.

ROBERT HERRICK

The Altar

A broken ALTAR, Lord, Thy servant reares,   *1*
Made of a HEART, and cimented with teares;
  Whose parts are as Thy hand did frame;
  No workman's tool hath touch'd the same.
     A HEART alone   *5*
     Is such a stone
     As nothing but
     Thy power doth cut.
     Wherefore each part
     Of my hard HEART   *10*
     Meets in this frame,
     To praise Thy name:
  That, if I chance to hold my peace,
  These stones to praise Thee may not cease.
O, let Thy blessed SACRIFICE be mine,   *15*
And sanctifie this ALTAR to be Thine!

GEORGE HERBERT

The Pulley

When God at first made man,   *1*
Having a glasse of blessings standing by,
'Let us,' said He, 'poure on him all we can;
Let the world's riches, which dispersed lie,
    Contract into a span.'   *5*

So strength first made a way,
Then beautie flow'd, then wisdome, honour, pleasure;
When almost all was out, God made a stay,
Perceiving that, alone of all His treasure,
    Rest in the bottome lay.   *10*

'For if I should,' said He,
'Bestow this jewell also on My creature,
He would adore My gifts in stead of Me,
And rest in Nature, not the God of Nature:
    So both should losers be.   *15*

Yet let him keep the rest,
But keep them with repining restlessnesse;
Let him be rich and wearie, that at least,
If goodnesse leade him not, yet wearinesse
    May tosse him to My breast.'   *20*

                          GEORGE HERBERT

Vertue

Sweet day, so cool, so calm, so. bright,   *1*
The bridall of the earth and skie,
The dew shall weep thy fall to-night;
       For thou must die.

Sweet rose, whose hue angrie and brave   *5*
Bids the rash gazer wipe his eye,
Thy root is ever in its grave,
       And thou must die.

Sweet spring, full of sweet days and roses,
A box where sweets compacted lie,   10
My musick shows ye have your closes,
        And all must die.

Onely a sweet and vertuous soul,
Like season'd timber, never gives;
But though the whole world turn to coal,   15
        Then chiefly lives.
GEORGE HERBERT

Song

Go, lovely rose!   1
Tell her that wastes her time and me
That now she knows,
When I resemble her to thee,
How sweet and fair she seems to be.   5

Tell her that's young
And shuns to have her graces spied,
That hadst thou sprung
In deserts where no men abide,
Thou must have uncommended died.   10

Small is the worth
Of beauty from the light retired;
Bid her come forth,
Suffer herself to be desired,
And not blush so to be admired.   15

Then die, that she
The common fate of all things rare
May read in thee;
How small a part of time they share
That are so wondrous sweet and fair!   20
EDMUND WALLER

On a Girdle

That which her slender waist confined   *1*
Shall now my joyful temples bind;
No monarch but would give his crown
His arms might do what this has done.

It was my heaven's extremest sphere,   *5*
The pale which held that lovely deer.
My joy, my grief, my hope, my love,
Did all within this circle move!

A narrow compass, and yet there
Dwelt all that's good and all that's fair;   *10*
Give me but what this riband bound,
Take all the rest the sun goes round.

EDMUND WALLER

L'Allegro

Hence loathed Melancholy   *1*
   Of *Cerberus* and blackest midnight born,
In *Stygian* Cave forlorn
    'Mongst horrid shapes, and shrieks, and sights unholy,
Find out some uncouth cell,   *5*
   Where brooding darkness spreads his jealous wings,
And the night-Raven sings;
   There under *Ebon* shades, and low-brow'd Rocks,
As ragged as thy Locks,
   In dark *Cimmerian* desert ever dwell.   *10*
But come thou Goddess fair and free,
In Heav'n yclep'd *Euphrosyne*,
And by men, heart-easing Mirth,
Whom lovely *Venus* at a birth
With two sister Graces more   *15*
To Ivy-crowned *Bacchus* bore;
Or whether (as some Sager sing)
The frolic Wind that breathes the Spring,

Zephyr with *Aurora* playing,
As he met her once a-Maying,   20
There on Beds of Violets blue,
And fresh-blown Roses washt in dew,
Fill'd her with thee a daughter fair,
So buxom, blithe, and debonair.
Haste thee nymph, and bring with thee   25
Jest and youthful Jollity,
Quips and Cranks, and wanton Wiles,
Nods, and Becks, and Wreathed Smiles,
Such as hang on *Hebe's* cheek,
And love to live in dimple sleek ;   30
Sport that wrinkled Care derides,
And Laughter holding both his sides.
Come, and trip it as ye go
On the light fantastic toe,
And in thy right hand lead with thee,   35
The Mountain Nymph, sweet Liberty ;
And if I give thee honour due,
Mirth, admit me of thy crew
To live with her, and live with thee,
In unreproved pleasures free ;   40
To hear the Lark begin his flight,
And singing startle the dull night,
From his watch-tow'r in the skies,
Till the dappled dawn doth rise ;
Then to come in spite of sorrow,   45
And at my window bid good morrow,
Through the Sweet-Briar, or the Vine,
Or the twisted Eglantine ;
While the Cock with lively din,
Scatters the rear of darkness thin,   50
And to the stack, or the Barn door,
Stoutly struts his Dames before ;
Oft list'ning how the Hounds and horn
Cheerly rouse the slumb'ring morn,
From the side of some Hoar Hill,   55
Through the high wood echoing shrill ;

Some time walking not unseen
By Hedge-row Elms, on Hillocks green,
Right against the Eastern gate,
Where the great Sun begins his state,   *60*
Rob'd in flames, and Amber light,
The clouds in thousand Liveries dight;
While the Plowman near at hand,
Whistles o'er the Furrow'd Land,
And the Milkmaid singeth blithe,   *65*
And the Mower whets his scythe,
And every Shepherd tells his tale
Under the Hawthorn in the dale.
Straight mine eye hath caught new pleasures
Whilst the Lantskip round it measures,   *70*
Russet Lawns and Fallows Gray,
Where the nibbling flocks do stray;
Mountains on whose barren breast
The labouring clouds do often rest;
Meadows trim with Daisies pied,   *75*
Shallow Brooks, and Rivers wide.
Towers and Battlements it sees
Bosom'd high in tufted Trees,
Where perhaps some beauty lies,
The Cynosure of neighbouring eyes.   *80*
Hard by, a Cottage chimney smokes,
From betwixt two aged Oaks,
Where *Corydon* and *Thyrsis* met,
Are at their savoury dinner set
Of Herbs, and other Country Messes,   *85*
Which the neat-handed *Phyllis* dresses;
And then in haste her Bow'r she leaves,
With *Thestylis* to bind the Sheaves;
Or if the earlier season lead
To the tann'd Haycock in the Mead.   *90*
Sometimes with secure delight
The up-land Hamlets will invite,
When the merry Bells ring round,
And the jocund rebecks sound

To many a youth, and many a maid,   *95*
Dancing in the Chequer'd shade;
And young and old come forth to play
On a Sunshine Holiday,
Till the live-long day-light fail;
Then to the Spicy Nut-brown Ale,   *100*
With stories told of many a feat,
How *Faery Mab* the junkets eat;
She was pincht and pull'd, she said,
And he, by Friar's Lanthorn led,
Tells how the drudging *Goblin* sweat   *105*
To earn his Cream-bowl duly set,
When in one night, ere glimpse of morn,
His shadowy Flail hath thresh'd the Corn
That ten day-labourers could not end;
Then lies him down the Lubber Fiend,   *110*
And, stretch'd out all the Chimney's length,
Basks at the fire his hairy strength;
And Crop-full out of doors he flings,
Ere the first Cock his Matin rings.
Thus done the Tales, to bed they creep,   *115*
By whispering Winds soon lull'd asleep.
Tow'red Cities please us then,
And the busy hum of men,
Where throngs of Knights and Barons bold,
In weeds of Peace high triumphs hold,   *120*
With store of Ladies, whose bright eyes
Rain influence, and judge the prize
Of Wit, or Arms, while both contend
To win her Grace, whom all commend.
There let *Hymen* oft appear   *125*
In Saffron robe, with Taper clear,
And pomp, and feast, and revelry,
With mask, and antique Pageantry—
Such sights as youthful Poets dream
On Summer eves by haunted stream.   *130*
Then to the well-trod stage anon,
If *Jonson's* learned Sock be on,

Or sweetest *Shakespeare*, fancy's child,
Warble his native Wood-notes wild.
And ever against eating Cares,   *135*
Lap me in soft *Lydian* Airs,
Married to immortal verse,
Such as the meeting soul may pierce
In notes, with many a winding bout
Of linked sweetness long drawn out,   *140*
With wanton heed, and giddy cunning,
The melting voice through mazes running;
Untwisting all the chains that tie
The hidden soul of harmony;
That *Orpheus'* self may heave his head   *145*
From golden slumber on a bed
Of heapt *Elysian* flow'rs, and hear
Such strains as would have won the ear
Of *Pluto*, to have quite set free
His half-regain'd *Eurydice*.   *150*
These delights if thou canst give,
Mirth, with thee I mean to live.

JOHN MILTON

Il Penseroso

Hence vain deluding joys,   *1*
   The brood of folly without father bred,
How little you bested,
   Or fill the fixed mind with all your toys;
Dwell in some idle brain,   *5*
   And fancies fond with gaudy shapes possess,
As thick and numberless
   As the gay motes that people the Sun-Beams,
Or likest hovering dreams,
   The fickle Pensioners of *Morpheus'* train.   *10*
But hail thou Goddess, sage and holy,
Hail divinest Melancholy,
Whose Saintly visage is too bright
To hit the Sense of human sight;

And therefore to our weaker view,   15
O'erlaid with black, staid Wisdom's hue.
Black, but such as in esteem,
Prince *Memnon's* sister might beseem,
Or that Starr'd *Ethiop* Queen that strove
To set her beauty's praise above   20
The Sea Nymphs, and their powers offended.
Yet thou art higher far descended;
Thee bright-hair'd *Vesta* long of yore,
To solitary *Saturn* bore;
His daughter she (in *Saturn's* reign,   25
Such mixture was not held a stain).
Oft in glimmering Bow'rs and glades
He met her, and in secret shades
Of woody *Ida's* inmost grove,
While yet there was no fear of *Jove*.   30
Come pensive Nun, devout and pure,
Sober, steadfast, and demure,
All in a robe of darkest grain,
Flowing with majestic train,
And sable stole of *Cypress* Lawn,   35
Over thy decent shoulders drawn.
Come, but keep thy wonted state,
With ev'n step, and musing gait,
And looks commercing with the skies,
Thy rapt soul sitting in thine eyes: 40
There held in holy passion still,
Forget thyself to Marble, till
With a sad Leaden downward cast,
Thou fix them on the earth as fast.
And join with thee calm Peace and Quiet,   45
Spare Fast, that oft with gods doth diet,
And hears the Muses in a ring
Aye round about *Jove's* Altar sing.
And add to these retired Leisure,
That in trim Gardens takes his pleasure;   50
But first, and chiefest, with thee bring
Him that yon soars on golden wing,

Guiding the fiery-wheeled throne,
The Cherub Contemplation;
And the mute Silence hist along,   *55*
'Less *Philomel* will deign a Song,
In her sweetest, saddest plight,
Smoothing the rugged brow of night.
While *Cynthia* checks her Dragon yoke,
Gently o'er th' accustom'd Oak;   *60*
Sweet Bird that shunn'st the noise of folly,
Most musical, most melancholy!
Thee Chantress oft the Woods among,
I woo to hear thy even-Song;
And missing thee, I walk unseen   *65*
On the dry smooth-shaven Green,
To behold the wand'ring Moon,
Riding near her highest noon,
Like one that had been led astray
Through the Heav'n's wide pathless way;   *70*
And oft, as if her head she bow'd,
Stooping through a fleecy cloud.
Oft on a Plat of rising ground,
I hear the far-off *Curfew* sound,
Over some wide-water'd shore,   *75*
Swinging slow with sullen roar;
Or if the Air will not permit,
Some still removed place will fit,
Where glowing Embers through the room
Teach light to counterfeit a gloom,   *80*
Far from all resort of mirth,
Save the Cricket on the hearth,
Or the Bellman's drowsy charm,
To bless the doors from nightly harm:
Or let my Lamp at midnight hour,   *85*
Be seen in some high lonely Tow'r,
Where I may oft out-watch the *Bear*,
With thrice great *Hermes*, or unsphere
The spirit of *Plato* to unfold
What Worlds, or what vast Regions hold   *90*

The immortal mind that hath forsook
Her mansion in this fleshly nook:
And of those *Dæmons* that are found
In fire, air, flood, or under ground,
Whose power hath a true consent   *95*
With Planet, or with Element.
Sometime let Gorgeous Tragedy
In Scepter'd Pall come sweeping by,
Presenting *Thebes*, or *Pelop's* line,
Or the tale of *Troy* divine,   *100*
Or what (though rare) of later age,
Ennobled hath the Buskin'd stage.
But, O sad Virgin, that thy power
Might raise *Musaeus* from his bower,
Or bid the soul of *Orpheus* sing   *105*
Such notes as, warbled to the string,
Drew Iron tears down *Pluto's* cheek,
And made Hell grant what Love did seek.
Or call up him that left half told
The story of *Cambuscan* bold,   *110*
Of *Camball*, and of *Algarsife*,
And who had *Canace* to wife,
That own'd the virtuous Ring and Glass,
And of the wond'rous Horse of Brass,
On which the *Tartar* King did ride;   *115*
And if aught else great Bards beside
In sage and solemn tunes have sung,
Of Tourneys and of Trophies hung,
Of Forests, and inchantments drear,
Where more is meant than meets the ear.   *120*
Thus night oft see me in thy pale career,
Till civil-suited Morn appear,
Not trickt and frounc't as she was wont
With the Attic Boy to hunt,
But Kerchieft in a comely Cloud,   *125*
While rocking Winds are Piping loud,
Or usher'd with a shower still,
When the gust hath blown his fill,

Ending on the rustling Leaves,
With minute drops from off the Eaves.   *130*
And when the Sun begins to fling
His flaring beams, me Goddess bring
To arched walks of twilight groves,
And shadows brown that *Sylvan* loves
Of Pine or monumental Oak,   *135*
Where the rude Axe with heaved stroke
Was never heard the Nymphs to daunt,
Or fright them from their hallow'd haunt.
There in close covert by some Brook,
Where no profaner eye may look,   *140*
Hide me from Day's garish eye,
While the Bee with Honied thigh,
That at her flow'ry work doth sing,
And the Waters murmuring
With such consort as they keep,   *145*
Entice the dewy-feather'd Sleep ;
And let some strange mysterious dream
Wave at his Wings in Airy stream,
Of lively portraiture display'd,
Softly on my eye-lids laid.   *150*
And as I wake, sweet music breathe
Above, about, or underneath,
Sent by some spirit to mortals good,
Or th'unseen Genius of the Wood.
But let my due feet never fail   *155*
To walk the studious Cloister's pale,
And love the high embowed Roof,
With antic Pillars massy proof,
And storied Windows richly dight,
Casting a dim religious light.   *160*
There let the pealing Organ blow
To the full voic'd Quire below,
In Service high and Anthems clear,
As may with sweetness, through mine ear,
Dissolve me into extasies,   *165*
And bring all Heav'n before mine eyes.

And may at last my weary age
Find out the peaceful hermitage,
The Hairy Gown and Mossy Cell,
Where I may sit and rightly spell   *170*
Of every Star that Heav'n doth shew,
And every Herb that sips the dew;
Till old experience do attain
To something like Prophetic strain.
These pleasures *Melancholy* give,   *175*
And I with thee will choose to live.

JOHN MILTON

Lycidas

Yet once more, O ye Laurels, and once more   *1*
Ye Myrtles brown, with Ivy never sere,
I come to pluck your Berries harsh and crude,
And with forc'd fingers rude,
Shatter your leaves before the mellowing year.   *5*
Bitter constraint, and sad occasion dear,
Compels me to disturb your season due:
For *Lycidas* is dead, dead ere his prime,
Young *Lycidas*, and hath not left his peer:
Who would not sing for *Lycidas?* he knew   *10*
Himself to sing, and build the lofty rhyme.
He must not float upon his wat'ry bier
Unwept, and welter to the parching wind,
Without the meed of some melodious tear.
    Begin then, Sisters of the sacred well,   *15*
That from beneath the seat of *Jove* doth spring,
Begin, and somewhat loudly sweep the string.
Hence with denial vain, and coy excuse,
So may some gentle Muse
With lucky words favour my destin'd Urn,   *20*
And as he passes turn,
And bid fair peace be to my sable shroud.
For we were nurst upon the self-same hill,
Fed the same flock, by fountain, shade, and rill.

Together both, ere the high Lawns appear'd   *25*
Under the opening eye-lids of the morn,
We drove afield, and both together heard
What time the Gray-fly winds her sultry horn,
Batt'ning our flocks with the fresh dews of night,
Oft till the Star that rose, at Ev'ning, bright   *30*
Toward Heav'n's descent had slop'd his westering wheel.
Meanwhile the Rural ditties were not mute,
Temper'd to th'Oaten Flute;
Rough *Satyrs* danc'd, and *Fauns* with clov'n heel,
From the glad sound would not be absent long,   *35*
And old *Damaetas* lov'd to hear our song.

But O the heavy change, now thou art gone,
Now thou art gone, and never must return!
Thee Shepherd, thee the Woods, and desert Caves,
With wild Thyme and the gadding Vine o'ergrown,   *40*
And all their echoes mourn.
The Willows and the Hazel Copses green
Shall now no more be seen,
Fanning their joyous Leaves to thy soft lays.
As killing as the Canker to the Rose,   *45*
Or Taint-worm to the weanling Herds that graze,
Or Frost to Flowers, that their gay wardrobe wear,
When first the White-thorn blows,
Such, *Lycidas*, thy loss to Shepherd's ear.

Where were ye Nymphs when the remorseless deep   *50*
Clos'd o'er the head of your lov'd *Lycidas?*
For neither were ye playing on the steep,
Where your old *Bards*, the famous *Druids*, lie,
Nor on the shaggy top of *Mona* high,
Nor yet where *Deva* spreads her wizard stream: *55*
Ay me, I fondly dream!
Had ye been there—for what could that have done?
What could the Muse herself that Orpheus bore,
The Muse herself, for her enchanting son
Whom Universal nature did lament,   *60*
When by the rout that made the hideous roar,
His gory visage down the stream was sent,
Down the swift *Hebrus* to the *Lesbian* shore?

Alas! What boots it with uncessant care
To tend the homely slighted Shepherd's trade,   65
And strictly meditate the thankless Muse?
Were it not better done as others use,
To sport with *Amaryllis* in the shade,
Or with the tangles of *Neaera's* hair?
Fame is the spur that the clear spirit doth raise   70
(That last infirmity of Noble mind)
To scorn delights, and live laborious days;
But the fair Guerdon when we hope to find,
And think to burst out into sudden blaze,
Comes the blind *Fury* with th'abhorred shears,   75
And slits the thin-spun life. But not the praise,
Phoebus repli'd, and touch'd my trembling ears;
Fame is no plant that grows on mortal soil,
Nor in the glistering foil
Set off to th'world, nor in broad rumour lies,   80
But lives and spreads aloft by those pure eyes
And perfect witness of all judging *Jove;*
As he pronounces lastly on each deed,
Of so much fame in Heav'n expect thy meed.

O Fountain *Arethuse,* and thou honour'd flood,   85
Smooth-sliding *Mincius,* crown'd with vocal reeds,
That strain I heard was of a higher mood:
But now my Oat proceeds,
And listens to the Herald of the Sea
That came in *Neptune's* plea.   90
He ask'd the Waves, and ask'd the Felon winds,
What hard mishap hath doom'd this gentle swain?
And question'd every gust of rugged wings
That blows from off each beaked Promontory.
They knew not of his story,   95
And sage *Hippotades* their answer brings,
That not a blast was from his dungeon stray'd,
The Air was calm, and on the level brine,
Sleek *Panope* with all her sisters play'd.
It was that fatal and perfidious Bark   100
Built in th'eclipse, and rigg'd with curses dark,
That sunk so low that sacred head of thine.

Next *Camus*, reverend Sire, went footing slow,
His Mantle hairy, and his Bonnet sedge,
Inwrought with figures dim, and on the edge   *105*
Like to that sanguine flower inscrib'd with woe.
Ah! Who hath reft (quoth he) my dearest pledge?
Last came, and last did go,
The Pilot of the *Galilean* lake.
Two massy Keys he bore of metals twain,   *110*
(The Golden opes, the Iron shuts amain).
He shook his Mitred locks, and stern bespake:
How well could I have spar'd for thee, young swain,
Enough of such as for their bellies' sake,
Creep and intrude and climb into the fold?   *115*
Of other care they little reck'ning make,
Than how to scramble at the shearers' feast,
And shove away the worthy bidden guest.
Blind mouths! that scarce themselves know how to hold
A Sheep-hook, or have learn'd aught else the least   *120*
That to the faithful Herdman's art belongs!
What recks it them? What need they? They are sped;
And when they list, their lean and flashy songs
Grate on their scrannel Pipes of wretched straw.
The hungry Sheep look up, and are not fed,   *125*
But swoln with wind, and the rank mist they draw,
Rot inwardly, and foul contagion spread:
Besides what the grim Wolf with privy paw
Daily devours apace, and nothing said;
But that two-handed engine at the door   *130*
Stands ready to smite once, and smite no more.
    Return *Alpheus*, the dread voice is past,
That shrunk thy streams; Return *Sicilian* Muse,
And call the Vales, and bid them hither cast
Their Bells and Flowrets of a thousand hues.   *135*
Ye valleys low where the mild whispers use
Of shades and wanton winds and gushing brooks,
On whose fresh lap the swart Star sparely looks,
Throw hither all your quaint enamell'd eyes,
That on the green turf suck the honied showers,   *140*
And purple all the ground with vernal flowers.

Bring the rathe Primrose that forsaken dies,
The tufted Crow-toe, and pale Jessamine,
The white Pink, and the Pansy freakt with jet,
The glowing Violet, 145
The Musk-rose, and the well attir'd Woodbine,
With Cowslips wan that hang the pensive head,
And every flower that sad embroidery wears:
Bid *Amaranthus* all his beauty shed,
And Daffadillies fill their cups with tears, 150
To strew the Laureate Hearse where *Lycid* lies.
For so to interpose a little ease,
Let our frail thoughts dally with false surmise.
Ay me! Whilst thee the shores, and sounding Seas
Wash far away, where'er thy bones are hurl'd, 155
Whether beyond the stormy *Hebrides*,
Where thou perhaps under the whelming tide
Visit'st the bottom of the monstrous world;
Or whether thou to our moist vows denied,
Sleep'st by the fable of *Bellerus* old, 160
Where the great vision of the guarded Mount
Looks toward *Namancos* and *Bayona's* hold;
Look homeward Angel now, and melt with ruth:
And, O ye *Dolphins*, waft the hapless youth.
    Weep no more, woeful Shepherds weep no more, 165
For *Lycidas* your sorrow is not dead,
Sunk though he be beneath the wat'ry floor,
So sinks the day-star in the Ocean bed,
And yet anon repairs his drooping head,
And tricks his beams, and with new spangled Ore, 170
Flames in the forehead of the morning sky:
So *Lycidas*, sunk low, but mounted high,
Through the dear might of him that walk'd the waves,
Where other groves, and other streams along,
With *Nectar* pure his oozy Locks he laves, 175
And hears the unexpressive nuptial Song,
In the blest Kingdoms meek of joy and love.
There entertain him all the Saints above,
In solemn troops, and sweet Societies
That sing, and singing in their glory move, 180

And wipe the tears for ever from his eyes.
Now Lycidas the Shepherds weep no more;
Henceforth thou art the Genius of the shore,
In thy large recompense, and shalt be good
To all that wander in that perilous flood.   *185*
    Thus sang the uncouth Swain to th'Oaks and rills,
While the still morn went out with Sandals gray.
He touch't the tender stops of various Quills,
With eager thought warbling his *Doric* lay:
And now the Sun had stretch't out all the hills,   *190*
And now was dropt into the Western bay;
At last he rose, and twitch't his Mantle blue:
Tomorrow to fresh Woods, and Pastures new.

JOHN MILTON

When I Consider How My Light Is Spent

When I consider how my light is spent,   *1*
  Ere half my days, in this dark world and wide,
  And that one Talent which is death to hide,
  Lodg'd with me useless, though my Soul more bent
To serve therewith my Maker, and present   *5*
  My true account, lest he returning chide;
  Doth God exact day-labour, light denied,
  I fondly ask; But patience to prevent
That murmur, soon replies, God doth not need
  Either man's work or his own gifts; who best   *10*
  Bear his mild yoke, they serve him best; his State
Is Kingly. Thousands at his bidding speed
  And post o'er Land and Ocean without rest:
  They also serve who only stand and wait.

JOHN MILTON

Out Upon It! I Have Loved

Out upon it! I have loved   *1*
  Three whole days together;
And am like to love three more,
  If it prove fair weather.

Time shalt moult away his wings, 5
   Ere he shall discover
In the whole wide world again
   Such a constant lover.

But the spite on 't is, no praise
   Is due at all to me; 10
Love with me had made no stays,
   Had it any been but she.

Had it any been but she,
   And that very face,
There had been at least ere this 15
   A dozen dozen in her place.
         SIR JOHN SUCKLING

To His Coy Mistress

Had we but world enough, and time, 1
This coyness, lady, were no crime.
We would sit down, and think which way
To walk, and pass our long love's day.
Thou by the Indian Ganges' side 5
Should'st rubies find: I by the tide
Of Humber would complain. I would
Love you ten years before the Flood,
And you should, if you please, refuse
Till the conversion of the Jews. 10
My vegetable love should grow
Vaster than empires, and more slow.
An hundred years should go to praise
Thine eyes, and on thy forehead gaze:
Two hundred to adore each breast: 15
But thirty thousand to the rest;
An age at least to every part,
And the last age should show your heart.
For, lady, you deserve this state,
Nor would I love at lower rate. 20

But at my back I always hear
Time's wingèd chariot hurrying near:
And yonder all before us lie
Deserts of vast eternity.
Thy beauty shall no more be found;   *25*
Nor, in thy marble vault, shall sound
My echoing song: then worms shall try
That long-preserved virginity,
And your quaint honor turn to dust,
And into ashes all my lust.   *30*
The grave's a fine and private place,
But none, I think, do there embrace.
    Now, therefore, while the youthful hue
Sits on thy skin like morning dew,
And while thy willing soul transpires   *35*
At every pore with instant fires,
Now let us sport us while we may;
And now, like amorous birds of prey,
Rather at once our Time devour,
Than languish in his slow-chapt power.   *40*
Let us roll all our strength and all
Our sweetness up into one ball,
And tear our pleasures with rough strife
Thorough the iron gates of life.
Thus, though we cannot make our sun   *45*
Stand still, yet we will make him run.

ANDREW MARVELL

Mac Flecknoe

or, *A Satire Upon the True-Blue-Protestant Poet T. S.*

All human things are subject to decay,   *1*
And when Fate summons, monarchs must obey,
This Flecknoe found, who, like Augustus, young
Was call'd to empire, and had govern'd long:
In prose and verse, was own'd, without dispute,   *5*
Thro' all the realms of *Nonsense*, absolute.

This aged prince, now flourishing in peace,
And blest with issue of a large increase,
Worn out with business, did at length debate
To settle the succession of the State;   10
And, pond'ring which of all his sons was fit
To reign, and wage immortal war with wit,
Cried: " 'T is resolv'd; for Nature pleads, that he
Should only rule, who most resembles me.
Sh—— alone my perfect image bears,   15
Mature in dulness from his tender years:
Sh—— alone of all my sons is he
Who stands confirm'd in full stupidity,
The rest to some faint meaning make pretense,
But Sh—— never deviates into sense.   20
Some beams of wit on other souls may fall,
Strike thro', and make a lucid interval;
But Sh——'s genuine night admits no ray,
His rising fogs prevail upon the day.
Besides, his goodly fabric fills the eye,   25
And seems design'd for thoughtless majesty:
Thoughtless as monarch oaks that shade the plain,
And, spread in solemn state, supinely reign.
Heywood and Shirley were but types of thee,
Thou last great prophet of tautology.   30
Even I, a dunce of more renown than they,
Was sent before but to prepare thy way:
And coarsely clad in Norwich drugget came
To teach the nations in thy greater name.
My warbling lute, the lute I whilom strung,   35
When to King John of Portugal I sung,
Was but the prelude to that glorious day,
When thou on silver Thames didst cut thy way,
With well-tim'd oars before the royal barge,
Swell'd with the pride of thy celestial charge;   40
And big with hymn, commander of a host,
The like was ne'er in Epsom blankets toss'd.
Methinks I see the new Arion sail,
The lute still trembling underneath thy nail.

At thy well-sharpen'd thumb from shore to shore   *45*
The treble squeaks for fear, the basses roar;
Echoes from Pissing Alley Sh—— call,
And Sh—— they resound from Aston Hall.
About thy boat the little fishes throng,
As at the morning toast that floats along.   *50*
Sometimes, as prince of thy harmonious band,
Thou wield'st thy papers in thy threshing hand.
St. André's feet ne'er kept more equal time,
Not ev'n the feet of thy own *Psyche's* rhyme:
Tho' they in number as in sense excel,   *55*
So just, so like tautology, they fell,
That, pale with envy, Singleton forswore
The lute and sword, which he in triumph bore,
And vow'd he ne'er would act Villerius more."
Here stopp'd the good old sire, and wept for joy   *60*
In silent raptures of the hopeful boy.
All arguments, but most his plays, persuade,
That for anointed dulness he was made.

   Close to the walls which fair Augusta bind,
(The fair Augusta much to fears inclin'd)   *65*
An ancient fabric rais'd t' inform the sight,
There stood of yore, and Barbican it hight:
A watchtower once; but now, so fate ordains,
Of all the pile an empty name remains.
From its old ruins brothel-houses rise,   *70*
Scenes of lewd loves, and of polluted joys,
Where their vast courts the mother-strumpets keep,
And, undisturb'd by watch, in silence sleep.
Near these a Nursery erects its head,
Where queens are form'd, and future heroes bred;   *75*
Where unfledg'd actors learn to laugh and cry,
Where infant punks their tender voices try,
And little Maximins the gods defy.
Great Fletcher never treads in buskins here,
Nor greater Jonson dares in socks appear;   *80*
But gentle Simkin just reception finds
Amidst this monument of vanish'd minds:

Pure clinches the suburbian Muse affords,
And Panton waging harmless war with words.
Here Flecknoe, as a place to fame well known,   *85*
Ambitiously design'd his Sh——'s throne;
For ancient Dekker prophesied long since,
That in this pile should reign a mighty prince,
Born for a scourge of wit, and flail of sense,
To whom true dulness should some *Psyches* owe,   *90*
But worlds of *Misers* from his pen should flow;
Humorists and hypocrites it should produce,
Whole Raymond families, and tribes of Bruce.
  Now Empress Fame had publish'd the renown
Of Sh——'s coronation thro' the town.   *95*
Rous'd by report of Fame, the nations meet,
From near Bunhill, and distant Watling Street.
No Persian carpets spread th' imperial way,
But scatter'd limbs of mangled poets lay;
From dusty shops neglected authors come,   *100*
Martyrs of pies, and relics of the bum.
Much Heywood, Shirley, Ogleby there lay,
But loads of Sh—— almost chok'd the way.
Bilk'd stationers for yeomen stood prepar'd
And Herringman was captain of the guard.   *105*
The hoary prince in majesty appear'd,
High on a throne of his own labors rear'd.
At his right hand our young Ascanius sat,
Rome's other hope, and pillar of the State.
His brows thick fogs, instead of glories, grace,   *110*
And lambent dulness play'd around his face.
As Hannibal did to the altars come,
Sworn by his sire a mortal foe to Rome;
So Sh—— swore, nor should his vow be vain,
That he till death true dulness would maintain;   *115*
And, in his father's right, and realm's defense,
Ne'er to have peace with wit, nor truce with sense.
The king himself the sacred unction made,
As king by office, and as priest by trade.
In his sinister hand, instead of ball,   *120*

He plac'd a mighty mug of potent ale ;
Love's *Kingdom* to his right he did convey,
At once his scepter, and his rule of sway ;
Whose righteous lore the prince had practic'd young
And from those loins recorded *Psyche* sprung.   *125*
His temples, last, with poppies were o'erspread,
That nodding seem'd to consecrate his head :
Just at that point of time, if fame nŏt lie,
On his left hand twelve reverend owls did fly.
So Romulus, 't is sung, by Tiber's brook,   *130*
Presage of sway from twice six vultures took.
Th' admiring throng loud acclamations make,
And omens of his future empire take.
The sire then shook the honors of his head,
And from his brows damps of oblivion shed   *135*
Full on the filial dulness : long he stood,
Repelling from his breast the raging god ;
At length burst out in this prophetic mood :
    "Heavens bless my son, from Ireland let him reign
To far Barbadoes on the western main ;   *140*
Of his dominion may no end be known,
And greater than his father's be his throne ;
Beyond *Love's Kingdom* let him stretch his pen !"
He paus'd, and all the people cried, "Amen."
Then thus continued he : "My son, advance   *145*
Still in new impudence, new ignorance.
Success let others teach, learn thou from me
Pangs without birth, and fruitless industry.
Let *Virtuosos* in five years be writ ;
Yet not one thought accuse thy toil of wit.   *150*
Let gentle George in triumph tread the stage,
Make Dorimant betray, and Loveit rage ;
Let Cully, Cockwood, Fopling, charm the pit,
And in their folly shew the writer's wit.
Yet still thy fools shall stand in thy defense   *155*
And justify their author's want of sense.
Let 'em be all by thy own model made
Of dulness, and desire no foreign aid,

That they to future ages may be known,
Not copies drawn, but issue of thy own.   *160*
Nay, let thy men of wit too be the same,
All full of thee, and differing but in name.
But let no alien S—dl—y interpose,
To lard with wit thy hungry *Epsom* prose.
And when false flowers of rhetoric thou wouldst cull,   *165*
Trust nature, do not labor to be dull;
But write thy best, and top; and, in each line,
Sir Formal's oratory will be thine:
Sir Formal, tho' unsought, attends thy quill,
And does thy northern dedications fill.   *170*
Nor let false friends seduce thy mind to fame,
By arrogating Jonson's hostile name.
Let father Flecknoe fire thy mind with praise,
And uncle Ogleby thy envy raise.
Thou art my blood, where Jonson has no part: *175*
What share have we in nature, or in art?
Where did his wit on learning fix a brand,
And rail at arts he did not understand?
Where made he love in Prince Nicander's vein,
Or swept the dust in *Psyche's* humble strain?   *180*
Where sold he bargains, 'whip-stitch, kiss my arse,'
Promis'd a play and dwindled to a farce?
When did his Muse from Fletcher scenes purloin,
As thou whole Eth'rege dost transfuse to thine?
But so transfus'd, as oil on water's flow,   *185*
His always floats above, thine sinks below.
This is thy province, this thy wondrous way,
New humors to invent for each new play:
This is that boasted bias of thy mind,
By which one way, to dulness, 't is inclin'd,   *190*
Which makes thy writings lean on one side still,
And, in all changes, that way bends thy will.
Nor let thy mountain-belly make pretense
Of likeness; thine's a tympany of sense.
A tun of man in thy large bulk is writ,   *195*
But sure thou 'rt but a kilderkin of wit.

Like mine, thy gentle numbers feebly creep;
Thy tragic Muse gives smiles, thy comic sleep.
With whate'er gall thou sett'st thyself to write,
Thy inoffensive satires never bite.   *200*
In thy felonious heart tho' venom lies,
It does but touch thy Irish pen, and dies.
Thy genius calls thee not to purchase fame
In keen iambics, but mild anagram.
Leave writing plays, and choose for thy command   *205*
Some peaceful province in acrostic land.
There thou may'st wings display, and altars raise,
And torture one poor word ten thousand ways;
Or, if thou wouldst thy diff'rent talents suit,
Set thy own songs, and sing them to thy lute."   *210*
    He said: but his last words were scarcely heard,
For Bruce and Longvil had a trap prepar'd,
And down they sent the yet declaiming bard.
Sinking he left his drugget robe behind,
Borne upwards by a subterranean wind.   *215*
The mantle fell to the young prophet's part,
With double portion of his father's art.

                                        JOHN DRYDEN

A Song for St. Cecilia's Day, 1687

I

From harmony, from heav'nly harmony   *1*
    This universal frame began:
    When Nature underneath a heap
        Of jarring atoms lay,
    And could not heave her head,   *5*
The tuneful voice was heard from high:
    "Arise, ye more than dead."
Then cold, and hot, and moist, and dry
In order to their stations leap,
    And Music's pow'r obey.   *10*
From harmony, from heav'nly harmony
    This universal frame began:
    From harmony to harmony

Thro' all the compass of the notes it ran,
The diapason closing full in Man.   *15*

II

What passion cannot Music raise and quell!
  When Jubal struck the corded shell,
 His list'ning brethren stood around,
 And, wond'ring, on their faces fell
 To worship that celestial sound: *20*
Less than a god they thought there could not dwell
  Within the hollow of that shell,
  That spoke so sweetly and so well.
What passion cannot Music raise and quell!

III

 The trumpet's loud clangor   *25*
  Excites us to arms
 With shrill notes of anger
  And mortal alarms.
 The double double double beat
  Of the thund'ring drum   *30*
Cries: "Hark! the foes come;
Charge, charge, 't is too late to retreat."

IV

 The soft complaining flute
 In dying notes discovers
 The woes of hopeless lovers,   *35*
Whose dirge is whisper'd by the warbling lute.

V

 Sharp violins proclaim
Their jealous pangs, and desperation,
Fury, frantic indignation,
Depth of pains, and height of passion,   *40*
 For the fair, disdainful dame.

VI

 But O! what art can teach,
 What human voice can reach

The sacred organ's praise?
  Notes inspiring holy love,   45
Notes that wing their heav'nly ways
  To mend the choirs above.

VII

Orpheus could lead the savage race,
And trees unrooted left their place,
  Sequacious of the lyre;   50
But bright Cecilia rais'd the wonder high'r:
When to her organ vocal breath was giv'n,
An angel heard, and straight appear'd,
  Mistaking earth for heav'n.

GRAND CHORUS

As from the pow'r of sacred lays   55
  The spheres began to move,
And sung the great Creator's praise
  To all the blessed above;
So, when the last and dreadful hour
This crumbling pageant shall devour,   60
The trumpet shall be heard on high,
The dead shall live, the living die,
And Music shall untune the sky.

JOHN DRYDEN

Alexander's Feast

or, *The Power of Music; An Ode in Honor of St. Cecilia's Day: 1697*

I

'T was at the royal feast, for Persia won   1
  By Philip's warlike son:
  Aloft in awful state
  The godlike hero sate
  On his imperial throne;   5
His valiant peers were plac'd around;
Their brows with roses and with myrtles bound:
  (So should desert in arms be crown'd.)

The lovely Thais, by his side,
Sate like a blooming Eastern bride   *10*
In flow'r of youth and beauty's pride.
   Happy, happy, happy pair!
   None but the brave,
   None but the brave,
   None but the brave deserves the fair.   *15*

      CHORUS
   Happy, happy, happy pair!
   None but the brave,
   None but the brave,
   None but the brave deserves the fair.

     II
Timotheus, plac'd on high   *20*
   Amid the tuneful choir,
    With flying fingers touch'd the lyre:
   The trembling notes ascend the sky,
     And heav'nly joys inspire.
The song began from Jove,   *25*
Who left his blissful seats above,
(Such is the pow'r of mighty love.)
A dragon's fiery form belied the god:
Sublime on radiant spires he rode,
   When he to fair Olympia press'd;   *30*
   And while he sought her snowy breast:
Then, round her slender waist he curl'd,
And stamp'd an image of himself, a sov'reign of the world.
The list'ning crowd admire the lofty sound,
"A present deity," they shout around: *35*
"A present deity," the vaulted roofs rebound.
    With ravish'd ears
    The monarch hears,
    Assumes the god,
    Affects to nod,   *40*
   And seems to shake the spheres.

CHORUS

With ravish'd ears
The monarch hears,
Assumes the god,
Affects to nod,   *45*
And seems to shake the spheres.

III

The praise of Bacchus then the sweet musician sung,
   Of Bacchus ever fair and ever young:
      The jolly god in triumph comes;
         Sound the trumpets; beat the drums;   *50*
            Flush'd with a purple grace
            He shews his honest face:
Now give the hautboys breath; he comes, he comes.
      Bacchus, ever fair and young
         Drinking joys did first ordain;   *55*
      Bacchus' blessings are a treasure,
      Drinking is the soldier's pleasure;
            Rich the treasure,
            Sweet the pleasure,
         Sweet is pleasure after pain.   *60*

CHORUS

Bacchus' blessings are a treasure,
Drinking is the soldier's pleasure;
      Rich the treasure,
      Sweet the pleasure,
   Sweet is pleasure after pain.   *65*

IV

Sooth'd with the sound, the king grew vain;
   Fought all his battles o'er again;
And thrice he routed all his foes; and thrice he slew the slain.
The master saw the madness rise,
His glowing cheeks, his ardent eyes;   *70*
And, while he heav'n and earth defied,
Chang'd his hand, and check'd his pride.

He chose a mournful Muse,
    Soft pity to infuse;
He sung Darius great and good,   75
    By too severe a fate,
Fallen, fallen, fallen, fallen,
    Fallen from his high estate,
        And welt'ring in his blood;
Deserted, at his utmost need   80
By those his former bounty fed;
On the bare earth expos'd he lies,
With not a friend to close his eyes.
With downcast looks the joyless victor sate,
    Revolving in his alter'd soul   85
        The various turns of chance below;
    And, now and then, a sigh he stole,
        And tears began to flow.

CHORUS

Revolving in his alter'd soul
    The various turns of chance below;   90
And, now and then, a sigh he stole,
    And tears began to flow.

V

The mighty master smil'd to see
That love was in the next degree;
'T was but a kindred sound to move,   95
For pity melts the mind to love.
    Softly sweet, in Lydian measures,
Soon he sooth'd his soul to pleasures.
"War," he sung, "is toil and trouble;
Honor, but an empty bubble.   100
    Never ending, still beginning,
Fighting still, and still destroying:
    If the world be worth thy winning,
Think, O think it worth enjoying.
    Lovely Thais sits beside thee,   105
        Take the good the gods provide thee."

The many rend the skies with loud applause;
So Love was crown'd, but Music won the cause.
    The prince, unable to conceal his pain,
      Gaz'd on the fair   *110*
      Who caus'd his care,
    And sigh'd and look'd, sigh'd and look'd,
    Sigh'd and look'd, and sigh'd again:
At length, with love and wine at once oppress'd,
The vanquish'd victor sunk upon her breast.   *115*

         CHORUS
    The prince, unable to conceal his pain,
      Gaz'd on the fair
      Who caus'd his care,
    And sigh'd and look'd, sigh'd and look'd,
    Sigh'd and look'd, and sigh'd again: *120*
At length, with love and wine at once oppress'd,
The vanquish'd victor sunk upon her breast.

         VI
Now strike the golden lyre again;
A louder yet, and yet a louder strain.
Break his bands of sleep asunder,   *125*
And rouse him, like a rattling peal of thunder.
    Hark, hark, the horrid sound
      Has rais'd up his head:
        As wak'd from the dead,
      And amaz'd, he stares around.   *130*
"Revenge, revenge!" Timotheus cries,
      "See the Furies arise!
      See the snakes that they rear,
      How they hiss in their hair,
    And the sparkles that flash from their eyes!   *135*
      Behold a ghastly band,
      Each a torch in his hand!
Those are Grecian ghosts, that in battle were slain,
        And unburied remain
          Inglorious on the plain: *140*

Give the vengeance due
To the valiant crew.
Behold how they toss their torches on high,
How they point to the Persian abodes,
And glitt'ring temples of their hostile gods!"   *145*
The princes applaud, with a furious joy;
And the king seiz'd a flambeau with zeal to destroy;
Thais led the way,
To light him to his prey,
And, like another Helen, fir'd another Troy.   *150*

CHORUS

And the king seiz'd a flambeau with zeal to destroy;
Thais led the way,
To light him to his prey,
And like another Helen, fir'd another Troy.

VII

Thus long ago,   *155*
Ere heaving bellows learn'd to blow,
While organs yet were mute;
Timotheus, to his breathing flute,
And sounding lyre,
Could swell the soul to rage, or kindle soft desire.   *160*
At last, divine Cecilia came,
Inventress of the vocal frame;
The sweet enthusiast, from her sacred store,
Enlarg'd the former narrow bounds,
And added length to solemn sounds,   *165*
With nature's mother wit, and arts unknown before.
Let old Timotheus yield the prize,
Or both divide the crown:
He rais'd a mortal to the skies;
She drew an angel down.   *170*

GRAND CHORUS

At last, divine Cecilia came,
Inventress of the vocal frame;

The sweet enthusiast, from her sacred store,
    Enlarg'd the former narrow bounds,
    And added length to solemn sounds,   *175*
With nature's mother wit, and arts unknown before.
   Let old Timotheus yield the prize,
     Or both divide the crown :
   He rais'd a mortal to the skies ;
     She drew an angel down.   *180*

                            JOHN DRYDEN

On the Death of Mr. Robert Levet

Condemn'd to hope's delusive mine,   *1*
   As on we toil from day to day,
By sudden blasts, or slow decline,
   Our social comforts drop away.

Well tried through many a varying year,   *5*
   See LEVET to the grave descend ;
Officious, innocent, sincere,
   Of every friendless name the friend.

Yet still he fills affection's eye,
   Obscurely wise, and coarsely kind ;   *10*
Nor, letter'd arrogance, deny
   Thy praise to merit unrefin'd.

When fainting nature call'd for aid,
   And hov'ring death prepar'd the blow,
His vig'rous remedy display'd   *15*
   The power of art without the show.

In misery's darkest caverns known,
   His useful care was ever nigh,
Where hopeless anguish pour'd his groan,
   And lonely want retir'd to die.   *20*

No summons mock'd by chill delay,
  No petty gain disdain'd by pride,
The modest wants of ev'ry day
  The toil of ev'ry day supplied.

His virtues walk'd their narrow round,   25
  Nor made a pause, nor left a void;
And sure th' Eternal Master found
  The single talent well employ'd.

The busy day, the peaceful night,
  Unfelt, uncounted, glided by;   30
His frame was firm, his powers were bright,
  Tho' now his eightieth year was nigh.

Then with no throbbing fiery pain,
  No cold gradations of decay,
Death broke at once the vital chain,   35
  And freed his soul the nearest way.

                              SAMUEL JOHNSON

Sonnet on the Death of Richard West

In vain to me the smileing Mornings shine,   1
  And redning Phoebus lifts his golden Fire:
The Birds in vain their amorous Descant joyn;
  Or chearful Fields resume their green Attire:
These Ears, alas! for other Notes repine,   5
  A different Object do these Eyes require.
My lonely Anguish melts no Heart, but mine;
  And in my Breast the imperfect Joys expire.
Yet Morning smiles the busy Race to chear,
  And new-born Pleasure brings to happier Men: 10
The Fields to all their wonted Tribute bear:
  To warm their little Loves the Birds complain:
I fruitless mourn to him, that cannot hear,
  And weep the more because I weep in vain.

                              THOMAS GRAY

Ode to Evening

If ought of Oaten Stop, or Pastoral Song,   *1*
May hope, O pensive *Eve*, to soothe thine Ear,
     Like thy own brawling Springs,
     Thy Springs, and dying Gales,
O *Nymph* reserv'd, while now the bright-hair'd Sun   *5*
Sits in yon western Tent, whose cloudy Skirts,
     With Brede ethereal wove,
     O'erhang his wavy Bed:
Now Air is hush'd, save where the weak-ey'd Bat,
With short shrill Shriek flits by on leathern Wing,   *10*
     Or where the Beetle winds
     His small but sullen Horn,
As oft he rises 'midst the twilight Path,
Against the Pilgrim born in heedless Hum:
     Now teach me, *Maid* compos'd,   *15*
     To breathe some soften'd Strain,
Whose Numbers stealing thro' thy darkning Vale,
May not unseemly with its Stillness suit,
     As musing slow, I hail
     Thy genial lov'd Return!   *20*
For when thy folding Star arising shews
His paly Circlet, at his warning Lamp
     The fragrant *Hours*, and *Elves*
     Who slept in Buds the Day,
And many a *Nymph* who wreaths her Brows with Sedge,   *25*
And sheds the fresh'ning Dew, and lovelier still,
     The *Pensive Pleasures* sweet
     Prepare thy shadowy Car.
Then let me rove some wild and heathy Scene,
Or find some Ruin 'midst its dreary Dells,   *30*
     Whose Walls more awful nod
     By thy religious Gleams.
Or if chill blustring Winds, or driving Rain,
Prevent my willing Feet, be mine the Hut,
     That from the Mountain's Side,   *35*
     Views Wilds, and swelling Floods,

And Hamlets brown, and dim-discover'd Spires,
And hears their simple Bell, and marks o'er all
    Thy Dewy Fingers draw
    The gradual dusky Veil.   *40*
While *Spring* shall pour his Show'rs, as oft he wont,
And bathe thy breathing Tresses, meekest *Eve!*
    While *Summer* loves to sport,
    Beneath thy ling'ring Light:
While sallow *Autumn* fills thy Lap with Leaves,   *45*
Or *Winter* yelling thro' the troublous Air,
    Affrights thy shrinking Train,
    And rudely rends thy Robes.
So long regardful of thy quiet Rule,
Shall *Fancy, Friendship, Science,* smiling *Peace,*   *50*
    Thy gentlest Influence own,
    And love thy fav'rite Name!

WILLIAM COLLINS

The Echoing Green

The Sun does arise,   *1*
And make happy the skies;
The merry bells ring
To welcome the Spring;
The skylark and thrush,   *5*
The birds of the bush,
Sing louder around
To the bells' chearful sound,
While our sports shall be seen
On the Echoing Green.   *10*

Old John, with white hair,
Does laugh away care,
Sitting under the oak,
Among the old folk.
They laugh at our play,   *15*
And soon they all say:
"Such, such were the joys
"When we all, girls and boys,

"In our youth time were seen
"On the Echoing Green."   *20*

Till the little ones, weary,
No more can be merry;
The sun does descend,
And our sports have an end.
Round the laps of their mothers   *25*
Many sisters and brothers,
Like birds in their nest,
Are ready for rest,
And sport no more seen
On the darkening Green.   *30*

WILLIAM BLAKE

London

I wander thro' each charter'd street,   *1*
Near where the charter'd Thames does flow,
And mark in every face I meet
Marks of weakness, marks of woe.

In every cry of every Man,   *5*
In every Infant's cry of fear,
In every voice, in every ban,
The mind-forg'd manacles I hear.

How the Chimney-sweeper's cry
Every black'ning Church appalls;   *10*
And the hapless Soldier's sigh
Runs in blood down Palace walls.

But most thro' midnight streets I hear
How the youthful Harlot's curse
Blasts the new born Infant's tear,   *15*
And blights with plagues the Marriage hearse.

WILLIAM BLAKE

To a Mouse, on Turning Her Up in Her Nest with the Plough, November 1785

Wee, sleekit, cow'rin', tim'rous beastie,   *1*
O what a panic's in thy breastie!
Thou need na start awa sae hasty,
   Wi' bickering brattle!
I wad be laith to rin an' chase thee   *5*
   Wi' murd'ring pattle!

I'm truly sorry man's dominion
Has broken Nature's social union,
An' justifies that ill opinion
   Which makes thee startle   *10*
At me, thy poor earth-born companion,
   An' fellow mortal!

I doubt na, whiles, but thou may thieve;
What then? poor beastie, thou maun live!
A daimen-icker in a thrave   *15*
   'S a sma' request:
I'll get a blessin' wi' the lave,
   And never miss 't!

Thy wee bit housie, too, in ruin!
Its silly wa's the win's are strewin'!   *20*
An' naething, now, to big a new ane,
   O' foggage green!
An' bleak December's winds ensuin',
   Baith snell an' keen!

Thou saw the fields laid bare and waste.   *25*
An' weary winter comin' fast,
An' cozie here, beneath the blast,
   Thou thought to dwell,
Till crash! the cruel coulter past
   Out thro' thy cell.   *30*

That wee bit heap o' leaves an' stibble
Has cost thee mony a weary nibble!
Now thou 's turn'd out, for a' thy trouble,
    But house or hald,
To thole the winter's sleety dribble,   *35*
        An' cranreuch cauld!

But, Mousie, thou art no thy lane,
In proving foresight may be vain:
The best laid schemes o' mice an' men
            Gang aft a-gley,   *40*
An' lea'e us nought but grief an' pain
            For promis'd joy.

Still thou art blest compar'd wi' me!
The present only toucheth thee:
But oh! I backward cast my e'e   *45*
            On prospects drear!
An' forward tho' I canna see,
        I guess an' fear!

                    ROBERT BURNS

Tam o' Shanter

When chapman billies leave the street,   *1*
And drouthy neibors neibors meet,
As market-days are wearing late,
An' folk begin to tak the gate;
While we sit bousing at the nappy,   *5*
An' getting fou and unco happy,
We think na on the lang Scots miles,
The mosses, waters, slaps, and styles,
That lie between us and our hame,
Where sits our sulky sullen dame,   *10*
Gathering her brows like gathering storm,
Nursing her wrath to keep it warm.
    This truth fand honest Tam o' Shanter,
As he frae Ayr ae night did canter—

(Auld Ayr, wham ne'er a town surpasses   *15*
For honest men and bonnie lasses).
  O Tam! hadst thou but been sae wise
As ta'en thy ain wife Kate's advice!
She tauld thee weel thou was a skellum,
A bletherin', blusterin', drunken blellum;   *20*
That frae November till October,
Ae market-day thou was na sober;
That ilka melder wi' the miller
Thou sat as lang as thou had siller;
That every naig was ca'd a shoe on,   *25*
The smith and thee gat roarin' fou on;
That at the Lord's house, even on Sunday,
Thou drank wi' Kirkton Jean till Monday.
She prophesied that, late or soon,
Thou would be found deep drown'd in Doon;   *30*
Or catch'd wi' warlocks in the mirk
By Alloway's auld haunted kirk.
  Ah, gentle dames! it gars me greet
To think how mony counsels sweet,
How mony lengthen'd sage advices,   *35*
The husband frae the wife despises!
  But to our tale: Ae market night,
Tam had got planted unco right,
Fast by an ingle, bleezing finely,
Wi' reaming swats, that drank divinely;   *40*
And at his elbow, Souter Johnny,
His ancient, trusty, drouthy crony;
Tam lo'ed him like a very brither;
They had been fou for weeks thegither.
The night drave on wi' sangs and clatter,   *45*
And aye the ale was growing better:
The landlady and Tam grew gracious,
Wi' favours secret, sweet, and precious;
The souter tauld his queerest stories;
The landlord's laugh was ready chorus: *50*
The storm without might rair and rustle,
Tam did na mind the storm a whistle.

Care, mad to see a man sae happy,
E'en drown'd himsel amang the nappy.
As bees flee hame wi' lades o' treasure,   55
The minutes wing'd their way wi' pleasure ;
Kings may be blest, but Tam was glorious,
O'er a' the ills o' life victorious !

But pleasures are like poppies spread—
You seize the flow'r, its bloom is shed ;   60
Or like the snow falls in the river—
A moment white, then melts for ever ;
Or like the borealis race,
That flit ere you can point their place ;
Or like the rainbow's lovely form   65
Evanishing amid the storm.
Nae man can tether time nor tide ;
The hour approaches Tam maun ride ;
That hour, o' night's black arch the key-stane,
That dreary hour, he mounts his beast in ;   70
And sic a night he taks the road in,
As ne'er poor sinner was abroad in.

The wind blew as 'twad blawn its last ;
The rattling show'rs rose on the blast ;
The speedy gleams the darkness swallow'd ;   75
Loud, deep, and lang, the thunder bellow'd :
That night, a child might understand,
The Deil had business on his hand.

Weel mounted on his gray mare, Meg,
A better never lifted leg,   80
Tam skelpit on thro' dub and mire,
Despising wind, and rain, and fire ;
Whiles holding fast his gude blue bonnet ;
Whiles crooning o'er some auld Scots sonnet ;
Whiles glow'ring round wi' prudent cares,   85
Lest bogles catch him unawares.
Kirk-Alloway was drawing nigh,
Whare ghaists and houlets nightly cry.

By this time he was cross the ford,
Where in the snaw the chapman smoor'd ;   90

And past the birks and meikle stane,
Where drunken Charlie brak's neck-bane;
And thro' the whins, and by the cairn,
Where hunters fand the murder'd bairn;
And near the thorn, aboon the well,   *95*
Where Mungo's mither hang'd hersel.
Before him Doon pours all his floods;
The doubling storm roars thro' the woods;
The lightnings flash from pole to pole;
Near and more near the thunders roll: *100*
When, glimmering thro' the groaning trees,
Kirk-Alloway seem'd in a bleeze;
Thro' ilka bore the beams were glancing;
And loud resounded mirth and dancing.
  Inspiring bold John Barleycorn!   *105*
What dangers thou canst make us scorn!
Wi' tippenny, we fear nae evil;
Wi' usquebae, we'll face the devil!
The swats sae ream'd in Tammie's noddle,
Fair play, he car'd na deils a boddle!   *110*
But Maggie stood right sair astonish'd,
Till, by the heel and hand admonish'd,
She ventur'd forward on the light;
And, vow! Tam saw an unco sight!
Warlocks and witches in a dance;   *115*
Nae cotillion brent new frae France,
But hornpipes, jigs, strathspeys, and reels,
Put life and mettle in their heels.
A winnock-bunker in the east,
There sat auld Nick, in shape o' beast—   *120*
A touzie tyke, black, grim, and large!
To gie them music was his charge:
He screw'd the pipes and gart them skirl,
Till roof and rafters a' did dirl.
Coffins stood round like open presses,   *125*
That shaw'd the dead in their last dresses;
And by some devilish cantraip sleight
Each in its cauld hand held a light,

By which heroic Tam was able
To note upon the haly table 130
A murderer's banes in gibbet-airns;
Twa span-lang, wee, unchristen'd bairns;
A thief new-cutted frae the rape—
Wi' his last gasp his gab did gape;
Five tomahawks, wi' blude red rusted; 135
Five scymitars, wi' murder crusted;
A garter, which a babe had strangled;
A knife, a father's throat had mangled,
Whom his ain son o' life bereft—
The gray hairs yet stack to the heft; 140
Wi' mair of horrible and awfu',
Which even to name wad be unlawfu'.

As Tammie glowr'd, amaz'd, and curious,
The mirth and fun grew fast and furious:
The piper loud and louder blew; 145
The dancers quick and quicker flew;
They reel'd, they set, they cross'd, they cleekit,
Till ilka carlin swat and reekit,
And coost her duddies to the wark,
And linkit at it in her sark! 150

Now Tam, O Tam! had thae been queans,
A' plump and strapping in their teens;
Their sarks, instead o' creeshie flannen,
Been snaw-white seventeen hunder linen!
Thir breeks o' mine, my only pair, 155
That ance were plush, o' gude blue hair,
I wad hae gi'en them off my hurdies,
For ae blink o' the bonnie burdies!

But wither'd beldams, auld and droll,
Rigwoodie hags wad spean a foal, 160
Louping and flinging on a crummock,
I wonder didna turn thy stomach.

But Tam kent what was what fu' brawlie,
There was ae winsome wench and walie
That night enlisted in the core, 165
Lang after kent on Carrick shore!

(For mony a beast to dead she shot,
And perish'd mony a bonnie boat,
And shook baith meikle corn and bear,
And kept the country-side in fear.)   *170*
Her cutty sark, o' Paisley harn,
That while a lassie she had worn,
In longitude tho' sorely scanty,
It was her best, and she was vauntie.
Ah! little kent thy reverend grannie   *175*
That sark she coft for her wee Nannie
Wi' twa pund Scots ('twas a' her riches)
Wad ever grac'd a dance of witches!
    But here my muse her wing maun cour;
Sic flights are far beyond her pow'r—   *180*
To sing how Nannie lap and flang,
(A souple jade she was, and strang);
And how Tam stood, like ane bewitch'd,
And thought his very een enrich'd;
Even Satan glowr'd, and fidg'd fu' fain,   *185*
And hotch'd and blew wi' might and main:
Till first ae caper, syne anither,
Tam tint his reason a' thegither,
And roars out 'Weel done, Cutty-sark!'
And in an instant all was dark!   *190*
And scarcely had he Maggie rallied,
When out the hellish legion sallied.
    As bees bizz out wi' angry fyke
When plundering herds assail their byke,
As open pussie's mortal foes   *195*
When pop! she starts before their nose,
As eager runs the market-crowd,
When 'Catch the thief!' resounds aloud.
So Maggie runs; the witches follow,
Wi' mony an eldritch skriech and hollow.   *200*
    Ah, Tam! ah, Tam! thou'll get thy fairin'!
In hell they'll roast thee like a herrin'!
In vain thy Kate awaits thy comin'!
Kate soon will be a woefu' woman!

Now do thy speedy utmost, Meg,   *205*
And win the key-stane o' the brig:
There at them thou thy tail may toss,
A running stream they darena cross,
But ere the key-stane she could make,
The fient a tail she had to shake!   *210*
For Nannie, far before the rest,
Hard upon noble Maggie prest,
And flew at Tam wi' furious ettle;
But little wist she Maggie's mettle!
Ae spring brought off her master hale,   *215*
But left behind her ain gray tail:
The carlin claught her by the rump,
And left poor Maggie scarce a stump.
   Now, wha this tale o' truth shall read,
Each man and mother's son, take heed;   *220*
Whene'er to drink you are inclin'd,
Or cutty-sarks rin in your mind,
Think! ye may buy the joys o'er dear;
Remember Tam o' Shanter's mare.

                     ROBERT BURNS

Ode

*Intimations of Immortality from Recollections of Early
Childhood*

I

There was a time when meadow, grove, and stream,   *1*
The earth, and every common sight,
    To me did seem
   Apparelled in celestial light,
The glory and freshness of a dream.   *5*
It is not now as it hath been of yore;—
   Turn wheresoe'er I may,
    By night or day,
The things which I have seen I now can see no more.

II

The Rainbow comes and goes,   *10*
  And lovely is the Rose,
  The Moon doth with delight
Look round her when the heavens are bare,
  Waters on a starry night
  Are beautiful and fair;   *15*
The sunshine is a glorious birth;
But yet I know, where'er I go,
That there hath past away a glory from the earth.

III

Now, while the birds thus sing a joyous song,
  And while the young lambs bound   *20*
    As to the tabor's sound,
To me alone there came a thought of grief:
A timely utterance gave that thought relief,
  And I again am strong:
The cataracts blow their trumpets from the steep;   *25*
No more shall grief of mine the season wrong;
I hear the Echoes through the mountains throng,
The Winds come to me from the fields of sleep,
  And all the earth is gay;
    Land and sea   *30*
  Give themselves up to jollity,
   And with the heart of May
Doth every Beast keep holiday;—
   Thou Child of Joy,
Shout round me, let me hear thy shouts, thou happy
    Shepherd-boy!   *35*

IV

Ye blessèd Creatures, I have heard the call
  Ye to each other make; I see
The heavens laugh with you in your jubilee;
  My heart is at your festival,
   My head hath its coronal,   *40*
The fulness of your bliss, I feel—I feel it all.

Oh evil day ! if I were sullen
While Earth herself is adorning,
 This sweet May-morning,
And the Children are culling   *45*
 On every side,
In a thousand valleys far and wide,
Fresh flowers ; while the sun shines warm,
And the Babe leaps up on his Mother's arm :—
 I hear, I hear, with joy I hear !   *50*
 —But there's a Tree, of many, one,
A single Field which I have looked upon,
Both of them speak of something that is gone :
 The Pansy at my feet
 Doth the same tale repeat :   *55*
Whither is fled the visionary gleam ?
Where is it now, the glory and the dream ?

v
Our birth is but a sleep and a forgetting :
The Soul that rises with us, our life's Star,
 Hath had elsewhere its setting,   *60*
  And cometh from afar :
 Not in entire forgetfulness,
 And not in utter nakedness,
But trailing clouds of glory do we come
 From God, who is our home :   *65*
Heaven lies about us in our infancy !
Shades of the prison-house begin to close
 Upon the growing Boy,
But He beholds the light, and whence it flows,
 He sees it in his joy ;   *70*
The Youth, who daily farther from the east
 Must travel, still is Nature's Priest,
 And by the vision splendid
 Is on his way attended ;
At length the Man perceives it die away, *75*
And fade into the light of common day.

VI

Earth fills her lap with pleasures of her own;
Yearnings she hath in her own natural kind,
And, even with something of a Mother's mind,
   And no unworthy aim,   80
   The homely Nurse doth all she can
To make her Foster-child, her Inmate Man,
   Forget the glories he hath known,
And that imperial palace whence he came.

VII

Behold the Child among his new-born blisses,   85
A six years' Darling of a pigmy size!
See, where 'mid work of his own hand he lies,
Fretted by sallies of his mother's kisses,
With light upon him from his father's eyes!
See, at his feet, some little plan or chart,   90
Some fragment from his dream of human life,
Shaped by himself with newly-learned art;
   A wedding or a festival,
   A mourning or a funeral;
    And this hath now his heart,   95
   And unto this he frames his song:
    Then will he fit his tongue
To dialogues of business, love, or strife;
   But it will not be long
   Ere this be thrown aside,   100
   And with new joy and pride
The little Actor cons another part;
Filling from time to time his "humorous stage"
With all the Persons, down to palsied Age,
That Life brings with her in her equipage;   105
   As if his whole vocation
   Were endless imitation.

VIII

Thou, whose exterior semblance doth belie
   Thy Soul's immensity;

Thou best Philosopher, who yet dost keep   *110*
Thy heritage, thou Eye among the blind,
That, deaf and silent, read'st the eternal deep,
Haunted for ever by the eternal mind,—
      Mighty Prophet! Seer blest!
      On whom those truths do rest,   *115*
Which we are toiling all our lives to find,
In darkness lost, the darkness of the grave;
Thou, over whom thy Immortality
Broods like the Day, a Master o'er a Slave,
A Presence which is not to be put by;   *120*
Thou little Child, yet glorious in the might
Of heaven-born freedom on thy being's height,
Why with such earnest pains dost thou provoke
The years to bring the inevitable yoke,
Thus blindly with thy blessedness at strife?   *125*
Full soon thy Soul shall have her earthly freight,
And custom lie upon thee with a weight,
Heavy as frost, and deep almost as life!

         IX
      O joy! that in our embers
      Is something that doth live,   *130*
      That nature yet remembers
      What was so fugitive!
The thought of our past years in me doth breed
Perpetual benediction: not indeed
For that which is most worthy to be blest;   *135*
Delight and liberty, the simple creed
Of Childhood, whether busy or at rest,
With new-fledged hope still fluttering in his breast:—
      Not for these I raise
      The song of thanks and praise;   *140*
      But for those obstinate questionings
      Of sense and outward things,
      Fallings from us, vanishings;
      Blank misgivings of a Creature
Moving about in worlds not realised,   *145*

High instincts before which our mortal Nature
Did tremble like a guilty Thing surprised:
      But for those first affections,
      Those shadowy recollections,
     Which, be they what they may,   *150*
Are yet the fountain-light of all our day,
Are yet a master-light of all our seeing;
     Uphold us, cherish, and have power to make
Our noisy years seem moments in the being
Of the eternal Silence: truths that wake,   *155*
        To perish never:
Which neither listlessness, nor mad endeavour,
       Nor Man nor Boy,
Nor all that is at enmity with joy,
Can utterly abolish or destroy.   *160*
      Hence in a season of calm weather
       Though inland far we be,
Our Souls have sight of that immortal sea
       Which brought us hither,
      Can in a moment travel thither,   *165*
And see the Children sport upon the shore,
And hear the mighty waters rolling evermore.

          x
Then sing, ye Birds, sing, sing a joyous song!
      And let the young Lambs bound
      As to the tabor's sound!   *170*
We in thought will join your throng,
      Ye that pipe and ye that play,
      Ye that through your hearts to-day
      Feel the gladness of the May!
What though the radiance which was once so bright   *175*
Be now for ever taken from my sight,
     Though nothing can bring back the hour
Of splendour in the grass, of glory in the flower;
      We will grieve not, rather find
      Strength in what remains behind;   *180*
      In the primal sympathy

Which having been must ever be ;
In the soothing thoughts that spring
Out of human suffering ;
    In the faith that looks through death,   *185*
In years that bring the philosophic mind.

XI

And O, ye Fountains, Meadows, Hills, and Groves,
Forebode not any severing of our loves !
Yet in my heart of hearts I feel your might ;
I only have relinquished one delight   *190*
To live beneath your more habitual sway.
I love the Brooks which down their channels fret,
Even more than when I tripped lightly as they ;
The innocent brightness of a new-born Day
        Is lovely yet ;   *195*
The Clouds that gather round the setting sun
Do take a sober colouring from an eye
That hath kept watch o'er man's mortality ;
Another race hath been, and other palms are won.
Thanks to the human heart by which we live,   *200*
Thanks to its tenderness, its joys, and fears,
To me the meanest flower that blows can give
Thoughts that do often lie too deep for tears.

WILLIAM WORDSWORTH

The World Is Too Much with Us

The world is too much with us ; late and soon,   *1*
Getting and spending, we lay waste our powers ;
Little we see in Nature that is ours ;
We have given our hearts away, a sordid boon !
This Sea that bares her bosom to the moon ;   *5*
The winds that will be howling at all hours,
And are up-gathered now like sleeping flowers ;
For this, for everything, we are out of tune ;
It moves us not.—Great God ! I'd rather be
A Pagan suckled in a creed outworn ;   *10*

So might I, standing on this pleasant lea,
Have glimpses that would make me less forlorn;
Have sight of Proteus rising from the sea;
Or hear old Triton blow his wreathèd horn.

WILLIAM WORDSWORTH

A Slumber Did My Spirit Seal

A slumber did my spirit seal;　　　　　1
　I had no human fears:
She seemed a thing that could not feel
　The touch of earthly years.

No motion has she now, no force;　　　　5
　She neither hears nor sees;
Rolled round in earth's diurnal course,
　With rocks, and stones, and trees.

WILLIAM WORDSWORTH

Kubla Khan
or *A Vision in a Dream*

In Xanadu did Kubla Khan　　　　　　　1
A stately pleasure-dome decree:
Where Alph, the sacred river, ran
Through caverns measureless to man
　Down to a sunless sea.　　　　　　　5
So twice five miles of fertile ground
With walls and towers were girdled round:
And there were gardens bright with sinuous rills,
Where blossomed many an incense-bearing tree;
And here were forests ancient as the hills,　　10
Enfolding sunny spots of greenery.

But oh! that deep romantic chasm which slanted
Down the green hill athwart a cedarn cover!
A savage place! as holy and enchanted
As e'er beneath a waning moon was haunted　　15
By woman wailing for her demon-lover!
And from this chasm, with ceaseless turmoil seething,
As if this earth in fast thick pants were breathing,

A mighty fountain momently was forced:
Amid whose swift half-intermitted burst   20
Huge fragments vaulted like rebounding hail,
Or chaffy grain beneath the thresher's flail:
And 'mid these dancing rocks at once and ever
It flung up momently the sacred river.
Five miles meandering with a mazy motion   25
Through wood and dale the sacred river ran,
Then reached the caverns measureless to man,
And sank in tumult to a lifeless ocean:
And 'mid this tumult Kubla heard from far
Ancestral voices prophesying war!   30
   The shadow of the dome of pleasure
   Floated midway on the waves;
   Where was heard the mingled measure
   From the fountain and the caves.
It was a miracle of rare device,   35
A sunny pleasure-dome with caves of ice!

   A damsel with a dulcimer
   In a vision once I saw:
   It was an Abyssinian maid,
   And on her dulcimer she played,   40
   Singing of Mount Abora.
   Could I revive within me
   Her symphony and song,
   To such a deep delight 'twould win me,
That with music loud and long,   45
I would build that dome in air,
That sunny dome! those caves of ice!
And all who heard should see them there,
And all should cry, Beware! Beware!
His flashing eyes, his floating hair!   50
Weave a circle round him thrice,
And close your eyes with holy dread,
For he on honey-dew hath fed,
And drunk the milk of Paradise.

SAMUEL T. COLERIDGE

Barbra Allen

In London City where I once did dwell, there's where I got my
    learning,   *1*
I fell in love with a pretty young girl, her name was Barbra
    Allen.
I courted her for seven long years, she said she would not
    have me;
Then straightway home as I could go and liken to a dying.

I wrote her a letter on my death bed, I wrote it slow and
    moving;   *5*
"Go take this letter to my old true love and tell her I am
    dying."
She took the letter in her lily-white hand, she read it slow and
    moving;
"Go take this letter back to him, and tell him I am coming."

As she passed by his dying bed she saw his pale lips quivering;
"No better, no better I'll ever be until I get Barbra Allen."   *10*
As she passed by his dying bed; "You're very sick and almost
    dying,
No better, no better you will ever be, for you can't get Barbra
    Allen."

As she went down the long stair steps she heard the death bell
    toning,
And every bell appeared to say, "Hard-hearted Barbra
    Allen!"
As she went down the long piney walk she heard some small
    birds singing,   *15*
And every bird appeared to say, "Hard-hearted Barbra
    Allen!"

She looked to the East, she looked to the West, she saw the
    pale corpse coming
"Go bring them pale corpse unto me, and let me gaze upon
    them.

Oh, mama, mama, go make my bed, go make it soft and narrow!
Sweet Willie died today for me, I'll die for him tomorrow!"   *20*

They buried Sweet Willie in the old church yard, they buried
    Miss Barbra beside him;
And out of his grave there sprang a red rose, and out of hers
    a briar.
They grew to the top of the old church tower, they could not
    grow any higher,
They hooked, they tied in a true love's knot, red rose around
    the briar.

ANONYMOUS

My Life Is Like the Summer Rose

My life is like the summer rose   *1*
  That opens to the morning sky,
But ere the shades of evening close,
  Is scatter'd on the ground—to die!
Yet on the rose's humble bed   *5*
The sweetest dews of night are shed,
As if she wept the waste to see—
But none shall weep a tear for me!

My life is like the autumn leaf
  That trembles in the moon's pale ray: *10*
Its hold is frail, its date is brief,
  Restless—and soon to pass away!
Yet ere that leaf shall fall and fade,
The parent tree will mourn its shade,
The winds bewail the leafless tree,   *15*
But none shall breathe a sigh for me!

My life is like the prints, which feet
  Have left on Tampa's desert strand;
Soon as the rising tide shall beat,
  All trace will vanish from the sand;   *20*

Yet, as if grieving to efface
All vestige of the human race,
On that lone shore loud moans the sea,
But none, alas! shall mourn for me!

RICHARD HENRY WILDE

Ode to the West Wind

I

O, wild West Wind, thou breath of Autumn's being,   1
Thou, from whose unseen presence the leaves dead
Are driven, like ghosts from an enchanter fleeing,

Yellow, and black, and pale, and hectic red,
Pestilence-stricken multitudes: O, thou,   5
Who chariotest to their dark wintry bed

The wingèd seeds, where they lie cold and low,
Each like a corpse within its grave, until
Thine azure sister of the spring shall blow

Her clarion o'er the dreaming earth, and fill   10
(Driving sweet buds like flocks to feed in air)
With living hues and odours plain and hill:
Wild Spirit, which art moving every where;
Destroyer and preserver; hear, O, hear!

II

Thou on whose stream, 'mid the steep sky's commotion,   15
Loose clouds like earth's decaying leaves are shed,
Shook from the tangled boughs of Heaven and Ocean,

Angels of rain and lightning: there are spread
On the blue surface of thine airy surge,
Like the bright hair uplifted from the head   20

Of some fierce Mænad, even from the dim verge
Of the horizon to the zenith's height
The locks of the approaching storm. Thou dirge

Of the dying year, to which this closing night
Will be the dome of a vast sepulchre,   *25*
Vaulted with all thy congregated might
Of vapours, from whose solid atmosphere
Black rain, and fire, and hail will burst : O, hear !

III

Thou who didst waken from his summer dreams
The blue Mediterranean, where he lay,   *30*
Lulled by the coil of his crystàlline streams,

Beside a pumice isle in Baiæ's bay,
And saw in sleep old palaces and towers
Quivering within the wave's intenser day,

All overgrown with azure moss and flowers   *35*
So sweet, the sense faints picturing them ! Thou
For whose path the Atlantic's level powers

Cleave themselves into chasms, while far below
The sea-blooms and the oozy woods which wear
The sapless foliage of the ocean, know   *40*
Thy voice, and suddenly grow grey with fear,
And tremble and despoil themselves : O, hear !

IV

If I were a dead leaf thou mightest bear ;
If I were a swift cloud to fly with thee ;
A wave to pant beneath thy power, and share   *45*

The impulse of thy strength, only less free
Than thou, O, uncontrollable ! If even
I were as in my boyhood, and could be

The comrade of thy wanderings over heaven,
As then, when to outstrip thy skiey speed   *50*
Scarce seemed a vision ; I would ne'er have striven

As thus with thee in prayer in my sore need,
Oh! lift me as a wave, a leaf, a cloud!
I fall upon the thorns of life! I bleed!

A heavy weight of hours has chained and bowed   *55*
One too like thee: tameless, and swift, and proud.

v

Make me thy lyre, even as the forest is:
What if my leaves are falling like its own!
The tumult of thy mighty harmonies

Will take from both a deep, autumnal tone,   *60*
Sweet though in sadness. Be thou, spirit fierce,
My spirit! Be thou me, impetuous one!

Drive my dead thoughts over the universe
Like withered leaves to quicken a new birth!
And, by the incantation of this verse,   *65*

Scatter, as from an unextinguished hearth
Ashes and sparks, my words among mankind!
Be through my lips to unawakened earth

The trumpet of a prophecy! O, wind,
If Winter comes, can Spring be far behind?   *70*

PERCY BYSSHE SHELLEY

Ode on a Grecian Urn

I

Thou still unravish'd bride of quietness,   *1*
  Thou foster-child of silence and slow time,
Sylvan historian, who canst thus express
  A flowery tale more sweetly than our rhyme:
What leaf-fring'd legend haunts about thy shape   *5*
  Of deities or mortals, or of both,
    In Tempe or the dales of Arcady?
  What men or gods are these? What maidens loth?
What mad pursuit? What struggle to escape?
    What pipes and timbrels? What wild ecstasy?   *10*

II

Heard melodies are sweet, but those unheard
    Are sweeter; therefore, ye soft pipes, play on;
Not to the sensual ear, but, more endear'd,
    Pipe to the spirit ditties of no tone:
Fair youth, beneath the trees, thou canst not leave   *15*
    Thy song, nor ever can those trees be bare;
        Bold Lover, never, never canst thou kiss,
Though winning near the goal—yet, do not grieve;
        She cannot fade, though thou hast not thy bliss,
    For ever wilt thou love, and she be fair!   *20*

III

Ah, happy, happy boughs! that cannot shed
    Your leaves, nor ever bid the Spring adieu;
And, happy melodist, unwearied,
    For ever piping songs for ever new;
More happy love! more happy, happy love!   *25*
    For ever warm and still to be enjoy'd,
        For ever panting, and for ever young;
All breathing human passion far above,
    That leaves a heart high-sorrowful and cloy'd,
        A burning forehead, and a parching tongue.   *30*

IV

Who are these coming to the sacrifice?
    To what green altar, O mysterious priest,
Lead'st thou that heifer lowing at the skies,
    And all her silken flanks with garlands drest?
What little town by river or sea shore,   *35*
    Or mountain-built with peaceful citadel,
        Is emptied of this folk, this pious morn?
And, little town, thy streets for evermore
    Will silent be; and not a soul to tell
        Why thou art desolate, can e'er return.   *40*

V

O Attic shape! Fair attitude! with brede
    Of marble men and maidens overwrought,

With forest branches and the trodden weed;
 Thou, silent form, dost tease us out of thought
As doth eternity: Cold Pastoral!   *45*
 When old age shall this generation waste,
  Thou shalt remain, in midst of other woe
 Than ours, a friend to man, to whom thou say'st,
"Beauty is truth, truth beauty,"—that is all
 Ye know on earth, and all ye need to know. *50*

        JOHN KEATS

The Snow-Storm

Announced by all the trumpets of the sky, *1*
Arrives the snow, and, driving o'er the fields,
Seems nowhere to alight: the whited air
Hides hills and woods, the river, and the heaven,
And veils the farm-house at the garden's end. *5*
The sled and traveller stopped, the courier's feet
Delayed, all friends shut out, the housemates sit
Around the radiant fireplace, enclosed
In a tumultuous privacy of storm.

 Come see the north wind's masonry. *10*
Out of an unseen quarry evermore
Furnished with tile, the fierce artificer
Curves his white bastions with projected roof
Round every windward stake, or tree, or door.
Speeding, the myriad-handed, his wild work *15*
So fanciful, so savage, nought cares he
For number or proportion. Mockingly,
On coop or kennel he hangs Parian wreaths;
A swan-like form invests the hidden thorn;
Fills up the farmer's lane from wall to wall, *20*
Maugre the farmer's sighs; and at the gate
A tapering turret overtops the work.
And when his hours are numbered, and the world
Is all his own, retiring, as he were not,

Leaves, when the sun appears, astonished Art   *25*
To mimic in slow structures, stone by stone,
Built in an age, the mad wind's night-work,
The frolic architecture of the snow.

RALPH WALDO EMERSON

The Lotos-Eaters

'Courage!' he said, and pointed toward the land,   *1*
'This mounting wave will roll us shoreward soon.'
In the afternoon they came unto a land
In which it seemed always afternoon.
All round the coast the languid air did swoon,   *5*
Breathing like one that hath a weary dream.
Full-faced above the valley stood the moon;
And like a downward smoke, the slender stream
Along the cliff to fall and pause and fall did seem.

A land of streams! some, like a downward smoke,   *10*
Slow-dropping veils of thinnest lawn, did go;
And some thro' wavering lights and shadows broke,
Rolling a slumbrous sheet of foam below.
They saw the gleaming river seaward flow
From the inner land: far off, three mountain-tops,   *15*
Three silent pinnacles of aged snow,
Stood sunset-flush'd: and, dew'd with showery drops,
Up-clomb the shadowy pine above the woven copse.

The charmed sunset linger'd low adown
In the red West: thro' mountain clefts the dale   *20*
Was seen far inland, and the yellow down
Border'd with palm, and many a winding vale
And meadow, set with slender galingale;
A land where all things always seem'd the same!
And round about the keel with faces pale,   *25*
Dark faces pale against that rosy flame,
The mild-eyed melancholy Lotos-eaters came.

Branches they bore of that enchanted stem,
Laden with flower and fruit, whereof they gave
To each, but whoso did receive of them,   *30*
And taste, to him the gushing of the wave
Far far away did seem to mourn and rave
On alien shores ; and if his fellow spake,
His voice was thin, as voices from the grave ;
And deep-asleep he seem'd, yet all awake,   *35*
And music in his ears his beating heart did make.

They sat them down upon the yellow sand,
Between the sun and moon upon the shore ;
And sweet it was to dream of Fatherland,
Of child, and wife, and slave ; but evermore   *40*
Most weary seem'd the sea, weary the oar,
Weary the wandering fields of barren foam.
Then some one said, 'We will return no more ;'
And all at once they sang, 'Our island home
Is far beyond the wave ; we will no longer roam.'   *45*

CHORIC SONG

I

There is sweet music here that softer falls
Than petals from blown roses on the grass,
Or night-dews on still waters between walls
Of shadowy granite, in a gleaming pass ;
Music that gentlier on the spirit lies,   *50*
Then tir'd eyelids upon tir'd eyes ;
Music that brings sweet sleep down from the blissful skies.
Here are cool mosses deep,
And thro' the moss the ivies creep,
And in the stream the long-leaved flowers weep,   *55*
And from the craggy ledge the poppy hangs in sleep.

II

Why are we weigh'd upon with heaviness,
And utterly consumed with sharp distress,
While all things else have rest from weariness ?

All things have rest: why should we toil alone,   *60*
We only toil, who are the first of things,
And make perpetual moan,
Still from one sorrow to another thrown:
Nor ever fold our wings,
And cease from wanderings,   *65*
Nor steep our brows in slumber's holy balm;
Nor hearken what the inner spirit sings,
'There is no joy but calm!'
Why should we only toil, the roof and crown of things?

III

Lo! in the middle of the wood,   *70*
The folded leaf is woo'd from out the bud
With winds upon the branch, and there
Grows green and broad, and takes no care,
Sun-steep'd at noon, and in the moon
Nightly dew-fed; and turning yellow   *75*
Falls, and floats adown the air.
Lo! sweeten'd with the summer light,
The full-juiced apple, waxing over-mellow,
Drops in a silent autumn night.
All its allotted length of days,   *80*
The flower ripens in its place,
Ripens and fades, and falls, and hath no toil,
Fast-rooted in the fruitful soil.

IV

Hateful is the dark-blue sky,
Vaulted o'er the dark-blue sea.   *85*
Death is the end of life; ah, why
Should life all labour be?
Let us alone. Time driveth onward fast,
And in a little while our lips are dumb.
Let us alone. What is it that will last?   *90*
All things are taken from us, and become
Portions and parcels of the dreadful Past.
Let us alone. What pleasure can we have

To war with evil? Is there any peace
In ever climbing up the climbing wave?   *95*
All things have rest, and ripen toward the grave
In silence; ripen, fall and cease:
Give us long rest or death, dark death, or dreamful ease.

V

How sweet it were, hearing the downward stream,
With half-shut eyes ever to seem   *100*
Falling asleep in a half-dream!
To dream and dream, like yonder amber light,
Which will not leave the myrrh-bush on the height;
To hear each other's whisper'd speech;
Eating the Lotos day by day,   *105*
To watch the crisping ripples on the beach,
And tender curving lines of creamy spray;
To lend our hearts and spirits wholly
To the influence of mild-minded melancholy;
To muse and brood and live again in memory,   *110*
With those old faces of our infancy
Heap'd over with a mound of grass,
Two handfuls of white dust, shut in an urn of brass!

VI

Dear is the memory of our wedded lives,
And dear the last embraces of our wives   *115*
And their warm tears: but all hath suffer'd change;
For surely now our household hearths are cold:
Our sons inherit us: our looks are strange:
And we should come like ghosts to trouble joy.
Or else the island princes over-bold   *120*
Have eat our substance, and the minstrel sings
Before them of the ten-years' war in Troy,
And our great deeds, as half-forgotten things.
Is there confusion in the little isle?
Let what is broken so remain.   *125*
The Gods are hard to reconcile:
'Tis hard to settle order once again.

There *is* confusion worse than death,
Trouble on trouble, pain on pain,
Long labour unto aged breath,   *130*
Sore task to hearts worn out with many wars
And eyes grown dim with gazing on the pilot-stars.

VII

But, propt on beds of amaranth and moly,
How sweet (while warm airs lull us, blowing lowly)
With half-dropt eyelids still,   *135*
Beneath a heaven dark and holy,
To watch the long bright river drawing slowly
His waters from the purple hill—
To hear the dewy echoes calling
From cave to cave thro' the thick-twined vine—   *140*
To watch the emerald-colour'd water falling
Thro' many a wov'n acanthus-wreath divine!
Only to hear and see the far-off sparkling brine,
Only to hear were sweet, stretch'd out beneath the pine.

VIII

The Lotos blooms below the barren peak: *145*
The Lotos blows by every winding creek:
All day the wind breathes low with mellower tone:
Thro' every hollow cave and alley lone
Round and round the spicy downs the yellow Lotos-dust is
    blown.
We have had enough of action, and of motion we. *150*
Roll'd to starboard, roll'd to larboard, when the surge was
    seething free,
Where the wallowing monster spouted his foam-fountains in
    the sea.
Let us swear an oath, and keep it with an equal mind,
In the hollow Lotos-land to live and lie reclined
On the hills like Gods together, careless of mankind.   *155*
For they lie beside their nectar, and the bolts are hurl'd
Far below them in the valleys, and the clouds are lightly
    curl'd

Round their golden houses, girdled with the gleaming world:
Where they smile in secret, looking over wasted lands,
Blight and famine, plague and earthquake, roaring deeps
    and fiery sands,   *160*
Clanging fights, and flaming towns, and sinking ships, and
    praying hands.
But they smile, they find a music centred in a doleful song
Steaming up, a lamentation and an ancient tale of wrong,
Like a tale of little meaning tho' the words are strong;
Chanted from an ill-used race of men that cleave the soil,   *165*
Sow the seed, and reap the harvest with enduring toil,
Storing yearly little dues of wheat, and wine and oil;
Till they perish and they suffer—some, 'tis whisper'd—down
    in hell
Suffer endless anguish, others in Elysian valleys dwell,
Resting weary limbs at last on beds of asphodel.   *170*
Surely, surely, slumber is more sweet than toil, the shore
Than labour in the deep mid-ocean, wind and wave and oar;
Oh rest ye, brother mariners, we will not wander more.
ALFRED, LORD TENNYSON

Ulysses

It little profits that an idle king,   *1*
By this still hearth, among these barren crags,
Match'd with an aged wife, I mete and dole
Unequal laws unto a savage race,
That hoard, and sleep, and feed, and know not me.   *5*
I cannot rest from travel: I will drink
Life to the lees: all times I have enjoy'd
Greatly, have suffer'd greatly, both with those
That loved me, and alone; on shore, and when
Thro' scudding drifts the rainy Hyades   *10*
Vext the dim sea: I am become a name;
For always roaming with a hungry heart
Much have I seen and known; cities of men
And manners, climates, councils, governments,
Myself not least, but honour'd of them all;   *15*

And drunk delight of battle with my peers,
Far on the ringing plains of windy Troy.
I am a part of all that I have met;
Yet all experience is an arch wherethro'
Gleams that untravell'd world, whose margin fades   *20*
For ever and for ever when I move.
How dull it is to pause, to make an end,
To rust unburnish'd, not to shine in use!
As tho' to breathe were life. Life piled on life
Were all too little, and of one to me   *25*
Little remains: but every hour is saved
From that eternal silence, something more,
A bringer of new things; and vile it were
For some three suns to store and hoard myself,
And this grey spirit yearning in desire   *30*
To follow knowledge, like a sinking star,
Beyond the utmost bound of human thought.

      This is my son, mine own Telemachus,
To whom I leave the sceptre and the isle—
Well-loved of me, discerning to fulfil   *35*
This labour, by slow prudence to make mild
A rugged people, and thro' soft degrees
Subdue them to the useful and the good.
Most blameless is he, centred in the sphere
Of common duties, decent not to fail   *40*
In offices of tenderness, and pay
Meet adoration to my household gods,
When I am gone. He works his work, I mine.

      There lies the port: the vessel puffs her sail:
There gloom the dark broad seas. My mariners,   *45*
Souls that have toil'd, and wrought, and thought with me—
That ever with a frolic welcome took
The thunder and the sunshine, and opposed
Free hearts, free foreheads—you and I are old;
Old age hath yet his honour and his toil;   *50*
Death closes all: but something ere the end,
Some work of noble note, may yet be done,
Not unbecoming men that strove with Gods.

The lights begin to twinkle from the rocks:
The long day wanes: the slow moon climbs: the deep   55
Moans round with many voices. Come, my friends,
'Tis not too late to seek a newer world.
Push off, and sitting well in order smite
The sounding furrows; for my purpose holds
To sail beyond the sunset, and the baths   60
Of all the western stars, until I die.
It may be that the gulfs will wash us down:
It may be we shall touch the Happy Isles,
And see the great Achilles, whom we knew.
Tho' much is taken, much abides; and tho'   65
We are not now that strength which in old days
Moved earth and heaven; that which we are, we are;
One equal temper of heroic hearts,
Made weak by time and fate, but strong in will
To strive, to seek, to find, and not to yield.   70

ALFRED, LORD TENNYSON

To Helen

Helen, thy beauty is to me   1
   Like those Nicéan barks of yore,
That gently, o'er a perfumed sea,
   The weary, way-worn wanderer bore
   To his own native shore.   5

On desperate seas long wont to roam,
   Thy hyacinth hair, thy classic face,
Thy Naiad airs have brought me home
   To the glory that was Greece
And the grandeur that was Rome.   10

Lo! in yon brilliant window-niche
   How statue-like I see thee stand,
   The agate lamp within thy hand!
Ah, Psyche, from the regions which
   Are Holy Land!   15

EDGAR ALLAN POE

The City in the Sea

Lo! Death has reared himself a throne   *1*
In a strange city lying alone
Far down within the dim West,
Where the good and the bad and the worst and the best
Have gone to their eternal rest.   *5*
There shrines and palaces and towers
(Time-eaten towers that tremble not!)
Resemble nothing that is ours.
Around, by lifting winds forgot,
Resignedly beneath the sky   *10*
The melancholy waters lie.

No rays from the holy heaven come down
On the long night-time of that town;
But light from out the lurid sea
Streams up the turrets silently—   *15*
Gleams up the pinnacles far and free—
Up domes—up spires—up kingly halls—
Up fanes—up Babylon-like walls—
Up shadowy long-forgotten bowers
Of sculptured ivy and stone flowers—   *20*
Up many and many a marvellous shrine
Whose wreathèd friezes intertwine
The viol, the violet, and the vine.

Resignedly beneath the sky
The melancholy waters lie.   *25*
So blend the turrets and shadows there
That all seem pendulous in air,
While from a proud tower in the town
Death looks gigantically down.

There open fanes and gaping graves   *30*
Yawn level with the luminous waves;
But not the riches there that lie
In each idol's diamond eye—

Not the gaily-jewelled dead
Tempt the waters from their bed;   35
For no ripples curl, alas!
Along that wilderness of glass—
No swellings tell that winds may be
Upon some far-off happier sea—
No heavings hint that winds have been   40
On seas less hideously serene.

But lo, a stir is in the air!
The wave—there is a movement there!
As if the towers had thrust aside,
In slightly sinking, the dull tide—   45
As if their tops had feebly given
A void within the filmy Heaven.
The waves have now a redder glow—
The hours are breathing faint and low—
And when, amid no earthy moans,   50
Down, down that town shall settle hence,
Hell, rising from a thousand thrones,
Shall do it reverence.

EDGAR ALLAN POE

Soliloquy of the Spanish Cloister

G-r-r-r—there go, my heart's abhorrence!   1
    Water your damned flower-pots, do!
If hate killed men, Brother Lawrence,
    God's blood, would not mine kill you!
What? your myrtle-bush wants trimming?   5
    Oh, that rose has prior claims—
Needs its leaden vase filled brimming?
    Hell dry you up with its flames!

At the meal we sit together:
    Salve tibi! I must hear   10
Wise talk of the kind of weather,
    Sort of season, time of year:

Not a plenteous cork-crop: scarcely
  Dare we hope oak-galls, I doubt:
What's the Latin name for "parsley"?   *15*
  What's the Greek name for Swine's Snout?

Whew! We'll have our platter burnished,
  Laid with care on our own shelf!
With a fire-new spoon we're furnished,
  And a goblet for ourself,   *20*
Rinsed like something sacrificial
  Ere 'tis fit to touch our chaps—
Marked with L for our initial!
  (He-he! There his lily snaps!)

Saint, forsooth! While brown Dolores   *25*
  Squats outside the Convent bank
With Sanchicha, telling stories,
  Steeping tresses in the tank,
Blue-black, lustrous, thick like horsehairs,
  —Can't I see his dead eye glow,   *30*
Bright as 'twere a Barbary corsair's?
  (That is, if he'd let it show!)

When he finishes refection,
  Knife and fork he never lays
Cross-wise, to my recollection,   *35*
  As do I, in Jesu's praise.
I the Trinity illustrate,
  Drinking watered orange-pulp—
In three sips the Arian frustrate;
  While he drains his at one gulp.   *40*

Oh, those melons! If he's able
  We're to have a feast! so nice!
One goes to the Abbot's table,
  All of us get each a slice.
How go on your flowers? None double?   *45*
  Not one fruit-sort can you spy?
Strange!—And I, too, at such trouble,
  Keep them close-nipped on the sly!

There's a great text in Galatians,
  Once you trip on it, entails   50
Twenty-nine distinct damnations,
  One sure, if another fails:
If I trip him just a-dying,
  Sure of heaven as sure can be,
Spin him round and send him flying   55
  Off to hell, a Manichee?

Or, my scrofulous French novel
  On grey paper with blunt type!
Simply glance at it, you grovel
  Hand and foot in Belial's gripe: 60
If I double down its pages
  At the woeful sixteenth print,
When he gathers his greengages,
  Ope a sieve and slip it in 't?

Or, there's Satan!—one might venture   65
  Pledge one's soul to him, yet leave
Such a flaw in the indenture
  As he'd miss till, past retrieve,
Blasted lay that rose-acacia
  We're so proud of! *Hy, Zy, Hine* . . .   70
'St, there's Vespers! *Plena gratia,*
  Ave, Virgo! Gr-r-r—you swine!

ROBERT BROWNING

Ah! Yet Consider it Again!

"Old things need not be therefore true,"   1
O brother men, nor yet the new;
Ah! still awhile the old thought retain,
And yet consider it again!

The souls of now two thousand years   5
Have laid up here their toils and fears,
And all the earnings of their pain,—
Ah, yet consider it again!

We! what do we see? each a space
Of some few yards before his face;   *10*
Does that the whole wide plan explain?
Ah, yet consider it again!

Alas! the great world goes its way,
And takes its truth from each new day;
They do not quit, nor can retain,   *15*
Far less consider it again.

ARTHUR HUGH CLOUGH

Pioneers! O Pioneers

    Come my tan-faced children,   *1*
Follow well in order, get your weapons ready,
Have you your pistols? have you your sharp-edged axes?
    Pioneers! O pioneers!

    For we cannot tarry here,   *5*
We must march my darlings, we must bear the brunt of
    danger,
We the youthful sinewy races, all the rest on us depend,
    Pioneers! O pioneers!

    O you youths, Western youths,
So impatient, full of action, full of manly pride and friend-
    ship,   *10*
Plain I see you Western youths, see you tramping with the
    foremost,
    Pioneers! O pioneers!

    Have the elder races halted?
Do they droop and end their lesson, wearied over there be-
    yond the seas?
We take up the task eternal, and the burden and the lesson,   *15*
    Pioneers! O pioneers!

All the past we leave behind,
We debouch upon a newer mightier world, varied world,
Fresh and strong the world we seize, world of labor and the
     march,
    Pioneers! O pioneers!   *20*

We detachments steady throwing,
Down the edges, through the passes, up the mountains steep,
Conquering, holding, daring, venturing as we go the un-
     known ways,
    Pioneers! O pioneers!

We primeval forests felling,   *25*
We the rivers stemming, vexing we and piercing deep the
     mines within,
We the surface broad surveying, we the virgin soil upheav-
     ing,
    Pioneers! O pioneers!

Colorado men are we,
From the peaks gigantic, from the great sierras and the high
     plateaus,   *30*
From the mine and from the gully, from the hunting trail we
     come,
    Pioneers! O pioneers!

From Nebraska, from Arkansas,
Central inland race are we, from Missouri, with the conti-
     nental blood intervein'd,
All the hands of comrades clasping, all the Southern, all the
     Northern,   *35*
    Pioneers! O pioneers!

O resistless restless race!
O beloved race in all! O my breast aches with tender love
     for all!
O I mourn and yet exult, I am rapt with love for all,
    Pioneers! O pioneers!   *40*

Raise the mighty mother mistress,
Waving high the delicate mistress, over all the starry
    mistress, (bend your heads all,)
Raise the fang'd and warlike mistress, stern, impassive,
    weapon'd mistress,
    Pioneers! O pioneers!

See my children, resolute children,   *45*
By those swarms upon our rear we must never yield or
    falter,
Ages back in ghostly millions frowning there behind us
    urging,
    Pioneers! O pioneers!

On and on the compact ranks,
With accessions ever waiting, with the places of the dead
    quickly fill'd,   *50*
Through the battle, through defeat, moving yet and never
    stopping,
    Pioneers! O pioneers!

O to die advancing on!
Are there some of us to droop and die? has the hour come?
Then upon the march we fittest die, soon and sure the gap is
    fill'd,   *55*
    Pioneers! O pioneers!

All the pulses of the world,
Falling in they beat for us, with the Western movement beat,
Holding single or together, steady moving to the front, all
    for us,
    Pioneers! O pioneers!   *60*

Life's involv'd and varied pageants,
All the forms and shows, all the workmen at their work,
All the seamen and the landsmen, all the masters with their
    slaves,
    Pioneers! O pioneers!

All the hapless silent lovers,   *65*
All the prisoners in the prisons, all the righteous and the
    wicked,
All the joyous, all the sorrowing, all the living, all the dying,
    Pioneers! O pioneers!

I too with my soul and body,
We, a curious trio, picking, wandering on our way,   *70*
Through these shores amid the shadows, with the appari-
    tions pressing,
    Pioneers! O pioneers!

Lo, the darting bowling orb!
Lo, the brother orbs around, all the clustering suns and
    planets,
All the dazzling days, all the mystic nights with dreams,   *75*
    Pioneers! O pioneers!

These are of us, they are with us,
All for primal needed work, while the followers there in
    embryo wait behind,
We to-day's procession heading, we the route for travel
    clearing,
    Pioneers! O pioneers!   *80*

O you daughters of the West!
O you young and elder daughters! O you mothers and you
    wives!
Never must you be divided, in our ranks you move united,
    Pioneers! O pioneers!

Minstrels latent on the prairies!   *85*
(Shrouded bards of other lands, you may rest, you have
    done your work,)
Soon I hear you coming warbling, soon you rise and tramp
    amid us,
    Pioneers! O pioneers!

Not for delectations sweet,
Not the cushion and the slipper, not the peaceful and the
    studious,   *90*
Not the riches safe and palling, not for us the tame enjoy-
    ment,
    Pioneers! O pioneers!

Do the feasters gluttonous feast?
Do the corpulent sleepers sleep? have they lock'd and bolted
    doors?
Still be ours the diet hard, and the blanket on the ground,   *95*
    Pioneers! O pioneers!

Has the night descended?
Was the road of late so toilsome? did we stop discouraged
    nodding on our way?
Yet a passing hour I yield you in your tracks to pause ob-
    livious,
    Pioneers! O pioneers!   *100*

Till with sound of trumpet,
Far, far off the daybreak call—hark! how loud and clear I
    hear it wind,
Swift! to the head of the army!—swift! spring to your
    places,
    Pioneers! O pioneers!

WALT WHITMAN

When Lilacs Last in the Dooryard Bloom'd

1

When lilacs last in the dooryard bloom'd,   *1*
And the great star early droop'd in the western sky in the
    night,
I mourn'd, and yet shall mourn with ever-returning spring.

Ever-returning spring, trinity sure to me you bring,
Lilac blooming perennial and drooping star in the west,   *5*
And thought of him I love.

2

O powerful western fallen star!
O shades of night—O moody, tearful night!
O great star disappear'd—O the black murk that hides the
    star!
O cruel hands that hold me powerless—O helpless soul of me!   *10*
O harsh surrounding cloud that will not free my soul.

3

In the dooryard fronting an old farm-house near the white-
    wash'd palings,
Stands the lilac-bush tall-growing with heart-shaped leaves
    of rich green,
With many a pointed blossom rising delicate, with the per-
    fume strong I love,
With every leaf a miracle—and from this bush in the door-
    yard,   *15*
With delicate-color'd blossoms and heart-shaped leaves of
    rich green,
A sprig with its flower I break.

4

In the swamp in secluded recesses,
A shy and hidden bird is warbling a song.

Solitary the thrush,   *20*
The hermit withdrawn to himself, avoiding the settlements,
Sings by himself a song.

Song of the bleeding throat,
Death's outlet song of life, (for well dear brother I know,
If thou wast not granted to sing thou would'st surely die.)   *25*

5

Over the breast of the spring, the land, amid cities,
Amid lanes and through old woods, where lately the violets
    peep'd from the ground, spotting the gray debris,
Amid the grass in the fields each side of the lanes, passing
    the endless grass,

Passing the yellow-spear'd wheat, every grain from its
 shroud in the dark-brown fields uprisen,
Passing the apple-tree blows of white and pink in the or-
 chards,   *30*
Carrying a corpse to where it shall rest in the grave,
Night and day journeys a coffin.

6

Coffin that passes through lanes and streets,
Through day and night with the great cloud darkening the
 land,
With the pomp of the inloop'd flags with the cities draped
 in black,   *35*
With the show of the States themselves as of crape-veil'd
 women standing,
With processions long and winding and the flambeaus of the
 night,
With the countless torches lit, with the silent sea of faces
 and the unbared heads,
With the waiting depot, the arriving coffin, and the sombre
 faces,
With dirges through the night, with the thousand voices ris-
 ing strong and solemn,   *40*
With all the mournful voices of the dirges pour'd around the
 coffin,
The dim-lit churches and the shuddering organs—where
 amid these you journey,
With the tolling tolling bells' perpetual clang,
Here, coffin that slowly passes,
I give you my sprig of lilac.   *45*

7

(Not for you, for one alone,
Blossoms and branches green to coffins all I bring,
For fresh as the morning, thus would I chant a song for
 you O sane and sacred death.

All over bouquets of roses,
O death, I cover you over with roses and early lilies,   *50*

But mostly and now the lilac that blooms the first,
Copious I break, I break the sprigs from the bushes,
With loaded arms I come, pouring for you,
For you and the coffins all of you O death.)

8

O western orb sailing the heaven,   55
Now I know what you must have meant as a month since I
     walk'd,
As I walk'd in silence the transparent shadowy night,
As I saw you had something to tell as you bent to me night
     after night,
As you droop'd from the sky low down as if to my side,
     (while the other stars all look'd on,)
As we wander'd together the solemn night, (for something I
     know not what kept me from sleep,)   60
As the night advanced, and I saw on the rim of the west how
     full you were of woe,
As I stood on the rising ground in the breeze in the cool
     transparent night,
As I watch'd where you pass'd and was lost in the nether-
     ward black of the night,
As my soul in its trouble dissatisfied sank, as where you sad
     orb,
Concluded, dropt in the night, and was gone.   65

9

Sing on there in the swamp,
O singer bashful and tender, I hear your notes, I hear your
     call,
I hear, I come presently, I understand you,
But a moment I linger, for the lustrous star has detain'd me,
The star my departing comrade holds and detains me.   70

10

O how shall I warble myself for the dead one there I loved?
And how shall I deck my song for the large sweet soul that
     has gone?
And what shall my perfume be for the grave of him I love?

Sea-winds blown from east and west,
Blown from the Eastern sea and blown from the Western
    sea, till there on the prairies meeting,   75
These and with these and the breath of my chant,
I'll perfume the grave of him I love.

11

O what shall I hang on the chamber walls?
And what shall the pictures be that I hang on the walls,
To adorn the burial-house of him I love?   80

Pictures of growing spring and farms and homes,
With the Fourth-month eve at sundown, and the gray smoke
    lucid and bright,
With floods of the yellow gold of the gorgeous, indolent,
    sinking sun, burning, expanding the air,
With the fresh sweet herbage under foot, and the pale green
    leaves of the trees prolific,
In the distance the flowing glaze, the breast of the river, with
    a wind-dapple here and there,   85
With ranging hills on the banks, with many a line against
    the sky, and shadows,
And the city at hand with dwellings so dense, and stacks of
    chimneys,
And all the scenes of life and the workshops, and the work-
    men homeward returning.

12

Lo, body and soul—this land,
My own Manhattan with spires, and the sparkling and hur-
    rying tides, and the ships,   90
The varied and ample land, the South and the North in the
    light, Ohio's shores and flashing Missouri,
And ever the far-spreading prairies cover'd with grass and
    corn.
Lo, the most excellent sun so calm and haughty,
The violet and purple morn with just-felt breezes,
The gentle soft-born measureless light,   95

The miracle spreading bathing all, the fulfill'd noon,
The coming eve delicious, the welcome night and the stars,
Over my cities shining all, enveloping man and land.

13

Sing on, sing on you gray-brown bird,
Sing from the swamps, the recesses, pour your chant from
    the bushes,   100
Limitless out of the dusk, out of the cedars and pines.

Sing on dearest brother, warble your reedy song,
Loud human song, with voice of uttermost woe.

O liquid and free and tender!
O wild and loose to my soul—O wondrous singer!   105
You only I hear—yet the star holds me, (but will soon de-
    part,)
Yet the lilac with mastering odor holds me.

14

Now while I sat in the day and look'd forth,
In the close of the day with its light and the fields of spring,
    and the farmers preparing their crops,
In the large unconscious scenery of my land with its lakes
    and forests,   110
In the heavenly aerial beauty, (after the perturb'd winds
    and the storms,)
Under the arching heavens of the afternoon swift passing,
    and the voices of children and women,
The many-moving sea-tides, and I saw the ships how they
    sail'd,
And the summer approaching with richness, and the fields all
    busy with labor,
And the infinite separate houses, how they all went on, each
    with its meals and minutia of daily usages,   115
And the streets how their throbbings throbb'd, and the cities
    pent—lo, then and there,
Falling upon them all and among them all, enveloping me
    with the rest,

Appear'd the cloud, appear'd the long black trail,
And I knew death, its thought, and the sacred knowledge of
    death.

Then with the knowledge of death as walking one side of me,   *120*
And the thought of death close-walking the other side of me,
And I in the middle as with companions, and as holding the
    hands of companions,
I fled forth to the hiding receiving night that talks not,
Down to the shores of the water, the path by the swamp in
    the dimness,
To the solemn shadowy cedars and ghostly pines so still.   *125*

And the singer so shy to the rest receiv'd me,
The gray-brown bird I know receiv'd us comrades three,
And he sang the carol of death, and a verse for him I love.

From deep secluded recesses,
From the fragrant cedars and the ghostly pines so still,   *130*
Came the carol of the bird.

And the charm of the carol rapt me,
As I held as if by their hands my comrades in the night,
And the voice of my spirit tallied the song of the bird.

Come lovely and soothing death,   *135*
Undulate round the world, serenely arriving, arriving,
In the day, in the night, to all, to each,
Sooner or later delicate death.

Prais'd be the fathomless universe,
For life and joy, and for objects and knowledge curious,   *140*
And for love, sweet love—but praise! praise! praise!
For the sure-enwinding arms of cool-enfolding death.

Dark mother always gliding near with soft feet,
Have none chanted for thee a chant of fullest welcome?
Then I chant it for thee, I glorify thee above all,   *145*
I bring thee a song that when thou must indeed come, come
    unfalteringly.

Approach strong deliveress,
When it is so, when thou hast taken them I joyously sing the
        dead,
Lost in the loving floating ocean of thee,
Laved in the flood of thy bliss O death.   *150*

From me to thee glad serenades,
Dances for thee I propose saluting thee, adornments and
        feastings for thee,
And the sights of the open landscape and the high-spread
        sky are fitting,
And life and the fields, and the huge and thoughtful night.

The night in silence under many a star,   *155*
The ocean shore and the husky whispering wave whose voice
        I know,
And the soul turning to thee O vast and well-veil'd death,
And the body gratefully nestling close to thee.

Over the tree-tops I float thee a song,
Over the rising and sinking waves, over the myriad fields
        and the prairies wide,   *160*
Over the dense-pack'd cities all and the teeming wharves and
        ways,
I float this carol with joy, with joy to thee O death.

15

To the tally of my soul,
Loud and strong kept up the gray-brown bird,
With pure deliberate notes spreading filling the night.   *165*

Loud in the pines and cedars dim,
Clear in the freshness moist and the swamp-perfume,
And I with my comrades there in the night.

While my sight that was bound in my eyes unclosed,
As to long panoramas of visions.   *170*

And I saw askant the armies,
I saw as in noiseless dreams hundreds of battle-flags,

Borne through the smoke of the battles and pierc'd with
    missiles I saw them,
And carried hither and yon through the smoke, and torn and
    bloody,
And at last but a few shreds left on the staffs, (and all in
    silence,)   *175*
And the staffs all splinter'd and broken.

I saw battle-corpses, myriads of them,
And the white skeletons of young men, I saw them,
I saw the debris and debris of all the slain soldiers of the war,
But I saw they were not as was thought,   *180*
They themselves were fully at rest, they suffer'd not,
The living remain'd and suffer'd, the mother suffer'd,
And the wife and the child and the musing comrade suffer'd,
And the armies that remain'd suffer'd.

16

Passing the visions, passing the night,   *185*
Passing, unloosing the hold of my comrades' hands,
Passing the song of the hermit bird and the tallying song of
    my soul,
Victorious song, death's outlet song, yet varying ever-alter-
    ing song,
As low and wailing, yet clear the notes, rising and falling,
    flooding the night,
Sadly sinking and fainting, as warning and warning, and
    yet again bursting with joy,   *190*
Covering the earth and filling the spread of the heaven,
As that powerful psalm in the night I heard from recesses,
Passing, I leave thee lilac with heart-shaped leaves,
I leave thee there in the door-yard, blooming, returning with
    spring.

I cease from my song for thee,   *195*
From my gaze on thee in the west, fronting the west, com-
    muning with thee,
O comrade lustrous with silver face in the night.

Yet each to keep and all, retrievements out of the night,
The song, the wondrous chant of the gray-brown bird,
And the tallying chant, the echo arous'd in my soul,   200
With the lustrous and drooping star with the countenance
    full of woe,
With the holders holding my hand nearing the call of the
    bird,
Comrades mine and I in the midst, and their memory ever to
    keep, for the dead I loved so well,
For the sweetest, wisest soul of all my days and lands—and
    this for his dear sake,
Lilac and star and bird twined with the chant of my soul,   205
There in the fragrant pines and the cedars dusk and dim.

WALT WHITMAN

To a Locomotive in Winter

Thee for my recitative,   1
Thee in the driving storm even as now, the snow, the winter-
    day declining,
Thee in thy panoply, thy measur'd dual throbbing and thy
    beat convulsive,
Thy black cylindric body, golden brass and silvery steel,
Thy ponderous side-bars, parallel and connecting rods,
    gyrating, shuttling at thy sides,   5
Thy metrical, now swelling pant and roar, now tapering in
    the distance,
Thy great protruding head-light fix'd in front,
Thy long, pale, floating vapor-pennants, tinged with deli-
    cate purple,
The dense and murky clouds out-belching from thy smoke-
    stack,
Thy knitted frame, thy springs and valves, the tremulous
    twinkle of thy wheels,   10
Thy train of cars behind, obedient, merrily following,
Through gale or calm, now swift, now slack, yet steadily
    careering;

Type of the modern—emblem of motion and power—pulse
of the continent,
For once come serve the Muse and merge in verse, even as
here I see thee,
With storm and buffeting gusts of wind and falling snow,   *15*
By day thy warning ringing bell to sound its notes,
By night thy silent signal lamps to swing.
Fierce-throated beauty!
Roll through my chant with all thy lawless music, thy swing-
ing lamps at night,
Thy madly-whistled laughter, echoing, rumbling like an
earthquake, rousing all,   *20*
Law of thyself complete, thine own track firmly holding,
(No sweetness debonair of tearful harp or glib piano thine,)
Thy trills of shrieks by rocks and hills return'd,
Launch'd o'er the prairies wide, across the lakes,
To the free skies unpent and glad and strong.   *25*

WALT WHITMAN

Youth, Day, Old Age and Night

Youth, large, lusty, loving—youth full of grace, force, fascination,
Do you know that Old Age may come after you with equal grace,
force, fascination?

Day full-blown and splendid—day of the immense sun, action,
ambition, laughter,
The Night follows close with millions of suns, and sleep and re-
storing darkness.

WALT WHITMAN

Dover Beach

The sea is calm to-night,   *1*
The tide is full, the moon lies fair
Upon the Straits;—on the French coast, the light
Gleams, and is gone; the cliffs of England stand,

Glimmering and vast, out in the tranquil bay. 5
Come to the window, sweet is the night air!
Only, from the long line of spray
Where the ebb meets the moon-blanch'd sand,
Listen! you hear the grating roar
Of pebbles which the waves suck back, and fling, 10
At their return, up the high strand,
Begin, and cease, and then again begin,
With tremulous cadence slow, and bring
The eternal note of sadness in.

Sophocles long ago 15
Heard it on the Ægæan, and it brought
Into his mind the turbid ebb and flow
Of human misery; we
Find also in the sound a thought,
Hearing it by this distant northern sea. 20

The sea of faith
Was once, too, at the full, and round earth's shore
Lay like the folds of a bright girdle furl'd;
But now I only hear
Its melancholy, long, withdrawing roar, 25
Retreating to the breath
Of the night-wind down the vast edges drear
And naked shingles of the world.

Ah, love, let us be true
To one another! for the world, which seems 30
To lie before us like a land of dreams,
So various, so beautiful, so new,
Hath really neither joy, nor love, nor light,
Nor certitude, nor peace, nor help for pain;
And we are here as on a darkling plain 35
Swept with confused alarms of struggle and flight,
Where ignorant armies clash by night.

MATTHEW ARNOLD

There's a Certain Slant of Light

There's a certain slant of light,   1
On winter afternoons,
That oppresses, like the weight
Of cathedral tunes.

Heavenly hurt it gives us ;   5
We can find no scar,
But internal difference
Where the meanings are.

None may teach it anything,
'Tis the seal, despair,—   10
An imperial affliction
Sent us of the air.

When it comes, the landscape listens,
Shadows hold their breath ;
When it goes, 'tis like the distance   15
On the look of death.

EMILY DICKINSON

I Taste a Liquor Never Brewed

I taste a liquor never brewed,   1
From tankards scooped in pearl ;
Not all the vats upon the Rhine
Yield such an alcohol!

Inebriate of air am I,   5
And debauchee of dew,
Reeling, through endless summer days,
From inns of molten blue.

When landlords turn the drunken bee
Out of the foxglove's door,   10
When butterflies renounce their drams,
I shall but drink the more!

Till seraphs swing their snowy hats,
And saints to windows run,
To see the little tippler   *15*
Leaning against the sun!

EMILY DICKINSON

Because I Could not Stop for Death

Because I could not stop for Death,   *1*
He kindly stopped for me;
The carriage held but just ourselves
And Immortality.

We slowly drove, he knew no haste,   *5*
And I had put away
My labor, and my leisure too,
For his civility.

We passed the school where children played
At wrestling in a ring;   *10*
We passed the fields of gazing grain,
We passed the setting sun.

We paused before a house that seemed
A swelling of the ground;
The roof was scarcely visible,   *15*
The cornice but a mound.

Since then 'tis centuries; but each
Feels shorter than the day
I first surmised the horses' heads
Were toward eternity.   *20*

EMILY DICKINSON

The Sky Is Low

The sky is low, the clouds are mean,   *1*
A travelling flake of snow
Across a barn or through a rut
Debates if it will go.

A narrow wind complains all day   *5*
How some one treated him ;
Nature, like us, is sometimes caught
Without her diadem.

EMILY DICKINSON

A Child's Laughter

All the bells of heaven may ring,   *1*
All the birds of heaven may sing,
All the wells on earth may spring,
All the winds on earth may bring
   All sweet sounds together ;   *5*
Sweeter far than all things heard,
Hand of harper, tone of bird,
Sound of woods at sundawn stirred,
Welling water's winsome word,
   Wind in warm wan weather,   *10*

One thing yet there is, that none
Hearing ere its chime be done
Knows not well the sweetest one
Heard of man beneath the sun,
   Hoped in heaven hereafter ;   *15*
Soft and strong and loud and light,
Very sound of very light
Heard from morning's rosiest height,
When the soul of all delight
   Fills a child's clear laughter.   *20*

Golden bells of welcome rolled
Never forth such notes, nor told
Hours so blithe in tones so bold,
As the radiant mouth of gold
   Here that rings forth heaven.   *25*
If the golden-crested wren
Were a nightingale—why, then

Something seen and heard of men
Might be half as sweet as when
    Laughs a child of seven.   *30*
        ALGERNON C. SWINBURNE

Some Sweet Day

Into all lives some rain must fall,   *1*
    Into all eyes some tear-drops start,
Whether they fall as gentle shower,
    Or fall like fire from an aching heart.
Into all hearts some sorrow must creep,   *5*
    Into all souls some doubtings come,
Lashing the waves of life's great deep
    From dimpling waters to seething foam.

Over all paths some clouds must lower,
    Under all feet some sharp thorns spring,   *10*
Tearing the flesh to bitter wounds,
    Or entering the heart with their bitter sting.
Upon all brows rough winds must blow,
    Over all shoulders a cross be lain,
Bowing the form in its lofty height   *15*
    Down to the dust in bitter pain.

Into all hands some duty's thrust;
    Unto all arms some burden's given,
Crushing the heart with its weary weight,
    Or lifting the soul from earth to heaven.   *20*
Into all hearts and homes and lives
    God's dear sunlight comes streaming down,
Gilding the ruins of life's great plain—
    Weaving for all a golden crown.
        LEWIS J. BATES

The Outcast

Bleak winds of the winter, sobbing and moaning,   *1*
    Pluck not my rags with your pitiless hand;

Here in the darkness, cold and despairing,
    Homeless, and friendless, and starving I stand.
Scourged by the white, icy whips of the tempest,   5
    I wander forlorn on my desolate way,
Forgotten of earth and forsaken of Heaven,
    Too frozen to kneel and too hungry to pray.

I look at the stately and palace-like dwellings
    That line with their grandeur the pathway I tread;   10
I fancy the brightness and warmth of the hearthstone,
    The plenteous board with the wine and the bread;
I see the heads bowed with a reverent meaning,
    A blessing is breathed o'er the sumptuous fare;
Will it rise to the ear of the pitiful Father,   15
    Or die of the cold, like the vagabond's prayer?

Hark! Midnight. The chime from the church-tower above me
    Drops solemnly down through the whirl of the storm;
If one could pass through the gate to the portal,
    Could sleep there, and dream it was lighted and warm!   20
Give away, cruel bars! let me through to a refuge!
    Give away! But I rave, and the fierce winds reply:
"No room in his house for his vagabond children,
    No room in his porch for an outcast to die."

No room in his dwelling—no room in the churches,   25
    No room in the prison—for hunger's no crime;
Is there room in the bed of the river, I wonder,
    Deep down by the pier in the ooze and the slime?
Mock on, taunting wind! I can laugh back an answer,
    An hour, and your bitterest breath I defy;   30
Since bars shut me out of God's house among mortals,
    I will knock at the gate of his home in the sky!

MARY L. RITTER

The Windhover:

To Christ our Lord

I caught this morning morning's minion, king-   1
    dom of daylight's dauphin, dapple-dawn-drawn Falcon, in
        his riding

Of the rolling level underneath him steady air, and striding
High there, how he rung upon the rein of a wimpling wing
In his ecstasy! then off, off forth on swing,   5
   As a skate's heel sweeps smooth on a bow-bend: the hurl
     and gliding
   Rebuffed the big wind. My heart in hiding
Stirred for a bird,—the achieve of, the mastery of the thing!

Brute beauty and valour and act, oh, air, pride, plume, here
   Buckle! AND the fire that breaks from thee then, a billion   10
Times told lovelier, more dangerous, O my chevalier!

   No wonder of it: shéer plód makes plough down sillion
Shine, and blue-bleak embers, ah my dear,
   Fall, gall themselves, and gash gold-vermilion.

GERARD MANLEY HOPKINS

What Is to Come

What is to come we know not. But we know   1
That what has been was good—was good to show,
   Better to hide, and best of all to bear.
   We are the masters of the days that were:
We have lived, we have loved, we have suffered . . . even so.   5

Shall we not take the ebb who had the flow?
Life was our friend. Now, if it be our foe—
   Dear, though it break and spoil us!—need we care
         What is to come?

Let the great winds their worst and wildest blow,   10
Or the gold weather round us mellow slow:
   We have fulfilled ourselves, and we can dare
   And we can conquer, though we may not share
In the rich quiet of the afterglow
         What is to come.   15

WILLIAM ERNEST HENLEY

Danny Deever

"What are the bugles blowin' for?" said Files-on-Parade.   1
"To turn you out, to turn you out," the Colour-Sergeant said.

"What makes you look so white, so white?" said Files-on-
  Parade.
"I'm dreadin' what I've got to watch," the Colour-Sergeant
  said.
  For they're hangin' Danny Deever, you can hear the Dead
    March play,   5
  The regiment's in 'ollow square—they're hangin' him to-
    day;
  They've taken of his buttons off an' cut his stripes away,
  An' they're hangin' Danny Deever in the mornin'.

"What makes the rear-rank breathe so 'ard?" said Files-on-
  Parade.
"It's bitter cold, it's bitter cold," the Colour-Sergeant said.   10
"What makes that front-rank man fall down?" says Files-on-
  Parade.
"A touch o' sun, a touch o' sun," the Colour-Sergeant said.
  They are hangin' Danny Deever, they are marchin' of 'im
    round,
  They 'ave 'alted Danny Deever by 'is coffin on the ground;
  An' 'e'll swing in 'arf a minute for a sneakin' shootin'
    hound—   15
  O they're hangin' Danny Deever in the mornin'!

" 'Is cot was right-'and cot to mine," said Files-on-Parade.
"E's sleepin' out an' far to-night," the Colour-Sergeant said.
"I've drunk 'is beer a score o' times," said Files-on-Parade.
"E's drinkin' bitter beer alone," the Colour-Sergeant said.   20
  They are hangin' Danny Deever, you must mark 'im to 'is
    place,
  For 'e shot a comrade sleepin'—you must look 'im in the
    face;
  Nine 'undred of 'is county an' the regiment's disgrace,
  While they're hangin' Danny Deever in the mornin'.

"What's that so black agin the sun?" said Files-on-Parade.   25
"It's Danny fightin' 'ard for life," the Colour-Sergeant said.
"What's that that whimpers over'ead?" said Files-on-Parade.

"Its Danny's soul that's passin' now," the Colour-Sergeant
  said.
  For they're done with Danny Deever, you can 'ear the
    quickstep play,
  The regiment's in column, an' they're marchin' us away;   *30*
  Ho! the young recruits are shakin', an' they'll want their
    beer to-day,
  After hangin' Danny Deever in the mornin'!

RUDYARD KIPLING

The Ladies

I've taken my fun where I've found it;   *1*
  I've rogued an' I've ranged in my time;
I've 'ad my pickin' o' sweet'earts,
  An' four o' the lot was prime.
One was an 'arf-caste widow,   *5*
  One was a woman at Prome,
One was the wife of a *jemadar-sais*,
  An' one is a girl at 'ome.

Now I aren't no 'and with the ladies,
  For, takin' 'em all along,   *10*
You never can say till you've tried 'em,
  An' then you are like to be wrong.
There's times when you'll think that you mightn't,
  There's times when you'll know that you might;
But the things you will learn from the Yellow an' Brown,   *15*
  They'll 'elp you a lot with the White!

I was a young un at 'Oogli,
  Shy as a girl to begin;
Aggie de Castrer she made me,
  An' Aggie was clever as sin;   *20*
Older than me, but my first un—
  More like a mother she were—
Showed me the way to promotion an' pay,
  An' I learned about women from 'er!

Then I was ordered to Burma,   25
   Actin' in charge o' Bazar,
An' I got me a tiddy live 'eathen
   Through buyin' supplies off 'er pa.
Funny an' yellow an' faithful—
   Doll in a teacup she were,   30
But we lived on the square, like a true-married pair,
   An' I learned about women from 'er !

Then we was shifted to Neemuch
   (Or I might ha' been keepin' 'er now),
An' I took with a shiny she-devil,   35
   The wife of a nigger at Mhow ;
Taught me the gypsy-folks' *bolee;*
   Kind o' volcano she were,
For she knifed me one night 'cause I wished she was white,
   An' I learned about women from 'er !   40

Then I come 'ome in the trooper,
   'Long of a kid o' sixteen—
Girl from a convent at Meerut,
   The straightest I ever 'ave seen.
Love at first sight was 'er trouble,   45
   She didn't know what it were ;
An' I wouldn't do such, 'cause I liked 'er too much,
   But—I learned about women from 'er !

I've taken my fun where I've found it,
   An' now I must pay for my fun,   50
For the more you 'ave known o' the others
   The less you will settle to one ;
An' the end of it's sittin' and thinkin',
   An' dreamin' Hell-fires to see ;
So be warned by my lot (which I know you will not),   55
   An' learn about women from me !

    What did the Colonel's Lady think?
    Nobody never knew.

Somebody asked the Sergeant's wife,
   An' she told 'em true!   *60*
When you get to a man in the case,
   They're like as a row of pins—
For the Colonel's Lady an' Judy O'Grady
   Are sisters under their skins!

RUDYARD KIPLING

Gloucester Moors

A mile behind is Gloucester town   *1*
Where the fishing fleets put in,
A mile ahead the land dips down
And the woods and farms begin.
Here, where the moors stretch free   *5*
In the high blue afternoon,
Are the marching sun and talking sea,
And the racing winds that wheel and flee
On the flying heels of June.

Jill-o'er-the-ground is purple blue,   *10*
Blue is the quaker-maid,
The wild geranium holds its dew
Long in the boulder's shade.
Wax-red hangs the cup
From the huckleberry boughs,   *15*
In barberry bells the grey moths sup,
Or where the choke-cherry lifts high up
Sweet bowls for their carouse.

Over the shelf of the sandy cove
Beach-peas blossom late.   *20*
By copse and cliff the swallows rove
Each calling to his mate.
Seaward the sea-gulls go,
And the land-birds all are here;
That green-gold flash was a vireo,   *25*
And yonder flame where the marsh-flags grow
Was a scarlet tanager.

This earth is not the steadfast place
We landsmen build upon;
From deep to deep she varies pace,   *30*
And while she comes is gone.
Beneath my feet I feel
Her smooth bulk heave and dip;
With velvet plunge and soft upreel
She swings and steadies to her keel   *35*
Like a gallant, gallant ship.

These summer clouds she sets for sail,
The sun is her masthead light,
She tows the moon like a pinnace frail
Where her phosphor wake churns bright.   *40*
Now hid, now looming clear,
On the face of the dangerous blue
The star fleets tack and wheel and veer,
But on, but on does the old earth steer
As if her port she knew.   *45*

God, dear God! Does she know her port,
Though she goes so far about?
Or blind astray, does she make her sport
To brazen and chance it out?
I watched when her captains passed: *50*
She were better captainless.
Men in the cabin, before the mast,
But some were reckless and some aghast,
And some sat gorged at mess.

By her battened hatch I leaned and caught   *55*
Sounds from the noisome hold,—
Cursing and sighing of souls distraught
And cries too sad to be told.
Then I strove to go down and see;
But they said, "Thou art not of us!"   *60*
I turned to those on the deck with me
And cried, "Give help!" But they said, "Let be:
Our ship sails faster thus."

Jill-o'er-the-ground is purple blue,
Blue is the quaker-maid,   *65*
The alder-clump where the brook comes through
Breeds cresses in its shade.
To be out of the moiling street
With its swelter and its sin!
Who has given to me this sweet,   *70*
And given my brother dust to eat?
And when will his wage come in?

Scattering wide or blown in ranks,
Yellow and white and brown,
Boats and boats from the fishing banks   *75*
Come home to Gloucester town.
There is cash to purse and spend,
There are wives to be embraced,
Hearts to borrow and hearts to lend,
And hearts to take and keep to the end,—   *80*
O little sails, make haste!

But thou, vast outbound ship of souls,
What harbor town for thee?
What shapes, when thy arriving tolls,
Shall crowd the banks to see?   *85*
Shall all the happy shipmates then
Stand singing brotherly?
Or shall a haggard ruthless few
Warp her over and bring her to,
While the many broken souls of men   *90*
Fester down in the slaver's pen,
And nothing to say or do?

WILLIAM VAUGHN MOODY

Patterns

I walk down the garden paths,   *1*
And all the daffodils
Are blowing, and the bright blue squills.

I walk down the patterned garden paths
In my stiff, brocaded gown.   5
With my powdered hair and jewelled fan,
I too am a rare
Pattern. As I wander down
The garden paths.

My dress is richly figured,   10
And the train
Makes a pink and silver stain
On the gravel, and the thrift
Of the borders.
Just a plate of current fashion,   15
Tripping by in high-heeled, ribboned shoes.
Not a softness anywhere about me,
Only whalebone and brocade.
And I sink on a seat in the shade
Of a lime tree. For my passion   20
Wars against the stiff brocade.
The daffodils and squills
Flutter in the breeze
As they please.
And I weep;   25
For the lime tree is in blossom
And one small flower has dropped upon my bosom.

And the plashing of waterdrops
In the marble fountain
Comes down the garden paths.   30
The dripping never stops.
Underneath my stiffened gown
Is the softness of a woman bathing in a marble basin,
A basin in the midst of hedges grown
So thick, she cannot see her lover hiding,   35
But she guesses he is near,
And the sliding of the water
Seems the stroking of a dear
Hand upon her.

What is summer in a fine brocaded gown!   40
I should like to see it lying in a heap upon the ground.
All the pink and silver crumpled up on the ground.

I would be the pink and silver as I ran along the paths,
And he would stumble after,
Bewildered by my laughter.   45
I should see the sun flashing from his sword-hilt and the
      buckles on his shoes.
I would choose
To lead him in a maze along the patterned paths,
A bright and laughing maze for my heavy-booted lover.
Till he caught me in the shade,   50
And the buttons of his waistcoat bruised my body as he
      clasped me,
Aching, melting, unafraid.
With the shadows of the leaves and the sundrops,
And the plopping of the waterdrops,
All about us in the open afternoon—   55
I am very like to swoon
With the weight of this brocade,
For the sun sifts through the shade.

Underneath the fallen blossom
In my bosom,   60
Is a letter I have hid.
It was brought to me this morning by a rider from the Duke.
"Madam, we regret to inform you that Lord Hartwell
Died in action Thursday se'nnight."
As I read it in the white, morning sunlight,   65
The letters squirmed like snakes.
"Any answer, Madam," said my footman.
"No," I told him.
"See that the messenger takes some refreshment.
No, no answer."   70
And I walked into the garden,
Up and down the patterned paths,
In my stiff, correct brocade.

The blue and yellow flowers stood up proudly in the sun,
Each one.   *75*
I stood upright too,
Held rigid to the pattern
By the stiffness of my gown.
Up and down I walked,
Up and down.   *80*

In a month he would have been my husband.
In a month, here, underneath this lime,
We would have broke the pattern;
He for me, and I for him,
He as Colonel, I as Lady,   *85*
On this shady seat.
He had a whim
That sunlight carried blessing.
And I answered, "It shall be as you have said."
Now he is dead.   *90*

In summer and in winter I shall walk
Up and down
The patterned garden paths
In my stiff, brocaded gown.
The squills and daffodils   *95*
Will give place to pillared roses, and to asters, and to snow.
I shall go
Up and down,
In my gown.
Gorgeously arrayed,   *100*
Boned and stayed.
And the softness of my body will be guarded from embrace
By each button, hook, and lace.
For the man who should loose me is dead,
Fighting with the Duke in Flanders,   *105*
In a pattern called a war.
Christ! What are patterns for?

AMY LOWELL

After Apple-Picking

My long two-pointed ladder's sticking through a tree   *1*
Toward heaven still,
And there's a barrel that I didn't fill
Beside it, and there may be two or three
Apples I didn't pick upon some bough.   *5*
But I am done with apple-picking now.
Essence of winter sleep is on the night,
The scent of apples : I am drowsing off.
I cannot rub the strangeness from my sight
I got from looking through a pane of glass   *10*
I skimmed this morning from the drinking trough
And held against the world of hoary grass.
It melted, and I let it fall and break.
But I was well
Upon my way to sleep before it fell,   *15*
And I could tell
What form my dreaming was about to take.
Magnified apples appear and disappear,
Stem end and blossom end,
And every fleck of russet showing clear.   *20*
My instep arch not only keeps the ache,
It keeps the pressure of a ladder-round.
I feel the ladder sway as the boughs bend.
And I keep hearing from the cellar bin
The rumbling sound   *25*
Of load on load of apples coming in.
For I have had too much
Of apple-picking : I am overtired
Of the great harvest I myself desired.
There were ten thousand thousand fruit to touch,   *30*
Cherish in hand, lift down, and not let fall.
For all
That struck the earth,
No matter if not bruised or spiked with stubble,
Went surely to the cider-apple heap   *35*

As of no worth.
One can see what will trouble
This sleep of mine, whatever sleep it is.
Were he not gone,
The woodchuck could say whether it's like his   *40*
Long sleep, as I describe its coming on,
Or just some human sleep.

ROBERT FROST

Birches

When I see birches bend to left and right   *1*
Across the lines of straighter darker trees,
I like to think some boy's been swinging them.
But swinging doesn't bend them down to stay.
Ice-storms do that. Often you must have seen them   *5*
Loaded with ice a sunny winter morning
After a rain. They click upon themselves
As the breeze rises, and turn many-colored
As the stir cracks and crazes their enamel.
Soon the sun's warmth makes them shed crystal shells   *10*
Shattering and avalanching on the snow-crust—
Such heaps of broken glass to sweep away
You'd think the inner dome of heaven had fallen.
They are dragged to the withered bracken by the load,
And they seem not to break; though once they are bowed   *15*
So low for long, they never right themselves:
You may see their trunks arching in the woods
Years afterwards, trailing their leaves on the ground
Like girls on hands and knees that throw their hair
Before them over their heads to dry in the sun.   *20*
But I was going to say when Truth broke in
With all her matter-of-fact about the ice-storm
I should prefer to have some boy bend them
As he went out and in to fetch the cows—
Some boy too far from town to learn baseball,   *25*
Whose only play was what he found himself,
Summer or winter, and could play alone.

One by one he subdued his father's trees
By riding them down over and over again
Until he took the stiffness out of them,   *30*
And not one but hung limp, not one was left
For him to conquer. He learned all there was
To learn about not launching out too soon
And so not carrying the tree away
Clear to the ground. He always kept his poise   *35*
To the top branches, climbing carefully
With the same pains you use to fill a cup
Up to the brim, and even above the brim.
Then he flung outward, feet first, with a swish,
Kicking his way down through the air to the ground.   *40*
So was I once myself a swinger of birches.
And so I dream of going back to be.
It's when I'm weary of considerations,
And life is too much like a pathless wood
Where your face burns and tickles with the cobwebs   *45*
Broken across it, and one eye is weeping
From a twig's having lashed across it open.
I'd like to get away from earth awhile
And then come back to it and begin over.
May no fate willfully misunderstand me   *50*
And half grant what I wish and snatch me away
Not to return. Earth's the right place for love:
I don't know where it's likely to go better.
I'd like to go by climbing a birch tree,
And climb black branches up a snow-white trunk   *55*
Toward heaven, till the tree could bear no more,
But dipped its top and set me down again.
That would be good both going and coming back.
One could do worse than be a swinger of birches.

ROBERT FROST

On the Beach at Fontana

Wind whines and whines the shingle,   *1*
The crazy pierstakes groan;

A senile sea numbers each single
Slimesilvered stone.

From whining wind and colder   5
Grey sea I wrap him warm
And touch his trembling fineboned shoulder
And boyish arm.

Around us fear, descending
Darkness of fear above   10
And in my heart how deep unending
Ache of love!

JAMES JOYCE

The Yachts

contend in a sea which the land partly encloses   1
shielding them from the too heavy blows
of an ungoverned ocean which when it chooses

tortures the biggest hulls, the best man knows
to pit against its beatings, and sinks them pitilessly.   5
Mothlike in mists, scintillant in the minute

brilliance of cloudless days, with broad bellying sails
they glide to the wind tossing green water
from their sharp prows while over them the crew crawls

ant like, solicitously grooming them, releasing,   10
making fast as they turn, lean far over and having
caught the wind again, side by side, head for the mark.

In a well guarded arena of open water surrounded by
lesser and greater craft which, sycophant, lumbering
and flittering follow them, they appear youthful, rare   15

as the light of a happy eye, live with the grace
of all that in the mind is feckless, free and
naturally to be desired. Now the sea which holds them

is moody, lapping their glossy sides, as if feeling
for some slightest flaw but fails completely.   *20*
Today no race. Then the wind comes again. The yachts

move, jockeying for a start, the signal is set and they
are off. Now the waves strike at them but they are too
well made, they slip through, though they take in canvas.

Arms with hands grasping seek to clutch at the prows.   *25*
Bodies thrown recklessly in the way are cut aside.
It is a sea of faces about them in agony, in despair

until the horror of the race dawns staggering the mind,
the whole sea become an entanglement of watery bodies
lost to the world bearing what they cannot hold. Broken,   *30*

beaten, desolate, reaching from the dead to be taken up
they cry out, failing, failing! their cries rising
in waves still as the skillful yachts pass over.

WILLIAM CARLOS WILLIAMS

Trees

I think that I shall never see   *1*
A poem lovely as a tree.

A tree whose hungry mouth is prest
Against the earth's sweet flowing breast;

A tree that looks at God all day,   *5*
And lifts her leafy arms to pray;

A tree that may in summer wear
A nest of robins in her hair;

Upon whose bosom snow has lain;
Who intimately lives with rain.   *10*

Poems are made by fools like me,
But only God can make a tree.

JOYCE KILMER

Aubade

Jane, Jane,   *1*
Tall as a crane,
The morning light creaks down again.

Comb your cockscomb-ragged hair;
Jane, Jane, come down the stair.   *5*

Each dull blunt wooden stalactite
Of rain creaks, hardened by the light,

Sounding like an overtone
From some lonely world unknown.

But the creaking empty light   *10*
Will never harden into sight,

Will never penetrate your brain
With overtones like the blunt rain.

The light would show (if it could harden)
Eternities of kitchen-garden,   *15*

Cockscomb flowers that none will pluck,
And wooden flowers that 'gin to cluck.

In the kitchen you must light
Flames as staring, red and white

As carrots or as turnips, shining   *20*
Where the cold dawn light lies whining.

Cockscomb hair on the cold wind
Hangs limp, turns the milk's weak mind. . . .

Jane, Jane,
Tall as a crane,   *25*
The morning light creaks down again!

EDITH SITWELL

Shine, Perishing Republic

While this America settles in the mould of its vulgarity, heavily thickening to empire,   *1*
And protest, only a bubble in the molten mass, pops and sighs
out, and the mass hardens,

I sadly smiling remember that the flower fades to make fruit,
the fruit rots to make earth.
Out of the mother; and through the spring exultances, ripeness and decadence; and home to the mother.

You making haste haste on decay: not blameworthy; life is
good, be it stubbornly long or suddenly   *5*
A mortal splendor: meteors are not needed less than mountains: shine, perishing republic.

But for my children, I would have them keep their distance
from the thickening center; corruption
Never has been compulsory, when the cities lie at the monster's feet there are left the mountains.

And boys, be in nothing so moderate as in love of man, a
clever servant, insufferable master.
There is the trap that catches noblest spirits, that caught—
they say—God, when he walked on earth.   *10*

ROBINSON JEFFERS

Hurt Hawks

I

The broken pillar of the wing jags from the clotted shoulder,   *1*
The wing trails like a banner in defeat,

No more to use the sky forever but live with famine
And pain a few days : cat nor coyote
Will shorten the week of waiting for death, there is game
    without talons.   5
He stands under the oak-bush and waits
The lame feet of salvation ; at night he remembers freedom
And flies in a dream, the dawns ruin it.
He is strong and pain is worse to the strong, incapacity is
    worse.
The curs of the day come and torment him   10
At distance, no one but death the redeemer will humble that
    head,
The intrepid readiness, the terrible eyes.
The wild God of the world is sometimes merciful to those
That ask mercy, not often to the arrogant.
You do not know him, you communal people, or you have for-
    gotten him ;   15
Intemperate and savage, the hawk remembers him ;
Beautiful and wild, the hawks, and men that are dying, re-
    member him.

II

I'd sooner, except the penalties, kill a man than a hawk ; but
    the great redtail
Had nothing left but unable misery
From the bone too shattered for mending, the wing that
    trailed under his talons when he moved.   20
We had fed him six weeks, I gave him freedom,
He wandered over the foreland hill and returned in the eve-
    ning, asking for death,
Not like a beggar, still eyed with the old
Implacable arrogance. I gave him the lead gift in the twilight.
    What fell was relaxed,
Owl-downy, soft feminine feathers ; but what   25
Soared : the fierce rush : the night-herons by the flooded river
    cried fear at its rising
Before it was quite unsheathed from reality.

ROBINSON JEFFERS

The Fish

wade   *1*
through black jade.
   Of the crow-blue mussel-shells, one keeps
   adjusting the ash-heaps;
      opening and shutting itself like   *5*

an
injured fan.
   The barnacles which encrust the side
   of the wave, cannot hide
      there for the submerged shafts of the   *10*

sun,
split like spun
   glass, move themselves with spotlight swiftness
   into the crevices—
      in and out, illuminating   *15*

the
turquoise sea
   of bodies. The water drives a wedge
   of iron through the iron edge
      of the cliff; whereupon the stars,   *20*

pink
rice-grains, ink
   bespattered jelly-fish, crabs like green
   lilies, and submarine
      toadstools, slide each on the other.   *25*

All
external
   marks of abuse are present on this
   defiant edifice—
      all the physical features of   *30*

ac-
cident—lack
  of cornice, dynamite grooves, burns, and
  hatchet strokes, these things stand
    out on it; the chasm-side is   *35*

dead.
Repeated
  evidence has proved that it can live
  on what cannot revive
    its youth. The sea grows old in it.   *40*

MARIANNE MOORE

The Love Song of J. Alfred Prufrock

> *S'io credesse che mia risposta fosse*
> *A persona che mai tornasse al mondo,*
> *Questa fiamma staria senza piu scosse.*
> *Ma perciocche giammai di questo fondo*
> *Non torno vivo alcun, s'i'odo il vero,*
> *Senza tema d'infamia ti rispondo.*

Let us go then, you and I,   *1*
When the evening is spread out against the sky
Like a patient etherised upon a table; .
Let us go, through certain half-deserted streets,
The muttering retreats   *5*
Of restless nights in one-night cheap hotels
And sawdust restaurants with oyster-shells:
Streets that follow like a tedious argument
Of insidious intent
To lead you to an overwhelming question . . .   *10*
Oh, do not ask, "What is it?"
Let us go and make our visit.

In the room the women come and go
Talking of Michelangelo.

The yellow fog that rubs its back upon the window-panes,   *15*
The yellow smoke that rubs its muzzle on the window-panes
Licked its tongue into the corners of the evening,
Lingered upon the pools that stand in drains,
Let fall upon its back the soot that falls from chimneys,
Slipped by the terrace, made a sudden leap,   *20*
And seeing that it was a soft October night,
Curled once about the house, and fell asleep.

And indeed there will be time
For the yellow smoke that slides along the street,
Rubbing its back upon the window-panes;   *25*
There will be time, there will be time
To prepare a face to meet the faces that you meet;
There will be time to murder and create,
And time for all the works and days of hands
That lift and drop a question on your plate;   *30*
Time for you and time for me,
And time yet for a hundred indecisions,
And for a hundred visions and revisions,
Before the taking of a toast and tea.

In the room the women come and go   *35*
Talking of Michelangelo.

And indeed there will be time
To wonder, "Do I dare?" and, "Do I dare?"
Time to turn back and descend the stair,
With a bald spot in the middle of my hair—   *40*
[They will say: "How his hair is growing thin!"]
My morning coat, my collar mounting firmly to the chin,
My necktie rich and modest, but asserted by a simple pin—
[They will say: "But how his arms and legs are thin!"]
Do I dare   *45*
Disturb the universe?
In a minute there is time
For decisions and revisions which a minute will reverse.

For I have known them all already, known them all:—
Have known the evenings, mornings, afternoons,   *50*
I have measured out my life with coffee spoons;
I know the voices dying with a dying fall
Beneath the music from a farther room.
    So how should I presume?

And I have known the eyes already, known them all—   *55*
The eyes that fix you in a formulated phrase,
And when I am formulated, sprawling on a pin,
When I am pinned and wriggling on the wall,
Then how should I begin
To spit out all the butt-ends of my days and ways?   *60*
    And how should I presume?

And I have known the arms already, known them all—
Arms that are braceleted and white and bare
[But in the lamplight, downed with light brown hair!]
Is it perfume from a dress   *65*
That makes me so digress?
Arms that lie along a table, or wrap about a shawl.
    And should I then presume?
    And how should I begin?

                    *   *   *

Shall I say, I have gone at dusk through narrow streets   *70*
And watched the smoke that rises from the pipes
Of lonely men in shirt-sleeves, leaning out of windows? . . .

I should have been a pair of ragged claws
Scuttling across the floors of silent seas.

                    *   *   *

And the afternoon, the evening, sleeps so peacefully!   *75*
Smoothed by long fingers,
Asleep . . . tired . . . or it malingers,
Stretched on the floor, here beside you and me.
Should I, after tea and cakes and ices,
Have the strength to force the moment to its crisis?   *80*

But though I have wept and fasted, wept and prayed,
Though I have seen my head [grown slightly bald] brought
     in upon a platter,
I am no prophet—and here's no great matter;
I have seen the moment of my greatness flicker,
And I have seen the eternal Footman hold my coat, and
     snicker,   85
And in short, I was afraid.

And would it have been worth it, after all,
After the cups, the marmalade, the tea,
Among the porcelain, among some talk of you and me,
Would it have been worth while,   90
To have bitten off the matter with a smile,
To have squeezed the universe into a ball
To roll it toward some overwhelming question,
To say: "I am Lazarus, come from the dead,
Come back to tell you all, I shall tell you all"—   95
If one, settling a pillow by her head,
    Should say: "That is not what I meant at all.
    That is not it, at all."

And would it have been worth it, after all,
Would it have been worth while,   100
After the sunsets and the dooryards and the sprinkled
     streets,
After the novels, after the teacups, after the skirts that trail
     along the floor—
And this, and so much more?—
It is impossible to say just what I mean!
But as if a magic lantern threw the nerves in patterns on a
     screen: 105
Would it have been worth while
If one, settling a pillow or throwing off a shawl,
And turning toward the window, should say:
    "That is not it at all,
    That is not what I meant, at all."   110

                *   *   *

No! I am not Prince Hamlet, nor was meant to be;
Am an attendant lord, one that will do
To swell a progress, start a scene or two,
Advise the prince; no doubt, an easy tool,
Deferential, glad to be of use,   *115*
Politic, cautious, and meticulous;
Full of high sentence, but a bit obtuse;
At times, indeed, almost ridiculous—
Almost, at times, the Fool.

I grow old . . . I grow old . . .   *120*
I shall wear the bottoms of my trousers rolled.

Shall I part my hair behind? Do I dare to eat a peach?
I shall wear white flannel trousers, and walk upon the beach.
I have heard the mermaids singing, each to each.

I do not think that they will sing to me.   *125*

I have seen them riding seaward on the waves
Combing the white hair of the waves blown back
When the wind blows the water white and black.

We have lingered in the chambers of the sea
By sea-girls wreathed with seaweed red and brown   *130*
Till human voices wake us, and we drown.

                                             T. S. ELIOT

The Hollow Men

MISTAH KURTZ—HE DEAD

A penny for the Old Guy

I

We are the hollow men   *1*
We are the stuffed men
Leaning together
Headpiece filled with straw. Alas!

Our dried voices, when   *5*
We whisper together
Are quiet and meaningless
As wind in dry grass
Or rats' feet over broken glass
In our dry cellar   *10*

Shape without form, shade without colour,
Paralysed force, gesture without motion ;

Those who have crossed
With direct eyes, to death's other Kingdom
Remember us—if at all—not as lost   *15*
Violent souls, but only
As the hollow men
The stuffed men.

II

Eyes I dare not meet in dreams
In death's dream kingdom   *20*
These do not appear :
There, the eyes are
Sunlight on a broken column
There, is a tree swinging
And voices are   *25*
In the wind's singing
More distant and more solemn
Than a fading star.

Let me be no nearer
In death's dream kingdom   *30*
Let me also wear
Such deliberate disguises
Rat's skin, crowskin, crossed staves
In a field
Behaving as the wind behaves   *35*
No nearer—

Not that final meeting
In the twilight kingdom

III

This is the dead land
This is cactus land   *40*
Here the stone images
Are raised, here they receive
The supplication of a dead man's hand
Under the twinkle of a fading star.

Is it like this   *45*
In death's other kingdom
Waking alone
At the hour when we are
Trembling with tenderness
Lips that would kiss   *50*
Form prayers to broken stone.

IV

The eyes are not here
There are no eyes here
In this valley of dying stars
In this hollow valley   *55*
This broken jaw of our lost kingdoms

In this last of meeting places
We grope together
And avoid speech
Gathered on this beach of the tumid river   *60*

Sightless, unless
The eyes reappear
As the perpetual star
Multifoliate rose
Of death's twilight kingdom   *65*
The hope only
Of empty men.

v

Here we go round the prickly pear
Prickly pear prickly pear
Here we go round the prickly pear   *70*
At five o'clock in the morning.

Between the idea
And the reality
Between the motion
And the act   75
Falls the Shadow
     For Thine is the Kingdom

Between the conception
And the creation
Between the emotion   80
And the response
Falls the Shadow
     Life is very long

Between the desire
And the spasm   85
Between the potency
And the existence
Between the essence
And the descent
Falls the Shadow   90
    For Thine is the Kingdom

For Thine is
Life is
For Thine is the

This is the way the world ends 95
This is the way the world ends
This is the way the world ends
Not with a bang but a whimper.
     T. S. ELIOT

March

Awake to the cold light   *1*
of wet wind running
twigs in tremors. Walls
are naked. Twilights raw—
and when the sun taps steeples   *5*
their glistenings dwindle
upward . . .

      March
slips along the ground
like a mouse under pussy   *10*
willows, a little hungry.

The vagrant ghost of winter,
is it this that keeps the chimney
busy still? For something still
nudges shingles and windows: *15*

but waveringly,—this ghost,
this slate-eyed saintly wraith
of winter wanes
and knows its waning.

HART CRANE

Barns in November

Along an empty road I watched the barns   *1*
Crouched on the hillsides while the morning light
Poured in among the trees like mist and fitted
Panes to the windows now locked winter tight.

And overhead a birdless waste went streaming   *5*
Missed the sharp trees and mirrored with its own
Our rolling hills, but not in that grey country
Rise roofs like these, low bent and rooted in stone.

The bare and tattered fields have long been empty.
Empty the pasture too of all save weather   *10*
Sowing his measure of snow where side by side
Fences and stones and furrows sleep together.

After the death of summer the barns inherit
Blossom and leaf and stem; granary and mow
Shoulder their loads in the darkness of timbers speaking   *15*
And pigeons sobbing, Winter is coming now.

And so the rafters arch to loosen the bony
Long fingers of the wind pressed toward the warm
And yellow pens where little calves lie sleeping
Rescued from their first snow. The heart of the farm   *20*

Beats a slow beat and is steady, the pulse awakens
Strength in the beams and sills, and the haymow floors
Stretch their feet to the walls and a staring window
Discovers the farmer hastily starting his chores.

Thus shall the heart against a bitter season   *25*
Guard countless doors and windows, bring to bin
The crops of its own raising and gather in
The fruit and seed of love, the stalks of reason,

And stand alone among the vacant meadows
Calmly awaiting the age of winter weather   *30*
When, through the air, a chill and cloudy heaven
Drops from its mantle of snow the first fine feather.

JAMES HEARST

The Fence Row

A ripple of ground still shows the line where   *1*
a fence once divided this field in two—
the habit of being divided fades slowly
and may not be smoothed out in one growing season.

Here where two fields shared a common boundary   *5*
that kept córn from oats and the meadow from rye
the limit set to please some farmer's business
has now been plowed over and planted to crops.

There were stones here once and woodchuck burrows,
these things belong to the edge of a field,   *10*
where perhaps wild grapevine had looped protection
around the nest where the hen pheasant sat,

and rested its vines on the barbed wire fence
that stood for authority once in this place
till the wire went slack and the barbs grew rusty   *15*
and posts rotted off, and soon nothing was left

in the wave of the ground but a few wild roses,
though lately I found a freshly dug den
where a fox of the old school loyal to his party
had refused to admit that the fence row was gone.   *20*

JAMES HEARST

A Summer Commentary

When I was young, with sharper sense,   *1*
The farthest insect cry I heard
Could stay me; through the trees, intense,
I watched the hunter and the bird.

Where is the meaning that I found?   *5*
Or was it but a state of mind,
Some old penumbra of the ground,
In which to be but not to find?

Now summer grasses, brown with heat,
Have crowded sweetness through the air;   *10*
The very roadside dust is sweet;
Even the unshadowed earth is fair.

The soft voice of the nesting dove,
And the dove in soft erratic flight
Like a rapid hand within a glove,   15
Caress the silence and the light.

Amid the rubble, the fallen fruit,
Fermenting in its rich decay,
Smears brandy on the trampling boot
And sends it sweeter on its way.   20

YVOR WINTERS

Now to Be with You, Elate, Unshared

Now to be with you, elate, unshared,   1
My kestrel joy, O hoverer in wind,
Over the quarry furiously at rest
Chaired on shoulders of shouting wind.

Where's that unique one, wind and wing married,   5
Aloft in contact of earth and ether;
Feathery my comet, Oh too often
From heav'n harried by carrion cares.

No searcher may hope to flush that fleet one
Not to be found by gun or glass,   10
In old habits, last year's hunting-ground,
Whose beat is wind-wide, whose perch a split second.

But surely will meet him, late or soon,
Who turns a corner into new territory;
Spirit mating afresh shall discern him   15
On the world's noon-top purely poised.

Void are the valleys, in town no trace,
And dumb the sky-dividing hills:
Swift outrider of lumbering earth
Oh hasten hither my kestrel joy!   20

C. DAY LEWIS

The Uninfected

I saw a man whose face was white as snow   *1*
Come slowly down the mall,
And he was followed by another one
Till there were seven in all.

Now this is very strange that lepers be   *5*
Allowed to walk abroad in broad daylight!
I shook myself, and quickly turned to call
A bluecoat, and as suddenly caught sight

Of one in blue ruling the thoroughfare,
Who made me passage through that brawling sea   *10*
With one raised hand. I spoke, and he inclined
To hear my word, the face of leprosy.

I turned and went straight on to search my own
Face in the next shop window mirror-glass—
Still no infection, not a single spot,   *15*
So I stood there and watched the lepers pass

Till four drove up to take me to a place
Where I live now, attended very well
By several strong male lepers dressed in white,
Eating what I like, sound as a bell.   *20*

E. L. MAYO

In Memory of W. B. Yeats

(D. JAN. 1939)

1

He disappeared in the dead of winter: *1*
The brooks were frozen, the airports almost deserted,
And snow disfigured the public statues;
The mercury sank in the mouth of the dying day.
O all the instruments agree   *5*
The day of his death was a dark cold day.

Far from his illness
The wolves ran on through the evergreen forests,
The peasant river was untempted by the fashionable quays;
By mourning tongues   10
The death of the poet was kept from his poems.

But for him it was his last afternoon as himself,
An afternoon of nurses and rumours;
The provinces of his body revolted,
The squares of his mind were empty,   15
Silence invaded the suburbs,
The current of his feeling failed: he became his admirers.

Now he is scattered among a hundred cities
And wholly given over to unfamiliar affections;
To find his happiness in another kind of wood   20
And be punished under a foreign code of conscience.
The words of a dead man
Are modified in the guts of the living.

But in the importance and noise of tomorrow
When the brokers are roaring like beasts on the floor of the
    Bourse,   25
And the poor have the sufferings to which they are fairly ac-
    customed,
And each in the cell of himself is almost convinced of his free-
    dom;
A few thousand will think of this day
As one thinks of a day when one did something slightly un-
    usual.
O all the instruments agree   30
The day of his death was a dark cold day.

2

You were silly like us: your gift survived it all;
The parish of rich women, physical decay,
Yourself; mad Ireland hurt you into poetry.
Now Ireland has her madness and her weather still,   35

For poetry makes nothing happen: it survives
In the valley of its saying where executives
Would never want to tamper; it flows south
From ranches of isolation and the busy griefs,
Raw towns that we believe and die in; it survives,   *40*
A way of happening, a mouth.

3

Earth, receive an honoured guest;
William Yeats is laid to rest:
Let the Irish vessel lie
Emptied of its poetry.   *45*

Time that is intolerant
Of the brave and innocent,
And indifferent in a week
To a beautiful physique,

Worships language and forgives   *50*
Everyone by whom it lives;
Pardons cowardice, conceit,
Lays its honours at their feet.

Time that with this strange excuse
Pardoned Kipling and his views,   *55*
And will pardon Paul Claudel,
Pardons him for writing well.

In the nightmare of the dark
All the dogs of Europe bark,
And the living nations wait,   *60*
Each sequestered in its hate;

Intellectual disgrace
Stares from every human face,
And the seas of pity lie
Locked and frozen in each eye.   *65*

Follow, poet, follow right
To the bottom of the night,
With your unconstraining voice
Still persuade us to rejoice;

With the farming of a verse   70
Make a vineyard of the curse,
Sing of human unsuccess
In a rapture of distress;

In the deserts of the heart
Let the healing fountain start,   75
In the prison of his days
Teach the free man how to praise.

W. H. AUDEN

September 1, 1939

I sit in one of the dives   1
On Fifty-second Street
Uncertain and afraid
As the clever hopes expire
Of a low dishonest decade: 5
Waves of anger and fear
Circulate over the bright
And darkened lands of the earth,
Obsessing our private lives;
The unmentionable odour of death   10
Offends the September night.

Accurate scholarship can
Unearth the whole offence
From Luther until now
That has driven a culture mad,   15
Find what occurred at Linz,
What huge imago made
A psychopathic god:
I and the public know

What all schoolchildren learn,   *20*
Those to whom evil is done
Do evil in return.

Exiled Thucydides knew
All that a speech can say
About Democracy,   *25*
And what dictators do,
The elderly rubbish they talk
To an apathetic grave;
Analysed all in his book,
The enlightenment driven away,   *30*
The habit-forming pain,
Mismanagement and grief:
We must suffer them all again.

Into this neutral air
Where blind skyscrapers use   *35*
Their full height to proclaim
The strength of Collective Man,
Each language pours its vain
Competitive excuse:
But who can live for long   *40*
In an euphoric dream;
Out of the mirror they stare,
Imperialism's face
And the international wrong.

Faces along the bar   *45*
Cling to their average day:
The lights must never go out,
The music must always play,
All the conventions conspire
To make this fort assume   *50*
The furniture of home;
Lest we should see where we are,
Lost in a haunted wood,
Children afraid of the night
Who have never been happy or good.   *55*

The windiest militant trash
Important Persons shout
Is not so crude as our wish:
What mad Nijinsky wrote
About Diaghilev   *60*
Is true of the normal heart;
For the error bred in the bone
Of each woman and each man
Craves what it cannot have,
Not universal love   *65*
But to be loved alone.

From the conservative dark
Into the ethical life
The dense commuters come,
Repeating their morning vow;   *70*
"I *will* be true to the wife
I'll concentrate more on my work,"
And helpless governors wake
To resume their compulsory game:
Who can release them now,   *75*
Who can reach the deaf,
Who can speak for the dumb?

Defenceless under the night
Our world in stupor lies;
Yet, dotted everywhere,   *80*
Ironic points of light
Flash out wherever the Just
Exchange their messages:
May I, composed like them
Of Eros and of dust,   *85*
Beleaguered by the same
Negation and despair,
Show an affirming flame.

W. H. AUDEN

Precursors

O that the rain would come—the rain in big battalions—   *1*
Or thunder flush the hedge a more clairvoyant green
Or wind walk in and whip us and strip us or booming
Harvest moon transmute this muted scene.

But all is flat, matt, mute, unlivened, unexpectant,   *5*
And none but insects dare to sing or pirouette;
That Man is a dancer is an anachronism—
Who has forgotten his steps or hardly learnt them yet.

Yet one or two we have known who had the gusto
Of wind or water-spout, and one or two   *10*
Who carry an emerald lamp behind their faces
And—during thunder-storms—the light comes shining
     through.

                              LOUIS MACNEICE

The Express

After the first powerful plain manifesto   *1*
The black statement of pistons, without more fuss
But gliding like a queen, she leaves the station.
Without bowing and with restrained unconcern
She passes the houses which humbly crowd outside,   *5*
The gasworks and at last the heavy page
Of death, printed by gravestones in the cemetery.
Beyond the town there lies the open country
Where, gathering speed, she acquires mystery,
The luminous self-possession of ships on ocean.   *10*
It is now she begins to sing—at first quite low
Then loud, and at last with a jazzy madness—
The song of her whistle screaming at curves,
Of deafening tunnels, brakes, innumerable bolts.
And always light, aerial, underneath   *15*
Goes the elate metre of her wheels.

Steaming through metal landscape on her lines
She plunges new eras of wild happiness
Where speed throws up strange shapes, broad curves
And parallels clean like the steel of guns.   20
At last, further than Edinburgh or Rome,
Beyond the crest of the world, she reaches night
Where only a low streamline brightness
Of phosphorus on the tossing hills is white.
Ah, like a comet through flame she moves entranced   25
Wrapt in her music no bird song, no, nor bough
Breaking with honey buds, shall ever equal.

STEPHEN SPENDER

Landscape Near an Aerodrome

More beautiful and soft than any moth   1
With burring furred antennae feeling its huge path
Through dusk, the air-liner with shut-off engines
Glides over suburbs and the sleeves set trailing tall
To point the wind. Gently, broadly, she falls   5
Scarcely disturbing charted currents of air.

Lulled by descent, the travellers across sea
And across feminine land indulging its easy limbs
In miles of softness, now let their eyes trained by watching
Penetrate through dusk the outskirts of this town   10
Here where industry shows a fraying edge.
Here they may see what is being done.

Beyond the winking masthead light
And the landing-ground, they observe the outposts
Of work: chimneys like lank black fingers   15
Or figures frightening and mad: and squat buildings
With their strange air behind trees, like women's faces
Shattered by grief. Here where few houses
Moan with faint light behind their blinds
They remark the unhomely sense of complaint, like a dog   20
Shut out and shivering at the foreign moon.

In the last sweep of love, they pass over fields
Behind the aerodrome, where boys play all day
Hacking dead grass: whose cries, like wild birds,
Settle upon the nearest roofs   *25*
But soon are hid under the loud city.

Then, as they land, they hear the tolling bell
Reaching across the landscape of hysteria
To where, larger than all the charcoaled batteries
And imaged towers against that dying sky,   *30*
Religion stands, the church blocking the sun.

STEPHEN SPENDER

To My Mother

Most near, most dear, most loved and most far,   *1*
Under the window where I often found her
Sitting as huge as Asia, seismic with laughter,
Gin and chicken helpless in her Irish hand,
Irresistible as Rabelais but most tender for   *5*
The lame dogs and hurt birds that surround her,—
She is a procession no one can follow after
But be like a little dog following a brass band.

She will not glance up at the bomber or condescend
To drop her gin and scuttle to a cellar,   *10*
To lean on the mahogany table like a mountain
Whom only faith can move, and so I send
O all my faith and all my love to tell her
That she will move from mourning into morning.

GEORGE BARKER

Poem in October

It was my thirtieth year to heaven   *1*
Woke to my hearing from harbour and neighbour wood
    And the mussel pooled and the heron
        Priested shore
    The morning beckon   *5*

With water praying and call of seagull and rook
And the knock of sailing boats on the net webbed wall
    Myself to set foot
      That second
In the still sleeping town and set forth.   *10*

My birthday began with the water—
Birds and the birds of the winged trees flying my name
    Above the farms and the white horses
      And I rose
      In rainy autumn   *15*
And walked abroad in a shower of all my days.
High tide and the heron dived when I took the road
    Over the border
      And the gates
Of the town closed as the town awoke.   *20*

A springful of larks in a rolling
Cloud and the roadside bushes brimming with whistling
    Blackbirds and the sun of October
      Summery
      On the hill's shoulder,   *25*
Here were fond climates and sweet singers suddenly
Come in the morning where I wandered and listened
    To the rain wringing
      Wind blow cold
In the wood faraway under me.   *30*

Pale rain over the dwindling harbour
And over the sea wet church the size of a snail
    With its horns through mist and the castle
      Brown as owls,
      But all the gardens   *35*
Of spring and summer were blooming in the tall tales
Beyond the border and under the lark full cloud.
    There could I marvel
      My birthday
Away but the weather turned around.   *40*

It turned away from the blithe country
And down the other air and the blue altered sky
　Streamed again a wonder of summer
　　　With apples
　　Pears and red currants   *45*
And I saw in the turning so clearly a child's
Forgotten mornings when he walked with his mother
　　Through the parables
　　　Of sun light
　　And the legends of the green chapels   *50*

　And the twice told fields of infancy
That his tears burned my cheeks and his heart moved in mine.
　These were the woods the river and sea
　　　Where a boy
　　In the listening   *55*
Summertime of the dead whispered the truth of his joy
To the trees and the stones and the fish in the tide.
　　And the mystery
　　　Sang alive
　　Still in the water and singing birds.   *60*

　And there could I marvel my birthday
Away but the weather turned around. And the true
　Joy of the long dead child sang burning
　　　In the sun.
　　It was my thirtieth   *65*
Year to heaven stood there then in the summer noon
Though the town below lay leaved with October blood.
　　O may my heart's truth
　　　Still be sung
　　On this high hill in a year's turning.   *70*

DYLAN THOMAS

Years-End

Now winter downs the dying of the year,   *1*
And night is all a settlement of snow;

From the soft street the rooms of houses show
A gathered light, a shapen atmosphere,
Like frozen-over lakes whose ice is thin   *5*
And still allows some stirring down within.

I've known the wind by water banks to shake
The late leaves down, which frozen where they fell
And held in ice as dancers in a spell
Fluttered all winter long into a lake;   *10*
Graved on the dark in gestures of descent,
They seemed their own most perfect monument.

There was perfection in the death of ferns
Which laid their fragile cheeks against the stone
A million years. Great mammoths overthrown   *15*
Composedly have made their long sojourns,
Like palaces of patience, in the gray
And changeless lands of ice. And at Pompeii

The little dog lay curled and did not rise
But slept the deeper as the ashes rose   *20*
And found the people incomplete, and froze
The random hands, the loose unready eyes
Of men expecting yet another sun
To do the shapely thing they had not done.

These sudden ends of time must give us pause.   *25*
We fray into the future, rarely wrought
Save in the tapestries of afterthought.
More time, more time. Barrages of applause
Come muffled from a buried radio.
The New-year bells are wrangling with the snow.   *30*

RICHARD WILBUR

GLOSSARY
PHONETIC SYMBOLS
AND NOTES

GLOSSARY

ACCENT. The same as stress.

ALEXANDRINE. A six-stress or twelve-syllable line in iambic meter; iambic hexameter. **Example:**

To Philomel the next the linnet we prefer.
MICHAEL DRAYTON

ALLEGORY. (1) As a figure of speech, an extended analogy which makes a point-by-point comparison of two things; an elaborate simile or metaphor. Example: Longfellow's *Nature*. (2) As a literary form, a story in which events and/or characters have a symbolic meaning. Example: Spenser's *The Faerie Queene*.

ALLITERATION. The repetition of identical consonant sounds. **Example:**

The lilies and languors of virtue,
    For the raptures and roses of vice.
ALGERNON C. SWINBURNE

ALLITERATION OF PATTERN. An alliteration of two or more different consonant sounds which fall into a pattern. Among the many patterns possible, some of the more simple that may occur are called: ternary, cancrizans, augmentative, diminutive, and rondo. See these terms in this glossary.

431

AMBIGUITY. In poetry, the deliberate use of words to express more than one meaning at the same time; multiple meaning.

ANAPEST. A foot consisting of two unstressed syllables followed by one stressed syllable. **Example:** *căvălíer.* The corresponding adjective is *anapestic.*

ANTICLIMAX. A drop in force or interest at the point where a climax is expected, or after the climax has been reached.

ANTISTROPHE. One of the stanza types of the Pindaric ode. Also called the counter-turn.

ANTITHESIS. Contrast; the placing of two opposing items in juxtaposition so that each gives emphasis to the other.

APOSTROPHE. A direct address to a person or thing not present. **Example:**

But come thou goddess fair and free.
JOHN MILTON

ARTICULATORY IMAGERY. The mental reproduction of movements made by the vocal apparatus in producing speech sounds.

ASSONANCE. The repetition of identical, related, or contrasting vowel sounds. **Example:**

Low on the sand and loud on the stone.
ALFRED, LORD TENNYSON

ASSONANCE OF CONTRAST. A series of contrasting assonanted vowels, often [u] or [o] as opposed to [i] or [e]. **Example:**

Sedate and slow and gay.
JAMES JOYCE

ASSONANCE OF IDENTITY. The repetition of identical vowel sounds or diphthongs. **Example:**

Oh, broken is the golden bowl!
EDGAR ALLAN POE

ASSONANCE OF PATTERN. Repetition of vowel sounds in a pattern. **Example:**

To deep and deeper blue.
JAMES JOYCE

ASSONANCE OF SIMILARITY. Repetition of vowel sounds that are closely related. **Example:**

If aught of oaten stop.
> WILLIAM COLLINS

AUGMENTATIVE ALLITERATION. Two consonant sounds in juxtaposition, repeated in the same order but separated by a vowel. **Example:**

So flashed and fell the brand Excalibur.
> ALFRED, LORD TENNYSON

BALLAD. A narrative poem composed in ballad stanzas, often made for singing. **Example:**

Get Up and Bar the Door.

BALLADE. A four-stanza poem usually in iambic five-stress. The first three stanzas rime *a b a b b c b C;* the fourth, called the envoi, rimes *b c b C.* The last line of each stanza is the same, and the same rimes are kept throughout.

BALLAD STANZA. A four-line stanza of which the first and third lines are four-stress iambic meter and the second and fourth lines three-stress iambic meter. The rime scheme is *a b c b.* See heptameter.

BLANK VERSE. Any unrimed verse. Usually applied to lines of five-stress iambic meter used continuously without rime. **Example:**

Five years have past; five summers with the length
Of five long winters! and again I hear
These waters, rolling from their mountain springs
With a soft inland murmur.
> WILLIAM WORDSWORTH

BURDEN. The same as refrain.

CACOPHONY. Harshness or unpleasantness of sound. **Examples:** *earth's furrowed face; pine-stump split deftly; irks care; petals flee, last gasp.* Cacophonous passages may be deliberately employed to achieve harsh effects and to suggest the sense of the words.

CANCRIZANS ALLITERATION. A series of consonant sounds repeated in reverse. **Example:**

The thundering rattle of slatting shook the sheaves.
JOHN MASEFIELD

CARMEN FIGURATUM. A poem whose visual shape on the page represents its subject. **Example:**

The Altar by George Herbert.

CESURA. A pause, usually grammatical, within the line, often near the middle but capable of occurring at any position. In scansion it is indicated by ||. **Examples:**

In words, as fashions, || the same rule will hold;
Alike fantastic, || if too new, or old:
Be not the first || by whom the new are tried,
Nor yet the last || to lay the old aside.
ALEXANDER POPE

CHANT ROYAL. A six-stanza variation of the ballade. The first five stanzas rime *a b a b c c d d e d E;* the envoi rimes *d d e d E.* The last lines of each stanza are the same.

CHIMING. The same as near-rime.

CLICHÉ. A trite, worn-out expression. **Examples:** *fluffy clouds; modest as a violet.*

CLIMAX. The culmination, in force or interest, of an ascending series.

CLOSED COUPLET. A unit of two lines riming *a a,* whose sense is complete within itself. **Example:**

Ladies, like variegated tulips, show;
'Tis to their changes half their charms we owe.
ALEXANDER POPE

COMMON METER, OR COMMON MEASURE. The same as the ballad stanza. Abbreviated C. M. in hymnals.

COMPENSATION. In metrical analysis, the substitution of a pause or a lengthened stressed syllable for a missing unstressed syllable. **Example:**

Should auld acquaintance be forgot,
  And auld lang syne?
ROBERT BURNS

CONCEIT. A fanciful and ingenious thought, and its expression, usually in a figure of speech, in a manner that is strained, far-fetched, and artificial. **Example:**

[DESCRIPTION OF RAVAGES OF SMALLPOX]
Blisters with pride swell'd, which thro's flesh did sprout
Like rose-buds, stuck i' th' lily-skin about,
Each little pimple had a tear in it,
To wail the fault its rising did commit.

JOHN DRYDEN

CONCRETE UNIVERSAL. The embodiment of the general and universal in a particular character, situation, or nodus of events.

CONNOTATION. The emotive tone of a word, its suggestiveness, the clusters of associations and vague memories that it conjures up.

CONSONANCE. The same as para-rime.

CONSONANTAL DISSONANCE. The same as para-rime.

CONSONANTAL RIME. The same as para-rime.

CONTEXT. The containing whole of which anything is a part; surroundings; environment. In poetry context means the verbal environment, that which precedes and follows a given word or word group.

CONVENTIONAL SYMBOL. A symbol which has been widely used and whose meaning is immediately understood. **Example:**

Up-hill by Christina Rossetti.

COUPLET. A unit of two lines which rime *a a.* **Example:**

As thy day grows warm and high,
Life's meridian flaming nigh,
Dost thou spurn the humble vale?
Life's proud summits wouldst thou scale?

ROBERT BURNS

DACTYL. A foot consisting of one stressed syllable followed by two unstressed syllables. **Example:** *mightĭlў.* The corresponding adjective is *dactylic.*

DEAD METAPHOR. A metaphor which has lost the element of similarity that originally prompted it. **Examples:** *the heart of the chapter; the foot of a ladder.*

DECASYLLABLE. A line of ten syllables or five stresses. Iambic pentameter is a decasyllabic meter.

DENOTATION. The agreed-upon sense of a word—what it refers to, stands for, or designates, apart from the feelings that it may call up.

DICTION. Selection of words.

DIMETER. A line of verse consisting of two metrical feet. **Example:**

Nŏr gréw| ĭt whíte
Ĭn ă sín|glĕ níght.
    LORD BYRON

DIMINUTIVE ALLITERATION. Two consonant sounds separated by a vowel, repeated in juxtaposition. **Example:**

To fields where flies no sharp and sided hail.
    G. M. HOPKINS

DIPODY. A meter in which the stressed syllables themselves form an alternating pattern of heavy and lighter stresses. **Example:**

She was boarded, she was looted, she was scuttled till she sank.
    JOHN MASEFIELD

DISTICH. The same as couplet.

DOUBLE RIME. The same as feminine rime.

DRAMATIC IRONY. The same as irony of audience.

DRAMATIC MONOLOGUE. A poem in which a situation or story is related through the words of a single participating person who in speaking reveals his own character. **Example:**

Soliloquy of the Spanish Cloister by Robert Browning.

DUPLE METER. Iambic or trochaic meter: in other words, meters made up of two-syllable metrical feet.

ELEGY. A poem that expresses a serious emotion, often a lament for the dead, in a formal and elaborate way. **Example:**

Elegy Written in a Country Churchyard by Thomas Gray.

ELISION. The omission of a final vowel in a word before a beginning vowel in the next word. **Example:** *Th'eternal night.* Also, the omission of a vowel within a word. **Example:** *hov'ring.*

EMOTIVE. Pertaining to emotion or feeling; affective. Words which refer to this area of experience—*feeling, attitude, sentiment, mood, emotion, emotional, emotive, affective*—are hard to use with precision. In discussion it is best to explain the meaning one intends for any particular term.

END-RIME. Rime at the ends of lines.

END-STOPPED LINE. A line which has a pause for meaning at the end.

ENGLISH SONNET. The same as Shakespearean sonnet.

ENJAMBEMENT. Continuation of the sense from one line to the next without any natural speech pause. The same as run-on line.

ENVOY. Also envoi and *l'envoi*. A short, concluding stanza, usually addressed to some person and serving as a pointed commentary or moral. See ballade.

EPIC. A narrative poem of great length. The action is on a grand scale, and some of the characters are of a heroic stature. **Example:**

Odyssey by Homer.

EPIGRAM. A short poem, usually in two or four lines. The subject is likely to be a neatly turned thought or a satirical thrust. **Example:**

Treason doth never prosper; what's the reason?
For if it prosper, none dare call it treason.

SIR JOHN HARINGTON

EPITAPH. A short poem for inscription on a gravestone or simply for honoring the dead. It may be given a humorous turn.

EPODE. One of the stanza types of the Pindaric ode. Also called the stand.

EUPHONY. Pleasantness of sound. **Example:**

Lulla, lulla, lullaby.

WILLIAM SHAKESPEARE

EYE-RIME. Agreement of rime in spelling but not in sound. **Example:** *love:prove*.

FALLING RHYTHM. A term applied to trochaic and dactylic meters. In other words, meters in which the syllables of the metrical feet move from stressed to unstressed. **Examples:**

Yóu ănd | Í wĭll | névĕr | sée thăt | píctŭre.

ROBERT BROWNING

and

Dáy wĭth ĭts | búrdĕn ănd | héat hăd dĕ|pártĕd.

H. W. LONGFELLOW

FEMININE ENDING.   A line-ending consisting of the addition of an extra syllable after the final iambus or anapest. **Example:**

Thĕ moún|tăin shéep | ăre swée|tĕr.

THOMAS L. PEACOCK

FEMININE RIME.   Rime of two syllables, the second of which is unstressed. **Example:** *notion:ocean.* Also called double rime.

FIGURE OF SIMILARITY.   A general term applied to metaphor, simile, personification, and allegory.

FIGURE OF SPEECH.   A form of expression in which words are used in an uncustomary and unliteral sense. Common figures of speech are metaphor, simile, personification, apostrophe, hyperbole, litotes, metonymy, synecdoche, allegory.

FOOT.   The smallest unit of meter, consisting of one stressed syllable and one or more unstressed syllables or a pause. Two kinds of feet, however, are exceptions: the spondee, consisting of two stressed syllables, and the pyrrhic, consisting of two unstressed syllables. Although many kinds of poetic feet have been invented by analysts, one can study meter satisfactorily using only six: the iambus (˘´), trochee (´˘), anapest (˘˘´), dactyl (´˘˘), pyrrhic (˘˘), and spondee (´´).

FREE VERSE.   Poetry in irregular form, not making consistent use of meter and rime and characterized by varying line lengths. **Example:**

Patterns by Amy Lowell.

HALF-STRESSED RIME.   Rime in which one of the words takes the rime on an unstressed syllable. **Examples:** *see:liberty; ring:stopping.*

HENDECASYLLABLE.   A line of eleven syllables. **Example:**

The brooks of Eden lazily murmuring.

ALFRED, LORD TENNYSON

HEPTAMETER.   A line of verse consisting of seven metrical feet.
Example:

Thĕ Gre|ciăns who|llў pút | ĭn róut, | thĕ Tro|jăns rou|tĭng still.

GEORGE CHAPMAN

This kind of line, called the septenary, is often broken into two
lines of four and three stresses respectively. Thus a couplet of
heptameter becomes a ballad stanza. **Example:**

"Ĭ féar | thĕe, an|cĭent Ma|rĭnĕr !
Ĭ féar | thў skin|nў hand !|
Ănd thóu | ărt lóng, | ănd lánk, | ănd brówn,|
Ăs ís | thĕ ríbbed | sea-sand.

SAMUEL T. COLERIDGE

HEROIC COUPLET.   A couplet in five-stress iambic meter, characterized by succinctness, balance, and flexibility. **Example:**

True ease in writing comes from art, not chance,
As those move easiest who have learned to dance.

ALEXANDER POPE

HEXAMETER.   A line of verse consisting of six metrical feet. **Example:**

Yĕ who bĕ|lieve ĭn ăf|fectĭon that | hópes, ănd en|dúres, ănd ĭs |
pátĭent.

H. W. LONGFELLOW

HIATUS.   The separation of a final vowel in a word from the beginning vowel of the next word. Such vowels were called "open vowels"
by Pope. **Example:**

Though oft the ear the open vowels tire.

ALEXANDER POPE

HOMOSTROPHIC ODE.   An ode in which each strophe (or stanza)
follows the same, or nearly the same pattern, which is usually
elaborate. **Example:**

Prothalamion by Edmund Spenser.

HOVERING ACCENT. In metrical analysis, an added stress given, for adequate sense reading, to a syllable that is unstressed in the subjective meter. **Example:**

The rude forefathers of the hamlet sleep.

THOMAS GRAY

Here there is a hovering accent on *fore*, the subjective meter being iambic.

HYPERBOLE. The same as overstatement.

IAMBIC PENTAMETER. Five-stress iambic meter, one of the great measures in English poetry. **Example:**

Ĭ lóng | tŏ tálk | wĭth sóme | óld lŏ|vĕr's ghóst,
Whŏ díed | befóre | thĕ gód | ŏf lóve | wăs bórn.

JOHN DONNE

IAMBUS. A foot consisting of one unstressed syllable followed by one stressed syllable. **Example:** *ăpárt.* The corresponding adjective is *iambic.*

IDENTICAL RIME. Rime in which the consonant sounds immediately preceding the accented vowels are the same. **Examples:** *pare:pair; refine:define.* Also called *rime riche.*

IMAGERY. The mental reproduction of sense perceptions.

IMPERFECT RIME. Any rime in which either the vowels of the accented syllables or the consonants which follow are not identical. The former is also caller near-rime. **Examples:** *moan:lawn; making:bacon.*

INADEQUATE RESPONSE. (1) A poem which does not offer enough material to create an adequate response, or poetic experience, in the reader. (2) The response of the reader created by such a poem.

INCREMENTAL REPETITION. In the popular ballad, the repetition, in a new context, of what has been said before, with some variation which moves the story forward. **Example:**

"O I hae killed my reid-roan steid,
            Mither, mither,
  O I hae killed my reid-roan steid,

              .   .   .

"O I hae killed my fadir deir,
      Mither, mither,
  O I hae killed my fadir deir.

INTERIOR RIME.   The same as internal rime.

INTERNAL RIME.   Rime that occurs between: (1) words within a line; (2) words within two or more lines; (3) an end word and a word within the line. Also called interior rime. The third type is also called Leonine rime.

INVERSION.   A change in the normal word order of a sentence. **Example:**

With them the seed of Wisdom did I sow.
        EDWARD FITZGERALD

IRONY.   A disparity or opposition between appearance and reality, or between expectation and realization. See below for five types of irony: irony of statement, irony of situation, irony of character, irony of audience, and irony of anticipation.

IRONY OF ANTICIPATION.   A form of irony of statement in which the ironical implications of a remark are not realized till later in the play or novel or poem.

IRONY OF AUDIENCE.   Possession of certain knowledge by the audience or reader, not shared by one or more participants in the action concerned. Also called dramatic irony.

IRONY OF CHARACTER.   In a character, the presence of qualities and traits that are the opposite of those we normally think of as typical; *e.g.*, timidity and gentleness in a metropolitan traffic cop.

IRONY OF SITUATION.   A state of affairs the opposite or reverse of what was expected.

IRONY OF STATEMENT.   A figure of speech in which the intended meaning is the opposite of that expressed by the words used. This may take the form of ridicule in which an expression of praise is used to condemn.

IRREGULAR ODE.   An ode with any number of stanzas, each one independent in its length, rime scheme, and metrical pattern. **Example:**

Intimations of Immortality by Wordsworth.

ITALIAN SONNET.   The same as Petrarchan sonnet.

ITERATION.   The repetition of a word, phrase, or sentence for emphasis or for musical effect.

LITOTES.   A figure of speech by which affirmation is expressed by the negative of its contrary. A form of understatement. **Example:**

He [The Puritan] had been wrested by *no common* deliverer from the grasp of *no common* foe. He had been ransomed by the sweat of *no vulgar* agony, by the blood of *no earthly* sacrifice.

T. B. MACAULAY

LONG METER, OR LONG MEASURE.   A four-line stanza in four-stress iambic meter, riming *a b a b* or *a b c d.* Abbreviated L. M. in hymnals.

LYRIC.   A poem that is expressive of emotion, usually that of the poet. The word is sometimes used in a narrower sense to denote a poem that is to be sung or that has singable qualities.

MADRIGAL.   The term *madrigal,* as used in the Elizabethan period, applies to three types of song. The madrigal proper is a contrapuntal song somewhat elaborate in texture. The ayre is a continuous melody accompanied by other voices. The ballett is a choral piece, with a *fa-la-la* refrain.

MASCULINE ENDING.   A line-ending consisting of a stressed syllable. **Example:**

Deep | within | the Au|gust woods.

DANTE G. ROSSETTI

MASCULINE RIME.   Single rime on a stressed final syllable. **Examples:** *buy:cry; remote:connote.*

MEASURE.   The same as meter.

METAPHOR.   An expression used in a new sense, on the basis of similarity between its literal sense and the new thing or situation to which it is applied; an implied simile. ". . . metaphor . . . is the supreme agent by which disparate and hitherto disconnected things are brought together in poetry for the sake of the effects upon attitude and impulse which spring from their collocation and from the combinations which the mind then establishes between them." I. A. Richards, *Principles of Literary Criticism* (New York: Harcourt, Brace, 1926), p. 240.

METER. A regular pattern of stressed and unstressed syllables. The
meter of a poem is described in terms of the number and kind of
metrical feet in a line. **Examples:**
Five-stress iambic meter

Remĕm|bĕr mé | whĕn Í | ăm góne | ăwáy.

Two-stress dactylic meter

Bríng ĭt fŏr | Génĕvĭeve.

Another set of descriptive terms for meter follows a slightly different pattern: adjective to describe the metrical foot + noun to indicate the number of feet in a line. With these terms the two lines
above would be named iambic pentameter and dactylic dimeter.
The adjectives are as follows:

Foot	Example
iambic	*ĕndéar*
trochaic	*dárknĕss*
anapestic	*ŏvĕrtáke*
dactylic	*téndĕrlў*

The nouns used to name lines of from one to seven metrical feet
are these: monometer, dimeter, trimeter, tetrameter, pentameter,
hexameter, and heptameter. For examples, see each of these terms
in the glossary.

METONYMY. A figure of speech in which a thing is designated by
the name of something which resembles or suggests it. Common
metonymic substitutions, with examples, are:
Cause for effect
   He spoke a strange tongue (language).
Material for product
   It costs a nickel (coin).
Sign for thing signified
   She accepted the cross (Christianity).
Container for thing contained
   The kettle (water) is boiling.
Instrument for agent
   The pen (writer) is mighty.

Attribute for subject

They sailed over the deep (ocean).

Author for works

Have you read Milton (works of Milton)?

The term metonymy is often used to include the meanings of synecdoche.

MIXED METAPHOR. A combination of the vehicles of two or more metaphors to form the vehicle of a single metaphor, with a resultant incongruous or ludicrous effect. **Example:**

One cog in a golden and singing hive.

STEPHEN SPENDER

MONOMETER. A line of verse consisting of only one metrical foot. **Example:**

Thus I

Pass by

And die.

ROBERT HERRICK

NEAR-RIME. Rime in which the accented vowels are similar but not identical. **Examples:** *stance:response; star:fur.* Also called oblique rime, slant rime, and chiming.

NONCE-SYMBOL. A symbol that is invented and used for a particular occasion.

OBJECTIVE CORRELATIVE. "The only way of expressing emotion in the form of art is by finding an 'objective correlative'; in other words, a set of objects, a situation, a chain of events which shall be the formula of that *particular* emotion; such that when the external facts, which must terminate in sensory experience, are given, the emotion is immediately evoked." T. S. Eliot, *Selected Essays* (New York: Harcourt, Brace, 1932), pp. 120–121. *Cf.* William James: "It is notorious that facts are compatible with opposite emotional comments, since the same fact will inspire entirely different feelings in different persons, and at different times in the same person; and there is no rationally deducible connection between any outer fact and the sentiments it may happen to provoke." *Varieties of Religious Experience* (New York: Modern Library), p. 147.

OBLIQUE RIME.   The same as near-rime.

OCTOSYLLABLE.   A line of eight syllables or four stresses. The corresponding adjective is octosyllabic. **Examples:**

Inspiring bold John Barleycorn!
What dangers thou canst make us scorn!
ROBERT BURNS

ODE.   A dignified poem on a serious subject. It is rather long and is intricate in structure. See homostrophic ode, irregular ode, and Pindaric ode.

ONOMATOPOEIA.   Speech sounds which suggest meaning through the imitation of other sounds. **Examples:** *buzz, hiss, crackle, whisper, murmur, bang, roar, thunder.*

OPEN VOWELS.   See Hiatus.

OTTAVA RIMA.   An eight-line stanza riming *a b a b a b c c*. **Example:** *Sailing to Byzantium* by W. B. Yeats.

OVERFLOW.   The same as enjambement.

OVERSTATEMENT.   A statement which exceeds the limits of fact or reason, which represents something as greater or more important than it really is, or which states something more strongly than the truth warrants. Not meant to be taken literally. Exaggeration for effect; hyperbole. **Example:**

Alack, it was I who leaped at the sun
    To give it my loving friends to keep!
Naught man could do, have I left undone;
ROBERT BROWNING

PAEON.   A foot consisting of one stressed and three unstressed syllables. Classified as first, second, third, or fourth paeon in accordance with the syllable which is stressed. **Example:**

Calling to the | angels and the | souls in their de|gree.
RUDYARD KIPLING

PARADOX.   A statement which seems to be self-contradictory, inconsistent, or opposed to common sense, but which may be nonetheless true. An example is: She won on the strength of her weakness.

PARA-RIME. A kind of rime consisting of differing vowels in a constant consonantal framework. **Examples:** *sipped:supped; knive us: nervous.* Also called consonance, consonantal rime, and consonantal dissonance.

PARODY. A poem which mimics with exaggeration another poem or a particular kind of style in such a way as to create a humorous effect.

PASTORAL. A poem of rustic life, real or affected; often with shepherds or poets in the guise of shepherds as leading figures. **Examples:** *Lycidas* by John Milton; *The Passionate Shepherd to His Love* by Christopher Marlowe.

PENTAMETER. A line of verse consisting of five metrical feet. **Example:**

And dost | with poi|son, war, | and sick|ness dwell.

JOHN DONNE

PERFECT RIME. Rimes in which the riming sounds are identical. **Examples:** *cry:buy; daisy:lazy; regretfully:forgetfully.*

PERSONIFICATION. A metaphor in which a lifeless object, an animal, or an abstract idea is made to act like a person. It imputes human life and motives to lifeless objects, animals, and abstract ideas and thereby endows with animation, vividness, and nearness those things that are normally thought of as impersonal and aloof from human affairs. **Example:**

The sea creeps to pillage,
She leaps on her prey.

ELINOR WYLIE

PETRARCHAN SONNET. A fourteen-line poem, in five-stress iambic meter, divided into two parts of eight and six lines each. The first part, called the octave, has a rime scheme of *a b b a a b b a*. The second *a* signals a strong pause or a stop and the fourth *a* a complete stop. The second part, called the sestet, employs three new rimes in any one of various schemes, such as *c d e c d e* or *c d d c e e.* In the sestet a new aspect of the thought or feeling or image is often taken up. Also called Italian sonnet. **Example:** *Remember* by Christina Rossetti.

PHONETIC INTENSIVES. Speech sounds which in themselves suggest meaning. For example, the vowel [ɚ], spelt -er, may suggest repetition when it is at the end of a word. **Examples:** *chatter, chitter, sputter, spatter, flutter, flicker, glimmer.*

PINDARIC ODE. An ode employing three kinds of stanza: the strophe (or turn), the antistrophe (or counter-turn), and the epode (or stand). The strophe and antistrophe have the same rime scheme and metrical pattern. The epode differs from these in form. The stanzas are often intricate in their arrangement of line lengths and rimes.

POEM. (1) A patterned arrangement of words creating an experience within a reader. (2) An experience within a reader which is an interaction between the words of a poem (1) and the total past experience and mental set of the reader.

POETIC DICTION. A selection of words that are believed to be especially appropriate for use in poetry and that set apart the language of poetry from that of everyday life.

POETIC EXPERIENCE. The same as poem (2).

POULTER'S MEASURE. A riming couplet consisting of a six-stress and a seven-stress line. **Example:**

Laid in my quiet bed, in study as I were,
I saw within my troubled head a heap of thoughts appear.

HENRY HOWARD, EARL OF SURREY

PYRRHIC. A foot consisting of two unstressed syllables. **Example:**

From the | great deep | to the | great deep | he goes.

ALFRED, LORD TENNYSON

QUATRAIN. A four-line stanza.

REFRAIN. A line or part of a line which is repeated at regular positions in the poem.

RESPONSE. The same as poem (2).

RHYTHM. In poetry, the regular recurrence of time-patterns and stress-patterns. It is sometimes used in a narrower sense to mean meter.

RIME. The identity or similarity, in two or more words, of the accented vowels and the sounds which follow, with different consonant sounds immediately preceding the accented vowels. **Examples:** *flowers:showers* and *pare:leer*.

RIME RICHE. The same as identical rime.

RIME ROYAL. A seven-line stanza in five-stress iambic meter riming *a b a b b c c*. **Example:** *The Rape of Lucrece* by William Shakespeare.

RISING RHYTHM. Iambic and anapestic meters; in other words, meters in which the syllables of the metrical feet move from unstressed to stressed syllables. **Examples:**

Ă skĭll|fŭl leá|dĕr, stoút, | sĕvére.

SAMUEL BUTLER

and

Ĭ ăm món|ărch ŏf áll | Ĭ sŭrvéy.

WILLIAM COWPER

RONDEAU. A thirteen-line poem, with a refrain after the eighth and thirteenth lines. The refrain is usually part of the first line. The rime scheme is *a a b b a   a a b R   a a b b a R*. **Example:** *What Is to Come* by W. E. Henley.

RONDEL. A fourteen-line poem in which two lines serve as refrain. Among the various rime schemes the most common is *A B b a   a b A B   a b b a A*.

RONDO ALLITERATION. Alternation of two or more consonant sounds. **Example:**

The league-long roller thundering on the reef.

ALFRED, LORD TENNYSON

RUN-ON LINE. A line whose meaning is continued without pause in the following line. See enjambement.

SCANSION. The analysis of the meter of poetry. The marks usually used are these:

´	over a stressed syllable
˘	over an unstressed syllable
∧	at the position of a pause or rest
|	between metrical feet
||	at a cesura

SENTIMENTAL RESPONSE. (1) A poem in which the emotion expressed seems too great for the objective occasion which is alleged as its source. (2) In the reader, the feeling of more emotion than is justified by the situation in the poem.

SEPTENARY. A line of seven feet. A septenary tends to break at the end of the fourth foot; hence two septenaries make up a ballad stanza, or the "common meter" of hymn books. See heptameter and ballad stanza.

SESTET. A six-line stanza. Usually applied to the second part of the Petrarchan sonnet.

SESTINA. A poem consisting of six stanzas of six lines each, and a concluding stanza of three lines. No rime is used. Instead, the lines of the six stanzas employ the same end words, each time in a different order. The order is as follows: 1. *a b c d e f;* 2. *f a e b d c;* 3. *c f d a b e;* 4. *e c b f a d;* 5. *d e a c f b;* 6. *b d f e c a.* The concluding three-line stanza uses the same words, ending its lines with *b d f* and using *a c e* in the middle of the lines or at the beginning.

SHAKESPEAREAN SONNET. A fourteen line poem consisting of three four-line units, called quatrains, and a concluding two-line unit, called a couplet. The meter is five-stress iambic. The rime scheme is *a b a b c d c d e f e f g g.* Each quatrain tends to be an individual unit within the whole. The couplet may give an epigrammatic finish to the poem.

SHAPED POEM. The same as carmen figuratum.

SHORT METER, OR SHORT MEASURE. Poulter's Measure written as a quatrain, the first, second, and fourth lines being three-stress iambic and the third line being four-stress iambic. The rime scheme is *a b a b* or *a b c b.* Abbreviated S. M. in hymnals.

SIMILE. A statement of similarity between unlike things introduced by *like* or *as*. **Example:**

Her feet beneath her petticoat,
Like little mice, stole in and out,
   As if they feared the light.
        JOHN SUCKLING

SLANT-RIME. The same as near-rime.

SOUND SYMBOLISM. A natural correspondence between sound and

sense. See onomatopoeia, euphony, cacophony, phonetic intensives, tempo.

SPENSERIAN SONNET.   A variation of the Shakespearean sonnet. The rime scheme is *a b a b b c b c c d c d e e*. **Example:** *Amoretti* by Edmund Spenser.

SPENSERIAN STANZA.   A nine-line stanza with eight lines in five-stress iambic meter and a final Alexandrine. The rime scheme is *a b a b b c b c c*. **Example:** *The Faerie Queene* by Edmund Spenser.

SPONDEE.   A foot consisting of two stressed syllables. **Example:**

From the | gréat déep | to the | gréat déep he | goes.
ALFRED, LORD TENNYSON

SPRUNG RHYTHM.   A rhythm consisting of stressed syllables with any number of unstressed syllables separating them. In theory this kind of rhythm would seem indistinguishable from prose but in practice sprung rhythm is decidedly a poetic rhythm.

STANZA.   A group of lines arranged in a special pattern and forming a unit of poetic discourse. Often characterized by a particular order of end-rimes.

STOCK RESPONSE.   An automatic, habitual, and stereotyped reaction; a conditioned response.

STRESS.   The prominence given to a syllable in reading, to make it stand out in auditory strength.

STROPHE.   (1) The same as stanza. (2) One of the stanza types in a Pindaric ode.

SUBJECTIVE METER.   The perfectly regular meter that a reader has in his mind as he reads a poem; a clock-like pattern of auditory expectancies.

SUBSTITUTION.   In metrical analysis, the replacement of an expected foot in the regular metrical pattern by a different kind of foot, *e.g.*, using a trochee in place of an expected iambus. **Example:**

Shákĭng | ănd quĭ|vérĭng, pále | ănd wán | fŏr féar.
CHRISTOPHER MARLOWE

SYMBOL.   A person, place, thing, relationship, or quality used to stand for something other than itself.

SYNECDOCHE. A figure of speech in which a thing is designated by using a substitute term in one of the following relationships:

Whole for part
  The scaly breed (fish).
Part for whole
  A hired hand (workman).
Material for thing
  He brought his rubbers, flannels, and linens.
Special for the general
  He looked like a cutthroat (murderer).
General for the special
  The engine (locomotive) stopped for water.
Individual for a general class
  She was a Circe (sorceress) in her wiles.

Since there is little agreement on the distinctions between synecdoche and metonymy, it is usual to use the term *metonymy* for both of these figures of speech.

SYNESTHESIA. Description of an item of sense perception in terms of a sense other than the usual one. **Examples:** *golden tones* (sound in terms of sight), *loud necktie* (sight in terms of sound).

TEMPO. The rapidity or slowness with which a passage is read. Extra unstressed syllables speed up a meter and extra stressed syllables slow it down.

TENOR. In a metaphor or simile, what the speaker is really talking about, the actual thing or situation, the original subject of discourse.

TERCET. (1) A three-line stanza. (2) One of the two parts in the sestet of a Petrarchan sonnet, when the sestet is divided into two equal halves.

TERNARY ALLITERATION. An initial consonant sound to be alliterated, a shift to other alliterated consonant sounds, and a return to the first sound. **Example:**

Down sunk a hollow bottom broad and deep.
                    JOHN MILTON

TERZA RIMA. A series of tercets linked by rime thus: *a b a b c b c d c* etc. Usually written in five-stress iambic meter. **Example:** *Ode to the West Wind* by Shelley.

TETRAMETER. A line of verse consisting of four metrical feet. **Example:**

The nĭght | ĭs chíll; | thĕ fó|rĕst báre.
SAMUEL T. COLERIDGE

THEME. A thought, idea, concept. In poems the theme is often implicit.

TRIMETER. A line of verse consisting of three metrical feet. **Example:**

Ănd Í | wĭll pledge | wĭth míne.
BEN JONSON

TRIOLET. An eight-line stanza in which the first two lines are repeated as the seventh and eighth lines and the first line is also repeated as the fourth. The rime scheme is $ABaAabAB$.

TRIPLE METER. Anapestic or dactylic meter; in other words, meters made up of three-syllable metrical feet.

TRIPLE RIME. Rime of three syllables. **Examples:** *intellectual: henpecked you all.*

TRIPLET. A group of three lines which rime aaa. Often used to vary a series of heroic couplets. **Example:**

Night came, but unattended with repose;
Alone she came, no sleep their eyes to close;
Alone, and black she came; no friendly stars arose.
JOHN DRYDEN

TROCHEE. A foot consisting of one stressed syllable followed by one unstressed syllable. **Example:** húrrў. The corresponding adjective is *trochaic.*

UNDERSTATEMENT. A statement which falls below the truth or fact, which represents something as less important than it really is, or which states something with less force than the truth warrants. Often used for purposes of irony.

UNITY. Singleness and coherence of experience, achieved by establishing relationships which fuse all parts into one meaningful whole.

VEHICLE. In a metaphor or simile, the part that is brought in because of its similarity in some respect to the tenor, the original subject of discourse.

VERS DE SOCIÉTÉ.   Light verse that is graceful, witty, and polished, and written in a playful and conversational tone.

VERSE.   This term has two generally used senses: (1) a single line of poetry; (2) poetry in general, especially that which follows regular metrical patterns, as distinguished from prose.

VERS LIBRE.   The same as free verse.

VILLANELLE.   A nineteen-line poem, based on two rimes, and divided into five tercets riming *a b a* and a quatrain riming *a b a a*. The first line is repeated as the sixth, twelfth, and eighteenth lines; the third line is repeated as the ninth, fifteenth, and nineteenth lines. **Example:** *The House on the Hill* by E. A. Robinson.

PHONETIC SYMBOLS

Speech sounds are represented throughout this book by the following symbols, which are a selection from the International Phonetic Alphabet. Though these symbols do not show finer shades of difference, they are adequate for our purpose.

VOWELS

Symbol		Key Word
1.	[i]	meet
2.	[ɪ]	mit
3.	[e]	mate
4.	[ɛ]	met
5.	[æ]	mat
6.	[a]	man, as pronounced in Scottish; a sound midway between [æ] and [ɑ]
7.	[ɑ]	father
8.	[ɔ]	saw
9.	[o]	note
10.	[ʊ]	full
11.	[u]	doom
12.	[ɝ]	fur, as pronounced in General American; used in accented syllables only.
13.	[ɜ]	fur, as pronounced in parts of the East and South; used in accented syllables only.
14.	[ɚ]	matter; used in unaccented syllables only.
15.	[ʌ]	love
16.	[ə]	alone, circus, sofa, gentleman, purpose; used in unaccented syllables only.

DIPHTHONGS

17.	[aɪ]	my
18.	[aʊ]	loud
19.	[ɔɪ]	boy
20.	[ɪʊ]	amuse
21.	[ˌjʊ]	use

CONSONANTS

Symbol		Key Word
	Stops	
22.	[p]	pie
23.	[b]	by
24.	[t]	to
25.	[d]	do
26.	[k]	came
27.	[g]	game
	Fricatives	
28.	[f]	five
29.	[v]	vat
30.	[θ]	thin
31.	[ð]	then
32.	[s]	see
33.	[z]	zone
34.	[ʃ]	shun
35.	[ʒ]	azure
36.	[h]	how
	Affricates	
37.	[tʃ]	chat
38.	[dʒ]	jug
	Sonorants	
39.	[m]	me
40.	[n]	thin
41.	[ŋ]	thing
42.	[l]	lilt
	Glides	
43.	[w]	way
44.	[hw]	whey
45.	[j]	you
46.	[r]	rate

NOTES TO PART I

44. *Bright Star, Would I Were Stedfast as Thou Art.*

Given below is the first version of this poem as recorded in *The Poetical Works and Other Writings of John Keats*, edited with notes and appendices by H. Buxton Forman, revised with additions by Maurice Buxton Forman (8 vols.; New York: Charles Scribner's Sons, 1939), IV, pp. 235–236.

Bright star, would I were steadfast as thou art!	*1*
Not in lone splendour hung amid the night,	*2*
Not watching, with eternal lids apart,	*3*
Like nature's devout sleepless eremite,	*4*
The morning waters at their priestlike task	*5*
Of pure ablution round earth's human shores;	*6*
Or, gazing on the new soft fallen mask	*7*
Of snow upon the mountains and the moors:—	*8*
No;—yet still steadfast, still unchangeable,	*9*
Cheek pillow'd on my love's white ripening breast,	*10*
To touch, for ever, its warm sink and swell,	*11*
Awake, for ever, in a sweet unrest,	*12*
To hear, to feel her tender taken breath,	*13*
Half passionless, and so swoon on to death.	*14*

The sestet of this version differs considerably from that of the final version; it is more passionate and physical.

46. *My Wife's a Winsome Wee Thing.*

7. *Neist.* Next.
8. *Tine.* Perish, be destroyed.
14. *warstle.* Struggle, tussle.

51. *Cousin Nancy.*

12. *Matthew and Waldo.* Matthew Arnold and Ralph Waldo Emerson.

57. Composed Upon Westminster Bridge.

Wordsworth received a criticism of lines 4 and 5 of this poem, to the effect that *like a garment* and *bare* are contradictory. In reply he wrote: "The contradiction is in the *words* only—bare, as not being covered with smoke or vapour;—clothed, as being attired in the beams of the morning. Tell me if you approve of the following alteration, which is the best I can do for the amendment of the fault.

The city now doth on her forehead wear
The glorious crown of morning; silent, bare,
Ships, towers, etc."

[*The Poetical Works of William Wordsworth,* edited by E. de Selincourt and Helen Darbishire (3 vols.; Oxford: The Clarendon Press, 1946), III, p. 431. Quoted by permission of The Clarendon Press.]

58. Dulce et Decorum.

The quotation *Dulce et decorum est pro patria mori* is from Horace's *Odes* (Bk. III, Ode 2, line 13), and means "It is sweet and proper to die for one's country."

79. Mr. Flood's Party.

5. When the poem first appeared in the *Nation,* November 24, 1920, this line read: *On earth again of home, paused and observed.*
11. *The bird is on the wing.* An allusion to the Bird of Time in the *Rubaiyat of Omar Khayyam,* a long meditative poem with a *carpe diem* philosophy. See p. 90.
20. *Roland's ghost.* A reference to the legendary figure of Roland, famed officer of Charlemagne. After a successful expedition, Charlemagne and his army were returning to France, with Roland as the leader of the rear-guard. Suddenly and treacherously the rear-guard was surprised at Ronce-vaux, Spain, by a band of Saracens. Oliver, Roland's best friend, at three different times urged him to blow his horn for help; but Roland because of pride refused to do so until it was too late.

85. Stopping by Woods on a Snowy Evening.

The original draft contained the following lines:
5.   The steaming horses think it queer
       The horse begins to think it queer
       The little horse must think it queer
7.   Between a forest and a lake

9. She gives her harness bells a shake
12. Of easy wind and fall of flake
15. That bid me give the reins a shake
    That bid me on, and there are miles
  From a holograph on p. 604 of *Preface to Poetry* by Charles W. Cooper
(N.Y.: Harcourt, Brace & Co., 1946. Cp. 1943 Charles W. Cooper, 1946,
Harcourt, Brace. Permission from Henry Holt & Co.).

87. John Anderson, My Jo.

1. *jo.* Sweetheart.
4. *brent.* Straight, unwrinkled.
5. *beld.* Bald.
7. *pow.* Head, pate.
11. *canty.* Cheerful, gladsome.

89. There Is a Garden in Her Face.

  See note to Herrick's *Cherry-Ripe* p. 474.

127. Lepanto.

  The Battle of Lepanto was a naval engagement fought on October 7,
1571, in the Gulf of Lepanto, or Corinth, which separates central from
southern Greece. On one side were the Mohammedan forces of Turkey
with about 300 ships. On the other were the forces of the Christian
League, with fewer ships, furnished largely by Venice and Spain. The
Christian nations had rallied together in response to a call from Pope
Pius V because the capture of Cyprus by the Turks constituted a threat
to Christendom. The Christian fleet was commanded by an experienced
Spanish general, Don John of Austria. Don John was a natural son of
Charles I, King of Spain, 1516–1556, who became Charles V, Emperor of
the Holy Roman Empire, 1519–1556. Don John was also the half-brother
of Philip II, King of Spain, 1556–1598. He had been acknowledged as a
son of Charles I only after Charles' death and in consequence did not
have a throne. The Christian fleet won the victory, with a loss of 8,000
dead. The greater part of the Turkish fleet was captured or destroyed,
and 25,000 Turks were killed. From the Turkish galleys 15,000 Christian
slaves, who had been used as oarsmen, were released.

2. *Soldan of Byzantium.* Sultan of Constantinople.

6. *inmost sea.* Mediterranean.

8. *Lion of the Sea.* The winged lion of St. Mark was the emblem of
Venice.

11. *cold queen.* Queen Elizabeth of England. As a Protestant she was
not interested.

12.   *shadow of the Valois.* The boy king of France, Charles IX, belonged to the royal family of the Valois. He was in the power of his mother, the Queen, Catherine de'Medici.

14.   *Golden Horn.* The harbor of Byzantium.

16.   *crownless prince.* Don John.

33.   *Death light of Africa!* Don John had previously fought in Africa.

36.   *Mahound.* Mohammed. In his paradise were beautiful women who were perpetually young, the houris.

47.   *Solomon.* Solomon was reputed to have power over spirits of the underworld by virtue of a seal on which was inscribed the name of God.

65.   *Richard, Raymond, Godfrey.* Leaders in the crusades of the 11th and 12th centuries.

73.   *Alcalar.* Don John's university was situated in Alcalar, Spain.

74.   *Mountain.* Mont St. Michel, a famous church on a rocky island off the coast of Northern France, the shrine of St. Michael.

84.   *Mary.* Reference to Protestant hatred of Catholicism.

92.   *Fleece.* King Philip II was a knight of the Order of the Golden Fleece.

95.   *dwarfs.* Dwarfs were kept at the Spanish court, as may be seen in paintings of Velasquez.

96.   *phial.* Philip was later charged with poisoning Don John.

112.   *mirror.* During the battle the Pope was thought to have had a vision of the battle and the victory.

114.   *Cross and Castle.* The emblems of Aragon and Castile.

115.   *galleys of St. Mark.* The Venetian ships.

116.   *swat.* Sweated.

123.   *horses.* Sculptured horses.

134.   *Vivat Hispania!* Long live Spain.

138.   *Cervantes.* Cervantes, the author of *Don Quixote,* fought at Lepanto.

141.   *knight.* Don Quixote.

135.   Inversnaid.

6.   *twindles.* A verb formed from the noun *twindle,* a twin; hence, to break into two parts. Or a coined word combining *twist, twin,* or *twine* with *dwindle* or *spindle.*

9.   *rounds.* Whispers.

154.   Wet Windy Night on a Pavement. The text is a recent revision. Originally the poem read as follows:

Light drunkenly reels into shadow   *1*
blurs, slurs uneasily
slides off the eyeballs
          the segments shatter
tree-branches cut arclight in ragged   *5*
          fluttering wet strips
the cup of the sky-sign is filled too full
          it slushes wine over
the street-lamps dance a tarantella
the street-lamps zig-zag down the street   *10*
the street-lamps fly away
          in a wind of lights.

164. Katharine Jaffray.

This poem is a popular ballad. The popular ballad had its origin, at least in part, in the literature of oral tradition. It is essentially a simple, spirited poem in which is narrated, usually by means of dialogue, a popular dramatic story. Most ballads are conventional in content and form. The story, whether legendary or historical, is often tragic. Many are concerned with violent death. The ballad is told impersonally, that is, the teller of the tale plays no role in the story and makes no comment on it. The story is not elaborated in great detail: the essential facts are given; the rest are left to inference. An essential characteristic is the use of repetition. This repetition may be simple, as in the use of a refrain; or it may be incremental, where what has been said before is, in a new context, repeated with some variation which moves the story forward. Certain "commonplaces," formulas of set words and phrases used in various situations, recur again and again. The form of the ballad is simple. It usually consists of a series of quatrains with alternating four-stress and three-stress iambic lines, the second and fourth of which rime.

Most of the early English ballads have come down to us in several versions. Compare the versions in this text with the variants given in Francis J. Child's *The English and Scottish Popular Ballads*, (5 vols.; Boston, 1882–98); or in *English and Scottish Popular Ballads*, edited by Helen C. Sargent and George L. Kittredge (Boston: Houghton Mifflin Co., 1904). The text of *Katharine Jaffray* used here is MS. A, Vol. IV, p. 219 in Child.

175.   Green Grow the Rashes.

1.   *rashes.* Rushes
9.   *warly.* Worldly.

13.   *canny.* Snug, comfortable and quiet.
16.   *tapsalteerie.* Topsy-turvy.
17.   *douce.* Sober, sedate.
19.   *wisest man.* Solomon.

176.   I Like to See It Lap the Miles.

Frederick J. Hoffman finds in *I Like to See It Lap the Miles* a prec-
edent for what he calls the "technological fallacy" in modern poetry, "a
failure of emotional grasp of the meaning implicit in a machine's purpose
and nature." Of this poem he writes, "Miss Dickinson reduces the size of
her machine and of its setting so that they are manageable in the same
way as a toy train must appear manageable to a child. Indeed, Miss Dickinson's machine may be said to be like many others of her poetic objects;
it is translated into an idiom and discussed on a scale which provide for
an easy, convenient attitude, within the range of her sensibility and taste.
The power of any locomotive depends in large part on its size as a moving, disciplined mechanism. Though the metaphoric resemblance to a
playful animal is not exceptional, in this poem it is used in such a way as
to reduce the size and significance of both the machine and the animal. In
short, Miss Dickinson's poem can easily be understood as a convenient
basis for an illustrated children's book." [Frederick J. Hoffman, "The
Technological Fallacy in Contemporary Poetry: Hart Crane and Mac-
Knight Black," *American Literature,* XXI, 97 (March, 1949). Quoted
by permission of *American Literature.*]
13.   *Boanerges.* The name Christ gave to James and John (Mark 3:17).
It means sons of thunder.

Compare this poem with Walt Whitman's *To a Locomotive in Winter,*
p. 377, and Stephen Spender's *The Express,* p. 422.

181.   Get Up and Bar the Door.

For a discussion of the popular ballad, see the note to *Katharine Jaffray,* p. 459. The text used here is MS. A, Vol. V, p. 98 in Child.

193.   I Wandered Lonely as a Cloud.

This poem stems from a scene described in Dorothy Wordsworth's
Journal as follows: "We saw a few daffodils close to the water-side. We
fancied that the lake had floated the seeds ashore, and that the little
colony had so sprung up. But as we went along there were more and yet
more; and at last, under the boughs of the trees, we saw that there was a
long belt of them along the shore, about the breadth of a country turn-
pike road. I never saw daffodils so beautiful. They grew among the

mossy stones about and about them; some rested their heads upon these stones, as on a pillow, for weariness; and the rest tossed and reeled and danced, and seemed as if they verily laughed with the wind, that blew upon them over the lake; they looked so gay, ever glancing, ever changing." [Quoted in *The Poetical Works of William Wordsworth,* edited by E. de Selincourt (3 vols.; Oxford: The Clarendon Press, 1944), II, p. 507. Used by permission of The Clarendon Press.]

The poem as first published differed from the final version:
4.   *golden* was *dancing.*
5–6.   These lines originally read:

Along the lake, beneath the trees,
Ten thousand dancing in the breeze.

7–12.   These lines did not appear in the original.
16.   *jocund* was *laughing.*

229.   *Upon Lazarus His Tears.*

See Luke 16:19–31 for the Biblical story behind the poem.
2.   *Dives.* Latin for rich man. Although the rich man is not named in the Biblical story, he is traditionally referred to as Dives.
4.   *purple.* As the context suggests, *purple* is not used in its present sense but in its older meaning of crimson or dark red.

229.   *Sonnet XXX.*

A detailed study of this poem appears in Stephen C. Pepper's *The Basis of Criticism in the Arts* (Cambridge: Harvard University Press, 1945), pp. 114 ff. The following comment is part of Mr. Pepper's discussion of the imagery in this sonnet: ". . . the inner ties among all the main images of the poem [are] all due to their connection with money and debts. . . . They are all details in the metaphor of a merchant's debts. Now [that] we have the key to the connections in terms of the merchant metaphor, consider 'sessions,' 'summon,' 'old,' 'new,' 'dear,' 'waste,' 'unused,' 'precious,' 'date,' 'long since cancelled,' 'expense,' 'grievances,' 'heavily,' 'Tell o'er,' 'account,' 'pay,' 'losses are restored.' These images springing from the metaphor are then all one connected image, and from it like leaves from branches of a tree depend all the other images of the poem. Moreover, notice how apt, how connected, this legal and commercial image is with the theme of the poem. From the misery of threatened bankruptcy all losses may be restored to the poor man if some one remaining piece of property proves sound in value."

230.   SONNET IV, *Fair Virtue.*

14.   *Turtle-dove or pelican.* Both are associated with gentleness and tenderness. The turtle-dove is noted for its affection for its mate; the pelican, according to fable, will peck its breast to get blood to feed its young.

Note the rimes in the following lines: 3–4, *care:are;* 11–12, *nature:feature;* 17–18, *move:love;* 37–38, *woo:go.* Note also that the *-ed* ending in *well-disposed,* line 11, and in *Joined,* line 12, must be pronounced for the sake of the meter.

231.   *Description of Spring.*

1.   *soote.* Sweet.
2.   *eke.* Also.
4.   *turtle.* Turtle-dove. See note above to George Withers' SONNET IV, *Fair Virtue.*

    make. Mate.
6.   *pale.* Paling, fence. Surrey is referring to the deer which were kept in parks or enclosures. When winter was over they would shed their antlers by rubbing them against the fence.
11.   *mings.* *Mings* here may have either the sense of mixes or calls to mind.

231.   SONNET XXIV, *Astrophel and Stella.*

The sonnet sequence *Astrophel and Stella* was addressed to Penelope Devereux, to whom Sidney was engaged for a while. In 1576 Penelope's father, the Earl of Essex, expressed the hope that Sidney might marry her. But in 1581 she married Robert, Lord Rich. It is possible that the marriage of Penelope's mother to Sidney's uncle, the Earl of Leicester, in 1577, was a deterrent to Penelope's marrying Sidney. SONNET XXIV puns on the word *Rich.*
3.   *Tantal's smart.* The reference is to the myth of Tantalus. For revealing secrets of his father Zeus, Tantalus was condemned to stand up to his chin in water. Overhead were trees heavily laden with fruit. Whenever Tantalus attempted to reach the fruit or to drink the water, they were drawn away from him.

232.   *The Good-Morrow.*

2.   *seaven sleepers den.* The seven sleepers were men who fled the city of Ephesus to escape Emperor Decius' persecution of the Christians in A.D. 252. They took refuge in a cave on Mount Celion. Finding their hiding place, Decius had the mouth of the cave walled up with stone so

that they would perish. They were put asleep by God. Two centuries later some stone masons opened the cave to get building materials. The companions then awakened and bid good-morrow to one another as if they had slept but a single night. The story is told in the *Golden Legend* by Jacopus de Voragine.

11.   The reference is to the sea voyages of discovery by Elizabethan explorers.

12.   *other.* A plural form without the *s*, which was common at this period.

14.   *is one.* The Elizabethans believed that the constitution of man closely resembles that of the universe, that man is a summing-up, or epitome, of the whole world; in short man is a microcosm. He has the power of reason possessed by divine beings; he has the sense and feeling of animals; he has the powers of growth and nourishment of plants. His body is composed of the four elements—earth, water, air, and fire—as was the rest of the world. His body contains vital heat, corresponding to the fires at the center of the earth. His food is transformed by the liver into four humours, life-sustaining liquids which must be properly mixed for good health, just as the four elements if properly proportioned bring about perfection and permanence in the substances they compose. He may be shaken by gusty passions just as earthquakes and storms upset the world. His veins resemble rivers, his breath air, his hair the grass. The analogy was carried to great lengths.

17.   *hemispheares.* In their eyes, which are hemispherical in appearance, each saw the reflection of the other. Two hemispheres make one sphere, which was considered the perfect shape. For example, around the earth as a center revolved the heavenly bodies in nine concentric, transparent spheres. These heavens were changeless and perfect and eternal and had the shape of perfection, the sphere.

19 ff.   A perfect mixture of the four elements produced immortality and perfection. The nine heavens were eternal because composed of a perfect mixture of the elements. For the same reason gold was the perfect metal.

232.   SONNET LV, *Amoretti.*

4.   *cruell faire.* A conventional conceit of the courtly love sonneteers.
    attonce. At once, at one and the same time.

5–8.   *earth, water, ayre, fyre.* The four basic elements, according to Elizabethan belief, which made up the world and the microcosm of man. For a fuller discussion, see the note above to *The Good-Morrow,* p. 462.

9.   *another element.* A variation of the idea that a perfect mixture of the four basic elements produced immortality and perfection was the belief that in addition to the four elements there was a fifth essence, the quintes-

sence, of which the heavenly bodies were composed, and which was thought to be latent in everything.

11. *haughty*. In addition to the sense of disdainful and arrogance, *haughty* also carries the older sense of noble or lofty.

aspire. Literally to breathe toward, to rise up as an exhalation.

13–14. Behind these lines, and implied in lines 1–4, is the Platonic notion that outward beauty is merely the reflection of inner beauty, which is heavenly and immortal. Since the lady can best be likened to heaven her actions toward her lover should correspond with her other heavenly qualities.

14. *mercy*. In the Christian sense, mercy is the heavenly reward granted to those who have no claim to such reward. In the context of the rejected lover and the Petrarchan convention, it might also mean a favor or reward of love granted by the lady to her lover.

233. Thomas Rymer.

One of many popular ballads concerned with fairy legend and the association of human beings with creatures of the other world. For a fuller discussion of the popular ballad, see the note to *Katharine Jaffray*, p. 459. The text used here is MS. A, Vol. I, pp. 323–324 in Child.

7. *At ilka tett*. At each lock.

17. *ye maun go wi me now*. There is a gap in the story between stanzas 4 and 5. In other versions of the tale, True Thomas at this point kissed or embraced the queen of Elfland and thus, according to the superstitions of fairy lore, put himself in her power.

34. If he ate other than earthly food, Thomas would not be able to return to earth and his soul would go to hell.

37–38. The loaf and bottle of claret wine are earthly food, which the queen of Elfland has considerately brought along.

57. *ye maun hold your tongue*. Another folk belief about fairies. To exchange speech with fairies would make Thomas one of them, and he would be unable to return to earth.

235. The Wild Swans at Coole.

The locale is Coole Park, the beautiful country estate of Lady Gregory to the southeast of Galway, Ireland. The eighteenth century house, white and symmetrical, was approached by an avenue of large trees whose branches intermingled overhead. On one side of the house were gray stone buildings of the stable yard. On the other were gardens surrounded by walls. At some distance behind the house in the midst of dark woods was a gray lake inhabited by wild swans. This lake, the scene of the poem, has been described by John Masefield: "In the afternoons, I used to row him [Yeats] out onto the lake to fish (for perch and pike). When I first went there, in the beauty of September, the lake was full. Under the burning sky, in the still shadows, the rocks of the lake had a grayness and strangeness of mirage. As we drifted into the lower lake, nine white swans rose up and clanked away from us. 'I have always thought,' Yeats said, 'that this is the most beautiful place in the world.'" [*Some Memories of William Butler Yeats* (New York: Macmillan, 1940), p. 21.] The lake is fed by a subterranean river, which is also described, together with the surrounding terrain, by Masefield: "'Near Coole, a strange river runs, disappears, reappears, forms a lake or chain of lakes, then disappears again, but may be heard talking underground, or even seen, at the bottom of occasional deep shafts and pot-holes. The woods in which these waters go are strange and uncanny. In the distance are low, strange, rocky, beautiful hills." [*Ibid.*, p. 20.]

When Yeats wrote this poem in 1916 he was a bachelor of 51. Nineteen years before, in 1897, he had first lived at Coole as the guest of his benefactress, Lady Gregory. At that time he was in very bad health and was sick with love for Maud Gonne, a famous Irish beauty, actress, and revolutionary. During the intervening years he had failed to make a conquest of Maud; she had steadfastly refused to marry him. And shortly before writing the poem Yeats "had been to France and been a 'little relieved' at Maud's refusal of his last offer of marriage." [Norman Jeffares, *W. B. Yeats Man and Poet* (New Haven: Yale University Press, 1949), p. 222.] Even this grand passion of his life was wearing thin with age. These observations help give substance to stanza four, in which the poet is really talking about himself under guise of speaking about the swans. A reading of lines 22 and 24 with emphasis on *their* and *them* will help to bring out the sense.

236. *You, Andrew Marvell.*

See Andrew Marvell's *To His Coy Mistress,* especially lines 21–24, pp. 309–310.

Concerning this poem Archibald MacLeish writes: "The poem was written in Paris in the Fall of 1926, after an extensive journey in Persia, followed by a rapid return to the United States. The fixed position of the poem is, of course, the American Continent—specifically Illinois on the shore of Lake Michigan. The surface meaning is thus geographic. The underlying meaning relates, equally of course, to the human situation— not necessarily of this age, but of all ages." [Letter to the authors, January 31, 1951.]

9. *Ecbatan.* Founded in 700 B.C., Ecbatan was the capital of ancient Media, in northwest Persia, and the residence of Cyrus the Great, founder of the Persian empire, and later the residence of Alexander the Great.

13. *Kermanshah.* Province in west Persia.

17. *Baghdad.* In southeast Iraq.

21. *Palmyra.* Ancient city of Syria, now the site of extensive ruins; it was destroyed by Aurelian, A.D. 273, and later sacked by Tamerlane, 1401.

23. *Lebanon.* Mountain in Syria.

240. *She Dwelt Among the Untrodden Ways.*

The variants are from *The Poetical Works of William Wordsworth,* edited by E. de Selincourt (3 vols.; Oxford: The Clarendon Press, 1944), II, p. 30.

241. *The Lads in Their Hundreds.*

The variant line is from Laurence Housman, *My Brother, A. E. Housman* (New York: Charles Scribner's Sons, 1938), p. 253.

242. *Sailing to Byzantium.*

Here Yeats, at the age of over 60, adjusts himself to his advancing old age. He deals with the problem symbolically, and the symbols are many-valued, having what he calls an "imaginative richness of suggestion." [A. Norman Jeffares, *W. B. Yeats* (New Haven: Yale University Press, 1949), p. 237.] His imagination had been quickened by the period of Justinian at Byzantium, the holy city of Eastern Christendom, with the great domed church of St. Sophia and its splendid mosaics of sacred figures set in a background of golden tesserae. It was the age, he believed, in which "Byzantine art was perfected." [*A Vision* (New York: Macmillan, 1938), p. 281.] In the poem Byzantium becomes a symbol of old age, intellect, permanence and immortality, and the created beauty of works of art. As such it contrasts with the Ireland of the first stanza, which symbolizes youth, sensual passion, decay and death, and the natural beauty of the living world.

1. *That.* Ireland.

4. *salmon-falls.* Yeats had seen the salmon in their grace and vigor leap the falls of the Sligo River in the spring.

4. *mackerel-crowded seas.* As a boy Yeats had sailed the Sligo Bay and the waters of northwestern Ireland; thus he was well acquainted with the shoals of mackerel that would excite the little fishing-village. It is also to be remembered that the fish is an ancient symbol of fertility and strength.

17, 18.   *O sages.* Saints pictured in the mosaics of St. Sophia. This image had its source in the Byzantine mosaics which Yeats had recently seen at Ravenna and in Sicily. The figures symbolize the great dead. Yeats had a belief that human souls go through a sequence of reincarnations, and that when the sequence comes to an end, the souls are "in the condition of fire," of rest. [W. B. Yeats, "Anima Mundi," *Essays* (New York: Macmillan, 1924), p. 524 and *passim.*]

19.   *perne in a gyre.* To perne is to spin or whirl; a gyre is a rotating or spiraling movement. Yeats knew that in folk lore the dead move in a whirl of wind. [*Letters on Poetry from W. B. Yeats to Dorothy Wellesley* (New York: Oxford University Press, 1940), p. 104.] Hence the phrase pictures the whirling movement of the sages, the great dead, as they might "come," in answer to his invocation, to be his singing-masters or teachers.

24.   *artifice of eternity.* The poet's eternity, that is, his immortality, he must make for himself. This he does by means of his art.

25.   *Once out of nature.* See note to line 17.

27 ff.   Yeats' note reads: "I have read somewhere that in the Emperor's palace at Byzantium was a tree made of gold and silver, and artificial birds that sang." [*The Poems of W. B. Yeats* (2 vols.; London: Macmillan, 1949), vol. 2, p. 277.] He expresses the wish to be himself a work of art, a bird of immortal gold, and in this form to sing immortal verse. This idea is in contrast to the mortal birds of the first stanza.

The earlier versions printed here are taken from A. Norman Jeffares' "The Byzantine Poems of W. B. Yeats," *Review of English Studies,* xxii (January, 1946) pp. 44–46. Used by permission of Mrs. Yeats.

244.   *Leda and the Swan.*

The variant octave is taken by permission of the Modern Language Association from Marion Witt's, "A Competition for Eternity: Yeats's Revisions of His Later Poems," PMLA, lxiv (March, 1949), p. 52.

According to Greek myth, Jove, disguised as a swan, ravished Leda, the wife of Tyndarus, king of Sparta. In the course of time Leda brought forth two eggs. From one came Pollux and Helen; from the other Castor and Clytemnestra. It was this Helen who became responsible for the burning of Troy. Clytemnestra, who became the wife of the Greek chieftain Agememnon, murdered her husband upon his return from the Trojan War. Yeats' treatment of the myth might have been influenced by Michelangelo's painting, of which he had a colored reproduction.

For Yeats the rape of Leda was the beginning of the historic cycle (2,000 B.C. to A.D. 1) of pagan civilization, as the annunciation of the birth of Christ to Mary began the second cycle of two millennia. He says in *A Vision:* "I imagine the annunciation that founded Greece as made to Leda . . . from one of her eggs came Love and the other War." [New York: Macmillan, 1938, p. 268.] The inception of the poem was described by Yeats: "After the individualistic, demagogic movements, founded by Hobbes and popularised by the Encyclopaedists and the French Revolution, we have a soil so exhausted that it cannot grow that crop again for centuries. Then I thought 'Nothing is now possible but some movement, or birth from above, preceded by some violent annunciation.' My fancy began to play with Leda and the Swan for metaphor, and I began this poem, but as I wrote, bird and lady took such possession of the scene that all politics went out of it. . . ." [quoted by A. Norman Jeffares, *W. B. Yeats, Man and Poet* (New Haven: Yale University Press, 1949, pp. 223–224.]

245.   On First Looking into Chapman's Homer.

The variants are from *The Poetical Works and Other Writings of John Keats,* edited with notes and appendices by H. Buxton Forman, revised with additions by Maurice Buxton Forman (8 vols.; New York: Charles Scribner's Sons, 1939), I, p. 85. By permission of the publisher.

246.   To Autumn.

The variants of *To Autumn* are a selection of those found in three sources: the original draft; a copy made by John Keats in the body of a letter to Woodhouse; a transcript in the British Museum Keats volume. They are recorded in the Buxton Forman edition cited in the note above, III, pp. 181–184.

247.   Ode to a Nightingale.

There is some reason to believe that this poem stems, at least in part, from the feelings aroused in Keats by the death of his brother Tom, who had died shortly before the poem was composed. In a letter to Miss Mitford, Benjamin Robert Haydon made the following comment: "The death of his Brother wounded him [Keats] deeply, and it appeared to me from that hour he began to droop—he wrote his exquisite ode to the Nightingale at this time, and as we were one evening walking in the meadows, he repeated it before he had put it to paper, in a low, tremulous undertone which affected me extremely." [Quoted in the Forman edition of Keats cited above, III, p. 142.] Line 6 of stanza three may have reference to the death of Keats' brother.

The variants given here are selected from those of four manuscript versions recorded in the Forman edition of Keats mentioned above, III, pp. 145–151.

250.   The Tiger.

The original version is taken by permission of the publisher from *The Poetical Works of William Blake,* edited by John Sampson (London: Oxford University Press, 1922), pp. 86–88.

253.   Lightning.

The final version is from D. H. Lawrence's *Collected Poems* (2 vols.; New York: Jonathan Cape, 1929), I, p. 54. The early version is from Lawrence's *Love Poems and Others* (London: Duckworth, 1913), p. 19. Used by permission of Viking Press, Mrs. Frieda Lawrence, and William Heinemann, Ltd.

255.   The House on the Hill.

The variants are taken from Charles Beecher Hogan, *A Bibliography of Edwin Arlington Robinson* (New Haven: Yale University Press, 1936), p. 100.

NOTES TO PART II

269. *Bonny Barbara Allan.*

A popular ballad. See the note to *Katharine Jaffray*, p. 459. The text used here is MS. A, Vol. II, p. 276 in Child. Cf. the American version of this poem on p. 345.

270. *Edward.*

A popular ballad. See the note to *Katharine Jaffray*, p. 459. The text used here is MS. B, Vol. I, p. 169 in Child.

271. *Fearewell Love and All Thy Lawes for Ever.*

In 1527 Wyatt visited Italy, where he was attracted by the love poems of several Italian poets, especially by those of Petrarch (1303–1374). Upon his return Wyatt introduced the Petrarchan sonnet form into England and helped to establish certain conventions which English poetry was to follow for some time.

The theme of love was predominant. Moreover, in the treatment of this theme certain conventions were followed. These were called "courtly love" conventions, and were derived in part from medieval concepts of Christianity and in part from Platonic ideas introduced early in the Renaissance. The concept of human love came from Christianity. At the same time, however, the ascetic elements of Christianity required the religious man to cast off mere human love for divine love. Plato, too, taught that man should strive not for earthly love but for heavenly love, that the highest form of love is not an appetite but a state of the soul contemplating beauty and wisdom. Hence there arose, during this time, two opposed views about women: in identification with the Virgin Mary, women were exalted as earthly representatives of divinity; women were disparaged as destroyers of inner peace and purity. This contrast between divine love and secular love was the basis of much of the poetry of the Elizabethans, and it appeared in a variety of forms.

We find at this time many poems in which the beauty of the lady was praised. Often her physical charms were listed in catalogue fashion. Since outward beauty, however, is only a reflection of inward beauty, the poet had occasion to catalogue the moral excellences of his beloved. Often, by association, he celebrated places and things connected with the lady, or he idealized her as the highest perfection, a mortal symbol of absolute virtue. Frequently the lover expressed pain at being separated from his lady and used the occasion to repeat his vows of love and to again stress her wisdom and beauty. Since, however, physical beauty is a transient thing, we find many poems concerned with the ravages of time and the idea of *carpe diem.* Often the rejected lover, in an outburst against love, renounced love as a snare which had brought him nothing but misery and destruction.

272.   SONNET LXXXI, *Amoretti.*

Cf. Sidney's SONNET VII, *Astrophel and Stella,* p. 281, and Shakespeare's *Sonnet* CXXX, p. 283.

272.   *The Faerie Queene,* BOOK II, CANTO XII.

In this long allegorical poem, the general end of which was "to fashion a gentleman or noble person in vertuous and gentle discipline," Spenser attempted "to represent all the moral vertues, assigning to every virtue a knight to be the patron and defender of the same; in whose actions and feates of armes and chivalry the operations of that virtue whereof he is the protector are to be expressed, and the vices and unruly appetites that oppose themselves against the same to be beaten down and overcome." Book II contains the "Legend of Sir Guyon," who represents Temperance; Canto XII marks the climax, in which Sir Guyon overcomes Acrasia (Intemperance or Incontinence personified as an enchantress). The stanzas printed here are part of the description of the "faire witch" Acrasia in her "Bowre of Blis." The Spenserian stanza consists of eight lines in five-stress iambic meter followed by an alexandrine, an iambic line of six feet. The rime scheme is *a b a b b c b c c.*

274.   *Prothalamion.*

The full title, which helps explain the situation, is: Prothalamion or a Spousall Verse Made by Edm. Spenser. In Honour of the Double Mariage of the Two Honorable and Vertuous Ladies, the Ladie Elizabeth and the Ladie Katherine Somerset, Daughters to the Right Honourable the Earle of Worcester and Espoused to the Two Worthie Gentlemen M. Henry Gilford, and M. William Peter Esquyers.

280. The Passionate Shepherd to His Love.

Many poets have used this poem as the basis for other poems on this theme. Cf. Raleigh's *The Nymph's Reply to the Shepherd,* p. 280; Donne's *The Baite,* p. 285; and Herrick's *To Phyllis, to Love and Live with Him,* p. 289.

280. The Nymph's Reply to the Shepherd.

This poem is a response to Marlowe's *The Passionate Shepherd to his Love.*

281. SONNET VII, *Astrophel and Stella.*

In the sonnet-cycle *Astrophel and Stella,* the poet expressed his love for Penelope Devereux, daughter of the first Earl of Essex. "Astrophel," which means "star-lover," refers to the poet; "Stella," which means "star," is Penelope. Cf. Spenser's SONNET LXXXI, *Amoretti,* p. 272, and Shakespeare's *Sonnet* CXXX, p. 283. See also Sidney's SONNET XXIV, *Astrophel and Stella,"* p. 231.

283. Sonnet CXXX.

Cf. Spenser's SONNET LXXXI, *Amoretti,* and Sidney's SONNET VII, *Astrophel and Stella.*

284. Song.

Louis J. Locke of *The Explicator* has written the following discussion of Donne's *Song:*

"Enjoyment of Donne's 'Song' is enhanced, we believe, when one recognizes Donne's art in creating just the right atmosphere in the first fifteen lines to shock the reader when the real theme of the poem, the inconstancy of women, is introduced.

"The first stanza, which creates the atmosphere of strangeness and anticipates the theme in lines 7–9 ('honest' meaning 'chaste,' 'true'?), may actually be considered a magical incantation, complete with the sorcerer's charmed number of seven impossibilities. In the beginning of the second stanza, Donne does not continue the incantation, since it is complete in the first, but he does continue the magical motif with his reference to the supernatural powers of vision known as second sight. The second stanza is also closely related to the first in that it, too, challenges the reader with two additional impossibilities, which like the seven of the incantation have the air of the supernatural about them. Thus is the reader bewitched before Donne confronts him with the last three lines of stanza two. All the elaborate hocus-pocus which precedes this statement of the theme serves to hypnotize the reader so that he is doubly shocked by the blunt statement of woman's inconstancy.

"The frailty of woman is thus underscored by the clever method of presentation: even though a man can accomplish all these impossible things by virtue of his magical endowments or knowledge, yet there is one thing he cannot find, Donne rollickingly asserts. Donne, therefore, has ironically used his magic to good purpose, namely, to surprise the reader and to make a much stronger statement of woman's inconstancy than would otherwise have been possible. (The reader experiences secondary shock at the end of the poem when he is told that the 'true and fair' woman will not only be found false, but false 'to *two* or *three*'!)

"The devil's cleft foot and the mermaid's singing contribute to the supernatural atmosphere, but 'Get with child a mandrake root' has already plunged us into the blackest of magic. The mandrake, according to the ancient herbals, was always associated with dark, weird, and nefarious practices. The mandrake, whose forked root was supposed to resemble the human body, was found in both sexes. According to superstitious belief, it grew under the gallows, where it was generated in connection with the execution of a man. . . .

"Although the mandrake was valued for various properties, the belief that a mandrake worn close to the body of a barren woman would insure her fertility (Cf. *Genesis*, XXX) is likely an implication that Donne had in mind in the line 'Get with child a mandrake root.' Yet this interpretation is not admitted by the syntax. Rather, what Donne says is that the mandrake, popularly associated with causing conception, was itself to be got with child—perhaps the most daringly fanciful impossibility which Donne proposed in the 'Song.'" [*The Explicator*, Vol. I, No. 4, February, 1943.]

285.   *The Baite.*

Cf. Marlowe's *The Passionate Shepherd to his Love*, p. 280.

286.   *The Canonization.*

For a provocative discussion of this poem see Cleanth Brooks' *The Well Wrought Urn* (New York: Reynal & Hitchcock, 1947), pp. 10–20.

287.   *A Valediction: Forbidding Mourning.*

The occasion appears to have been Donne's separation from his wife upon his departure for France.

6.   In conventional love poetry of the Petrarchan tradition, separation of

lovers was accompanied by floods of tears, tempests of sighs, and other exaggerated protestations of love.

7, 8. The words *prophanation* and *layetie* suggest that their love is sacred or spiritual.

9. *Moving of th'earth.* Earthquakes, which were thought to be ill omens. Or, the movement of the earth around the sun, according to the new Copernican astronomy; this new concept caused men to fear and to wonder what it meant.

11. *trepidation of the spheares.* See note to *The Good-Morrow,* p. 463. Latin *motus trepidationis;* according to the old Ptolemaic astronomy, a tremendous heavenly movement of the eighth sphere. The eighth sphere, that of the fixed stars, was believed to have three motions: 1. a diurnal east-to-west motion; 2. a centennial west-to-east motion; 3. the trepidation, a north and south motion, the poles of the eighth sphere describing a circle which was completed only once in 7000 years. This would be much greater than the movement of the earth around the sun.

12. *innocent.* Harmless.

13. *sublunary.* Below the sphere of the moon, that is, on earth, all is imperfect, mortal, and subject to decay. Above the moon, throughout the spheres, all is perfect, immortal, and immutable.

14. (*Whose soule is sense*). Man was believed to have three souls: a rational soul, a sensible soul, and a vegetative soul. The sensible soul, also possessed by animals, was concerned with sensation and feeling. See note to *The Good-Morrow,* p. 463.

19. The implication is that their love is controlled by the rational soul, which is also possessed by divine beings, and which concerns understanding and will.

289.   Cherrie-Ripe.

Cf. Campion's *There is a garden in her face,* p. 89. *Cherry-Ripe* is the call of the London street vendors.

289.   To Phillis, to Love, and Live with Him.

Cf. Marlowe's *The Passionate Shepherd to his Love,* p. 280.

292.   The Pulley.

"Without the pulley conceit," writes D. S. Mead, "the purport of the poem is quite clear. But how visualize a pulley that will permit 'weariness' to 'toss' man to God's breast?

"A simple pulley consists usually of a wheel over which a rope is suspended. Perfect balance is maintained if the weights on either end of the rope are equal. If one end is heavier the wolf descends and the fox rises.

"To make use of the pulley in the poem, God must be thought of as threading the rope through the wheel. On one side he lets down man and from his 'glass of blessings' he gives man strength, beauty, wisdom, honor, pleasure—all but rest. Rest He withholds in His glass so that man without it will experience restlessness. Man can climb up the rope to God by virtue of his goodness, but in case he does not, and, spurning his earthly riches yearns in his weariness for peace, God need but release His rest on the other side of the pulley and its weight, greater than man's unburdened soul, will hoist or 'toss' man to His level." [D. S. Mead, *The Explicator,* Vol. IV, No. 3, December, 1945.]

294. L'Allegro.

L'Allegro is a companion piece to *Il Penseroso*. L'Allegro is The Joyous Man; Il Penseroso is The Thoughtful Man.

According to James Holly Hanford, "The poems are a comprehensive record of aesthetic pleasures. The two imaginary personalities which Milton creates for purposes of expression are in reality one. L'Allegro is Milton dreaming. . . . L'Allegro delights in the morning. Long before sunrise he wakens and lies dreamily listening to the pure bird notes. The lark from his high station is his watchman to warn him of approaching dawn. At length he rises and is the solitary witness of the birth of a new day. . . .

"The companion poem records the satisfactions of solitary meditation. . . . The scene . . . is largely the same; the spirit that walks among them is for the moment changed. Il Penseroso courts only those aspects of the world which create the poetic *Stimmung* and quickly lose their substance to become part of the baseless fabric of a dream. The nightingale, the moon, the curfew,

Over some wide watered shore
Swinging slow with sullen roar,

above all firelight and candle, the hearth cricket, and the bellman's drowsy call from out of doors." [James Holly Hanford, *John Milton, Englishman* (New York: Crown Publishers, 1949), pp. 54–55. Quoted by permission of the publisher.]

Although Cleanth Brooks also considers these poems as companion pieces, he disagrees to some extent with Mr. Hanford as to the relationship between the two poems: "A little consideration, however, will show that Milton could not afford to exploit mere contrast. If he had, the two halves would have been driven poles apart. They would have ceased to be twin halves of *one* poem, for the sense of unity in variety would have been lost. . . .

". . . 'L'Allegro,' as we know, is not consistently a daylight poem, just as 'Il Penseroso' is not consistently a night poem . . . in neither of the poems do we get the flaring sunbeam in which the dust motes swim or the unrelieved blackness of midnight. In both poems the spectator moves through what are predominantly cool half-lights. It is as if the half-light were being used in both poems as a sort of symbol of the aesthetic distance which the cheerful man, no less than the pensive man, consistently maintains." [Cleanth Brooks, *The Well Wrought Urn* (New York: Reynal & Hitchcock, 1947), pp. 50; 55–56.]

298.   Il Penseroso.

See note above.

303.   Lycidas.

In a prefatory note to *Lycidas* Milton wrote: "In this monody the author bewails a learned friend, unfortunately drowned in his passage from Chester on the Irish Seas, 1637. And by occasion foretells the ruin of our corrupted clergy then in their height." The "learned friend" was Edward King, a former classmate of Milton's at Christ College, Cambridge.

Lycidas is a pastoral elegy, a form which has become traditional during the course of many centuries. The outstanding feature of the pastoral elegy is that the subject is thinly veiled as a shepherd amidst his rural surroundings. The poet himself is also a shepherd who tended his flock with the subject of the poem. On the death of his companion, the poet feels that he is the poetical successor to the dead shepherd.

The pastoral elegy usually opens with an introduction giving the setting. Throughout the poem there is much use of refrain and repetition. On the death of the shepherd all of nature mourns his loss. The nymphs are called upon and questioned: "Where were ye Nymphs when the shepherd died?" They in turn ask why everyone and everything is in mourning. There is also a passage describing the decking of the grave with flowers. Because of the personal relationship of the poet to the other shepherd, the pastoral elegy offers a means of expressing personal comments and digressions. The poem concludes on a note of hope and a suggestion of immortality.

Although the occasion for this poem was the death of King, many critics assert that King is not the real subject of the poem. E. M. W. Tillyard writes in part: "Most criticism of *Lycidas* is off the mark, because it fails to distinguish between the nominal and the real subject, what the poem professes to be about and what it is about. It assumes that Edward King is the real, whereas he is but the nominal subject. Fundamentally *Lycidas* concerns Milton himself; King is but the excuse for one of Milton's most personal poems." [E. M. W. Tillyard, *Milton* (New York: The Dial Press, 1930), p. 80.]

For some of the circumstances of Milton's life at the time the poem was written, the student is referred to the rest of Tillyard's discussion in the work cited above (pp. 80–85), and to James Holly Hanford's *John Milton, Englishman* (New York: Crown Publishers, 1949), pp. 66–71.

308.   *When I Consider How My Light Is Spent.*

This sonnet is an expression of deep personal emotion and thought. Milton's eyesight began to fail when he was about thirty-three years old. This poem was probably written in 1652, when Milton was forty-four and totally blind. Milton, however, did more than "only stand and wait." In fact, he wrote more poetry and prose after the loss of his vision than before. Nearly all of his epic poem *Paradise Lost* was written after he had lost his sight.

The attitude expressed in this poem has been interpreted in various ways. George Serrell writes: "In that noble sonnet on his blindness, which has furnished a topic of consolation for countless sufferers incapacitated by bodily affliction from active service of God and their kind, we seem to trace in the poet's mind a very natural conflict of somewhat inconsistent thoughts." [George Serrell, "Milton as Seen in His Sonnets," *Temple Bar*, cxxi (1900), p. 38]

E. M. W. Tillyard feels that "There is in it a tone of self-abasement. . . . In *Lycidas* the deed is personal, the exercise of Milton's creative faculty: in the sonnet it is the passive yielding to God's command. Milton crouches in humble expectation, like a beaten dog ready to wag its tail at the smallest token of its master's attention." [E. M. W. Tillyard, *Milton* (New York: The Dial Press, 1930), p. 190.]

Eleanor Gertrude Brown, a blind scholar, takes exception to both the views expressed above: "There is, I believe, in English literature no human tragedy so simply depicted as that of the foregoing sonnet. It is a tragedy because, though the end is peaceful, it is the renunciation of poetic achievement seemingly impossible in blindness. It is a tragedy because it contains a conflict, controlled and well-ordered, but obviously a struggle. It is likewise a tragedy because it is the expression of one who has suffered almost beyond human endurance and has emerged without bitterness of spirit of reproach against his grievous fate. . . . I agree with Serrell that there is a conflict of thought, but to me the thoughts are in no sense inconsistent. There are two very definite elements: on the one hand, the 'talent which is death to hide'; on the other, the inability to use this talent. This conflict ends in calm submission to the sacrifice of all he holds dear. 'They also serve who only stand and wait.' . . . It should always be borne in mind that in Milton's day God was supposed to be the bestower of blessings and punishments. Even if we do not agree with such a belief, we cannot but respect Milton for his acquiescence to the seemingly inevitable. The 'beaten dog' attitude portrayed by Tillyard is to me not apparent and is in no sense compatible with the lofty resignation which his majority of readers usually find in this sonnet." [Eleanor Gertrude Brown, *Milton's Blindness* (New York: Columbia University Press, 1934), p. 52. Quoted by permission of the publisher.]

309.   To His Coy Mistress.

Cf. MacLeish's *You, Andrew Marvell*, p. 236.

310.   Mac Flecknoe.

This mock-epic, written in 1682, is a bitter personal satire. In order to understand the animosity expressed in the poem, it is necessary to know something of its background. "T. S." refers to Thomas Shadwell, a contemporary poet and dramatist with whom Dryden was in open feud. The previous year Dryden had written his famous satire *Absolom and Achitophel,* in which he attacked Lord Shaftesbury, who was on trial for treason for attempting to establish the claims of the Duke of Monmouth as successor to the throne. Part of the poem was a satirical caricature of Shadwell. After the charges against Shaftesbury had been dropped a medal was struck in honor of the event. Because of this Dryden wrote another satire, *The Medal,* to which Shadwell replied with a coarse poem, *The Medal of John Bayes,* in which he ridiculed Dryden. To this Dryden replied with *Mac Flecknoe.*

For a fuller discussion of the Dryden-Shadwell dispute, see R. Jack Smith, "Shadwell's Impact Upon John Dryden," *Review of English Studies,* XX (Jan., 1944), 29–44.

3.   *Flecknoe.* A minor Irish writer, who earlier had been lampooned by Andrew Marvell.

15.   *Sh——.* Shadwell. Shadwell, ironically, succeeded Dryden as Poet Laureate.

33.   *drugget.* Coarse woolen cloth.

36.   *King John of Portugal.* Flecknoe had been at the court of the King of Portugal.

42.   *Epsom.* Probably a reference to *Epsom Wells,* one of Shadwell's plays.

53.   *St. André's.* St. André was a French dancing master.
54.   *Psyche's rhyme.* Psyche was another of Shadwell's works.
57.   *Singleton.* A contemporary actor.
59.   *Villerius.* A character in *The Siege of Rhodes,* earliest English opera, written by Sir William D'Avenant.
64.   *Augusta.* Dryden is referring to London.
65.   *fears.* A reference to the political intrigue to put a Catholic on the throne.
74.   *Nursery.* A school for training actors.
78.   *Maximin.* A character in Dryden's *Tyrannic Love.*
79.   *in buskins.* In ancient Greece tragic actors wore buskins, that is, high boots, to give them added stature and dignity; hence, buskin has come to mean tragedy or tragic drama.
80.   *in socks.* Socks were low-heeled light shoes worn by actors of comedy in ancient Greece; hence, in socks means in comedy.
83.   *clinches.* Puns.
91, 92.   *Misers; Humorists.* Plays by Shadwell.
97.   *Bunhill.* An old cemetery near the center of London.
       Watling Street. An old street on the edge of London.
105.   *Herringman.* A contemporary publisher.
122.   *Love's Kingdom.* Another play by Shadwell.
149.   *Virtuosos.* The reference is to *The Virtuoso* by Shadwell.
151.   *gentle George.* Sir George Etherege, a contemporary dramatist.
152, 153.   *Dorimant, Loveit, Cully, Cockwood, Fopling.* Characters in contemporary plays.
163.   *S-dl-y.* Sir Charles Sedley, a minor writer supposed to have assisted Shadwell in some of his work.
168.   *Sir Formal.* A character in *The Virtuoso.*
179.   *Nicander.* A character in *Psyche.*
196.   *kilderkin.* A small barrel.
212.   *Bruce and Longvil.* Characters in *The Virtuoso.*

316.   A Song for St. Cecilia's Day, 1687.

   A Song for St. Cecilia's Day (1687) and *Alexander's Feast* (1697) were written for a London musical society which held a celebration each year in honor of St. Cecilia, the patroness of music. Both poems were set to music and given public performances.

318.   Alexander's Feast.

   See note above.
2.   *warlike son.* Alexander.
9.   *Thais.* A famous Greek courtesan.

20. *Timotheus*. Alexander's favorite musician.
30. *Olympia*. The mother of Alexander.
75. *Darius*. Darius III, King of Persia, conquered by Alexander.

325. Sonnet on the Death of Richard West.

Richard West was one of the poet's closest friends. West's early death in 1742 affected Gray deeply.

Wordsworth, in his famous Preface to the second edition of *Lyrical Ballads* (1800), used this sonnet to substantiate his thesis that "there neither is, nor can be, any *essential* difference between the language of prose and metrical composition." "To illustrate the subject in a general manner," Wordsworth wrote, "I will here adduce a short composition of Gray, who was at the head of those who, by their reasonings, have attempted to widen the space of separation betwixt Prose and Metrical composition, and was more than any other man curiously elaborate in the structure of his own poetic diction. . . .

"It will easily be perceived, that the only part of this Sonnet which is of any value is the lines printed in Italics;

[*A different object do these eyes require;*
My lonely anguish melts no heart but mine;
And in my breast the imperfect joys expire;

. . . . .

I fruitless mourn to him that cannot hear,
And weep the more because I weep in vain.]

it is equally obvious, that, except in the rhyme, and in the use of the single word 'fruitless' for fruitlessly, which is so far a defect, the language of these lines does in no respect differ from that of prose."

327. The Echoing Green.

E. M. W. Tillyard gives the following as his interpretation of this poem:
"I believe that Blake in this poem is expressing . . . the idea that there is a virtue in desire satisfied. Though desire is not mentioned, yet the keynote of the poem is fruition. Nature fulfills itself in the cycle of a perfect day. Old John gets a perfect vicarious satisfaction, the little ones are entirely played out and ready for rest. And at the end the 'echoing green' is the 'darkening green' because its function is fulfilled. The very completeness of formal balance points the same way. The poem . . . expresses the profound peace of utterly gratified desire. . . . The main sense is stated in no particular whatever, but is diffused through every part of the poem and can only be apprehended as a whole through the

synthesis of all those parts. [E. M. W. Tillyard, *Poetry Direct and Oblique* (London: Chatto and Windus, 1934), pp. 11–12. Quoted by permission of The Macmillan Company and Chatto and Windus.]

329.   To a Mouse.

 1.   *sleekit*. Sleek.
 4.   *bickering brattle*. Hurrying scamper.
 6.   *pattle*. Plow-staff.
15.   *daimen . . . thrave*. An occasional ear of wheat in a pile of twenty-four sheaves.
17.   *lave*. Remainder.
21.   *big*. Build.
24.   *snell*. Sharp, biting.
34.   *But*. Without.
35.   *thole*. Endure.
36.   *cranreuch*. Hoar-frost.
37.   *no thy lane*. Not the only one.
40.   *a-gley*. Awry, askew.

330.   Tam o' Shanter.

 1.   *chapman billies*. Peddlers.
 2.   *drouthy*. Thirsty.
 4.   *tak the gate*. Take the road, go home.
 5.   *bousing . . . nappy*. Drinking ale.
 6.   *fou*. Full.
       unco. Uncommonly.
 8.   *slaps*. Gaps, narrow passages.
19.   *skellum*. Rogue, good-for-nothing.
20.   *blellum*. Babbler.
23.   *ilka melder*. Every grinding.
24.   *siller*. Silver.
25.   *ca'd*. Nailed.
31.   *warlocks*. Wizards.
33.   *gars me greet*. Makes me weep.
39.   *ingle*. Fireplace.
40.   *reaming swats*. Foaming new beer.
41.   *Souter*. Cobbler.
78.   *Deil*. Devil.
81.   *skelpit*. Galloped.
       dub. Puddle.
86.   *bogles*. Hobgoblins.

88. *houlets.* Owls.
90. *smoor'd.* Smothered.
91. *meikle stane.* Great stone.
93. *whins.* Brush, furze.
    cairn. Pile of stones.
94. *bairn.* Child.
103. *ilka bore.* Every opening or chink.
107. *tippenny.* Two-penny ale.
108. *usquebae.* Whiskey.
110. *car'd . . . boddle.* Cared not a farthing for devils.
116. *brent new.* Brand new.
119. *winnock-bunker.* Window-seat.
121. *touzie tyke.* Shaggy dog.
123. *gart them skirl.* Made them squeal or scream.
124. *dirl.* Vibrate.
127. *cantraip sleight.* Magic trick.
131. *gibbet-airns.* Gallows-irons.
133. *rape.* Rope.
134. *gab.* Mouth.
147. *cleekit.* Clutched.
148. *ilka . . . reekit.* Every hag sweat and reeked.
149. *coost her duddies.* Cast off her clothes.
150. *linkit.* Tripped, danced.
    sark. Shirt.
153. *creeshie.* Greasy.
155. *Thir.* These.
157. *hurdies.* Buttocks.
160. *Rigwoodie.* Ancient.
    spean. Wean.
161. *crummock.* Crooked staff.
163. *brawlie.* Well, finely.
164. *walie.* Well-built, buxom.
165. *core.* Corps, company.
169. *bear.* Barley.
171. *cutty sark.* Short shirt.
    harn. Coarse fabric.
174. *vauntie.* Proud.
176. *coft.* Bought.
185. *fidg'd.* Fidgeted.
186. *hotch'd.* Hitched, squirmed.
188. *tint.* Lost.

193.   *fyke*. Fuss.
194.   *byke*. Hive.
195.   *pussie's*. Hare's.
200.   *fairin'*. Reward.
206.   *brig*. Bridge.
210.   *fient*. Fiend, devil.
213.   *ettle*. Aim, intent.
217.   *carlin*. Witch.

336.   Ode: Intimations of Immortality.

The following is Wordsworth's note to this poem:

"This was composed during my residence at Town-end, Grasmere. Two years at least passed between the writing of the four first stanzas and the remaining part. To the attentive and competent reader the whole sufficiently explains itself; but there may be no harm in adverting here to particular feelings or *experiences* of my own mind on which the structure of the poem partly rests. Nothing was more difficult for me in childhood than to admit the notion of death as a state applicable to my own being. I have said elsewhere—

'A simple child,
That lightly draws its breath,
And feels its life in every limb,
What should it know of death!'—

But it was not so much from feelings of animal vivacity that *my* difficulty came as from a sense of the indomitableness of the Spirit within me. I used to brood over the stories of Enoch and Elijah, and almost to persuade myself that, whatever might become of others, I should be translated, in something of the same way, to heaven. With a feeling congenial to this, I was often unable to think of external things as having external existence, and I communed with all that I saw as something not apart from, but inherent in, my own immaterial nature. Many times while going to school have I grasped at a wall or tree to recall myself from this abyss of idealism to the reality. At that time I was afraid of such processes. In later periods of life I have deplored, as we have all reason to do, a subjugation of an opposite character, and have rejoiced over the remembrances, as is expressed in the lines—

'Obstinate questionings
Of sense and outward things,
Fallings from us, vanishings;' etc.

To that dream-like vividness and splendor which invest objects of sight in childhood, every one, I believe, if he would look back, could bear testimony, and I need not dwell upon it here: but having in the poem regarded it as presumptive evidence of a prior state of existence, I think it right to protest against a conclusion, which has given pain to some good and pious persons, that I meant to inculcate such a belief. It is far too shadowy a notion to be recommended to faith, as more than an element in our instincts of immortality. But let us bear in mind that, though the idea is not advanced in revelation, there is nothing there to contradict it, and the fall of Man presents an analogy in its favor. Accordingly, a pre-existent state has entered into the popular creeds of many nations; and, among all persons acquainted with classic literature, is known as an ingredient in Platonic philosophy. Archimedes said that he could move the world if he had a point whereon to rest his machine. Who has not felt the same aspirations as regards the world of his own mind? Having to wield some of its elements when I was impelled to write this poem on the 'Immortality of the Soul,' I took hold of the notion of pre-existence as having sufficient foundation in humanity for authorizing me to make for my purpose the best use of it I could as a poet.

'The Child is Father of the Man;
And I could wish my days to be
Bound each to each by natural piety.' "

343.   Kubla Khan: or, A Vision in a Dream.

The composition of this poem has been described by the poet himself: "The following fragment is here published at the request of a poet of great and deserved celebrity, and, as far as the Author's own opinions are concerned, rather as a psychological curiosity, than on the ground of any supposed *poetic* merits.

"In the summer of the year 1797, the Author, then in ill health, had retired to a lonely farmhouse between Porlock and Linton, on the Exmoor confines of Somerset and Devonshire. In consequence of a slight indisposition, an anodyne had been prescribed, from the effects of which he fell asleep in his chair at the moment he was reading the following sentence, or words of the same substance, in *Purchas's Pilgrimage:*—'Here the Khan Kubla commanded a palace to be built, and a stately garden thereunto: and thus ten miles of fertile ground were inclosed with a wall.' The Author continued for about three hours in a profound sleep, at least of the external senses, during which time he has the most vivid confidence that he could not have composed less than from two to three hundred lines; if that indeed can be called composition in which all the images rose up before him as *things,* with a parallel production of the correspondent expressions, without any sensation or consciousness of effort. On awaking he appeared to himself to have a distinct recollection of the whole, and taking his pen, ink, and paper, instantly and eagerly wrote down the lines that are here preserved. At this moment he was unfortunately called out by a person on business from Porlock, and detained by him above an hour, and on his return to his room, found, to his no small surprise and mortification, that though he still retained some vague and dim recollection of the general purport of the vision, yet, with the exception of some eight or ten scattered lines and images, all the rest had passed away like the images on the surface of a stream into which a stone had been cast, but, alas! without the after restoration of the latter."

For an interesting study of the poem, the student is referred to John Livingston Lowes' *The Road to Xanadu, A Study in the Ways of the Imagination* (Boston: Houghton Mifflin Company, 1930).

345. Barbra Allen.

The popular ballad of Barbra Allen appears in many versions. This American version is from the R. W. Gordon collection as recorded in Carl Sandburg's *The American Songbag* (New York: Harcourt, Brace & Company, 1927), p. 57. Sandburg feels that perhaps "the paradox of tender and cruel forces operating together in life . . . has kept the Barbra Allen story alive and singing through three centuries and more." Cf. an older version of this poem on p. 269. For a fuller discussion of the popular ballad, see the note to *Katharine Jaffray,* p. 459.

351. The Snow-Storm.

F. O. Matthiessen has made the following comment about this poem: "The onset of the poem conveys breathless speed, but then, as the snow itself delays actions, shuts out or encloses, the movement of the verse also slows down. But the exciting sound of the storm still remains uppermost, and in presenting it, Emerson's ear has been sensitive to his impression. The trumpets are high pitched: the thin vowel in 'sky' is dominant through the following lines, especially in the phrases, 'driving o'er the fields' and 'the whited air hides hills.' And the echo of the piercing wind, which is itself nowhere directly named, is still heard in the phrase 'tumultuous privacy,' wherein the full vowel-sounds again give way to the piercing notes.

"Emerson goes on [in stanza two] to develop his most lucid and graceful expression of the doctrine of organic form: . . . The rhythm is not so successfully sustained as in the more immediately descriptive stanza, and limps very badly in the next to last line, only to rally, to recapture once more the vibrating excitement that the poem has been designed to express." [F. O. Matthiessen, *American Renaissance, Art and Expression in the Age of Emerson and Whitman* (New York: Oxford University Press, 1941), p. 139.]

352. The Lotos-Eaters.

Homer's *Odyssey*, a long epic poem, describes the adventurous wandering homeward to Ithaca of Ulysses and his men following the Trojan War. Tennyson's poem is based on the following passage from Book IX: "Thence for nine whole days was I borne by ruinous winds over the teeming deep; but on the tenth day we set foot on the land of the lotus-eaters, who eat a flowery food. So we stepped ashore and drew water, and straightway my company took their midday meal by the swift ships. Now when we had tasted meat and drink I sent forth certain of my company to go and make search what manner of men they were who here live upon the earth by bread, and I chose out two of my fellows, and sent a third with them as a herald. Then straightway they went and mixed with the men of the lotus-eaters, and so it was that the lotus-eaters devised not death for our fellows, but gave them of the lotus to taste. Now whosoever of them did eat the honey-sweet fruit of the lotus, had no more wish to bring tidings nor to come back, but there he chose to abide with the lotus-eating men, ever feeding on the lotus, and forgetful of his homeward way. Therefore I led them back to the ships weeping, and sore against their will, and dragged them beneath the benches, and bound them in the hollow barques. But I commanded the rest of my well-loved company to make speed and go on board the swift ships, lest haply any should eat of the lotus and be forgetful of returning." [Translation of S. H. Butcher and A. Lang. Quoted by permission of the publishers, Macmillan and Company, Ltd., and the translators' representatives.]

The text of *The Lotos-Eaters* is that of the 1842 edition of Tennyson's *Poems*. The original version, 1833, was considerably different. The most significant changes are given below:

    7.   Above the valley burned the golden moon;
    16. Three thundercloven thrones of oldest snow.
    69–87. These lines did not appear in the version of 1833.
    88. Or propt on lavish beds of amaranth and moly,
    98. Only to watch and see the far-off sparkling brine,

100.   The Lotos blooms below the flowery peak:
105 ff.   The section from line 105 to the end was considerably different:

We have had enough of motion,
Weariness and wild alarm,
Tossing on the tossing ocean,
Where the tuskèd sea-horse walloweth
In a stripe of grass-green calm,
At noontide beneath the lee;
And the monstrous narwhale swalloweth
His foam-fountains in the sea.
Long enough the wine-dark wave our weary bark did carry.
This is lovelier and sweeter,
Men of Ithaca, this is meeter,
In the hollow rosy vale to tarry,
Like a dreamy Lotos-eater, a delirious Lotos-eater!
We will eat the Lotos, sweet
As the yellow honeycomb,
In the valley, some, and some
On the ancient heights divine;
And no more roam,
On the loud hoar foam,
To the melancholy home
At the limit of the brine,
The little isle of Ithaca, beneath the day's decline.
We'll lift no more the shattered oar,
No more unfurl the straining sail;
With the blissful Lotos-eaters pale
We will abide in the golden vale
Of the Lotos-land till the Lotos fail;
We will not wander more.
Hark! how sweet the horned ewes bleat
On the solitary steeps,
And the merry lizard leaps,
And the foam-white waters pour;
And the dark pine weeps,
And the lithe vine creeps,
And the heavy melon sleeps
On the level of the shore:
Oh! islanders of Ithaca, we will not wander more,
Surely, surely, slumber is more sweet than toil, the shore

Than labour in the ocean, and rowing with the oar:
Oh, islanders of Ithaca we will return no more.

357.   Ulysses.

After ten years of adventurous wandering following the Trojan War, Ulysses returned home to Ithaca, rejoining his wife, Penelope, and his son, Telemachus. Here he ruled again as king. It is this Ulysses who speaks in the poem.

About this poem Tennyson is reported to have said: " 'Ulysses' . . . was written soon after Arthur Hallam's death, and gave my feeling about the need of going forward and braving the struggle of life perhaps more simply than anything in *In Memoriam*." [*Alfred Lord Tennyson a Memoir by His Son* (2 vols.; New York: The Macmillan Company, 1905) I, p. 196.]

359.   To Helen.

Poe, who was much concerned with problems of artistic form, felt that the poet "should limit his endeavors to the creation of novel moods of beauty in form, in color, in sound, in sentiment." Toward these ends he continually revised his total output of forty-eight poems. Earlier versions of *To Helen* contained the following lines in place of the ones finally adopted:

9.   To the beauty of fair Greece.
10.   And the grandeur of old Rome.
11.   Lo! in that little window-niche
13.   The folded scroll within thy hand!

The "Helen" of the poem was Mrs. Jane Stith Stanard, a woman who had been friendly and kind to Poe when he was a boy, and whom he described as "the first purely ideal love of my soul."

360.   The City in the Sea.

First published as *The Doomed City* this poem later appeared under the titles of *The City of Sin* and *The City in the Sea. A Prophecy*. Various interpretations of the poem have been given; and the City in the Sea has been variously associated with "The City of Death" (symbolically identified with Babylon) and with the ruins of an ancient city in the Dead Sea, probably Gomorrah. For a study of these interpretations of the poem, and of the possible sources and influences, see Killis Campbell, *The Poems of Edgar Allan Poe* (Boston, 1917), pp. 207–210; Louise Pound, "On Poe's 'The City in the Sea,' " *American Literature*, VI, 22–27 (1934); Henry M. Belden, "Poe's 'The City in the Sea' and Dante's City of Dis," *American Literature*, VII, 332–334 (1935); Louise Pound, "On Poe's 'The City in the Sea,'" *American Literature*, VIII, 70–71 (1936); T. O. Mabbott, "Poe's 'City in the Sea,'" *The Explicator*, IV, October, 1945; and Roy P. Basler, "Poe's Dream Imagery," *Sex, Symbolism, and Psychology in Literature* (New Brunswick: Rutgers University Press, 1948), pp. 192–195.

The first two versions of this poem differ extensively from the final version. The most significant differences are listed below:

7.   This line preceded line 9.
8.   This line read
"Are—not like anything of ours,"
followed by

O! no— O! no—*ours* never loom
To heaven with that ungodly gloom!

11.   After this line, the earliest version has the following:

A heaven that God doth not contemn
With stars is like a diadem—
We liken our ladies' eyes to them—
But there! that everlasting pall!
It would be mockery to call
Such dreariness a heaven at all.

14.   *lurid* was *deep* in the earliest version.
21.   *marvellous* was *melancholy.*
22.   *wreathed friezes* was *entablatures.*
23.   This line read
"The *mask*—the viol—and the vine."
28.   *a proud tower in* was *the high towers of.*
31.   This line read
"Are on a level with the waves."
44.   *thrust* was *thrown.*
47.   *void within* was *vacuum in.*
53.   This line was followed by

And death to some more happy clime
Shall give his undivided time.

For all the variants to this poem, see Killis Campbell, *The Poems of Edgar Allan Poe* (Boston: Ginn and Company, 1917), pp. 59–62, from which those above were taken by permission.

364. Pioneers! O Pioneers!

The metrical pattern of this poem has been the subject of controversy. In his *Walt Whitman Handbook,* Gay W. Allen writes: "One of the most metrical poems in *Leaves of Grass* is the trochaic 'Pioneers! O Pioneers!,' 1865. The number of stresses in the second and third lines varies from seven to ten, and occasionally an iamb is substituted for a trochee, but the pattern is almost as regular as in conventional verse." Edward G. Fletcher, although he agrees that the poem is "more regular than most of Whitman's poems," takes exception to Allen's view that the poem is basically trochaic. He asserts that the regularity of *Pioneers! O Pioneers!* is "not because of a conventional metrical regularity; the regularity of the poem is a regularity of stanzaic form. This stanzaic form, moreover, depends upon a careful and skilful manipulation of accents, not upon a handling of conventional metrical units. To try to stretch out the poem on a Procrustean bed of trochees or iambics is to misread it."

For the details of the argument and for examples of differences in scansion, see Gay W. Allen, *Walt Whitman Handbook* (Chicago: Packard and Company, 1946), pp. 426–427; Edward G. Fletcher, "Pioneers! O Pioneers!," *American Literature,* XIX, pp. 259–261 (November, 1947); Gay W. Allen, "On the Trochaic Meter of 'Pioneers! O Pioneers!,'" *American Literature,* XX, pp. 449–451 (January, 1949).

368. When Lilacs Last in the Dooryard Bloom'd.

This poem is an elegy on the death of Abraham Lincoln. Whitman was in Washington during the Civil War and often saw Lincoln, heard him speak, and occasionally spoke with him. To Whitman, Abraham Lincoln was "the grandest figure yet, on all the crowded canvas of the Nineteenth Century." In *Specimen Days,* Whitman records the note he made shortly after Lincoln's death: "*April 16, '65.*—I find in my notes of the time, this passage on the death of Abraham Lincoln: He leaves for America's history and biography, so far, not only its most dramatic reminiscence —he leaves, in my opinion, the greatest, best, most characteristic, artistic, moral personality. Not but that he had faults, and show'd them in the Presidency; but honesty, goodness, shrewdness, conscience, and (a new virtue, unknown to other lands, and hardly yet really known here, but the foundation and tie of all, as the future will grandly develop), UNIONISM, in its truest and amplest sense, form'd the hard-pan of his character. These he seal'd with his life. The tragic splendor of his death, purging, illuminating all, throws round his form, his head, an aureole that will remain and will grow brighter through time, while history lives, and love of country lasts. By many has this Union been help'd; but if one name, one man, must be pick'd out, he, most of all, is the conservator of it, to the future. He was assassinated—but the Union is not assassinated—*ça ira!* One falls, and another falls. The soldier drops, sinks like a wave—but the ranks of the ocean eternally press on. Death does its work, obliterates a hundred, a thousand—President, general, captain, private—but the Nation is immortal."

377.   To a Locomotive in Winter.

The following comments about this poem are somewhat at variance. Esther Shephard writes: "Not only did the steam engine become, in all seriousness, no bad symbol of the American people but to Whitman it became the symbol of the beauty of modern progress, and in a sense the symbol of his verse." [Esther Shephard, *Walt Whitman's Pose* (New York: Harcourt, Brace and Company, 1938), p. 83.]

G. W. Arms writes: "It is the last phrase of Miss Shephard's sentence that seems to me basic in interpreting the poem. . . . The interpretation proposed here is of the locomotive as primarily a symbol of Whitman's poetry. Largely through the poetry—and only slightly of itself alone—is the locomotive a symbol of America and of modern progress." And he goes on to comment, "The locomotive is adequate as a symbol because it is also satisfactory as a locomotive." [G. W. A., "Whitman's 'To a Locomotive in Winter,'" *The Explicator*, V, November, 1946.]

Frederick J. Hoffman writes: "In this poem Whitman's treatment alternates between the specific and the symbolic, as well as between dry precision and vague personification. That he is thinking of the locomotive as a worshipful symbol of America's cultural strength and promise is suggested by the archaism of address. The poem exhibits the kind of confusion so often found in Whitman's poetry when he attempts to specify objects as supporting evidence for his semiphilosophic generalizations about American culture. The locomotive as machine has an appearance quite often precisely given ('black cylindric body,' 'parallel and connecting rods,' etc.); at other times, the poet speaks of it as a 'Fierce-throated beauty!' whose power and noise assert its domination over hills, prairies, and lakes. There are at least three points of view in the poem, and they are not unified; nor are they given in an arrangement which allows one to anticipate a shift from one to another." [Frederick J. Hoffman, "The Technological Fallacy in Contemporary Poetry," *American Literature*, XXI, p. 98 (March, 1949). Quoted by permission of *American Literature*.]

Cf. Emily Dickinson's *I Like to See It Lap the Miles,* p. 176, and Stephen Spender's *The Express,* p. 422.

378. Dover Beach.

Matthew Arnold in this poem uses light symbolism to support his theme. This symbolism can be simply described: the light imagery moves from brightness to darkness, reinforcing by this shift the theme of loss of faith and its attendant evils.

In the moonlight scene of the first stanza, the light-bearing words— *moon, light, moon-blanched, gleams, glimmers*—interact with the others —*sea, cliffs, et al.*—to drench the opening lines with a dusky brilliance. This visual effect is strengthened by the phonetic intensives in *gleams* and *glimmers*. Phonetic intensives are speech sounds which in themselves suggest meaning, when such attributable meaning is related to the sense of the words in which they occur. In *gleams* and *glimmers* we find several phonetic intensives. The *gl-* suggests light (as in *glow, glare, glitter, glisten, glint, glossy*); the *ea* and *i* suggest smallness (as in *sip, chip, bit, peep, teeny, thin, slim, piddle, fib*); the *-er* suggests repeated movement (as in *twitter, flicker, flutter, sputter, spatter, chatter*). These palimpsestic meanings interplay to suggest small moving light, and this suggestiveness gives to the words extraordinary imaginal power. We may further remark (1) that each word, *gleams* and *glimmers*, occupies the emphatic opening position in the line, and (2) that *gleams* is a replacement for the *shines* of an earlier version, perhaps because the poet felt its intensive power.

Contrasted with the brightness of the opening lines is the darkness of the closing scene: the world is *darkling*, and the last word of the poem is *night*. The contrast is striking and, dominating the poem, can hardly be unmeaningful. Confirmation of this interpretation is intimated in the third stanza. Here we see the nexus of *faith* and *bright*; then follows a contrastive *but*, which implies the absence of light as well as of faith, and in so doing equates darkness with loss of faith. [Slightly changed, this note by Norman C. Stageberg appeared in the *Explicator*, IX, March, 1951.]

Some variants from an earlier draft are of interest:
  6.   *sweet* was *hush'd*
 11.   *high* was *steep*, then *barr'd*
 13.   *tremulous* was *regular*, then *mournful*
 17.   *turbid* was *troubled*
 23.   *girdle* was *garment*.
These are reported by C. B. Tinker and H. F. Lowry, *Matthew Arnold a Commentary* (New York: Oxford University Press, 1940), pp. 173–174.

380.   *I Taste a Liquor Never Brewed.*

Shortly after Emily Dickinson's first volume of poems appeared in 1890, Thomas Bailey Aldrich wrote: "The English critic who said of Miss Emily Dickinson that she might have become a fifth-rate poet 'if she had only mastered the rudiments of grammar and gone into metrical training for about fifteen years,'—the rather candid English critic who said this somewhat overstated his case. He had, however, a fairly good case. If Miss Dickinson had undergone the austere curriculum indicated, she would, I am sure, have become an admirable lyric poet of the second magnitude. In the first volume of her poetical chaos is a little poem which needs only slight revision in the initial stanza in order to make it worthy of ranking with some of the odd swallow flights in Heine's lyrical *intermezzo*. I have ventured to desecrate this stanza by tossing a rhyme into it, as the other stanzas happened to rhyme, and here print the lyric, hoping the reader will not accuse me of overvaluing it:—

'I taste a liquor never brewed
In vats upon the Rhine;
No tankard ever held a draught
Of alcohol like mine.' . . ."

["In Re Emily Dickinson," The Contributors' Club, *The Atlantic Monthly*, LXIX, p. 143 (January, 1892).]

385.   *The Windhover: To Christ Our Lord.*

This poem, like many of Hopkins' other poems, is written in what he called "sprung rhythm." The basic principles of this rhythm have been stated by the poet himself: "Sprung Rhythm . . . is measured by feet of from one to four syllables, regularly, and for particular effects any number of weak or slack syllables may be used. It has one stress, which falls on the only syllable, if there is only one, or, if there are more, then scanning as above, on the first, and so gives rise to four sorts of feet, a monosyllable and the so-called accentual Trochee, Dactyl, and the First Paeon [´ ⌣ ⌣ ⌣]. And there will be four corresponding natural rhythms; but nominally the feet are mixed and any one may follow any other. . . . In Sprung Rhythm . . . the feet are assumed to be equally long or strong and their seeming inequality is made up by pause or stressing." [*Poems of Gerard Manley Hopkins*, edited by W. H. Gardner, Third edition (New York: Oxford University Press, 1948), pp. 7–8. Quoted by permission of the publisher.]

As in very early English poetry, Hopkins used alliteration to reinforce rhythmic stress. In addition he used assonance and rime to help structure the poem and to bring out relationships between sound and sense. Greater freedom was achieved by an increased use of what he called "rove-over" lines, that is, "for the scanning of each line immediately to take up that of the one before, so that if the first has one or more syllables at its end the other must have so many the less at its beginning; and in fact the scanning runs on without break from the beginning, say, of a stanza to the end and all the stanza is one long strain though written in lines asunder." [*Ibid.*, p. 8.]

In a letter to Robert Bridges, Hopkins gave his reasons for using sprung rhythm in preference to others: "Why do I employ sprung rhythm at all? Because it is the nearest to the rhythm of prose, that is the native and natural rhythm of speech, the least forced, the most rhetorical and emphatic of all possible rhythms, combining, as it seems to me, markedness of rhythm—that is rhythm's self—and naturalness of expression—for why, if it is forcible in prose to say 'lashed:rod' am I obliged to weaken this in verse, which ought to be something stronger, not weaker, into 'lashed birch-rod' or something?" [*The Letters of Gerard Manley Hopkins to Robert Bridges*, edited with notes and an introduction by Claude Colleer Abbott (London: Oxford University Press, 1935,) p. 46.]

For further information about Hopkins, see the discussion of *Harry Ploughman* in Chapter 11.

The interpretations of *The Windhover* have been numerous and varied. W. H. Gardner writes: "*The Windhover* is yet another of those poems which make a profound appeal long before their full significance is grasped. The whole octave may be read with little difficulty as a vigorous and colourful piece of nature-poetry, a description of the kestrel in action. . . .

"One phrase, in line 7 of the octave, has provoked some speculation among critics:

> '*My heart in hiding*
> Stirred for a bird,—'

The sonnet carried the unique dedication *To Christ Our Lord*, so that even a reader who knew not Hopkins could have no doubt about the religious and specifically Christian connotation of 'heart' in this passage. The poet's emotions—sympathy, admiration, love—were ever aroused by all natural or 'mortal' beauty, but principally by the supreme pattern of 'immortal' beauty—the character of Christ. For this ideal, the poet had renounced worldly ambition, the fullest life of the senses; hence his heart was 'in hiding' with Christ, wholly dedicated to His love, praise and service.

"'My heart in hiding' is the first giving out of the essential moral theme of the poem. The whole poem, it must be remembered, is addressed not to the bird, or to the reader, or to the poet himself, but primarily and deliberately to Christ. . . . The truth is that in the sestet Hopkins holds up to a passionate but critical judgment two conflicting sets of values, one represented by the 'kingdom of daylight's dauphin'—the windhover, the other by the Kingdom of Heaven's 'chevalier'—Christ." [W. H. Gardner, *Gerard Manley Hopkins, A Study of Poetic Idiosyncrasy in Relation to Poetic Tradition*, Vol. I (London: Martin Secker & Warburg, and New Haven: Yale University Press, 1948), pp. 180–81. Quoted by permission of its publishers.]

W. A. M. Peters, S. J., on the other hand, has this to say about the poem: "There is in my opinion nothing very obscure about the thought of these lines [the sestet]. The poet's ecstasy reaches a climax when he inscapes the bird displaying all its majestic splendours in its flight; it is the bird in action that strikes the poet as ever so much more beautiful than the bird just hanging on the wing. In the last three lines he exemplifies whence this increase in beauty comes by means of two very fine images. . . . It is hardly believable that these lines could have given rise to speculations most astonishing in their far-fetchedness. Critics have overlooked what must appear to be the meaning intended by Hopkins himself and have chosen their own way of interpreting these lines: the chevalier refers to Christ; the expression 'gash gold-vermilion' calls up the 'symbol of the climax of Christ's task' and thus suggests the crucifixion; the exclamation 'ah my dear' is addressed to Christ, etc. Now Hopkins dedicated this sonnet to Christ Our Lord and at this hint critics have set to work to discover why it was that Hopkins dedicated this poem to Christ. They forget that it was the best thing he ever wrote (Hopkins stated this in a letter to Robert Bridges, June 22, 1879) and that is the only reason why he gave this, his best, to Christ. Obvious as this explanation is, it cannot satisfy many critics; they think there must have been other reasons, preferably subconscious ones. I leave them alone; be it only remembered that Hopkins did not dedicate this poem to Christ until some six years after he had written it!" [W. A. M. Peters, S. J., *Gerard Manley Hopkins, A Critical Essay towards the Understanding of his Poetry* (London: Oxford University Press, 1948), pp. 85–86. Quoted by the publisher's permission.]

Part of the difficulty—and richness—of the poem is the result of Hopkins' use of unfamiliar words and images, some of which may have multiple meanings. It may be of help, therefore, to consider the following:

4. *rung upon the rein of a wimpling wing:ring*. To rise spirally in flight; to make a circle or ring; to cause a horse to circle around one in a long rein.

wimpling. Veiling, concealing, winding or rippling. A wimple is "A garment of linen or silk formerly worn by women, so folded as to envelop the head, chin, sides of the face, and neck; now retained in the dress of nuns. Also *gen.* a veil." (OED) Hence, to wimple is to envelop in a wimple; "to fall in folds; to ripple; to move shiftily or unsteadily."

10. *Buckle*. 1) To fasten with a buckle; hence to fasten in any way. 2) With allusion to the fastening on of armor: to equip, prepare (for battle, and expedition, etc.); hence, to gird oneself, to apply oneself resolutely. 3) To join closely; to close, come to close quarters with; to grapple or engage. 4) To bend under stress or pressure; to give way to; to submit, cringe, or truckle.

12. *sillion*. Furrow.

For additional comment about this poem, the student is referred to I. A. Richards, "Gerard Hopkins," *The Dial*, Vol. 81 (Sept. 1926), pp. 195–203; Herbert Marshall McLuhan, "The Analogical Mirrors," in *Gerard Manley Hopkins* (Norfolk, Conn.: New Directions, 1945), pp. 15–27; William Empson, *Seven Types of Ambiguity* (London: Chatto & Windus, 1930), Chapter VII.

389. Gloucester Moors.

The text is that of Moody's *Poems*, 1901. When *Gloucester Moors* was first published, in *Scribner's Magazine*, December, 1900, the last two lines of the first stanza read as follows:

Or where the choke-cherry lifteth up
Its bowls of shy carouse.

Reviewing Moody's *Poems*, Rollo Ogden made the following comment about this poem: ". . . Mr. Moody has followed a sure instinct in giving the place of honor in his volume to a poem, 'Gloucester Moors,' which affords a fairer because broader test of his powers. It shows him, by so much, to have—in addition to the technical mastery of his craft—imagination, sympathy, ability to see the large in the little and the universal in the particular, and originality combined with fidelity to the great poetical tradition. . . . It is all finely imagined, sympathetically rendered, with frequent flash and charm of phrase; and, at the end, Mr. Moody shows how true a son of our best poets he is by rising to a strain of religious fervor, even if the religion be only that of humanity." ["Mr. William Vaughn Moody's Poems," *The Atlantic Monthly*, LXXXVIII (July, 1901), pp. 132–133.]

Recently, when asked for an opinion of Moody's poetry, a well-known contemporary poet and critic replied: "Moody never quite achieved great poetry for several reasons: he never quite defined even to himself what he was talking about, therefore his diction rises only through gassy abstractions of rhetoric at the climax instead of achieving a firm elevation; his expression suffers from the typical faults of late nineteenth century minor poetry of heroic intention in that all the natural effects seem laboured and the poet is only at ease among stock phrases; and, lastly, his technique is naïve without achieving true simplicity.

"Just one example: the famous 'Gloucester Moors.' The particular catalogue of natural objects which opens the passage remains merely a catalogue, because it never comes to a focus. (It is also highly doubtful that scarlet tanagers frequent marsh-grasses; it was probably a red-winged blackbird.) Then suddenly the world is seen as a most unlikely fishing schooner, and ploughs along in a welter of archaisms, exclamations, invocations of a papier maché deity, awkward inversions, and half-baked social sentimentalism of the most mawkish kind. It is the same sort of verse that made Felicia Hemans famous in her time and forgotten in ours.

"It is sad that I should have to write this for candour's sake, . . . [Moody] represents both in spirit and even in execution, a far finer conception of poetry and its function than is current today. But he was a weak poet." [Letter to Wallace L. Anderson, December 9, 1947.]

400. Aubade.

In this poem the poet makes use of a device called synesthesia, the description of an item of sense perception in terms of a sense other than the usual one. Miss Sitwell feels that "The senses of many people are practically unused—not through their fault, but because they have been taught that inherited ideas are best. . . . The modernist poet's brain is becoming a central sense, interpreting and controlling the other five senses; . . . When the speech of one sense is insufficient to convey his entire meaning, he uses the language of another. He knows, too, that every sight, touch, sound, smell of the world we live in has its meanings; and it is the poet's duty to interpret those meanings."

Miss Sitwell's own comments, written in the third person, reveal quite clearly her synesthetic sensibility: " *'The morning light creaks down again.'* The author said 'creaks' because, in a very early dawn, after rain, the light has a curious uncertain quality, as though it does not run quite smoothly. Also, it falls in hard cubes, squares, and triangles, which, again, give one the impression of a creaking sound, because of the association with wood. *'Each dull, blunt wooden stalactite of rain creaks, hardened by the light.'* In the early dawn, long raindrops are transformed by the light, until they have the light's own quality of hardness; also they have the dull and blunt and tasteless quality of wood; as they move in the wind, they seem to creak. *'Sounding like an overtone from some lonely world unknown.'* Though it seems to us as though we heard them sensorily, yet the sound is unheard in reality; it has the quality of an overtone from some unknown and mysterious world. *'But the creaking, empty light will never harden into sight, will never penetrate your brain with overtones like the blunt rain.'* The poem is about a country servant, a girl on a farm, plain and neglected and unhappy, and with a sad bucolic stupidity, coming down in the dawn to light the fire; and this phrase means that to her poor mind the light is an empty thing which conveys nothing. It cannot bring sight to her—she is not capable of seeing anything; it can never bring overtones to her mind, because she is not capable of hearing them. She scarcely knows even that she is suffering. *'The light would show, if it could harden, eternities of kitchen garden, cockscomb flowers that none will pluck, and wooden flowers that 'gin to cluck.'* If she were capable of seeing anything, still she would only see the whole of eternity as the world of kitchen gardens to which she is accustomed, with flowers red and lank as cockscombs (uncared for, just as she is uncared for), and those hard flowers that dip and bend beneath the rain till they look (and seem as though they must sound) like hens clucking. *'In the kitchen you must light flames as staring red and white as carrots or as turnips— shining where the cold dawn light lies whining.'* To the author's sight, the shivering movement of a certain cold dawn light upon the floor suggests a kind of high animal whining or whimpering, a kind of half-frightened and subservient urge to something outside our consciousness. *'Cockscomb hair on the cold wind hangs limp, turns the milk's weak mind,'* is obviously a joke, and a joke may be permitted even to a poet." [Edith Sitwell, *Poetry and Criticism* (New York: Henry Holt and Company, 1926), 22–26. Copyright 1926 by Edith Sitwell. Reprinted by permission of Hogarth Press.]

401.   Shine, Perishing Republic.

Jeffers has rather consistently maintained a philosophy that he calls Inhumanism. What Inhumanism is and what some of its values are, Jeffers has stated in his preface to *The Double Axe:* "Inhumanism [is] a shifting of emphasis and significance from man to not-man; the rejection of human solipsism and recognition of the transhuman magnificence. It seems time that our race began to think as an adult does, rather than like an egocentric baby or insane person. This manner of thought and feeling is neither misanthropic nor pessimist, though two or three people have said so and may again. It involves no falsehoods, and is a means of maintaining sanity in slippery times; it has objective truth and human value. It offers a reasonable detachment as rule of conduct, instead of love, hate and envy. It neutralizes fanaticism and wild hopes; but it provides magnificence for the religious instinct, and satisfies our need to admire greatness and rejoice in beauty." [Robinson Jeffers, *The Double Axe and Other Poems* (New York: Random House, 1948), p. vii. Quoted by permission of the publisher.]

401.   Hurt Hawks.

See note above. The hawk is Jeffers' favorite animal, and he often uses it as a symbol of the beauty, grace, and strength of the non-human world.

403.   The Fish.

About this poem Vivienne Koch writes: "I believe insufficient attention has been given to the fact that her verse is, on the whole, syllabic, rather than accentual. 'The Fish' (one of her most exquisitely worked-out metaphors) will serve as a useful illustration of this practice. There are eight stanzas of five lines, each with a recurring syllabic pattern of 1, 3, 9, 6, 8, the final longish line of each stanza connecting with and carrying over to the first two or three short lines of the next stanza. What this accomplishes is a run-on pattern of movement very much like that of 'prose with a heightened consciousness,' or speech. For it should be noted that contrary to the historical confusions about the possibilities for syllabic verse in English, in actuality, experimental studies have shown that stress and syllabic length tend to coincide; and, in addition, both the *heard* patterns of accent, normal to speech, as well as Miss Moore's generous usage of end rimes (in this poem aabbc, ddeef, etc.) set up a counterpoint against which the syllabic pattern makes its way. The result is a very complex and rich range of metrical possibilities within the given syllabic scheme of any poem." [Vivienne Koch, "The Peaceable Kingdom of Marianne Moore," *Quarterly Review of Literature*, IV, No. 2, p. 163. Quoted by permission of the *Quarterly Review of Literature*.]

404.   The Love Song of J. Alfred Prufrock.

The quotation which introduces the poem is from Dante's *Inferno*, XXVII, 61–66. Dante, making a journey through hell, the world of the dead, encounters the "flame" or spirit of Count Guido da Montefeltro, an unrepentant sinner condemned to suffer for having given fraudulent counsel. When Dante asks him why he is being punished, the flame of Guido replies:

If I might believe that my answer were made
to some one who would ever return to the world [of living men]
this flame [in which I am imprisoned] would cease to quiver;
but since no one ever returned alive from this
depth [of Hell], if I hear the truth,
I answer you without fear of infamy [in the world above].

Guido would not have answered had he thought Dante would return to the land of the living, for he feared what the living would say of him.

In *The Love Song of J. Alfred Prufrock*, Prufrock, realizing that he is growing older and fearing an old age of loneliness without love, carries on a conversation with himself. What he "says" in the poem he can say only to himself, for he is afraid of what the people in his world will say about him. But these people, though existing, are not really alive; Prufrock's world is a world of the living-dead. The epigraph sets up the life-death opposition in the poem and intensifies the irony. Guido is afraid of the living; Prufrock is afraid of the dead.

408.   The Hollow Men.

Mistah Kurtz—he dead is from Joseph Conrad's novel *Heart of Darkness*. The speaker is a negro cabin boy contemptuously announcing the death of Mr. Kurtz, an ivory hunter who had gone into the African jungles with nobility of purpose; but "the wilderness had found him out early" and changed him to a man of evil, "hollow at the core." Kurtz's dying words, "The horror! The horror!," were "a judgment upon the adventures of his soul on this earth." Commenting upon Kurtz's death, the narrator of the story remarks: "This is the reason why I affirm that Kurtz was a remarkable man. He had something to say. He said it. Since I had peeped over the edge myself, I understand better the meaning of his [death] stare, that could not see the flame of the candle, but was wide enough to embrace the whole universe, piercing enough to penetrate all the hearts that beat in the darkness. He had summed up—he had judged. 'The horror!' He was a remarkable man. After all, this was the expression of some sort of belief; it had candour, it had conviction, it had a vibrating note of revolt in its whisper, it had the appalling face of a glimpsed truth —the strange commingling of desire and hate. . . . I like to think my summing-up would not have been a word of careless contempt. Better his cry—much better. It was an affirmation, a moral victory paid for by abominable satisfactions. But it was a victory." The point is that Mr. Kurtz, though evil, was a remarkable and forceful man; he was a "lost violent soul" who "crossed with direct eyes, to death's other kingdom."

A penny for the Old Guy is a reference to Guy Fawkes, who was executed for his part in the Gunpowder Plot to blow up the English House of Parliament when it was in session on November 5, 1605. Like Mr. Kurtz, Fawkes, though evil, was at least a man of action. On Guy Fawkes day the English children, carrying effigies of Fawkes, parade the streets shouting "A penny for the Old Guy." With the pennies they collect, they buy fireworks, which are set off when the effigies are hanged and burned. The character of Fawkes, the Gunpowder Plot, and the fireworks all have a direct relationship to the *bang* of the last line of the poem.

412.   Barns in November.

James Hearst has written the following comment about this poem: "This poem began in a feeling that came to me early one November morning as I returned from meeting a train. It was a raw cold morning with a low ceiling of fast moving clouds. The light was pale and grey. Gritty snow covered the fields where cornstalks showed their broken knees in grotesque attitudes of resignation. Or so it seemed to me. And there along the country road stood the barns, solid, dependable, the preservers against the cold of the farm life and harvest. As the feeling churned around in me I wondered if we all didn't need some kind of shelters in which to store our treasured experiences against catastrophe. Harriet Monroe of POETRY magazine suggested the stanza where the world of clouds seems a reflection of our own—but without the barns. The illusion, she called it, contrasted with what for the farmer is the reality." [Letter to the authors, January 8, 1951.]

Note that the rime scheme of stanza seven differs from the rest of the poem.

413.   The Fence Row.

The inception of this poem has been described by the poet: "It's hard to nail down in words the beginning of this piece. The situation is plain enough: there was a fence row on our farm where my brother and I had decided to throw two fields into one. What interested me was how evidence of it persisted. We kept hitting rock with the plow, and the buried part of fence posts; the ridge of ground didn't level out; even the soil was of a different texture. It was that way year after year, you can still see it. It remained like a scar or an ingrown prejudice, or anything that marks you deeply. The fox den set me off, though, it was too pat a chance to say something about old party members who won't give up." [Letter to the authors, January 8, 1951.]

416.   *In Memory of W. B. Yeats.*

Yeats, a poet of great power and versatility, was born June 13, 1865, near Dublin, Ireland. He was one of the founders of the Abbey Theater, and was one of the leaders in the Irish Renaissance. In all his work his deep love for Ireland is apparent. He died on January 28, 1939, in France, and his body was returned to Ireland for burial.

59.   *All the dogs of Europe bark.* At the time of Yeats' death, fear that the dogs of war might be unleashed at any moment was intense. See the note to MacNeice's *These Days Are Misty,* p. 214.

419.   *September 1, 1939.*

The date that Hitler invaded Poland and precipitated World War II.

422.   *The Express.*

Cf. Walt Whitman's *To a Locomotive in Winter,* p. 377, and Emily Dickinson's *I Like to See It Lap the Miles,* p. 176.

INDEX OF AUTHORS, TITLES, AND FIRST LINES

Names of authors are in capitals, titles of poems are in italics, and first lines are in roman type. Notes to poems are indicated by the letter **n** after the page number.

503